WHY REVOLUTION?

Theories and Analyses

Edited with Introductions
by
CLIFFORD T. PAYNTON
San Bernardino State College

and

ROBERT BLACKEY
San Bernardino State College

SCHENKMAN PUBLISHING COMPANY, INC.
Cambridge, Massachusetts, U.S.A. and London, England

distributed by
General Learning Press
Morristown, New Jersey, U.S.A.

To

Gladys, Cheralyn & Scott

and

Phyllis, Richard & Jeffrey

Library of Congress Catalog Card No. 77-145964

Printed in the United States of America

CONTENTS

Contents

ACKNOWLEDGEMENTS

Aristotle, *Man and Revolution*
Reprinted from Aristotle, *The Politics of Aristotle*. Translated by B. Jowett (1885), pp. 144–153.

Karl Griewank, *Emergence of the Concept of Revolution*
Reprinted from *Der Neuzeitliche Revolutionsbergriff* (Frankfurt am Main, 1969), pp. 143–151, by permission of Europäische Verlagsanstalt. Translation reprinted with permission of The Macmillan Company from *Revolutions in Modern European History* by Heinz Lubasz. Copyright © 1966 by Heinz Lubasz. With one exception, the footnotes have been eliminated.

George Pettee, *The Process of Revolution*
Abridged from pp. ix–xi, 1–29, 61–63, 95–97 in *The Process of Revolution* by George Sawyer Pettee. Copyright 1938 by Political Science Associates; copyright renewed 1966 by George Sawyer Pettee. Reprinted by permission of Harper and Row, Publishers, Inc.

Peter Amann, *Revolution: A Redefinition*
Reprinted with permission from the *Political Science Quarterly*, vol. 77 (March 1962), 36–53.

Lyford P. Edwards, *Advanced Symptoms of Revolution*
Abridged from pp. 38–68 in *The Natural History of Revolution* by Lyford P. Edwards (1927). Reprinted by permission of L. P. Edwards.

Crane Brinton, *The Anatomy of Revolution*
From the book *The Anatomy of Revolution* by Crane Brinton. © 1962 by Prentice-Hall, Inc. Published by Prentice-Hall, Inc., Englewood Cliffs, New Jersey.

Louis Gottschalk, *Causes of Revolution*
Reprinted with permission from The University of Chicago Press and *The American Journal of Sociology*, vol. L, no. 1 (July 1944), 1–8.

Sigmund Neumann, *The International Civil War*
Sigmund Neumann, "The International Civil War," *World Politics*, vol. 1, no. 3 (April 1949), 333–350. Copyright © 1948–1949 by Princeton University Press. Reprinted by permission of Princeton University Press. Some of the footnotes have been eliminated.

Harry Eckstein, *On The Etiology of Internal Wars*
Copyright © 1965 by Wesleyan University. Reprinted from *History and Theory*, Volume IV, Number 2, by permission of the author and Wesleyan University Press. Abridged with permission of the author.

Charles A. Ellwood, *A Psychological Theory of Revolutions*
Reprinted with permission from The University of Chicago Press and *The American Journal of Sociology*, vol. XI (July 1905), 49–59.

Acknowledgments

Gustave Le Bon, *The Psychology of Revolutions*
Abridged from pp. 60–105 in *The Psychology of Revolutions* by Gustave Le Bon (1913). Reprinted by permission of Ernest Benn Limited.

James C. Davies, *Toward a Theory of Revolution*
Reprinted from *The American Sociology Review*, vol. 27, no. 1 (February 1962), 5–19, by permission of J. C. Davies and *The American Sociology Review*.

Chalmers Johnson, *Revolution and The Social System*
Reprinted from Johnson, Chalmers, *Revolution and The Social System* (1964), with the permission of The Hoover Institution on War, Revolution and Peace, Stanford University. © 1964 by the Board of Trustees of Leland Stanford Junior University. Some of the footnotes have been eliminated.

Robert C. Tucker, *The Marxian Revolutionary Idea*
Robert C. Tucker, "The Marxian Revolutionary Idea" in Carl J. Friedrich (ed.), *Revolution (Nomos VIII)*. Reprinted by permission of the publishers, Atherton Press, Inc. Copyright © 1966, Atherton Press, Inc. New York. All Rights Reserved.

Rex D. Hopper, *The Revolutionary Process*
Reprinted from *Social Forces*, vol. 28 (1950), 270–279, by permission of *Social Forces*. One footnote has been eliminated.

Heinz Lubasz, *What is Revolution?*
Reprinted with permission of The Macmillan Company from *Revolutions in Modern European History* by Heinz Lubasz. Copyright © 1966 by Heinz Lubasz.

Lawrence Stone, *Theories of Revolution*
Lawrence Stone, "Theories of Revolution," *World Politics*, vol. XVIII, no. 2 (June 1966), 159–175. Copyright © 1966 by Princeton University Press. Reprinted by permission of Princeton University Press.

INTRODUCTION

Revolution! The word probably evokes a greater intensity and variety of responses than any other in the vocabulary of man. Revolution serves as the foundation for some societies and as the final act of others. To many revolution is a horror to be avoided; to others it is a necessary step in the direction of utopia; while for some it is an end in itself. Written in 1949, the eighth selection in this book begins: "This is the age of revolutions. No longer are they the domain of the theorizer or the peripheral plotter. They have moved into the center of the average man's thought. They are on everybody's mind and in every newspaper's headline." What was a reasonably adequate description in 1949 is virtually an understatement today. More than ever before we are involved, if not immersed, in an age of revolution.

With international war meaning almost certain worldwide destruction, revolutions have become practically the only means by which combatants can maneuver for power. Thus, a new pattern of world politics is emerging in which revolution is replacing war.[1] But revolution is not a phenomenon just of the twentieth century; it has been a characteristic of the history of man almost from the beginning.

Few will deny the fascinating nature of the subject of revolution. How may we account for this? The study of revolution is vital for an understanding of both the past and present. Compared to other forms of political and social action, revolution is a most unique event. It seeks to reconstruct

1

the entire social order; it challenges the existing mores and proposes a new scheme of moral values.[2] Its study tells us about aspects of the nature of man which cannot be learned from observing virtually any other phenomena. It arouses emotions to an intensity not otherwise observed and reveals acts of man which do not occur under any lesser stimulation. A further reason for this fascination with revolution is the fact that its most important ingredient is the human element — man's behavior is infinitely variable. This is why revolutions are not predictable, and why each particular one differs from all others. However, just as the study of human behavior enables us to anticipate human action, similarly the study of revolutions allows us to anticipate future ones.

Although most published and unpublished material is available to the student of revolution, little of it is devoted to broad theoretical considerations. That is, while many writers have discussed one or more revolutions, not many have presented theoretical explanations of revolutions in general. This may seem surprising in view of the fact that revolution is a topic of interest to both laymen and scholars. Whether one speaks to historians, sociologists, political scientists, philosophers or others, it is possible to find those who are interested in general theories of revolution, and not in analyses of particular revolutions only.

To understand why a paucity of material of this nature exists is not easily explained. Partly it may lie with the difficulty of classifying and defining what should be included within the concept of revolution. The word itself has been used by writers from the time of Plato and Aristotle. From then until today its definition has never been consistently applied. It has, for example, been used to refer to historical eras, such as the Scientific Revolution and the Industrial Revolution, to political crises, such as the 1830 and 1848 Revolutions, to great societal upheavals, such as the French Revolution and the Russian Revolution, and to lesser changes, such as the Fashion Revolution and the Sexual Revolution. The variety of applications and definitions of the term are practically endless, as these examples indicate.

Confining ourselves to socio-political conflicts we still find no agreement. Definitions run the gamut: they may include any minor illegal changes in government (e.g., coups d'etat or palace revolutions) or they may exclude everything but those major upheavals which affect all areas of government and society (e.g., the Russian Revolution). To claim there are common elements among these diverse events which permit them to be classified under a single label requires considerable justification. Justification under these circumstances, however, has proven to be a demanding and frustrating task for those who undertake it.

Many scholars have attempted to avoid the problem by abandoning the term "revolution" and its confusing array of definitions. A variety of other concepts has consequently been substituted, such as "internal war," "politics of violence" and "international civil war." Along with these terms, however, have come new definitions and classifications not clearly superior to those associated with the concept of revolution. So even though the word "revolution" has been popularized and journalized to the point where it has become a cliché, it may still be preferable, if for no other reason than because it is familiar, and because terms and definitions which are new are not necessarily better.

In recent years scholars have come increasingly to recognize the interdependence of their different disciplines. The study of any subject from the narrow confines of one perspective alone has been recognized as necessarily incomplete. Undeniably, materials from several of the fields of the social sciences have in the past often been utilized, but without the researcher intending an eclectic approach. Of late, the trend has been by conscious design.[3] In order for the concept of revolution to be understood as completely as possible the ideas and insights from all relevant sources must be employed. Consequently, we have included selections from a variety of disciplinary approaches: history, sociology, political science, psychology, and philosophy.

Although we have of necessity chosen a limited number of papers on the subject, we have attempted to discover and include some of the more thought provoking and meaningful examples of the writings available. Unfortunately, there are some rather interesting and well conceived theoretical treatments of our subject which could not be included. Some of these are too lengthy and complicated for a book of readings, the ideas having been developed throughout an entire volume.[4]

The quality and utility of our collection is not completely uniform, but it does, in our judgment, provide a reasonably comprehensive sample of manuscripts that are available and that meet our criteria for selection. The criteria are obviously somewhat subjective and arbitrary. The two most important are:

1. The selection must not be limited to a particular revolution, but must apply to revolutions in general.
2. The selection must be theoretical in nature, either definitional or explanatory.

The book is divided into four parts. The first section reveals the development of the concept of revolution. In part two is included the bulk of the readings under the heading "Determinants of Revolution." Within this category we have attempted to establish three broad emphases or theoretical orientations. The editors recognize that these are not clearly delineated divisions of thought, but represent, we hope, a useful framework for approaching the subject. Part three includes two works in which the authors see revolutions as developmental processes divided into specific stages. Finally, the last part provides two summary statements of current views, the first by historian Lawrence Stone and the second by the editors. The former is a critical examination of some of the more prominent works on the subject, many of which are selections in this book. It is hoped that Stone's study will help the reader in his own assessment of analyses of revolutions. The latter is a bibliographical essay that summarizes several important works which the editors were unable to include. The intention in this case is to add further breadth to the volume.

The purpose of this book is not to present a particular point of view or to promote a given cause. But rather it is to broaden the body of knowledge concerning the nature of revolution and to help in the understanding of revolutions, both past and present. If the reader leaves this volume more informed and with conceptions that are more flexible, then the editors will have achieved their purpose.

[1] C. E. Black, "The Anticipation of Communist Revolutions," in C. E. Black and T. Thornton, *Communism and Revolution* (Princeton: Princeton University Press, 1964), p. 431.

[2] Herbert Blumer, "Social Movements," in Barry McLoughlin, *Studies in Social Movements* (New York: The Free Press, 1969), p. 21.

[3] See S. Lipset and R. Hofstadter, eds., *Sociology and History: Methods* (New York: Basic Books, 1968); W. J. Cahnman and A. Boskoff, eds., *Sociology and History: Theory and Research* (Glencoe, Ill.: The Free Press, 1964); H. S. Hughes, "The Historian and the Social Scientist," *American Historical Review*, LXVI, 1 (1960), 20–46; A. Cobban, "History and Sociology," *Historical Studies*, III (1961), 1–8; M. G. Smith, "History and Social Anthropology," *Journal of the Royal Anthropological Institute*, XCII (1962); K. V. Thomas, "History and Anthropology," *Past and Present*, 24 (April 1963), 3–18.

[4] Neil J. Smelser, *Theory of Collective Behavior* (New York: The Free Press, 1962) and Hannah Arendt, *On Revolution* (New York: The Viking Press, 1963) are two examples.

I

ORIGINS OF A CONCEPT

INTRODUCTION

INTRODUCTION

One of the aims of this book is to generate an interest in, and therefore an understanding of the causes of revolutions. Just as an awareness of the causes of past revolutions should solve some of the problems in comprehending contemporary revolutions, so it is hoped that an awareness of the historical origins of the word "revolution" should serve the purpose of clarifying the problem of its use and misuse.

The phenomenon of revolution has been of interest to political philosophers, theorizers, and historians from classical times. It was from the Greeks that "revolution" came to us as a political conception. Its meaning was associated with the turning of the wheel of Fortune, elevating one government and eliminating another. Yet, the Greeks had no single word for the event. Herodotus and Thucydides wrote of "uprisings," whereas Plato applied the words "change" and "revolution" without making any significant distinction between them.[1] The same observations may be made for Aristotle. Nevertheless, as the selection from his *Politics* illustrates, Aristotle was an astute commentator. Despite seemingly simplified statements, he presents in a systematic and analytical fashion a set of sound ideas revealing an understanding of some of the basic causes of revolutions. However, he does not define his terms, and his handling of the subject may be insufficiently sophisticated for present day social scientists. For example, Aristotle does not distinguish between revolutions and rebellions, nor does he recognize the complicated interplay of political, economic, social, and ideological forces.

The Romans were little different from the Greeks in their application of a variety of terms for comparable occurrences. In fact, since the history of Rome is virtually void of anything we would label a revolution, it is no wonder that the Roman contribution is negligible. The same is true for the period of the Middle Ages where a universally accepted rigid life-style allowed no room for revolution.

The Renaissance was a period of rebirth, and not merely in the cultural sphere. The Italian city-states were responsible for a host of political upheavals and with them came the reapplication of the word "revolution." From that time revolution has been an effective form of action, rating the keen attention of political observers. In the second selection Karl Griewank, late Dean of the Philosophical Faculty at the University of Jena (East Germany), traces the evolution of the word from its initial usage adapted from the natural sciences in the sixteenth and seventeenth centuries to its more modern meaning. Griewank states that for the astronomer a revolution was a circular or elliptical movement with the heavenly body in question predictably returning to place. At first political observers viewed revolutions in a similar fashion; that is, revolutions signaled the reestablishment or restoration of a more desirable past. He goes on to say that following the French Revolution of 1789 the word came to be used in the more modern sense. It referred to massive popular movements strong enough to overthrow formidable administrations and to political and societal alterations and reversals. Revolution meant disruption of the army, mobs in the streets, communes, and the flowing of blood. This section demonstrates the origin of a term that has evolved in the twentieth century to mean everything and anything to everybody.

[1] For more detail see Arthur Hatto, " 'Revolution': An Enquiry Into the Usefulness of an Historical Term," *Mind*, LVIII, 232 (October 1949), 498f.

I. Man and Revolution

ARISTOTLE

In the first place we must assume as our starting point that in the many forms of government which have sprung up there has always been an acknowledgment of justice and proportionate equality, although mankind fail in attaining them, as indeed I have already explained. Democracy, for example, arises out of the notion that those who are equal in any respect are equal in all respects; because men are equally free, they claim to be absolutely equal. Oligarchy is based on the notion that those who are unequal in one respect are in all respects unequal; being unequal, that is, in property, they suppose themselves to be unequal absolutely. The democrats think that as they are equal they ought to be equal in all things; while the oligarchs, under the idea that they are unequal, claim too much, which is one form of inequality. All these forms of government have a kind of justice, but, tried by an absolute standard, they are faulty; and, therefore, both parties, whenever their share in the government does not accord with their preconceived ideas, stir up revolution. Those who excel in virtue have the best right of all to rebel (for they alone can with reason be deemed absolutely unequal), but then they are of all men the least inclined to do so. There is also a superiority which is claimed by men of rank; for they are thought noble because they spring from wealthy and virtuous ancestors. Here then, so to speak, are opened the very springs and fountains of revolution; and hence arise two sorts of changes in governments; the one affecting the constitution, when men seek to change from an existing form into some

9

other, for example, from democracy into oligarchy, and from oligarchy into democracy, or from either of them into constitutional government or aristocracy, and conversely; the other not affecting the constitution, when, without disturbing the form of government, whether oligarchy, or monarchy, or any other, they try to get the administration into their own hands. Further, there is a question of degree; and oligarchy, for example, may become more or less oligarchical, and a democracy more or less democratical; and in like manner the characteristics of the other forms of government may be more or less strictly maintained. Or, the revolution may be directed against a portion of the constitution only, e.g. the establishment or overthrow of a particular office: as at Sparta it is said that Lysander attempted to overthrow the monarchy, and king Pausanias, the ephoralty. At Epidamnus, too, the change was partial. For instead of phylarchs or heads of tribes, a council was appointed; but to this day the magistrates are the only members of the ruling class who are compelled to go to the Heliaea when an election takes place, and the office of the single archon [survives, which] is another oligarchical feature. Everywhere inequality is a cause of revolution, but an inequality in which there is no proportion, for instance, a perpetual monarchy among equals; and always it is the desire of equality which rises in rebellion.

Now equality is of two kinds, numerical and proportional; by the first I mean sameness or equality in number or size; by the second, equality of ratios. For example, the excess of three over two is equal to the excess of two over one; whereas four exceeds two in the same ratio in which two exceeds one, for two is the same part of four that one is of two, namely, the half. As I was saying before, men agree about justice in the abstract, but they differ about proportion; some think that if they are equal in any respect they are equal absolutely, others that if they are unequal in any respect they are unequal in all. Hence there are two principal forms of government, democracy and oligarchy; for good birth and virtue are rare, but wealth and numbers are more common. In what city shall we find a hundred persons of good birth and of virtue? whereas the poor everywhere abound. That a state should be ordered, simply and wholly, according to either kind of equality, is not a good thing; the proof is the fact that such forms of government never last. They are originally based on a mistake, and, as they begin badly, cannot fail to end badly. The inference is that both kinds of equality should be employed; numerical in some cases, and proportionate in others.

Still democracy appears to be safer and less liable to revolution than oligarchy. For in oligarchies there is the double danger of the oligarchs falling out among themselves and also with the people; but in democracies there is only the danger of a quarrel with the oligarchs. No dissension

worth mentioning arises among the people themselves. And we may further
remark that a government which is composed of the middle class more
nearly approximates to democracy than to oligarchy, and is the safest of the
imperfect forms of government.

In considering how dissensions and political revolutions arise, we must
first of all ascertain the beginnings and causes of them which affect constitutions generally. They may be said to be three in number; and we have
now to give an outline of each. We want to know (1) what is the feeling?
and (2) what are the motives of those who make them? (3) whence arise
political disturbances and quarrels? The universal and chief cause of this
revolutionary feeling has been already mentioned; viz. the desire of equality;
when men think that they are equal to others who have more than themselves; or, again, the desire of inequality and superiority, when conceiving
themselves to be superior they think that they have not more but the same
or less than their inferiors; pretensions which may and may not be just.
Inferiors revolt in order that they may be equal, and equals that they may
be superior. Such is the state of mind which creates revolutions. The
motives for making them are the desire of gain and honour, or the fear of
dishonour and loss; the authors of them want to divert punishment or dishonour from themselves or their friends. The cause and reasons of these
motives and dispositions which are excited in men, about the things which
I have mentioned, viewed in one way, may be regarded as seven, and in
another as more than seven. Two of them have been already noticed; but
they act in a different manner, for men are excited against one another by
the love of gain and honour — not, as in the case which I have just supposed,
in order to obtain them for themselves, but at seeing others, justly or unjustly, engrossing them. Other causes are insolence, fear, love of superiority,
contempt, disproportionate increase in some part of the state; causes of
another sort are election intrigues, carelessness, neglect about trifles, dis-
similarity of elements.

What share insolence and avarice have in creating revolutions, and how
they work, is plain enough. When the magistrates are insolent and grasping
they conspire against one another and also against the constitution from
which they derive their power, making their gains either at the expense of
individuals or of the public. It is evident, again, what an influence honour
exerts and how it is a cause of revolution. Men who are themselves dis-
honoured and who see others obtaining honours rise in rebellion; the honour
or dishonour when undeserved is unjust; and just when awarded according
to merit. Again, superiority is a cause of revolution when one or more
persons have a power which is too much for the state and the power of the
government; this is a condition of affairs out of which there arises a monarchy, or a family oligarchy. And, therefore, in some places, as at Athens

and Argos, they have recourse to ostracism. But how much better to provide from the first that there should be no such preeminent individuals instead of letting them come into existence and then finding a remedy.

Another cause of revolution is fear. Either men have committed wrong, and are afraid of punishment, or they are expecting to suffer wrong and are desirous of anticipating their enemy. Thus at Rhodes the notables conspired against the people through fear of the suits that were brought against them. Contempt is also a cause of insurrection and revolution; for example, in oligarchies — when those who have no share in the state are the majority, they revolt, because they think that they are the stronger. Or, again, in democracies, the rich despise the disorder and anarchy of the state; at Thebes, for example, where, after the battle of Oenophyta, the bad administration of the democracy led to its ruin. At Megara the fall of the democracy was due to a defeat occasioned by disorder and anarchy. And at Syracuse the democracy was overthrown before the tyranny of Gelo arose; at Rhodes before the insurrection.

Political revolutions also spring from a disproportionate increase in any part of the state. For as a body is made up of many members, and every member ought to grow in proportion, that symmetry may be preserved; but loses its nature if the foot be four cubits long and the rest of the body two spans; and, should the abnormal increase be one of quality as well as of quantity, may even take the form of another animal: even so a state has many parts, of which some one may often grow imperceptibly; for example, the number of poor in democracies and in constitutional states. And this disproportion may sometimes happen by an accident, as at Tarentum, from a defeat in which many of the notables were slain in a battle with the Iapygians just after the Persian War, the constitutional government in consequence becoming a democracy; or, as was the case at Argos, where, after the battle at Hebdomè, the Argives, having been cut to pieces by Cleomenes the Lacedaemonian, were compelled to admit to citizenship some of their perioeci; and at Athens, when, after frequent defeats of their infantry in the times of the Peloponnesian War, the notables were reduced in number, because the soldiers had to be taken from the roll of citizens. Revolutions arise from this cause in democracies as well as in other forms of government, but not to so great an extent. When the rich grow numerous or properties increase, the form of government changes into an oligarchy or a government of families. Forms of government also change — sometimes even without revolution, owing to election contests, as at Heraea (where, instead of electing their magistrates, they took them by lot, because the electors were in the habit of choosing their own partisans); or owing to carelessness, when disloyal persons are allowed to find their way into the highest offices, as at Oreum, where, upon the accession of Heracleodorus to office, the oligarchy was overthrown, and changed by him into a constitutional and democratical government.

Again, the revolution may be accomplished by small degrees; I mean that a great change may sometimes slip into the constitution through neglect of a small matter; at Ambracia, for instance, the qualification for office, small at first, was eventually reduced to nothing. For the Ambraciots thought that a small qualification was much the same as none at all.

Another cause of revolution is difference of races which do not at once acquire a common spirit; for a state is not the growth of a day, neither is it a multitude brought together by accident. Hence the reception of strangers in colonies, either at the time of their foundation or afterwards, has generally produced revolution; for example, the Achaeans who joined the Troezenians in the foundation of Sybaris, being the more numerous, afterwards expelled them; hence the curse fell upon Sybaris. At Thurii the Sybarites quarrelled with their fellow-colonists; thinking that the land belonged to them, they wanted too much of it and were driven out. At Byzantium the new colonists were detected in a conspiracy, and were expelled by force of arms; the people of Antissa, who had received the Chian exiles, fought with them, and drove them out; and the Zancleans, after having received the Samians, were driven by them out of their own city. The citizens of Apollonia on the Euxine, after the introduction of a fresh body of colonists, had a revolution; the Syracusans, after the expulsion of their tyrants, having admitted strangers and mercenaries to the rights of citizenship, quarrelled and came to blows; the people of Amphipolis, having received Chalcidian colonists, were nearly all expelled by them.

Now, in oligarchies the masses make revolution under the idea that they are unjustly treated, because, as I said before, they are equals, and have not an equal share, and in democracies the notables revolt, because they are not equals, and yet have only an equal share.

Again, the situation of cities is a cause of revolution when the country is not naturally adapted to preserve the unity of the state. For example, the Chytrians at Clazomenae did not agree with the people of the island; and the people of Colophon quarrelled with the Notians; at Athens, too, the inhabitants of the Piraeus are more democratic than those who live in the city. For just as in war, the impediment of a ditch, though ever so small, may break a regiment, so every cause of difference, however slight, makes a breach in a city. The greatest opposition is confessedly that of virtue and vice; next comes that of wealth and poverty; and there are other antagonistic elements, greater or less, of which one is this difference of place.

In revolutions the occasions may be trifling, but great interests are at stake. Trifles are most important when they concern the rulers, as was the case of old at Syracuse; for the Syracusan constitution was once changed by a love-quarrel of two young men, who were in the government. The story is that while one of them was away from home his beloved was gained over by his companion, and he to revenge himself seduced the other's wife. They then drew all the members of the ruling class into their quarrel and made a revolution. We learn from this story that we should be on our guard against the beginnings of such evils, and should put an end to the quarrels of chiefs and mighty men. The mistake lies in the beginning — as the proverb says — 'Well begun is half done;' so an error at the beginning, though quite small, has the proportion of a half to the whole matter. In general, when the notables quarrel, the whole city is involved, as happened in Hestiaea after the Persian War. The occasion was the division of an inheritance; one of two brother refused to give an account of their father's property and the treasure which he had found: so the poorer of the two quarrelled with him and enlisted in his cause the popular party, the other, who was very rich, the wealthy classes.

At Delphi, again, a quarrel about a marriage was the beginning of all the troubles which followed. In this case the bridegroom, fancying some occurrence to be of evil omen, came to the bride, and went away without taking her. Whereupon her relations, thinking that they were insulted by him, put some of the sacred treasure [among his offerings] while he was sacrificing, and then slew him, pretending that he had been robbing the temple. At Mitylene, too, a dispute about heiresses was the beginning of many misfortunes, and led to the war with the Athenians in which Paches took their city. A wealthy citizen, named Timophanes, left two daughters; Doxander, another citizen, wanted to obtain them for his sons; but he was rejected in his suit, whereupon he stirred up a revolution, and instigated the Athenians (of whom he was proxenus) to interfere. A similar quarrel about an heiress arose at Phocis between Mnaseas the father Mnason, and Euthycrates the father of Onomarchus; this was the beginning of the Sacred War. A marriage-quarrel was also the cause of a change in the government of Epidamnus. A certain man betrothed his daughter secretly to a person whose father, having been made a magistrate, fined the father of the girl, and the latter, stung by the insult, conspired with the unenfranchised classes to overthrow the state.

Governments also change into oligarchy or into democracy or into a constitutional government because the magistrates, or some other section of the state, increase in power or renown. Thus at Athens the reputation gained by the court of the Areopagus, in the Persian War, seemed to tighten the reins of government. On the other hand, the victory of Salamis, which was gained by the common people who served in the fleet, and won for the Athenians the empire of the sea, strengthened the democracy. At Argos, the notables, having distinguished themselves against the Lacedaemonians in the battle of Mantinea, attempted to put down the democracy. At Syracuse, the people having been the chief authors of the victory in the war with the Athenians, changed the constitutional government into democracy. At Chalcis, the people, uniting with the notables, killed Phoxus the tyrant, and then seized the government. At Ambracia, the people, in like manner, having joined with the conspirators in expelling the tyrant Periander, transferred the government to themselves. And generally, it should be remembered that those who have secured power to the state, whether private citizens, or magistrates, or tribes, or any other part or section of the state, are apt to cause revolutions. For either envy of their greatness draws others into rebellion, or they themselves, in their pride of superiority, are unwilling to remain on a level with others.

Revolutions break out when opposite parties, e.g. the rich and the poor, are equally balanced and there is little or nothing between them; for, if either party were manifestly superior, the other would not risk an attack upon them. And, for this reason, those who are eminent in virtue, do not stir up insurrections, being always a minority. Such are the beginnings and causes of the disturbances and revolutions to which every form of government is liable.

Revolutions are effected in two ways, by force and by fraud. Force may be applied either at the time of making the revolution or afterwards. Fraud, again, is of two kinds; for (1) sometimes the citizens are deceived into a change of government, and afterwards they are held in subjection against their will. This was what happened in the case of the Four Hundred, who deceived the people by telling them that the king would provide money for the war against the Lacedaemonians, and when the deception was over, still endeavoured to retain the government. (2) In other cases the people are persuaded at first, and afterwards, by a repetition of the persuasion, their goodwill and allegiance are retained. The revolutions which affect constitutions generally spring from the above-mentioned causes.

2. Emergence of the Concept of Revolution

KARL GRIEWANK

The word *revolution* entered the domain of political thought proper by way of natural philosophy [science]. The growing importance of the word for astronomy, and for science generally, coupled with an inclination to fit each change of the heavenly bodies into an astrological or scientific scheme, helped to make the word *revolution* an ever more popular term and paved the way for its introduction into the language of politics. Sixteenth- and seventeenth-century theorizers were very prone to link both the name and the course of every kind of cosmically-determined upheaval with that regular circulation of the firmaments to which Nicholas Copernicus had devoted his principal work, *De Revolutionibus Orbium Celestium* [*On the Revolutions of the Heavenly Bodies*]. People were taking it for granted that the world they lived in was full of change. They could detect change most readily in political affairs, but there was no mistaking it in religion, mores, institutions and inventions as well: after all, a change in religion was often the evident cause of political change. Scientists, political theorists, and statesmen alike came to occupy themselves with the question of how these changes, the decisive and sweeping political changes especially, were related to the motions of the heavens. So sober a thinker as Bodin did not disdain such endeavors [nor did the brilliant Johannes Kepler]. Kepler had, through observation and mathematics, discovered the laws of planetary motion, the foundation of celestial mechanics, which had hitherto been inaccessible to the purely speculative Aristotelian conceptions that had

16

prevailed. Yet this same Kepler, for all that he fought against the superstitious pseudo-prophecies of the astrologers, constantly tried to puzzle out in what way the fluctuations in the affairs of men were connected with the motions of stars and constellations, believing as he did that the creator had instilled the same geometry and harmony into all things, creatures possessed of a soul and heavenly bodies alike. This pioneer of the new physico-mathematical science sought gratification for his intellectual longings in a speculative system deriving from Platonic and Neo-Platonic ideas, a system in which earthly creatures and heavenly bodies were embraced in a single universal harmony and were also jointly subject to disturbances. He associated the appearance of comets with the genesis of "protracted evil doings" (*langwirige böse Händel*) which [according to him] were not to be attributed solely to the "departure of a potentate and the changes in government ensuing thereon" (*Abgang eines Potentatens ond darauff erfolgende Newerung im Regiment.*) To be sure, Kepler himself was on his guard against the attempts of the "great crowd of astrologers" (*grossen Haufen der Astrologen* [*vulgus astrologorum*]) to conclude from the "revolution" of an astronomical year to a *Revolutio Mundana* [earthly revolution], to a lawlike regularity [*Gesetzmässigkeit*] in earthly affairs during the same time-span. But the belief in a very precise correlation between celestial motions and worldly changes nevertheless took root far and wide. It found expression, for example, in a dictum attributed to Kepler's Italian contemporary, Galileo Galilei: "The revolutions of the globe we inhabit give rise to the mishaps and accidents of human existence."

This new picture of a universe of stars rotating in regular motion, and of the earth moving within it, gave many people something to hold onto in their attempts to understand life and the world at a time when they no longer found security in the medieval-Christian doctrine of a harmonious world order. The astronomical conception of *revolution* suggested that it was possible to fit worldly changes into an orderly scheme; and this thought provided one important impetus, though not the only one, for the introduction of this conception into the language of politics. This despite the fact that the traditional desire prevailed for a time to conceive of change as circular, as a return to the good old ways, and so to think of *revolution* — akin to the ancient idea of *reformation* — as a turning away from abuses, lapses, and aberrations. Bodin, for example, sought to interpret the "conversion" to monarchy of insecure democratic and aristocratic regimes as the *re*-establishment of a stable and felicitous state of affairs. When Henry IV (Bodin's ideal king) disarmed his enemies, the League, by converting to Catholicism, and they all one by one went over to his side, it was widely said, "This is a revolution" — meaning that a reversion to a state of affairs similar or equivalent to an earlier one had taken place as irresistibly as a star rotates, so that resistance to it had become pointless. The contemporary *Histoire des dernières troubles de France* of 1599 observed that the king had accomplished a salutary change in the state (*changement en l'Estat*) at a moment when sun and moon were propitiously placed.

The great English Revolution of the seventeenth century (a term which may be used to designate the whole course of development from the outbreak of the Great Rebellion in 1640 to the Glorious Revolution of 1688) has often been made the basis of a cyclical conception of revolutions, following Polybius' old cyclical theory of constitutions: from the collapse of monarchy and aristocracy through a more and more democratic republic to military dictatorship and eventually back to monarchy. A cycle of this sort did indeed recur in the great French Revolution, and one can find it adumbrated in classical antiquity, in the Greek city-states and in the Roman Republic. But this must not be allowed to obscure the fact that modern revolutions [do not simply return to their starting points; they] always have further effects which shape and direct the subsequent development of the nation, and of those nations connected with it. We must understand the English Revolution in terms of the same preconditions as the Dutch struggles for independence from Spain which began in the sixteenth century (and which, in their turn, strike us as so much more modern than the Swiss struggles of the fifteenth). The thrust of political revolution took several directions, which stemmed from a spectrum extending all the way from conservative Calvinism to the anti-ecclesiastical, chiliastic sectarian movements of religious Puritanism. These revolutionary assaults were directed against the royal, episcopal, established church; against the monarchy itself; against compulsory religious institutions; and, finally, against every sort of political discrimination against the less powerful. The common objective of these endeavors was to secure the personal rights of individuals — rights which were derived from the birthright of free Englishmen (a right supposedly dating from Saxon times, but not extended to Papists or unbelievers); from the divinely-ordained right to freedom of conscience; and from the natural right to life, liberty, and property — three kinds of right that largely merged into one another. Chiliastic movements — which, incidentally, were increasingly coming to accept the principle of private property — were defeated by socially more conservative movements like Cromwell's which aimed only to change the social and political situation of certain segments of society without altering the structure of society as a whole. Parliament, which was evolving from an assembly of estates into the acknowledged organ of popular representation, gained the ascendant over king and church. At the same time it accepted as the fundamental principle of the constitution, if not the explicitly democratic ideas of the Rebellion, then at least the inherent individual rights of all Christian

Englishmen (Catholics excepted). These changes acted as powerful forces making for the integration of the English nation and of that growing number of nations in the old world and the new which followed its example.

It has been shown elsewhere, in conjunction with some striking texts,[1] that it was not the — to us — revolutionary events of the years 1640 to 1660, but rather the return to tranquil conditions and to the old order, which some people at the close of the "Great Rebellion" connected with the motions of the firmaments and welcomed as a *revolution*. In the House of Commons Clarendon introduced the restoration of the monarchy with the following words: "The good genius of this kingdom is become superior and hath mastered that malignity, and our good old stars govern us again." And Hobbes, the sworn enemy of all insurrection against a political authority [which he conceived of as having been] created by a contract of all the citizens — Hobbes writes at the close of his *Behemoth* concerning the acts of the Long Parliament, on the occasion of Charles II's return: "I have seen in this revolution a circular motion of the sovereign power through two usurpers, father and son, from the late king to his son." In fact, he was overjoyed to see that now, at the close of the upheaval, Parliament was definitively conceding to the king a right which hitherto he had only been able to derive unilaterally from his sovereign title. This it was that Hobbes regarded as the positive outcome of the whole matter. The republican Commonwealth of 1649 had, for its own part, sought to legitimate itself with the claim that it represented the restoration of ancient liberties. In that way it had made allowance for the still deep-seated desire for a return to the olden ways; the legend inscribed on the Great Seal of 1651 read: "In the third year of freedom by God's blessing restored." In just the same way Charles VIII of France, upon the overthrow of the Medici in 1494, had had himself fêted as the restorer and protector of the freedom of Florence (*restitutor et protector libertatis fiorentinae*). In all these instances the concept of the cycle was employed for the purpose of justifying a new state of affairs which, following upon an upheaval, was looked upon as final.

But the concept of revolution which astronomy had made familiar did not remain restricted to such conservative usage in the quest for tranquility and permanence and, thus, in a restorative sense. It would in fact be completely wrong to ascribe the introduction of the concept of revolution into politics and statecraft to astrological speculations and astronomical parallels exclusively, or even to regard these as having played a decisive and enduring role in the transmission of the concept. At a time when political thinking was becoming more flexible, the keen political mind could see a variety of possible applications for the simple notions of revolving, rotating [*Umwälzung, Umdrehung*]. In the seventeenth century the word *revolution* was already linked with that objective, non-evaluative conception of *transfor-*

mation introduced by Machiavelli on the basis of classical models, and subsequently extended to the social realm — albeit, once again in a more limited and conservative sense — by certain French statesmen. A new, dynamic conception of political change underlies the words which the Duke de Rohan used in dedicating his *Interest des Princes et Etats de la Chrestienté* to Richelieu in 1634, a conception of change that is no longer bounded by fixed conditions and that flies in the face of every known piece of political wisdom, ancient or medieval: "Whatever it is that causes the cyclical revolutions of the things of this world, also causes the basic principles of good government to change." Revolution here becomes synonymous with reversal and alteration in things political, and with alteration in the world generally. The word *revolution* replaces the old terms *mutazione, commutatio, conversion,* and *changement* to denote alterations that have taken or are taking place on the objective plane; and though it does not denote subjective manifestations such as insurrections and conspiracies, still it carries with it that overtone of restlessness and movement which attaches to it from earlier and vulgar usage. Therewith the word *revolution* becomes the standard term for the doctrine of political and worldly change whose emergence we have been able to trace from the sixteenth century on.

The most important step in the history of the term was the event which permanently introduced the word *revolution* into historical writing and political theory — the Glorious Revolution of 1688. In contrast to the period of the civil war (1640–1660), which had been introduced into historiography by its first historian, Clarendon, as "the Great Rebellion," the later event, which brought about lasting political changes with far less internal turmoil, was unequivocally labeled a *revolution.* Historically, that was in keeping with current usage. A history of *England's Revolutions from the Death of the Protector Oliver to the Restoration of the King* (Charles II) appeared in Paris in 1689. It was a very superficial chronicle, most deferential to monarchy in general and to the French monarchy in particular. The author takes it for granted that his readers will take transformations of the kind he describes to be *revolutions,* not in the modern sense, as being manifestations of insurrection and disintegration, but simply as being turbulent changes in the body politic. The undertaking which had led to yet one more revolution of this kind was termed *glorious* because of its successful outcome: writers of biographical and political apologias for William of Orange thought it important to call his domestic and foreign policy illustrious because it was successful. By calling it "the Glorious Revolution" they meant that it was really just one more change of sovereigns, albeit one that had taken place in circumstances reflecting glory on the king and on the nation represented in Parliament. An apologetic tract in Latin, published in London, correctly translated the phrase into the ancient wording:

"insignis nostra rerum commutatio" or *"rerum conversio." "La dernière Révolution d'Angleterre"* [England's latest revolution] — with this phrase one more change was added to a long line of changes.

For all that, the Glorious Revolution constituted a new point of departure for the political significance of the concept of revolution. The application of the word *revolution* to this event may be regarded as a counterblow to the restorationist concept of revolution held by Clarendon and Hobbes: a victorious Parliament was snatching from the hands of a king who had jeopardized the laws of the land, from the hands of a king in flight, the very concept of revolution that had been used in behalf of his predecessor! In the same way the concept of restoration, which had first been used by rebels, in Florence and then in London, to signify a "restoration of liberty," had subsequently been turned against them and used in behalf of the restored monarch.

The Settlement of 1688–89 was not an act of reversal. It was the confirmation of a constitutional state of affairs which Parliament considered it essential to legitimize in accord with all extant principles of English law, historical and natural. It was, therefore, a revolution only in the sense that it was a return to stable conditions after a period of fluctuation. It was a "liberation" of the Church of England and of the English nation from the arbitrary will of the monarch, a revolution without rebels or rebellions. But it was at the same time an event of the kind hitherto known as a *mutation:* a transition to a new dynasty upon new conditions which, with whatever foundation in law, had been laid down by Parliament. As an historical event the Revolution of 1688 itself soon came to be looked upon as something final and unrepeatable and, thus, as something not to be drawn into precedent [*"etwas theoretisch nicht weiter Verwertbares"*]. At the end of the eighteenth century Hume and Burke were still speaking of *revolution* as a unique historical event — and what they had in mind was the event of 1688. The naming of the "Glorious Revolution" was the beginning of the successful career of the modern meaning of *revolution* as a non-evaluative term for great tranformative events, first and foremost in the political realm, but also for natural cataclysms and intellectual changes.

The American Revolution, which created another new nation by severing the ties of external dependence, was later to build upon the intellectual arsenal of the English Revolution. But with the Declaration of Independence and the founding of the United States that arsenal was once again enlarged in characteristic fashion. The equality of all men, their inherent and inalienable rights, and the sovereign right of peoples to institute their own governments were now no longer derived from historical or divinely ordained rights but exclusively from the rational right of nature which had been elaborated in west European thought. The French Revolution, however, being a process of purely internal transformation, was to have a truly incalculable impact upon the moulding of old and new nations in Europe and throughout the world. Its impact proceeded from a number of enduring fundamental principles. These principles were not drawn from the peculiar right of a particular people, as they had been in England; they were formulated in comprehensible terms of universal validity.

[1] E. Rosenstock, "Revolution als politischer Begriff in der Neuzeit," *Festgabe der rechts- und staatswissenschaftlichen Fakultät in Breslau für Paul Heilborn*, Abhandlungen der Schlesischen Gesellschaft für väterländische Cultur, Geisteswissenschaftliche Reihe, 5. Heft (Breslau: 1931), pp. 83–124, at p. 90f.

II

DETERMINANTS OF REVOLUTION

INTRODUCTION

Definitional Orientation

General Orientation

Specific Orientation

INTRODUCTION

Abundantly demonstrated in the general introduction to this volume is the endless variety of definitions and applications associated with the term "revolution." Nevertheless, an assumption usually made about the subject of revolution is that while it is complex and composed of many sub-types, it is nevertheless a unitary variable and not a series of separate events. In other words, it is assumed the term "revolution" refers to a coherent social event that can be studied as a singular whole. Implicit in the selections of this section, however, would seem to be the possibility that the authors are discussing behavior which is different enough in some instances to be more profitably studied as quite separate kinds of things.

The innumerable factors involved in a revolution and the variety of valid scholarly approaches that have subsequently arisen point to the difficulties involved in forming a consistent and workable definition for the term. The example of our first author in this section, George Pettee, points to this difficulty. Pettee, a political scientist, indicates that according to a common definition, "A revolution is a change in the constitution by illegal means." But, then he goes on to state,

> . . . where it seemed worth the trouble a revolution could be carried out with no formal breach of law at any point, through the enaction of radical amendments in due form.

Pettee proceeds to relate the idea of change to the type of society. In the process, he makes a distinction between palace revolutions — which he contends occur in backward societies with a large element of inert consent in the state association — and social revolutions — which are considered characteristic of advanced societies where the active element is large.

Most definitions do incorporate such factors as violence and power. Historian Peter Amann, for instance, is specifically concerned with power. He first defines the sovereign state in such terms, identifying it as, ". . . a political organization exercising, or able to exercise, a monopoly of armed force, justice and administration over a given area and population . . . a postulate of the state in terms of power, a postulate which I am here stating explicitly." Amann then goes on to place revolution within a similar kind of framework — that is, one of power. He contends that once several power blocs have been identified (e.g., army, national guard, police, etc.) one can begin to construct a meaningful framework for studying revolutionary politics. Using the politics of the French Revolution of 1848 as an example, Amann outlines the events supporting his contention that the exercise of power depends not on the consent of the people, but on their habit of obedience.

Thus, while some elements in the definitions of revolution have a degree of commonness, still no single one is to be found common to all. In the final analysis the range of definitions is very great — bringing us back to the problem with which we began this section. Should what is commonly labeled "revolution" be treated as if it were a complex, but still unitary and singular variable? Or is revolution different kinds of social phenomena that do not belong under one label? Would it make more sense and be more profitable scientifically to recognize that people may be talking about completely different things, even though the term "revolution" is applied in each instance?

It should be strongly emphasized that what is being suggested here, that the term "revolution" may refer to a complex of social processes which could be more suitably treated separately and individually, is not a new and different hypothesis. As we have already pointed out, some of the authors of our selections have suggested the variety of distinct social processes being dealt with. The authors themselves intend to present their discussion of revolutionary social action as merely sub-categories of a more general phenomena. This sort of holistic approach is often associated with areas of study that have not as yet reached a highly refined and developed state of knowledge. The implication is that as the study of revolution reaches a systematic and scientific level the holistic approach will be dropped. Nevertheless, the insights of these contributions are invaluable for further progress on research into the subject.

For a moment let us consider one additional piece of evidence in support of the hypothesis that we can lump very distinct social phenomena under a single concept. Pettee's point that revolutions are not necessarily illegal opposes, as has been previously pointed out, a commonly applied definition that they are. Also implied by Pettee and Louis Gottschalk is the point that revolution is not necessarily a violent form of social change. For in Gottschalk's definition a revolution may be no more than ". . . a popular movement whereby a significant change in the structure of a nation or society is effected." Perhaps this might bring us to a minor resolution of the definitional and conceptualizing difficulties that we are encountering.

If there seems to be any single trait that is common to or constant in all meanings of revolution, it would have to be that of social change. But social change itself is so broadly conceived in sociological writings as to be unsuitable as the definitive and defining characteristic of such a specifically discussed and detailed topic as revolution. If "revolution" in the end refers to nothing more specific than some form of social change not consistently specified, then a redirecting of studies on revolution, to consider the variety of different social processes included within the concept, seems inevitable and desirable.

In order to adequately test the hypothesis of whether revolutionary phenomena do in fact represent a common core of social behavior, it would seem particularly important to determine if a consistent and systematic theoretical framework can be devised to explain revolution satisfactorily and completely. Among the articles in this book the two which most explicitly approach this question are Chalmers Johnson's and Louis Gottschalk's. Neither of these authors go so far as to develop a complete and unalterable systematic theory about revolution. But both of them provide at least the beginning. Their articles discuss specifically the significance of systematic theory in general and its relationship particularly to revolution. Less definitive is the actual application of the theoretical formula to the specific phenomenon. This, of course, is the crux of the matter. It is all very well to talk of a theory of revolution, but how it is to proceed is by far the more difficult assignment.

Chalmers Johnson, a political scientist, in his functionalist approach probably moves a little further and more specifically in this direction. Johnson applies the notion of structural functionalism to the extent that he uses it as a point of departure in analyzing revolutionary social change. His model is of a "functionally integrated social system — a system whose members cooperate with each other by 'playing' various 'roles' that, taken together, permit the whole system to 'function.'" Johnson goes on to state,

> Within the framework of this model, we hope to show that revolution is a form of social change undertaken in response to specific conditions of the social system, and that it occurs at a particular stage in the system's efforts to resolve functional difficulties.

Since structural functionalism is an equilibrium model, a changing social system is one that has moved out of equilibrium, according to Johnson. Whether one agrees entirely with this assessment or not,[1] it is clearly an application of the structural functional framework to the problem of revolutionary social change.

Historian Louis Gottschalk's outline of the nature of historical causes provides a theoretical framework which permits him to develop in a systematic fashion an analysis of causes of revolution. There are, he finds, five basic causes: (1) the demand for change resulting from provocations, (2) the demand for change voiced by solidified public opinion, (3) the hope for success as revealed in programs for reform, (4) faith in revolutionary leadership, and (5) weakness of the groups in power. While the framework employed by Gottschalk is of a more general nature than structural functionalism, it does lead in the direction of examining revolutionary phenomena from a particular and consistent perspective. It is this type of approach we contend which will be most fruitful in determining the real nature of revolution.

In this vein Robert C. Tucker, in his discussion of the Marxian revolutionary idea, provides an excellent summary of the background, progress, and systematic nature of Marxist theory on revolution. Tucker, who is a political scientist, clearly presents the depth and insight of Marxian thought as well as some of its weaknesses. His is a fitting commentary on one of the most widely known theoretical statements on revolution. Not the least of Tucker's contributions is the revelation of some less well-known and controversial aspects of Marx. Disputed by some, for example, is Marx's view on the division of labor. Evidence strongly suggests that Marx was opposed to the division of labor and occupational specialization, which he saw as slavery. There is by no means complete agreement about Marx's position on this point, as Tucker indicates.

While the editors recognize their dated nature, particularly from a psychological point of view, the contributions of Charles A. Ellwood and Gustave LeBon are nevertheless valuable. Psychological factors in revolutionary activity cannot be ignored by anyone interested in developing a general theory of revolution. The classic discussions by Ellwood and LeBon remind us of this fact, as well as provide some provocative insights into the revolutionary mentality. Ellwood arrives at an explanation in terms of habit and adaptation. His theory essentially is that revolutions occur when interferences or disturbances in society arise because of a rapid breakdown of social habits, and a new social order is not easily formed. LeBon develops his ideas on the part played by the people in revolutions, the influence of revolution in transforming personality and mentality, and the kinds of mentalities that characterize people involved in revolution.

James C. Davies, a political scientist, also indicates an interest in the more individualistic psychological factors of revolution. Davies argues, "It is the dissatisfied state of mind rather than the tangible provision of 'adequate' or 'inadequate' supplies of food, equality, or liberty which produces the revolution." In fact, he contends that preoccupation with physical survival militates *against* the "revolutionary state of mind." After examining several revolutions Davies finds that they are most likely to arise when a long period of economic and social advances is succeeded by a relatively sudden reversal. As a result, hard earned gains appear to be totally lost and people become susceptible to revolution.

Of course, part of any systematic theory is a logically consistent classification system of the elements of the subject under consideration. The problem in the social sciences is that agreement by a majority of scholars in the field to accept a classification scheme is next to impossible to attain. The classifications of Lyford P. Edwards and Crane Brinton are no exception to this rule, but they probably do have wider acceptance than most. The utility of their classification schemes is revealed by the fact that present day scholars still employ from time to time the ideas developed by these two authors.

Our concern with Edwards, a sociologist, is his chapter that deals with the advanced symptoms of revolution, including the transfer of allegiance of the intellectuals, the gradual concentration of public dissatisfaction upon some one institution, the exposure of an attack upon the dominant class, and the *oppression psychosis*.

In his well-known work *The Anatomy of Revolution,* historian Crane Brinton analyzes four of history's *great* revolutions. The selection by Brinton summarizes his findings. He comes to the conclusion that history is not necessarily a series of unique events. Instead, his study reveals some important uniformities which are of value for the study of man in society, though not for the purposes of prediction.

While the selections by political scientists Sigmund Neumann and Harry Eckstein both have elements of classification, though in a quite different vein from Edwards and Brinton, this is not their main focus. Neumann balances psychological or individual considerations with the sociological. His concern with the realistic phase of modern revolutions leads him to describe today's revolutionary attitudes as cold, calculated, and coordinated in contrast to earlier revolutions where super-human forces and the whim of individual action played significant roles. He characterizes the broad social or sociological factors in today's movements as totalitarianism, institutionalization, and a mass basis. Neumann also believes that if revolutions are to be considered significant they must necessarily have an international character. In fact, it would be extremely difficult today to distinguish between wars and revolutions since the over-lapping is great. Thus, Neumann suggests the term *international civil war*.

Eckstein contributes the term *internal war* as another substitute for the word "revolution." He discusses the problems involved in determining the causes of internal wars. He makes important distinctions between a number of crucial factors: preconditions and precipitants; the roles of incumbents and insurgents; and theories of particular conditions and general processes. He concludes by asserting that the anticipation of internal wars depends upon a ratio between the positive forces working towards them and the negative forces working against them.

Although specification of a particular theoretical framework is absent from Eckstein's discussion, his concern with propositions toward explaining revolutionary behavior is thoroughly theoretical. It is especially significant for the development of a general theory of revolution that the author is able to demonstrate that many of the propositions on revolution are simply different ways of saying essentially the same thing. The possibility of demonstrating this fact about more of the presently available and future propositions will be particularly important in determining the extent to which revolution should be studied as a complex but singular social phenomenon and not a series of discrete, separate events.

FOOTNOTE

[1] George C. Homans' conception of moving equilibrium suggests the possibility of an equilibrium of change. ". . . what if the system is . . . in a process of change? Shall we abandon the idea of equilibrium in these circumstances?" The implication is that we should not. Take for example "the job of the leader as he tries with conscious interest, to bring his group from one social state to another. . . . We may think of the leader as causing the group, by the orders he gives, to follow a path leading from the initial state of the group to the final one. One path, moreover, may be better than another."

In a reference to a problem situation in an electrical equipment company which Homans had earlier described in detail he now points out that, ". . . increasing complexity of its organization had results that ended in the discontent of the design engineers. If the leaders of the company, while trying to increase the size of the firm, had carried out compensatory changes in other aspects of its social organization, changes tending, for instance, to maintain the rank of the design engineers and to keep the norms of the firm in line with realities; they might have brought about the expansion of the firm and kept the morale of its members unimpaired as well. For any group moving toward a goal, there may be some one path, some changing *balance of conditions* (italics ours), in which the willingness of its members to cooperate with one another and obey orders is most fully maintained." This latter condition then would represent a state of moving equilibrium, of change occurring without equilibrium being disturbed. See George C. Homans, *The Human Group* (New York: Harcourt, Brace and World, Inc., 1950), pp. 421–23.

3. The Process of Revolution

GEORGE SAWYER PETTEE

Nothing is more needed, or more lacking, today than a clear understanding of the real nature of revolution. A revolution represents at least the political failure of a government. In the great cases it represents the general failure of a social system. Every statesman would avoid them by every means if he could. That we do not know how to avoid them is made clear by the fact that at least half of the people living now have seen their governments changed by revolution. At the same time revolution is seriously prophecied for many countries which have not had one recently.

Meanwhile there is no reasonably adequate theory as to the nature of revolutions. Utterly contradictory theories enjoy wide acceptance. None of them can make pretenses to scientific realism or detailed analysis, except the Marxist, which is both unable to win acceptance, and imperfect from the point of view of science. It is superior to any other theory of revolutions now available, but not good enough.

Outside of Marxism there are only some rudimentary efforts at a sociological theory of revolutions. Some of them are useful and suggestive, but they are far from complete. There are also numerous pretentious accounts based on mystical intuition, describing revolutions figuratively as the work of the devil, or of his agents, working through conspiracy to take advantage of human weakness, and some of these find wide favor. They ignore the canons of social science however, and thereby make themselves useless for

31

all the purposes for which science is useful. They give us no real understanding by which to guide our acts more effectively.

The Marxist theory is by all odds the best of those now available. For the crisis stage of a great revolution it is very good. The discipline and success of the Bolshevik Party in 1917 was the reflection of the adequate relation between their ideas and the facts of the situation. But even for the crisis it seems to me that the Marxist picture can be improved on, while for the process before and after the crisis it is quite helpless to illuminate the facts. The Bolsheviks did not call the turn before February 1917 with any precision. The effect of the war was unpredictable for them. And since the N.E.P. in 1921, the disciplined party has been shattered repeatedly by facts on which there could be no obvious and agreed Marxist interpretation. The present multiplicity of Marxist sects is a monument to the failings of Marxist social theory.

A useful theory of revolutions would do more to save us from social ills than anything else could. It would arm social policy with clear criteria for the economy of good to be achieved through mastery of the social order. If we are even partially to substitute intelligent adaptation for helpless drift, or even occasionally to avoid paving hell with good intentions, it can only be through understanding. And the abstract mastery of single aspects of the social process cannot suffice. A general social science is needed, not separate sciences such as economics. Economics, political science, education and others, cannot explain history to us, because the human material has no constant and separable aspects. In history the economic man, for example, behaves in anti-economic ways for reasons unmanageable by the economist.

There is a very considerable knowledge of revolutions available now in books. My notes will indicate to some extent where I have found what seemed to me to be useful. At the same time however, such knowledge, even though rather complete in the aggregate, is at present quite uncommunicable. Only by long and intense selective study can anyone gather today the fragments of a complete theory. Some few have done so, but none of them have restated the whole picture in coherent form.

In trying to construct a coherent and realistic theory of revolution I have tried most of all to conform to sound sociological theory and to the best historical descriptions of the great revolutions. After all, any complete theory of society must describe a society which could have a revolution, since human societies do. And any description of revolution must describe a process of human society, since that is what they are.

It seems to me that the findings of sociology can offer an account of revolution much more illuminating than any existing one, and with no violence to logic. Society as so pictured is no organism but only the relationships between conscious social beings. Every social fact is a fact of individual human personality. Such social facts are partially but imperfectly ordered by the important aspects of human nature into what is recognized as an economic system, and what are less perfectly recognized as a political system, a moral system, etc. All of these alike are governed by the forces of habit and purpose, and are subject to the limitations of human consciousness and of human energy.

DEFINITION

In order to understand revolution we must understand what is the state, since the state is the field of action; and this is most clearly set forth in the description of the state as an association. Every association is a self conscious group possessing common institutions which have grown up to serve common purposes, or to serve the vicarious and incidental interests which spring up around a common purpose. It also must possess a common system or aggregate of symbolic expressions of its purpose and of its identity. This system is its myth, more or less coherent and artistic as the case may be.

An association is commonly taken to mean a defined group of people. Those who are associated are the list of members. But it should be taken as a much less rigid conception than this. Its members are not equals in their membership. An association is a group whose members are conscious of their membership, who act in conformity with that membership, who are aware of common purposes and act under common directives. It is a relationship between men, varying vastly in degree from the case of the member who is suspended for not attending meetings to the member who gladly gives his life for the cause involved in a great association. The state is most variable of all associations, requiring of many of its members, not that they should conform in any way, but only that they should not violate certain rules. The state reaches its highest development, simply as an association, in fascism, where membership becomes most uniform and definite. Since the state is not an end in itself, this of course carries no implication that it is the best state because the most developed.

The *state* as an association is very nearly the same as the ordinary condition of an organized society. To take association in too narrow a sense is extremely easy, but leads to many false conclusions, especially in relation to the problem of the function of the state. The state is not merely a club of good citizens for the maintenance of social order. Its purposes, institutions, and relation to its members can vary with circumstances as much as the circumstances given by human society may vary.

In the case of the state the purpose is closely dependent upon the culture of the society in question. The state protects and serves all the recognized values defined in the general mythology. It does so through its institutions and organs, mainly identifiable as its government. Its minimal purpose is internal peace, but it may, and does, undertake any useful function which its members recognize.

As with any association, its members may be classed as active and passive and coerced, according as they participate or merely conform, or by non-conformity bring penalties upon themselves.

Such a great association as the state with an immense momentum of the "force of habit" in its favor, has a very large historical persistence, but occasionally a state association is violently modified by a partial revolution, changing some of its institutions, and partly changing the classes of members, and in a few cases, the great revolutions, the association has broken down completely, and the society in question has created a new one.

When any association is transformed it means that it has new officers, a new constitution and by-laws, and a rearrangement of its members. Some of its former active members, insiders, become less active, or are thrown out altogether. The reorganization of a corporation is a clear enough example. Further, there are new purposes, or the original purposes are given new effect against mis-directed purposes which had become dominant before the reorganization. The association is made up very largely of the same people, and in it they work together for the same fundamental reasons as before; but in the expression of its purposes, in its official personnel, and in the pattern of its membership, it has been reconstituted. When this occurs in the state it is called a revolution. In the greatest revolutions there is a period between the destruction of the old and acceptance of the new, when by any significant test there is no state.

In revolution we have to deal with "a mysterious, lustful virago, who gives herself to all, intoxicates all, promises all things, and calls herself Revolution."[1] It is high time that some of this lust and mystery and intoxication and many of the promises should be dissolved. Marcu has also said that "All great events that stir men's emotions are accompanied by the most wonderful lying." This is perhaps the main reason why it is so difficult to find reasonable discussions of revolution.

A great revolution is a reconstitution of the state. This means a change in the purpose and institutions of the state, and in the arrangement of its members in political classes. During a revolution there is a short time when there is no complete state association in the community. The idea that a realignment of classes is involved is accepted generally. But in most of the prevalent theories this recognition is marred by a failure to take account of the fact that political classes are derivative from, and not identical with, social classes.

Before such an event can take place the complex of active purpose and passive consent which ordinarily maintains the state must have declined in strength and an opposed purpose must have developed, even if not clearly expressed. The organization of the society under the force of one purpose, or purpose complex, dissolves and is replaced by another. The realignment of classes does not take place without a realignment of ideas; a disintegrated moral order is abandoned and a new one built.

Owing to the peculiar position of the state in society, a great change in social conditions cannot take place without a change in the composition of the state. Given the tendency of mankind to the association of ideas, this also means that old institutional forms will be changed because they are associated in men's minds with the purposes which must be changed, even if they are not, taken by themselves, incapable of serving the new purposes equally well. Hence revolutions always have changed the organization of government, and from this arises the common definition: a revolution is a change in the constitution by illegal means. This is based on an almost perfect correlation, but not on the real nature of revolutions. Revolutions do strive to change everything that is old, but in any case where it seemed worth the trouble a revolution could be carried out with no formal breach of law at any point, through the enaction of radical amendments in due form. The fact that they always have violated the constitution, and that this is the most conspicuous and determinable aspect for study, has led to the rather superficial theories that they also change everything in the culture, with its counterpart, that they change only the superficials and leave the essentials unaltered.

Among the causes of revolution, in a changing culture, may be the progressive dislocation or maladjustment between the forms of economic production and the forms of property, and other analogously related elements in the total culture. A second class of factors may arise in a perfectly stable culture because of the progressive isolation and decay of the governing class, requiring a political revolution without cultural change, and without any implication of evolution or progress. In such a case a revolution is truly restorative, as all revolutions make some pretense of being. Or, thirdly, a series of revolutions might occur due to cyclical spoiling and chastening of classes as in the theories by which Plato and Aristotle explained the Greek revolutions, and which the critics of democracy tend to suggest today. The second and third types of causes are real, and have occurred, but the first type may be taken as of basic significance for the great modern revolutions. As is frequently pointed out, although positive progress upward and onward is not provable, cumulative change in a given direction is a fact of modern history, at least in science and technology, and it causes continuous maladjustment, tension, and readjustment in modern culture and society.

Every revolution is wasteful, "one of the overhead expenses of historic progress," as Trotsky says.[2] One of the hoped for results of a scientific understanding of society would certainly be a degree of social control sufficient to eliminate them. That would require a balance of reason and habit in public life, such as has hitherto been beyond the capacity of any except extraordinary individuals even in private life.

PERSONNEL

One of the necessary steps in any revolution is to remove from office all supporters of the ideas which are being replaced. The old ideas cannot be destroyed, and the old purpose with them, unless the seats of habitual power are cleared of conservatives, and a new personnel installed. This is what is called "the seizure of power." Sometimes it is indeed a seizure of power, but in an advanced society it partakes quite largely the character of a destruction and re-creation of power. Typically a palace revolution is a seizure of power, and occurs in backward societies with a very large element of inert consent in the state association, while social revolutions occur in advanced societies where the active element is large, and are typified by the destruction and re-creation rather than the seizure of power. In any case the whole responsible personnel of government, which is the most active political class, is changed.

The character of this change has been much misunderstood, partly due to failure to appreciate the difference between palace and social revolutions, partly due to the failure to clarify the problem of the elite. The new association which replaces the old is itself, like the old, composed only partly on the basis of active purpose. In so far as it is based on passive consent such consent is granted partly to the new ideas (this is the new power) and partly to the old seats of authority (this is the old power which has been seized). Thus the really effective force is the minority who actively participate in the purpose of the new state. The example of peasant revolts which by themselves never accomplish a revolution or found a new state, is sufficient illustration. The new ruling personnel have power because there is a new association, or because they better represent the purposes of the old association. A Jacquerie which merely burns and pillages in bitter retribution sets up no state, no power, no rulers. However the rulers may also be replaced by others having no object in view but to enjoy the power and perquisites of office.

Obviously revolution may occur in a great variety of forms in this respect. The common error is to suppose that the easiest of these forms to understand must be the universal. This leads to the assumption that all revolutions are carried out by small conspiracies draped in dark and esoteric mystery, seeking to seize office and power without any other significant change. Malaparte has expounded this doctrine with the greatest vigor and show of sophistication.[3] But Trotsky devotes considerable space to an exhibition of the charlatanry at the bottom of it, and to exploding the errors of Blanquism, the older conspiratorial theory from which Malaparte derives.[4]

✳ Such a theory has a romantic appeal . . . and a very consoling effect on the minds of those who are victimized by a revolution, since it makes any account of their own failings unnecessary, but it is a pure fiction so far as an appreciation of what happens in a real revolution is concerned. It rests on the erroneous unilateral theory of political power, which treats power as the attribute of the power holder alone, instead of as a relationship of which authority and consent are coincident aspects. Such a view of the nature of power would indeed reduce the problem of revolution to the problem of conspiracy and the seizure of power.

The transfer of consent by the passive members, in an advanced society is a great act, the fundamental constituent act, in which the majority for once violate the "iron law of oligarchy." In this connection the active class is much larger than in any other social act, no great revolution can take place without it, and through it the state is given a new form which it could never achieve through conspiracy.

As Trotsky asserts, "The most indubitable feature of a revolution is the direct interference of the masses in historic events."[5] This outburst of participation is certainly a fact. The recession of participation after the revolution when life becomes once more habitual, is omitted from Trotsky's analysis however, even in his recent writings, with the exception of his complaints against it as he sees it, only as the Thermidorian reaction.

The change in the personnel of government is one of the most definite and conspicuous points in the process and therefore very important for the whole subject. The only phenomenon in a revolution which is more precisely determinable is the formal change in the constitutional law, which can be dated and documented with great precision, and is therefore beloved of historians. But the going into effect of laws after they are promulgated, like the building of power after office has been seized, is a gradual and time consuming process, because it rests upon the development of habits by the masses of people.

A revolutionary change in the personnel of government is generally the occasion of violence. As Burke puts it, "The ceremony of cashiering Kings . . . can rarely, if ever, be performed without force."[6] The former tenants generally resist, and must be defeated in a military sense. Even when some of them abdicate, some of them resist. This makes the most useful point by which to mark or label a revolution. At the same time no violent change in personnel can take place without violating the existing law defining the tenure of the supreme offices. This means that simultaneously with the change in personnel there is a change in the constitutional law by methods not provided in the constitution. This has sometimes been offered as a general definition of revolution. But the Japanese revolution of the last century, and the German revolution of 1933, show that a real modification of the state could take place without any formally legal break, and even without a complete change in personnel which would by itself serve to give a precise date to the revolution. Indeed it would be possible for a revolution to occur through mass conversion, giving a state constituted entirely around a new purpose, without any necessary change in either the makeup of the political classes or in the form of the governing institutions. Then the ruling class would have the same membership, yet would be transformed by a new ideology. Such a possibility is of course remote, yet it serves to indicate the inadequacy of formalistic definition.

CHANGES IN LAW

No revolution can actually occur unless the state has become a barrier to change, and the state cannot become a barrier to change unless its own form is in some way out of adjustment to the society it is supposed to serve. As Aristotle said, a state does not generally fall unless it is misrepresentative of the society under it and is preserving some injustice. Machiavelli and Harrington follow Aristotle, but like him, they fail to make explicit exactly what maladjustments can occur in a formal constitution of government.

Revolutions occur when most people feel that many of the old laws of business, property, and family relationships have become barriers to life, and have then found that the constitutional laws form a bulwark against changes in ordinary law, because the constituted authorities are interested in the maintenance of the cramping institutions. They can be overcome only through united action, and this united action occurs only when there is already by implication a new norm which is the amorphous material of the new constitution and legal system. This does not mean that the new already must exist as a clearly expressed doctrine. It only means that people are clearly conscious of the ways in which they wish to act upon their normal impulses in the circumstances of their present, and are prevented by instituted norms. From the complex picture of the behavior they feel proper, will come the norms of the new order.

Law as a norm makes uniformity and order possible in society. The legal system with its sanctions, is the standard of reference by which order is preserved in the social system. Once accepted it is immensely powerful, especially as vested interests grow up around it. The problem of social change therefore inevitably becomes a problem of legal change, and also in many cases a problem of change in the constitution and personnel of the ruling offices.

Any refusal to adjust laws to changing customs, where the great majority feel that the new customs are justifiable, must be due to a lack of coherence between the composition and purposes of the ruling class and of the society as a whole. The commonest of such cases can occur only where political participation is closed in some way. It is not a matter of the arrangement of the organic constitution of the state within itself, but of the relation of the government to the society. If social flexibility is to prevent the governing class from becoming a closed and isolated and decadent group, government must be open to class circulation. This is the minimum provision, and exit as well as entrance must be provided for. If office is open to the talents in the widest possible way, then at least the active citizens are allowed to aspire to the highest degree of participation. Where office is closed or restricted in any arbitrary way, in a society in which social mobility is otherwise possible, the composition of society can change while the composition of the government does not, so that an eventual readjustment must take place. This usually is a concomitant feature of a great revolution, as in Russia where the governing classes were so lacking in the necessary qualities of an elite and so isolated from Russian society.

A more typical example of purely constitutional maladjustment was the composition of the Estates General in France when called in 1789. It was based upon an approximate adjustment to the French society of several centuries earlier, and the first step in the revolution was to redress the balance by uniting the three houses so that the Tiers could hold the balance instead of being outvoted by the other two. "This, rather more than the lurid later affair of the Bastille, was a revolution," as Brinton says.[7]

Erroneous conclusions have sometimes been reached by writers who found false clarity in this confusion. Martin has decided that there really is no relation between the forms of government and the ends of revolution. As he sees it, every revolution begins with the cry of liberty and ends in tyranny. Therefore they are all a great waste of time. His argument is based on limited conceptions of liberty and of revolution as purely political in a narrow sense. This extremely superficial attitude has considerable prevalence today.

Another strange idea is the one which passes as a theory that there is a legal "right" of revolution. This, even more than the extreme forms of the theory of sovereignty shows the dire results of an attempt to make a complete sociology out of juristic materials. Law does consist of formal expressions founded on social facts. But it cannot be a complete picture of all social facts. Upon the reality of a promise may be raised the artificial conception of contract. But revolution, like crime, must remain outside legal expression. Law is after all the product of social forces above and beyond its own scheme of reference. The only practical applications of the legal theory of a right of revolution have been judicial review, and the "vocation of the lesser magistrates" of Calvinist theory. Each is meant to empower certain offices to restore the fundamental law in case of violation by the supreme political power. Whatever one may think of judicial review, the vocation of the magistrate has found its only historical realization in such coups as those of the two Napoleons, and has proved a fruitful source of perversion, but not of correction. All such theories grow out of the universal pretense of revolutionists, most conspicuous in the Fronde, that they are really the pious restorers of the original constitution.

One of the assumptions without which law cannot operate is that of the unique power field. It is one of the outstanding features of a great revolution that it temporarily destroys this power field when it destroys the state association. Law rests upon the fundamental agreement of the community. When a community is in fundamental disagreement, and men's wills are involved to the point of fighting, there occurs a condition of dual or multiple power, an unresolved conflict of forces in which there is no unique power. Until coercion becomes an effective control determining the behavior of the losers in conformance to the will of the victors, there is no state, and no general legal system. The intervening process is not subject to legal considerations.

The fact remains that the constitution of government as well as the composition of the state association and the personnel of government, is generally changed in a revolution. The reasons why this is necessary are of two orders: first, the constitution has a greater or less degree of logical appropriateness to the composition of the old society, secondly, in addition to any logical objections to the old constitution as a form for the new government, it is generally associated in men's minds with policies that have come to be hated and which have been overthrown. Only the detailed study of particular cases can show how far each of these reasons enters into a given case.

SOCIAL CHANGES

Changes in the personnel and form of government are means to ends. Governments are overthrown only when desired changes in ordinary law cannot be accomplished by any other means. Law, as a formalization of the social system is the level on which the real grievances leading to political action occur, and on which the remedies are sought. There are two main ways in which a social system and a system of law can be out of harmony with the life that men are trying to lead under them. One is involved in privilege. The other is represented by general maladjustments which bind and constrict the whole society without class distinction.

Where privilege leads to revolution it is because the lack of social mobility leaves a large portion of the intrinsic elite barred from the use of their talents, or denied appropriate rewards. If members of the intrinsic elite can find no other outlet for their talents they will always revolt. This is sometimes pictured as a perfect somersault in society, the former ruling class becoming coerced, and the former suppressed class becoming the ruling one. Such a picture is useful for propaganda, and is also a source of some of the phobias of such critics as Burke. It is naturally a very difficult subject to treat quantitatively. The situation involves a great reallocation of social status, and only an army of sociologists on the spot at the time could measure what is happening. The great mass of passive citizens transfer their allegiance or consent from the old leaders and institutions to a new ruling class made up on a more nearly intrinsic basis. The new elite is not absolutely exclusive of elements of the old. It is in the transfer of allegiance that the masses become for a short time active participants in the historical process.

In any social system the adjustment of intrinsic to extrinsic factors determining social status is subject to some friction and is time consuming. The greater the degree of identity between the intrinsic and the socially recognized extrinsic elite, the less tension in society, all other things being equal.

The specific content of the maladjustments and cramps may be found in any side of social life, since there are many forms of privilege. Marx founded his system on an implicit psychology of the subconscious in which acquisitiveness is the only basic motive of human nature. But only a complete psychology can account for all of the things that men want, and only such a psychology can account for all of man's possible frustrations, and no less than all of these may play a part in revolt. Inequalities in the distribution of the social income and of existing wealth of course play a major role.

Specific groups become rebellious when they are cramped or coerced. Cramp is basically subjective, depending upon a consciousness of barriers to full self expression. In most cases men feel cramped only when others no better than themselves enjoy greater perquisites, or when the direct expression of a blameless impulse collides with convention, but in many cases ambitious men feel cramped in any position which denies them unique power. Aristotle and Machiavelli were more conscious of this than Marx.

It is commonly supposed that revolutions are a means of redress of the specific advantages of one class and specific disadvantages of another. Yet the Russian and French revolutions each commenced with an astonishing display of unanimity by the whole of society. The truth is that such a revolution can only be carried out by an alliance of several classes under

the leadership mainly of one of them, and occurs only when almost the
entire society has reached the point of consent to the destruction of the
old state. In such a case the existing social system has reached a point at
which not one but all classes without exception find it impossible to go on.
The decadence of the rulers plays a part in such a situation, and economic
factors assist. But as Trotsky says, "The fundamental premise of a revolution is that the existing social structure has become incapable of solving
the urgent problems of development of the nation." [8] The collapse does
not occur until the old system has exhausted all its possibilities.

There are certain prescribed preventives of revolution on the social plane.
One is the encouragement of the middle class. Another is the maintenance
of social services, with a basic attitude in the rulers which inclines them
to yield to pressures before instead of after they become extreme. The last
is the resort to repression under the guise of Fascism, which destroys
problems instead of solving them. This last, if it can avoid ending as the
Marxists claim it must, having merely played out a losing hand to the
last bitter end, is under suspicion of fundametal decadence.

The effects of revolution in the social sphere are less due to policy and
more largely due to the violence of the process itself than is generally
thought. The Bolsheviks did indeed alter the pattern of Russian social and
economic relations to a great degree. And the French revolution carried
out some of the reforms suggested in the Cahiers of 1789. But the complete
disorder of the process alone is sufficient to discharge a great many of the
tensions which have caused a revolution. Mere temporary disorder suffices
to eliminate cumulative maladjustments. Monetary inflation serves to redis-
tribute property for instance, and has served this purpose in each of the
great revolutions. But social ills and social cures are themselves parts of
the larger area of the culture, and factors outside the area of the purely
social or economic or political may have a deep effect on the problem,
both as to the causes and the nature and effect of revolution.

CULTURAL CHANGES

It is a commonplace to ascribe to Rousseau a profound influence in the
movement which made the French Revolution. This sort of argument
carries us at once from the plane of particular political or economic ills
and rational remedies into the equally real one where the interworking
of will and imagination give us an infinite variety of products.

Outside of any question of the growth of a revolutionary movement
which works to change social organization, is the question of what happens
to the rulers that they can permit insoluble contradictions to arise, and a
movement outside the ruling elite to grow up and displace them. Every

revolution represents a failure of the ruling class, decadence in at least a limited sense. Apparently the same forces which operate to create a new elite tend also toward the simultaneous decrepitude of the old rulers.

One such mechanism is the one noted by Aristotle, by which such oligarchies as the Spartan tended through the concentration of land holding to become too small in numbers to contain enough of the intrinsic elite to go on holding power. In his own words, oligarchies "passed into tyrannies and tyrannies into democracies; for love of gain in the ruling class was always tending to diminish their number, and so to strengthen the masses, who in the end set upon their masters and established democracies." [9]

Among the many writers who deal with this question of the failure of the ruling class, Pareto has probably the most elaborate and formal explanation. At the same time he furnishes an interpretation which might be used to support the Marxist one. The Marxist theory requires something like mutually exclusive ideologies and mentalities in the capitalist class and in the proletariat. Pareto emphasizes that just such a differentiation of basic attitudes may occur through the predominence of what he calls residues of group-persistence in one class and of residues of combination in the other.[10] What his argument amounts to is that when solidarity declines and individual hedonism increases in the ruling class, and the opposite happens in the subject class, a transfer of power is also on the cards. This is an integral part of the Marxist argument, and may be restated in terms of social entropy as by Brooks Adams, or of its outward effects on the distribution of property, as by Aristotle.

Even when such a process is pursued to its end it is not a smooth glide into oblivion by the decadent elite. The elite itself is complex and not homogeneous. There is always a fraction of it which tries to regain the old morale. Nock has given a good picture of the religious side of the attempt of the Roman elite to salvage something, to return to group residues. But he also shows how fatally tardy and finally inadequate such a restoration of the cultural character of the Roman elite was.[11]

Coincident with the decline of the elite in those cultural qualities essential to its survival occurs the development of those same qualities in some other sector of society, really in members of the intrinsic elite who are excluded from membership in the extrinsic elite, and who, if all Pareto says of them is true, naturally act upon residues of group persistence and demand rule for the class in which extrinsic social factors have placed them rather than solely on behalf of themselves. Pareto at this point gives a better account of the class loyalty of the proletarian elite than the Marxists. In the typical great revolution the rising elite act under the guidance of a definite though unfinished myth, with strong solidarity and a very large degree of individual self-abnegation.

Another element in any great revoluton and in many abortive revolts is the aggression of the desperate. Trotsky and others have insisted that without the revolt of the peasants in Russia in 1917 the proletarian revolt could not have been successful. This would be sufficient to prove that such a revolt is not unimportant. It is true that no successful revolution has been carried out by a class repressed to the level of ignorance and starvation. It is also true that there are very few actual outbreaks by such classes. But the present tendency to discount them altogether would certainly leave one open to some shocking surprises. Carlyle overdid the argument that the French revolution was a revolt of a frightfully repressed people, but the correction should be taken with moderation. The whole argument about distress and expansive ambition as causes of revolution may be resolved if one remembers that a shoe may pinch, either because the foot has grown, or because the shoe has shrunken. Distress alone has not sufficed to cause a full dress revolution, but it has played a mighty role in the two greatest ones.

Connected directly with the theories that account for revolution on a rational interest basis are the theories of cyclical revolution which assume alternations of expansive ambition and chastened moderation on the part of the masses of men. The stage of chastened moderation is accounted for in various ways. Plato suggests a sequence of forms of government from aristocracy, through timocracy, oligarchy, democracy, to tyranny, which would appear to rest in its early steps upon a gradual transformation of the elite from a condition in which the intrinsic and extrinsic elite are identical, to one in which the extrinsic elite become based first on honor and then on wealth, whereupon they are overthrown by the mob which eventually lays the burden of power in the lap of the tyrant. In the early stages the decline of character and low social mobility would appear to be the causes of the decay of the rulers while in the later stages the expansive ambition of the mass followed by disillusionment would appear to have the major role.[12]

Quite aside from the objective changes which disintegrate a social order, and the changes brought by revolution to reintegrate it, we have the ideological products of a revolution, largely created before the political revolution takes place, though not accepted until afterwards. Mass action with destructive aims needs no common ideas, since any common impulse, however elementary, will suffice. But the constructive phase of revolution requires the power of common will guided by common ideas. Every revolution develops such common ideas, or a myth, before it accomplishes any positive political action.

A community cannot shed its old form and reintegrate itself by new purposes, without an accepted expression of these purposes in a myth. This means no more than that a new social order is real only when men behave regularly and coherently in the new patterns, which thereby are made the new institutions. This condition can be reached only through the common direction of the wills of a multitude of individuals by common directives, which for the innovations cannot be habits, and so must be ideas. These are the new myth. The only *tertium quid* is the abandoning of both conventional habit and rational thought for blind instinct. The existence of a common myth requires a long and complicated development from original conception or invention through elucidation and elaboration and diffusion, until it is received by a considerable number of individuals in the given society. This does not mean that the new myth is already widely received before the revolution. But it is accepted by a nucleus capable of receiving the consent of the great majority as leaders, after the revolution begins. Such a process is individual in all its stages. Single persons experience dissatisfaction with existing conditions, conceive in imagination a better order, express both their criticism of the old and their picture of the new in a literary form, often largely symbolic, and others adhere or are converted to the new doctrine. The classic form is that of the prophet who carries the movement through all its stages in his own life, but such a case is relevant only to primitive cultural conditions in a small community. Modern culture is more complicated, so that it requires the work of many minds to build an adequate body of doctrine, as in the case of Marxism. And modern community is huge, and varies from place to place in its stage of development, so that diffusion is a more complicated and time consuming process. Hence for any great revolution the guiding myth is certain to be the product of many hands, and to contain within itself sometimes irrelevant and even contradictory elements. But in general a successful revolutionary myth must be logically integrated, and have artistic literary form, though not necessarily assembled as such in a single book, and must be seriously antagonistic to the last previous myth which has given a general stamp to the society through its function as a common rule by which individuals govern their behavior.

Such a myth is at its center a picture of man. That is the simple reason why the older myths generally were woven as a story around an individual protagonist. It is perhaps the basic weakness of the modern myths that they possess no clear picture of human nature. Both Rousseau and Marx did indeed make clear assertions about the character of man, but in the one case the portrait of Emile was badly messed up by the superimposition of the physiognomies of Robespierre and Napoleon, and in the Marxist case there is an obvious contradiction between man as a materialist and man as exemplified in Marx or Lenin. Some of the literary Marxists have done much recently to clarify the Marxist picture of man, especially such writers as Malraux, Ralph Bates, Auden, and Macleish. But they have certainly not yet fully overcome this weakness of the doctrine. Such confusion blurs the myth as a work of art, and causes confusion in its effects as a guide to conduct. This illustrates what was meant by the statement above that a myth may itself contain contradictions. At the same time such complexity greatly aids the myth in diffusion by making it to a degree pass tender as all things to all men.

A myth possesses force only through the individuals whose wills it governs. It can govern behavior only through becoming the focus of their wills, and this only through a sort of monopoly of the imagination. Those whose imaginations are so monopolized are the converted, and very often become so through the emotional crisis called conversion, common in religious history. The less completely controlled are those who may be classed as adherents. It is in relation to individual psychology that a social or political myth has something in common with a religious one, although its content may have very little of a strictly theological quality.

The central point here is that the personality of the true revolutionary is integrated by the principles which have won his devotion. This gives him what all men recognize as integrity of character. He will be dependable, and will be trusted, either as a follower or as a leader. This is the true type of the professional revolutionary in the Marxist movement. Anyone who has read much of the literature of revolution is familiar with the type, illustrated by such a figure as Lenin himself and many others. At the same time, the same symbols may have different meanings to different converts, and internal misunderstandings and disputes grow up in the movement in spite of agreement on the symbols. AE's book, *The Interpreters*,[13] gives an extraordinary picture of the variety of meanings which can be united by a single vague idea.

The basic function of a myth is always to govern present action towards future hopes. Very often the future hopes are pictured in an altogether too far off divine event. Such a myth will secure less devotion, and even for its fanatic devotees it will be an escape, a vicarious purpose, not a way of life. There may well be times when a whole people will eagerly accept false gods, but in the long run such faiths fail. As Henri De Man argues, the justification of a myth must be found in its service as a way of present action, and in the value of the way of present life of its followers. To serve only the future is a way of life only for those who place no value on themselves, the already defeated.[14]

The success of a myth in uniting human wills may depend upon a great many factors. Its completeness and internal coherence, its comforting pretenses of the restoration of some good old time, its gorgeous vision of the future, and its pretense to provide a universal frame of reference of good and evil, will all contribute. If it is narrow or inconsistent, unconvincing in its criticism of the present or in its picture of the future, or in any way too much open to counter-criticism, it will be weaker.

Especially in the present world must a myth pass a barrage of critical examination which it can survive only if the builders of it have done their job well. This is the point at which it becomes possible to place comparative values upon different myths. In general it is a survival test. That myth which can best survive criticism must have the fewest internal flaws and the fewest contradictions of the known facts of human nature, and must therefore be the best guide for conduct in the same sense of truth as that by which we judge the scientific. A myth is not scientific in the sense of being explicitly logical and lucid. In general myth making is more a task for a man with great perceptions than for a man with great logical faculties. It is always, at least hitherto, expressed in terms quite different from those of science, allegory or metaphor rather than precise theorems. But the criteria remain the same. Thus the most dangerous weapon against any myth is the charge that it violates the facts of human nature. Such is the charge of Burke against what he took to be the ideas of the French Revolution. And such in turn is the charge of Irving Babbitt against both Burke and democracy.[15]

A newer weapon, almost equally dangerous, is that of skepticism armed by modern psychology with explanations of how myths may grow as compensations in maladjusted minds. In a given case this may of course be a valid attack, but it is also a much too convenient instrument of cynical relativism. If there are any standards possible it is also possible for conditions to exist in which any well adjusted man must be a revolutionist, and in which it is the comfortable people who feel well adjusted to the existing system who are in fact psychopathic cases.

The ability to pass critical examination is a relative and not an absolute test. There never has been an absolutely perfect myth. Perhaps the meaning behind the symbols of Roman Christianity has reached as high as any, but even taken at its best and not in its corruption, sound criticism can find flaws. That has been true of all myths, and after all remains true of all science. The impossibility of perfection is balanced by the necessity of effort as a condition of living, and by the possibility of improvement, and criticism is essential to improvement.

The creation of myths is a function of the elite. At the same time it is the elite who have the least need of anything like a rule book for conduct. Lenin for example knew how to act according to circumstances, breaking rules and making new ones by the precedent of his own decisions, where the average Bolshevik was often enough at a loss to know how to follow even the existing rule.

A great revolution is one in which the reconstitution of the state association is coincident with the substitution of one myth for another as the main integrating guide in the culture. It is often asserted that such a revolution is a complete or total change in the culture of the community. Burke expressed this attitude very clearly in his writings on the French Revolution.

This idea of total change colors a great deal of the criticism of revolution, and also bolsters the eschatological ideas of the most devoted revolutionists. But if culture, and the social system, are always complex, only imperfectly integrated, always containing contradictions, how could a change in even the most dominant of all single integrating factors, the myth, actually change the total system in a total way? The answer is that it will doubtless cause repercussions into even the farthest corners, nothing will escape altogether. Change in a revolution is neither insignificant nor total, but something in between. A myth is a great force for uniformity of style and spirit in a culture, and a change in the dominant myth does bring changes in a great deal of the way of life. It it doubtless the most important thing that can happen in human history. But society is not so constituted that anything can change it all at once, nor completely in any determinate time.

All this is assuming that the old and the new myths are directly contradictory to each other, the extreme case. But this extreme case does not occur. Only a demigod or a lunatic could conceive a new myth which was really out of all relation to the old one. It is one of the scientific elements in Marxism that it conceives of the old system as the parent of the new, and of the new myth as bearing a definite relationship to the old one, changing certain fundamental features but carrying on many others in modified form. The victory of Marxism would not represent anything like a total cultural change, but it is nevertheless the extreme type of case for practical purposes.

Revolution may then change the whole tone or style of a society, and change the direction of development. In so far as the new myth does contradict the old there must also be a conflict between individuals who are devoted to the new and other individuals devoted to the old. When a new myth has become accepted by the bulk of the society, which is to say, when the period of dictatorship has passed and the reconstitution of the state has been completed by the consent of the mass of the members, then of course the individual must be living to a degree under the guidance of the new myth. To the degree that he does so he is a different man from the typical citizen before the revolution.

GRADUALNESS AND SUDDENNESS

Revolutions involve operations on many different levels, from the replacement of the personnel of government, and the replacement of formal laws, to the replacement of the dominant myth, and the changes in all the ways of human life which are restyled by the new myth. For each of these levels of operation the time scale is quite different. A change of law is conceptually instantaneous. A change in personnel may be extremely abrupt. But the replacement of a myth requires generations, and the full adaptation of life to a new myth (or of the myth to life), may need centuries. Hence the controversy as to the suddenness or gradualness of revolution. There are the widest discrepancies between various treatments of this question. It is closely related to the question of the importance of conspiracy and insurrection. The emphasis on gradualness in one of its forms is an emotional application of the truth that construction takes time, and that violence is destructive. This is no more meaningful however, than it is to call attention to the fact that surgery is not constructive. In its more reasoned form it insists simply that the deeper changes take time.

Against the gradual aspects which are often overemphasized, are the sudden aspects. The overemphasis on these is the basis of Blanquism, already mentioned. An underemphasis on them is one of the bases of reformism in the derogatory sense as the evasion of unpleasant facts. The truth comes back to the point that man is governed largely by habit, that common habits are institutions, and that institutions generally rest partly upon some formal expression. From the point of view of behavior an individual can only follow a habit or not follow it. He cannot for any length of time wobble between two habits or institutions in any one of the essential patterns of life. In his habitual granting of consent to a recognized authority, particularly, he must eventually grant it only to one, though he may for some time not entirely make up his mind. The transfer or recreation of power, or reconstitution of the state association, represents the critical point at which a sudden but superficial change takes place. The masses at this point shift their habitual consent. This is part of what Marx meant by his formula, "quantity becomes quality," though this phrase is generally misused in a sense of organic integration of the culture, connected with the stage-theory aspects of Marx's thought.

This sudden change is very conspicuous, is indeed the change which is taken by some to be all there is in a revolution. It is the easiest part of the descriptive historical problem of a particular revolution because it gives rise to specific events which can be easily described and dated, and of which everyone is conscious. It remains superficial for those who seek deeper and more remote causes, but only in such a sense as that in which law is more superficial than custom. Russia was only superficially socialistic in 1920, let us say, yet such a superficial change of myth, with the accompanying change in the field of power, is as fundamental in its later effects as anything that can happen. After all, the inseparable phases of a single process cannot be distinguished as more or less significant.

Many of the most adverse criticisms of revolution are founded on just this sort of distinction. There may be ways to avoid much of the wastefulness of revolution but the assumption that the superficial changes in personnel and organs, and the violence that accompanies them, are unnecessary and pointless, is quite unfounded. All the violence of revolution can be avoided if and when men can be induced to be so reasonable or so indifferent that they can live without the mediation of myths which are at best approximate truths, or when man can perceive perfect truth.

One school of writers condemn revolution mainly for its wastefulness.[16] Another condemns it for always ending in the opposite of what it professes.[17] A third simply holds it altogether unnecessary and bad. They all have the degree of truth which Trotsky admits, that revolution is wasteful and destructive beyond what may be the necessity of normal human failing, but their conclusions are Utopian. The best examples of such writers might be Burke, J. Ferrari, G. L. Dickinson, and E. D. Martin. They all alike analyze revolution as if it were a purely political event, but criticize it and evaluate it as if it were a broad social and cultural process. They thus fail to analyze and evaluate the same thing. This irrelevance weakens both their analysis and their judgement, since neither can be guided by the other. Value judgements which go beyond the political plane can only be supported by an analysis which is fully as broad as the thing to be judged. All of these critics fall into what is really the error of Blanquism, almost making the revolutionist the sole cause of revolution. It is, unfortunately, an error only too easy to fall into in an age when political science and sociology have been artificially divided.

The necessity of revolution rests on the conservatism of man and the contrast between the gradualness with which he changes habits which are superficial to his personality, and the suddenness and strain with which he changes his governing beliefs. The violence of revolution is due to the resistance of a ruling class which is devoted to forms which no longer are tolerable to others who are already living under new habits and by new purposes. The defense of revolution against its critics is based on the argument that it represents vitality and progress triumphing over decay and death. That is doubtless as the case may be. But it possesses no less possibility of truth in a given case than the criticism.

The written defenses of revolution are generally based upon a much more realistic analytic approach than are the anti-revolutionary arguments. Admitting all the waste and horror, a revolution may still operate for the economy of human good. The waste of revolution must be weighed against the waste of an *ancien régime,* and the benefits of revolution against the recognized good things of the old system. The judgement is not easy to make. The sober judgement of mankind has held them to be worthwhile, but only as *faut de mieux*. The chief causes of revolution, and the greatest crimes against society are those which make it impossible to obtain the benefits more cheaply.

THE KINDS OF REVOLUTION

If what has gone before has been at all clear it should appear by now that an organized society is so complex that it can undergo quite a variety of operations, politically similar, yet differing from each other in nature and importance. The principles upon which society is built are essentially simple, but like any function of a dozen variables, it may in total have an infinite variety of values. Therefore the superficial aspects of revolution, such as the change in the constitution by methods not provided in the constitution, or the violent change in the personnel of government, may take place as the outward signs of a great variety of different processes. We have the French and Russian revolutions as one type, in which the state association is reconstituted in order to adapt it to a society which has already widely departed from its former constitution. That is what I call a great revolution. We have also the rebellion of a section of the passive membership of the state, not in order to overthrow the existing state, but in order to separate from it and establish a new state beside the old one. It's common and useful to refer to such as rebellions. A rebellion is rather an intercommunal struggle, if not formally international, than an intra-communal struggle.

Dealing only with intra-communal violence as revolutionary we are left with a great variety still. It is at this point that the levels of operation become really important. A violent political change may be carried out only to change the personnel of government, violating no part of the constitution except the laws defining the tenure of office. Or it may be meant to alter the organic structure of the government in order better to serve the same purposes of the same intact state association. Or it may find its real objectives and tasks on the level of the social system, to be achieved through changes in the legal system, in which case it is to some degree a social revolution, though not necessarily a great one.

There are three main types then to distinguish. First and least significant is the private coup d'etat or palace revolution, which is common in the plays of Shakespeare, and in South America. Secondly comes what may more properly be called a public coup d'etat which is common in more advanced societies, in which the large size of the ruling elite gives an aspect of mass action and publicity to a seizure of existing power where no shift of classes beyond the expulsion of a fragment of the elite is contemplated, and no change in the social system is sought. The coup of Louis Napoleon in 1851 was of this type. Thirdly and most important are the social revolutions in which the whole extrinsic social system is to be readjusted to the intrinsic social life, formed by a new purpose expressed in a new myth.

Of course no social revolution is ever likely to take place without a coup d'etat at some point. When social changes do take place without any political crisis they are not revolutions. But a social revolution cannot be grasped through a study of the change of government affected. Anyone who tries to study the French Revolution from a purely constitutional angle will find not one but many coups d'etat. A social revolution includes coup d'etat as a part of its process, but coups d'etat can and do occur independently. There are many possible objectives for a coup d'etat beside the reconstitution of the state.

There is one exceptional type of social revolution which must be distinguished. That is a revolution by which the state association is reconstituted in its purpose, and the social system is changed, without any great displacement of political or social classes. Such an occurrence is rare in history, but it did take place in Japan in the late nineteenth century. In such a case a revolution as according to Aristotle has taken place; that is, the country has a new constitution, and the ruling class has been transformed yet the personnel of the active elite remains much the same. In such a case the immediate cause of revolution is not the disparity between the intrinsic and the extrinsic social classes but the inadequacy of the social system as felt by the elite itself. In such a case as the Japanese a part of the old elite resist and are coerced. But otherwise there is very little dislocation of classes. The American Civil War is a partial parallel, with the elite splitting on geographical lines and thus giving the conflict the form of a rebellion. Such cases are priceless as illustrations of the variety of possibilities, and as checks against too narrow exclusions, such as the Marxists particularly indulge in.

Their common error is to deal with the most probable outcome of a social situation as if it were the only possibility. They make a mistake when they take the French and Russian revolutions as the inevitable form. The great revolution is an actual and possible form, but far from inevitable as the outcome of any situation.

There are still the successful and the unsuccessful to distinguish, as well as the partially successful. Every attempted coup d'etat is an insurrection. But insurrection is subject to the fortune of war, and the balance of the other social forces may be entirely upset by the role of the army. Insurrection is the military phase of the class struggle or of the group struggle for power. There are many failures, of which the Paris Commune of 1871 is one of the most famous.

In all of these differences between revolutions the variations are of degree rather than absolutely of kind. Yet the commonest historical cases are of the logically typical varieties.

PRE-REVOLUTIONARY SOCIETY

The failure of a state may be due to its failure to serve the purposes of men in the form which the culture makes appropriate, or to the loss of coherent correspondence between the organization of the state association and the existing structure of society itself, or to plain bad engineering in the organization of the government. Cramp thus occurs on the same set of levels as those dealt with in discussing the kinds of revolutionary change in the previous chapter. If the cramp is only in the organization of the state a palace revolution discharges it, if it extends to the composition of the state as an association, or to the social system, a social revolution is the necessary outcome.

Cramp may arise in every social relationship, and so may be infinitely complex and varied. Societies are, as said before, never perfectly integrated, so that the same cramps have different effects and degrees of importance in different communities, even in going through the same phases of a joint cultural development. The significance of any single factor depends upon its interaction with the total matrix, and the total is never identical, so that the equation never can be identical in two cases. Trotsky's "law of uneven development" is a form of statement of this fact. The discharge of a major secular maladjustment is always accompanied by a release of all restraints which allows a simultaneous discharge of all sorts of minor and perhaps wholly unrelated cramps. This is why a revolution may turn out to be more violent than any examination of its major causes can account for.

A revolution is the opportunity for the discharge not only of those cramps which affect the society as a whole, but of every local or even private abuse or vengeance. Cyclical cramps can actually be corrected for a long time to come by a period of pure anarchy. This is why an apparently irresistible revolt is sometimes suppressed shortly afterward by a well timed reaction. The cyclical cramps which gave to the revolt much of its force have been discharged in the period of disorder, property has been shuffled, debts canceled. After the burning of the chateaux in France by the peasants, for instance, destroying the documents on which many of the privileges and abuses rested, the peasants never again had as much interest in the revolution, and never really supported the Jacobins. The power of the revolution declined like that of a wave on a beach, as one after another of the actual cramps was removed, and many of them beyond the power of restoration. Robespierre's power on the eve of Thermidor was practically only that of the very brief tradition of the revolution. There were no longer any important purposes which required changes in the social order.

Only a very broad view can give a clear picture of the whole of a revolutionary situation. Burke's failure to grasp the meaning of the French revolution was due simply to a narrow preoccupation with the political process and therefore with the political causes, which rightly enough appeared to him an inadequate justification of it. When a society has reached the last stage before a revolution it is in a state of pseudo-morphosis, living under forms determined by purposes long dead, and striving to live already by new purposes so frustrated by the old forms that they cannot be understood, much less pursued, by the majority. The system of mediation and the actual way of life have become irrelevant to each other. This if anything, may be called social neurosis. It has a part of its base in widespread individual neurosis, and faction.

A resort of those conservatives armed with the jargon of modern psychology is to call all revolutionists maladjusted cases, and by implication dispose of them as abnormal. This is typical of a good deal of post war ideology in its washed out relativism and basic cynicism. It is true that in any given case the presumption is that maladjustment between an individual and a social system is due to the abnormality of the individual rather than to that of the system. But this probability is by no means overwhelming. Revolutionists may be and sometimes are the most normal members of their societies in every respect except blindness and lazy acquiescence toward conventions.

It is revolutionists, finally, as persons, who actually do the work of rebuilding a social order amid the ruins of the old one. This is always done through organized groups or a party, which develops a new myth, criticizes the old one, and finally attempts to destroy the old power and create a new one in its place. The whole work of recreation is performed by individuals, and the death of the old system takes place as it loses its hold upon individual wills, just as the new is born and grows in individual minds and wills. Cramp is the original motivation, but the discharge of cramp and development of a new system take place through a mass process of propagation and reception as well as through the formal changes of institutions and laws which follow.

PRE-REVOLUTIONARY LOYALTY

Viewed historically a revolution appears as the reconstitution of a state to serve human purposes newly expressed, with new rules dictated by a new sense of proportion. The conflict appears in retrospect to be one between only two great antagonists. The principal characteristic of the French Revolution was thus the liquidation of feudalism and the introduction of a political and legal system in which capitalist relationships would be free to develop. The Russian Revolution viewed superficially appears as a destruction of the old mingled feudalism and capitalism by Marxism. Actually the process of growth of the new purposes is utterly complicated, and while an integrated doctrine such as Communism may reach the finished form of a myth it is by no means the only myth on the revolutionary side, and much less is it the expression of all the revolutionary purposes. The elaboration and propagation of the revolutionary ideas is carried on by a group of competing revolutionary sects, with all kinds of straddlers and stragglers between and around them. There is a great division of labor in a revolution, those who contribute one idea may be all unaware of some other; those who criticize the old may have no conscious sympathy with those who are trying to plan the new. In the French Revoluton there was no integrated doctrine whatever, only a few flexible and half understood guiding ideas about a rational ordering of society, and a great accumulation of specific opposition to specific old institutions.

The French Revolution was the revolution which cracked the modern consciousness and made men realize that revolution is a fact, that a great revolution may occur in a modern progressive society. After the French Revolution no other revolution could ever be carried out by men so innocently naive about the significance of their own acts. It is after the French Revoluton that we find professed revolutionists working for revolutions in the future and studying those of the past. Therefore, after the French Revolution we find a conscious development of revolutionary doctrines in anticipation of revolutions to come, and the spread of a more active attitude toward conscious control over institutions in general. The English Revolution, and even the American succeeded so well in maintaining their own conservative and legitimate pretensions that the idea of social transformation did not enter in. The idea of a revolution as a willed destruction and replacement of a whole system of controlling institutions did not occur until after the French Revolution, and it necessarily changed the course of development of all succeeding revolutions. Revolution has become one of the techniques of social control, the most wasteful, the most expensive, the last to be chosen; but also the most powerful, and therefore always appealed to in what men feel to be a last resort.

The process of diffusion-reception of the new picture and the critical destruction of the old proceeds in society as it exists, and therefore is extremely complicated, and worked out with cross purposes, inversions, compensations, associations of ideas, and all the infinite resultants which even a limited number of independent factors can produce.

Society on the brink of revolution is in a crisis, a truly critical point, swinging like a ship under its rudder to a new course. It is just starting a re-volution, not a revolving motion, but a new direction of development; one might call it a re-volition. The forces working for continuity and maintenance are no longer superior to the forces working at cross purposes to them. It is already accepted by society that certain new forms of behavior are the correct ones for their special circumstances, although they contradict the older rules. With no complete consciousness of the whole implications, or even of the nature of the contradictions, men are more strongly impelled by the new directives than by the old ones which are contradicted by the new. They are therefore giving more of their energies, and more of their loyalty to them. The point is reached at which the new forces overpower the old. There is no new coherent system ready to replace the old, however. How could there be, when the vast system of education, style, law, has not yet been put to work to make one. There are a few individuals who have thought out a definite picture for the future, but these do not agree. There are a few who still are wholly devoted to the old. But the vast bulk of society are dropped out of one ordered pattern into semi-anarchy. It is not surprising that revolutions should be disorderly, wasteful, violent, and should require time to work out, and should consume energies and men. It would be astonishing if they were less so.

The new myth or myths, and the revolutionary parties, are not the leaders of the revolution in its first phase. They are only the little crystals around which the new organization of society, into a new moral and social and political pattern, a new state, will grow; when any differences between them have been settled by reconciliation, or by the survival of the fittest.

---

[1] Marcu, *Lenin*, p. 121.
[2] Trotsky, *History of the Russian Revolution*, II, p. 36.
[3] Malaparte, *Coup d'Etat, The Technique of Revolution*, N.Y., 1932.
[4] See Trotsky, *History*, III, p. 167 ff., p. 295.
[5] Trotsky, *History*, I, p. xvii.
[6] Burke, *Reflections on the Revolution in France*, Works, Boston, 1865, III, p. 270.
[7] Brinton, *A Decade of Revolution*, p. 5.
[8] Trotsky, *History*, III, p. 173.
[9] Aristotle, *Politics*, 1286 b16.
[10] Pareto, *The Mind and Society*.
[11] Nock, A. D., *Conversion, The Old and the New in Religion from Alexander the Great to Augustine of Hippo*, N.Y., 1933.
[12] See *The Republic*, Book VIII.
[13] AE, *The Interpreters*, N.Y., Macmillan, 1923.
[14] De Man, *The Psychology of Socialism*.
[15] Babbitt, *Democracy and Leadership*.
[16] See for examples, Sorokin, *The Sociology of Revolution*, Gilbert Seldes, *Against Revolution*, John Day Co. N.Y., 1932. Ortega y Gassett, *The Revolt of the Masses*, p. 102.
[17] J. Ferrari, *Histoire de la raison d'état*, p. 35; Chateaubriand, *Essai sur les revolutions*, p. 383; G. L. Dickinson, *Revolution and Reaction in Modern France*, p. 35, Sorokin, *The Sociology of Revolution*, p. 79.

4. Revolution: A Redefinition

PETER AMANN

Historians traditionally insist that they must carry out their work without benefit of presuppositions. In spite of the shadows which Marx, Freud and Mannheim (not to speak of such American historians as Beard and Becker) have cast over "objectivity," the dominant Rankean tradition still requires the historian to enter into his subject with unsullied, if not blank, mind until such time as he is permitted to re-emerge, pure as Botticelli's Venus, clutching history "as it really happened" to his bosom. If this burlesque is unfair, it is not groundless. Although some historians are quietly making good use of concepts borrowed from the social sciences, a majority continue to frown on any schematic approach to history as fraught with prejudice and dogma.

The limitations of the traditional methodology become obvious in the study of political revolution. Aside from assessing the impact of revolution, the historian is surely concerned with a rational understanding of the dynamics of a revolution. Merely "reliving" the chaos "as it really was" is unlikely to provide such an understanding. Actually, though the advocates of Rankean detachment also want to draw conclusions and discover patterns, they feel that they can do this without bringing to their study any conceptual apparatus at all — merely a healthy curiosity and the canons by which they were trained. I believe that they are deceiving themselves. The real alternative lies between a conceptual framework which is never made explicit and therefore remains beyond the reach of criticism, and one which is open to critical inspection.

The aim of this article is to suggest a framework for studying the course of a revolutionary movement, irrespective of its ideological content or specific historical significance. This analytical framework hinges on a redefinition of the term "revolution." This is not to claim some superiority inherent in my particular definition. There is no "true" definition of an abstraction: such a term is a semantic device which may or may not be useful, not a reflection of some absolute Platonic prototype. A term that during the seventeenth century referred to the revolving Wheel of Fortune casting down one prince and raising up another has since been broadened to the point of hopeless imprecision. If I suggest a narrowing of the definition of revolution, it is in order to provide a useful analytic tool for the study of revolutionary politics in the west since the seventeenth century. This definition will in turn permit a schematic approach, helping the historian to distinguish the politically crucial from the insignificant, without attempting to impose the pattern, timing and ideology of one revolution on what may well be the unique pattern of another.

Some preliminaries must first be considered. What is the modern state? On what base does its stability rest? The sovereign state, as I define it here, is a political organization exercising, or able to exercise, a monopoly of armed force, justice and administration over a given area and population. It is true that this state monopoly is merely a tendency which may never be completely fulfilled and which does not preclude the delegation of military, judicial and administrative functions to subordinate bodies, provided the latter recognize their subordination and act accordingly. The national government of a federal state such as the United States or Switzerland may be circumscribed in its inner dynamic by a constitutional separation of powers; yet this constitutes at most a difference in degree rather than in kind from centralized states. While this expansive tendency, this inner dynamic of the state, undoubtedly varies, the variations seem to have little to do with the ideological coloring of the government. I am aware that where the influence of Rousseau or Hegel has prevailed, the definition of the state as a moral or metaphysical being has been widely accepted. The rationale of my definition is not metaphysical: it is rather, in its way, empirical. Most political historians appear in practice to accept a postulate of the state in terms of power, a postulate which I am here stating explicitly.

In addition to this definition of the state as an incipient power monopoly, I wish to submit a further working hypothesis which seems verified by experience. I maintain that the power monopoly of the state depends largely, not on the consent of the governed, but on their habit of obedience, whatever its motive. It is the habit of obedience that, extended to institutions like the army and the bureaucracy, makes it possible for the state to delegate vital functions without jeopardizing its own effective monopoly of military, judicial and administrative power.

To summarize: the ensuing argument will rest on a definition of the state as a monopoly of power and on the crucial importance of the habit of obedience in assuring the stability of the state. We find, therefore, that the political historian's usual assumption of an identity of politics and government makes sense just so long as such a government enjoys a power monopoly resting in turn on an undisturbed habit of obedience. From the point of view of historical method, revolution may be said to be a breakdown, momentary or prolonged, of the state's monopoly of power, usually accompanied by a lessening of the habit of obedience. The sequence of this breakdown varies: in the Russian March Revolution the withdrawal of obedience preceded the appearance of any organized blocs that challenged the power of the state and led to the creation of such para-governments. By contrast, however sullen the popular attitude toward the Batista administration may have been, most Cubans transferred their habit of obedience to the Castro regime only after its seizure of power.

In a *coup d'état* or in a revolution not directly involving large sections of the population, the transfer of the habit of obedience from the old to the new government may be virtually automatic. If this is the case, the traditional methods of the political historian are adequate. From this specific point of view, once the transfer of power is effected the revolution is over — even though drastic social changes may yet follow the consolidation of the new regime. Once again the case of the Cuban revolution may be cited. As long as Batista's power was effectively unchallenged, Cuban politics could be studied in terms of his administration. As soon as Castro established himself as a para-governmental power in Oriente province, Cuban politics became, by my definition, revolutionary — that is, the historian was faced with more than one power center. Until Castro had succeeded Batista, only the study of *both* power centers, in their internal development as well as in their interaction, could reveal the history of Cuban politics. Once Castro's government had gained the monopoly of power formerly enjoyed by the Batista administration, Cuban politics ceased to be revolutionary, that is, they could once again be adequately documented in terms of the activities of the central government.

What emerges from this discussion is a new definition of revolution which serves a clearer function for the historian than the "common sense" one, being more precise, comprehensive and relatively independent of ideological value judgments. As I define it, revolution prevails when the state's monopoly of power is effectively challenged and persists until a monopoly of power is re-established. Such a definition avoids a number of traditional problems: the fine distinction between a *coup d'état* and a revolution; the degree of social change necessary before a movement may be called revolutionary; the possibility of a conservative revolution; the uncertain differentiation between wars of independence, civil wars and revolutions. By this definition the Algerian crisis is clearly revolutionary, since the French monopoly of armed force, justice and administration has been breached.

The definition also recognizes what might be called a suspended revolution: the prolonged co-existence of two or more antagonistic governmental power centers which are unable or unwilling to eliminate each other. This situation has, for instance, prevailed in Argentina since the ouster of the Perón dictatorship: the army has exercised a veto power over the Frondizi regime without displacing it. The relationship between government and army in the Weimar Republic of the late 1920's might also be cited as such an example of suspended revolution. This is not to assert that this definition of revolution makes it automatically possible to pinpoint a revolutionary situation. It would, for instance, be difficult at the present time to determine whether the French army has regained its habit of obedience to the state or whether it continues to exercise para-governmental powers, thus creating a revolutionary situation. In this respect the task of the historian with access to all available sources is considerably lighter than that of the student of contemporary politics hemmed in by a curtain of secrecy.

As we have already seen, in a revolutionary change carried out with little popular participation, the population may shift its habit of obedience without much disruption. If an established government is overthrown by a massive popular uprising, the chances of a revolutionary situation prevailing long after the actual overthrow of the established government are much greater. If a broadly based insurrection succeeds in capturing power, the prior involvement of a substantial segment of the people is likely to extend the time span of revolution, that is, the length of time during which state power is dispersed among several centers. The very act of insurrection is the most drastic break possible in the habit of obedience; hence the greater number of combatants and active sympathizers engaged in insurrection, the greater the number of people who have decisively cast off their habit of obedience. The new government, which may crown the successful efforts of the insurgents, may well command their immediate loyalty, yet the fact that this government is their own personal creation deprives it of the *mystique* of impersonal power in which an established government is clothed. Obedience based on loyalty independent of habit or fear is, as Machiavelli saw, an insecure basis of state power. Loyalty freely given may be freely withdrawn. It may be argued that the messianic expectations aroused by most revolutions are likely to lead some disappointed supporters to challenge sooner or later the government which they had helped to establish. At the very least the insurrectionists who remain outside the new "establishment" are likely to keep in abeyance some of their power in order to make their influence felt should the new government betray their ideals. In this sense the rising of the Kronstadt sailors against the Bolshevik regime is no historical accident; the bitterness of the insurgents was directed not against government in general, but against a government of their own creation which had, they felt, betrayed their aspirations.

Mass insurrection shatters the habit of obedience on a large scale and therefore tends to perpetuate revolution even after it is "officially" over. The rebel military build-up that made seizure of power possible also has the paradoxical effect of prolonging the revolutionary conditions after rebel victory. Lenin was quite right, though for the wrong reasons, in asserting that "the revolution" (as defined in Marxist terms) cannot take over the pre-revolutionary state as a going concern but can only destroy it to make room for its own. The new insurrectionary state cannot simply inherit what it has destroyed. While it inherits the still functioning parts of the administration — the judiciary, the armed forces — it must also bring under control its own armed adherents, a task made more difficult by the wide dispersion of weapons which a successful mass insurrection may require. Other things remaining equal, the larger the number of armed supporters the greater the likelihood of future armed opponents.

The number of insurgents is not by itself the sole criterion of the magnitude of the task confronting the successful insurrectionary government. Much depends on the state of organization or organizability of the insurgents and the degree of control exercised by an insurrectional leadership. If, as was true during the March Revolution in St. Petersburg, certain military units defected to the rebellious rioters, this was no assurance of automatic future support. The Parisian National Guard legions, which in February, 1848, refused to disperse the barricade builders, did not surrender their future freedom of action or blindly pledge themselves thereby to a successful insurrectionary government. Very clearly this collective withdrawal of the habit of obedience from an estalished government, while it may prove decisive in bringing victory to the insurrection, may also pose an explicit threat to the future authority of the new government.

Autonomous support is dangerous support, for the future of an insurrectionary government depends heavily on the disciplined unity of the rebels prior to their success and on the extent to which they have been conditioned to accept the decisions of a recognized leadership. It is possible that in the mid-twentieth century, the totalitarian party had succeeded in solving the dilemma of power seizure by controlling the revolutionary impetus from its very inception. The technique has involved not merely the creation of a highly centralized elite party but of a full-fledged state within a state in the very process of carrying on insurrection against the established regime. The examples of the Chinese Communists and the Viet Minh in Indochina come to mind — westernizing movements in an Oriental setting — though in both cases the accidents of prolonged conflict rather than deliberate policy may account for the blossoming of a full-fledged insurrectionary state with its own military, judicial and administrative powers long before final victory. In such a case the insurrection replaces the political power of the recognized state by its own within the area which it controls, thus conditioning a new habit of obedience both among its supporters and among the mass of the indifferent, the cautious and the hostile.

It may be objected that the foregoing discussion is no more than an elaborate semantic game, which, after conjuring up an artificial definition of political revolution, tests its suitability in a variety of historical settings. This new definition is not meant as a quixotic attempt to change common usage, even the common usage of historians. Just as professional economists will casually speak of capital and labor in connection with an industrial dispute, yet employ the term "capital" in a technical and much more specific meaning as well, historians may still use "revolution" in its undefinable sense, yet recognize the usefulness of a narrow and technical meaning of the word. The utility is two-fold: (1) revolution defined in terms of a dispersion of political power can be ascertained fairly readily and with reasonable objectivity; (2) once the historian has defined a situation as revolutionary, he is forewarned that he may have to shift his attention from the study of one power monopoly, the sovereign state, to two or more competing power blocs. This admonition will not, however, be very meaningful unless he has also defined a power bloc and has some idea where to look for one.

By a power bloc I refer to a group, too strong to be suppressed by ordinary police action, which has usurped military, administrative or judicial power traditionally held by the state. Such a group, defined in terms of its dynamics rather than its organization, may be a highly cohesive paramilitary formation such as the Nazi S. A. after 1930, an inspired improvisation like the workers' councils in the Russian Revolution of 1905 or a completely spontaneous *jacquerie*. It may be a cluster of state governments emerging as a Confederacy against a Federal Government; it may be a bureaucracy systematically sabotaging the policies of its government or a national army that has escaped civilian tutelage. Since the power traditionally held by the central government varies according to country and period, what may be a revolutionary power bloc in one instance may not be recognized as such in another. While in the context of French centralization the Paris Commune of 1871 constituted a revolutionary power bloc, similar actions on the part of a Netherlands province of the seventeenth century would have been viewed as part and parcel of the established order.

Although this definition does not eliminate all ambiguities, the historian is able to identify readily the main power blocs where power has been dispersed by insurrection. Such a situation is most likely to occur, as our earlier discussion brought out, where the violent seizure of power has been accomplished by a loosely organized mass movement. Since insurrection substitutes armed force for the gentler art of political compromise, the major power blocs emerging before or after a successful uprising are likely also to rely on force or the threat of force. The exercise of military force by a substantial group unresponsive to state influence is the most obvious hallmark of a revolutionary power bloc. To identify such blocs, the historian may well begin with the traditional agencies of governmental power — army, national guard, police, administration, judiciary — to determine whether any of these agencies have departed from their customary role of executors of state policy and become autonomous power centers. He must also survey new or revived organizations which have emerged from the insurrectional turmoil — political clubs, labor organizations, armed leagues — to assess the power at their disposal and the authority by which they exercise it.

Once several power blocs have been identified, the historian can construct a meaningful framework for studying revolutionary politics, whatever their ideological content. He should trace the internal structure and policies of each of these blocs as well as their interaction. Although among these the insurrectionary state is only one of several power centers, we may expect the state, regardless of ideology, to bend every effort toward reimposing obedience on its para-governmental competitors. In short, if an insurrection has been successful in toppling an established government, yet is unable to assume the traditional monopoly of power peculiar to the state, the very dynamic of the state *qua* state will prolong the contest. While stability under such circumstances is unlikely, the direction of change is by no means determined. What the historian will witness may be either the reconquest of power by the state, or the displacement of the state by one of the competing power blocs, or the disintegration of the country into smaller political units or into political chaos. The instability of revolution in the common sense meaning of the word and the tendency of most insurrectional governments to rely heavily on force even after they have come to power may thus be explained without recourse to some special revolutionary mentality or the implicit dialectics of a particular ideology. In the face of barriers to its power erected by Left or Right, the insurrectional state, regardless of program or ideology, will seek to surmount them by force if necessary.

The test of such a conceptual framework should be pragmatic: does it work? Does the use of such a device facilitate the historian's grasp of the politics of upheaval, or is this no more than a spelling out of what the historian does with or without conscious methodology? In the case of a revolution which has engaged the undivided attention of an army of historians over many decades, it may well be that such an approach may not provide any startling new insights. Even in the case of the French Revolution, however, it should be noted that not until very recent years has one of the decisive power blocs, the Parisian *sans-culottes,* been seriously examined despite a wealth of surviving documentary evidence. The type of attack which I have suggested would not have relegated such analysis to the haphazard inducements of Marxist piety. Where revolutions have been studied less exhaustively, an analysis in terms of power blocs may be more fruitful, if only in uncovering significant gaps in our knowledge.

By way of illustration, I would like to sketch the politics of the Parisian revolution of February to June 1848, in terms of the internal development and interplay of power blocs. If I confine myself to narrowly political considerations, this does not imply a disregard of economic, social, cultural and ideological influences. In any full-length study these would deserve attention, yet since they can readily be fitted into a framework of power blocs, I shall concentrate on the methodology of revolutionary *politics.* For the sake of greater clarity, I shall also omit events in the French provinces, some of which had considerable impact on the course of the revolution of 1848.

By March 1, 1848, the revolution was over; the revolution had begun. The position of the Provisional Government reflected this paradox: a product of insurrection, the government had entrenched itself without as yet succeeding to the traditional power enjoyed by any nineteenth century French government. Although there was no organized opposition to the Republic in the provinces, the new authorities did not yet govern the country. Holdover appointees, or, occasionally, locally improvised revolutionary commissions, were in charge of the departments, while the localities remained virtually untouched. In Paris the government had occupied and now administered the various traditional ministries, except for the post office, a little empire independently conquered by Etienne Arago. The routine of judicial administration was yet to be upset by the replacement of state procurators and minor modifications in the legislation of the preceding regime. While the government also controlled the mayoralty of Paris with its twelve subdivisions, it lacked armed force and effective police power within the capital. The large garrison of Paris which, together with the hated municipal guard, had unsuccessfully defended the monarchy, had been expelled from Paris under pressure from the revolutionary rank and file. The dissolution of the surviving municipal guards had left the insurrectionary government completely bereft of any professional and reliable force at its disposal. By February 27, it had struck out in two directions toward the re-creation of an effective military force. On that day there appeared both the decree organizing the *garde nationale mobile* (in practice the military enrollment of young unemployed workers), and the National Workshops, also envisaged from the beginning along para-military lines.

The anomalous position of the Provisional Government is underlined by its relationship with the Paris police under Caussidière. Marc Caussidière, long an activist in republican secret societies, had literally conquered the police prefecture for himself and his friends in the course of the February insurrection. His official appointment by the Provisional Government was merely the confirmation of a *fait accompli*, negotiated between two sovereign powers. If Caussidière proved a surprisingly competent police administrator in safeguarding life and property in the capital, this did not alter the fact that his two thousand Montagnards, recruited from among militant republicans, answered to him only. Politically Caussidière pursued a policy sufficiently cautious and tortuous to baffle both contemporaries and later historians. Whatever its merits, however, this policy was his own, thus depriving the government of any automatic police support in the face of political opposition. Throughout the revolutionary period, the prefecture of police played the role of an essentially negative power bloc, withholding obedience yet without clear aims of its own.

At the beginning of March, the position of the Paris National Guard was as ambiguous as that of the police and is even less known. Under the July Monarchy, the Paris National Guard had been confined to some forty thousand taxpayers willing and able to purchase their own uniforms and equipment. During the February Days, the Guard's refusal to die for Louis Philippe had proved decisive in determining the outcome of the insurrection. If, however, there were instances of individual guards and even whole units siding with the insurgents, such active support was far from unanimous. Few, if any, guards had consciously fought for a republic and their adherence to this republic was at best qualified. While they might endorse *la république sage*, guarantor of property and order, such an endorsement was a long way from habitual obedience to a government simply because it was the government. Despite a certain *esprit de corps*, the individual legions of the guard, organized according to district, largely reflected the varying political complexion of the capital. At the beginning of March, we can only conclude, on the basis of our very scanty knowledge, that the National Guard's attitude toward the government was uncertain.

Both the Paris police looming on the Left and the Paris National Guard threatening on the Right constituted power blocs subordinated in ordinary times to the national government, now cut loose through insurrection. The emergence of the *corporations ouvrières,* the organized crafts, was a different kind of phenomenon since labor organizations had never led a more than vaguely recognized underground existence. Their emergence as a major power center, able to sway policy through street demonstrations by armed workers, followed almost immediately the installation of the Provisional Government, long before the establishment of the Luxembourg Labor Commission furnished the organized workers a centralized organization and a recognized leadership. Much of the early social legislation, including the admission by the Provisional Government of the "right to work" itself, were concessions exacted by craft street demonstrations.

Still another power bloc was as yet inchoate — the club movement. While Blanqui's *Société républicaine centrale* had met as early as February 25, the centralizing trend which was to see numerous political clubs agree on a common policy did not set in until the second week of March. By March 1, a number of political clubs, most of them of leftward orientation, had been founded or were in the process of organization.

In March 1848, the power blocs began to move. The pre-revolutionary National Guard balked at its dilution in a mass of newcomers as the number of Paris guards increased almost five-fold to nearly two hundred thousand. The discontent led to a mass demonstration on March 16, ostensibly directed against the dissolution of certain élite companies but possibly aiming for more ambitious political objectives. In the face of government firmness, the demonstrators backed down and ceased to play an independent role as a conservative threat to the government.

The role of the organized crafts and of the gathering club movement was considerably more militant. Throughout March, these two blocs acted in concert even if they did not merge. They pursued a policy which sought to give the working class a substantial representation in the political life of the nation as well as a generally leftward social orientation distasteful to the moderates of the Provisional Government. To implement this policy, two parallel and perhaps incompatible methods were followed: direct pressure by mass demonstration and electoral organization and propaganda. The link between the two showed through the demands voiced by the monster demonstration of March 17 (which, by pure coincidence, appeared as a radical response to the conservative pressure of the previous day). The demonstrators of March 17 called above all else for a major postponement in the date of elections, which would give them sufficient time for proselytizing. It is also notable that on this occasion the Provisional Government resisted the popular pressure through its spokesman, Louis Blanc, whose ideological sympathies were with the working class demonstrators; the government's compulsion to govern was stronger than the ideological inclinations of its members. After the partial failure of March 17, both clubs and organized crafts continued to cooperate in their electoral agitation. The Club of Clubs represented essentially a political holding company embracing most of the socially oriented clubs and the Electoral Committee of the Workers of Seine organized by the *corporations ouvrières.*

By the end of March, therefore, the relative position of these power blocs had somewhat altered. The Provisional Government had succeeded in extending its rule in fact as well as in theory over all of France; its special commissioners had begun the type of purge which had recurrently thinned French administrative personnel since Napoleon's departure to Elba. The government's acceptance in the provinces, as well as its survival in Paris in the face of stormy, half-threatening demonstrations, had lent the Provisional Government a spurious air of legitimacy which belied its insurrectional origin. Its power position was improving: while the police remained firmly in Caussidière's hands, the government had begun the surreptitious reintroduction of regular troops into the capital. The *garde nationale mobile,* though lacking in both uniforms and discipline, was a potential military support, while the absence of the unemployed from the demonstration of March 17 testified to the effectiveness of the National Workshops as a government instrument. The police under Caussidière, on the other hand, continued its policy of political non-intervention.

By May 1, the position of the Provisional Government had improved dramatically, although its success was much less inevitable than it appeared in retrospect. Substantial units of the army had been re-introduced into the capital and if the police prefecture still played an independent role, such independence could no longer be decisive. More important, the government had survived another crisis, not as on March 17 by sheer bluff, but by successfully calling on armed support. The motives of the demonstration of April 16 remain obscure though we know that it was almost solely confined to elements of the organized crafts without much support from the clubs, which were preoccupied with political campaigning. In any case, the demonstrators, while protesting their loyalty, also sought to commit the government to a social policy more favorable to the workers. Against this pressure the government, in the person of Ledru-Rollin, called out the Paris National Guard in a general alarm. As on March 17, the Minister of the Interior's action testifies to the solidarity of the government *qua* government in the face of pressure, since Ledru-Rollin was loud in proclaiming his social sympathies on other occasions. The government's appeal hinged on the dependability of the enlarged citizens' militia. Early in April, elections for officers had placed convinced republicans in some of the higher ranks, yet a number of these high-ranking guard officers sought collaboration with the Electoral Committee of the Workers of Seine which was to be in the thick of the April 16 demonstration. The demonstration was a disaster. The organized workers found themselves hemmed in by rows of booing national guards. Within a few days the government's reconquest of power appeared virtually complete: a festival of reconciliation served also to introduce regular army units into Paris, and the general elections legitimized moderate republicanism. Discounting minor symptoms of disaffection in the *garde nationale mobile* and the National Workshops and the continued inscrutable neutrality of the prefecture of police, the government's monopoly of power seemd assured.

April had seen the elimination of the *corporations ouvrières* as a power bloc and the apparent taming of the club movement. The month of May witnessed a revival of club militancy and the government's gradual awareness that in the National Workshops it had bred a Frankenstein monster which was becoming harder and harder to control. The clubs' new line was to revive in rather unpromising circumstances the direct democracy of the Great Revolution by insuring progressive legislation through direct pressure on the National Assembly. The dissolution of the Assembly on May 15 by a club-led crowd of demonstrators was the unintended culmination of retaining influence by popular pressure.

The result was disastrous: with few exceptions, the top leadership of the major clubs was arrested, some of the clubs were dissolved and those that survived were subjected to semi-official harassment. While a number of the clubs had revived by the end of May and once again made common front, their leadership ceased flirting with violence and throughout June sought to restrain its restive followers. April 16 had jolted the organized crafts into non-revolutionary channels; May 15 finished the clubs as a power bloc. The crisis had also served to end the sovereignty of the prefecture of police: this time Caussidière's studied neutrality led to his removal from office and to the disbanding of his private army. While the events of May 15 had confirmed the adherence of the National Guard — or at least of those who responded to the drum-call of the *rappel* — they had pointed up the rising disaffection in the National Workshops, an estimated 14,000 of whose members had participated in the day's demonstration. During the month following May 15, the problem of how to neutralize the National Workshops became the chief preoccupation of the government. Its policy moved simultaneously toward the short-term objective of regaining administrative control over the workshops and toward the "final solution" of liquidating them altogether.

In March the government had weathered challenges from the unreformed National Guard on the Right and the alliance of organized crafts and clubs on the Left. In April it had defeated the crafts; in May the clubs had been broken by the National Guard. The crushing of the June insurrection by the government forces, re-establishing decisively the government's monopoly of power, marked the end of the revolution. This uprising has usually been interpreted as a class struggle — in Tocqueville's phrase, a servile war. This interpretation may shed light on the motives of the participants and their social origin, yet it does nothing to explain *how* such class antagonism could crystallize into major organized rebellion.

The June insurrection became possible, not simply because of widespread popular discontent, but because such discontent could find effective expression through armed, organized power blocs. The dissolution of the National Workshops proved the catalyst which transformed a substantial segment of this militarized institution into such an aggressive bloc. The other major insurrectional contingent emerged when the National Guard of Paris split along geographical — and, by implication, class — lines. The appearance of entire National Guard units from the eastern, working class sections of Paris behind the barricades held by the insurgents goes far toward explaining the effectiveness of their organization which mystified contemporary observers. The citizens' militia of the wealthier, western half of Paris, on the other hand, enthusiastically supported the government's cause. The *garde nationale mobile,* an incipient power bloc deemed unreliable by both sides, opted for the government, perhaps for very trivial reasons. The main direction and burden of the combat fell on the reintroduced Paris garrison whose loyalty had never come into question. Significantly, neither the organized crafts nor the clubs participated in the insurrection as coherent units, although specific industrial establishments such as the railroad repair shops, contributed numerous recruits. The government, in any case, used the opportunity of the proclaimed state of siege to suppress remaining clubs which henceforth played no more than a shadowy role. When on June 26, 1848, the smoke lifted over the Faubourg St. Antoine, last stronghold of the rebels to fall, the government had at last succeeded in eliminating all its rivals: the dissident elements of the National Guard filled the prisons to overflowing; the eastern districts of Paris were to be permanently demilitarized; National Workshops and political clubs had been dissolved; the *garde mobile* had been brought under control; the organized crafts were cowed and about to launch into the harmless dead end of producers' cooperatives. The government had restored obedience as well as re-establishing its monopoly of power: four months after it had begun, the revolution was over.

How does this view of the French revolution of 1848, seen in terms of power blocs struggling for dominion, compare with other accounts? It avoids, first of all, some of the mystification inherent in many accounts of revolution. Since in many works, such as, for example, Gaston-Martin's *La Révolution de 1848,* the government occupies the center of the stage, forces outside the government make their appearance unannounced, having neither antecedents nor future. By tracing the genesis, emergence and development of all power blocs, the historian can dispel some of the romantic mist in which revolution is half hidden. What we may lose in romantic appeal, we gain in clarity.

Secondly, the technique which I have illustrated counteracts the historian's quest for the tragic flaw. History can and should be literature, provided the flux of events is not subordinated to a literary device, such as it is in H. Guillemin's *La tragédie de 1848.* Revolution offers a particularly acute temptation to the historian: even before he begins his work, he knows that in 1848, for example, June will follow February. It is much easier simply to work backward and to personify the revolution as the tragic hero doomed from the start to self-destruction — a fetching attention-getter, yet bad history. Once the premise of the drama is accepted, the tendency to prune the dramatically irrelevant becomes irresistible, until what was in fact an intricate process has been transmuted into the starkness of Greek tragedy. By viewing revolution as a many-centered power struggle, the historian, though he may still come to view history as tragedy, will be less likely to underrate the contingent, the dead ends and backtracks, that have no place in a well-constructed play but may be the stuff of life.

Thirdly, by analyzing the structure of revolution, the historian is less likely to impose without qualification a prefabricated, monistic pattern on revolutionary events. A Marxist historian, such as J. Dautry, would have to explain why the middle class leadership of the National Guard came so close to supporting the workers' demonstration of April 16; he would have to face the problem of why the National Workshops joined and the *corporations ouvrières* abstained from the June insurrection though both were "proletarian"; he might, in connection with the club movement, have to ask himself whether the bourgeois-proletarian dichotomy is meaningful for 1848 or whether the old *sans-culotte* amalgam of artisans, small shopkeepers and workers did not come closer to the reality of mid-ninteenth century Paris. Whatever his answers, the historian would be forced to qualify his borrowed preconceptions.

By viewing revolution as a contest for state power in which all the contestants are on show, we may succeed in keeping the great simplifiers in check. We may at the same time become aware of how little is known about significant revolutionary movements: in the case of 1848, for example, the history of the National Guard and that of the prefecture of police under Caussidière is virtually blank. We may also wish to take a second look at ideology as the motor of an insurrectionary government once we accept its drive for power as literally "natural," that is, in the nature of the state. Yet of itself this way of looking at revolution provides no answers. Though the framework may be new and even an improvement over the old, this is no guarantee that the completed structure for which we bear responsibility will be sound. What I offer is a tool, not a nostrum.

5. Advanced Symptoms
of Revolution

LYFORD P. EDWARDS

There now come up for consideration those more important phenomena which never occur unless a revolution does follow. There are a considerable number of these advanced symptoms of revolution, but they are all more or less dependent upon two master-symptoms — symptoms which, once clearly recognized, enable the social diagnostician to predict with a great degree of assurance the certainty of coming upheaval.

The first master-symptom of revolution is the "transfer of the allegiance of the intellectuals." The authors, the editors, the lecturers, the artists, the teachers, the priests, the preachers, and all those whose function it is to form and guide public opinion become infected with the discontent of the repressed classes of society. In order to appreciate the great importance of this intellectualist change of feeling it is necessary to recall the social function of the intellectuals.

All societies above the lower stages of barbarism have been composed of three classes of people: exploiters, non-productive laborers, and productive laborers. Exploiters are those who control, direct, and live by the labor of others, "without giving," as the revolutionists claim, "any equivalent labor in return." Productive laborers are those who do the work necessary to maintain society at the given level of culture. The non-productive laborers (the intellectuals) are the intermediate class whose work consists very largely in maintaining and transmitting the system intact to future generations.

The exploiters are relatively few in number but they control a great part, generally the greater part, of the capital and labor of society. Their essential characteristic is that they constitute, with the intellectuals, the "overhead," and so become a charge upon the producers in any society in which they exist.

The intellectuals are about as numerous as the exploiters — that is, they form only a small percentage of society. They own little, and live mostly by wages received from the exploiters. Their essential function is the creation and maintenance of the institution of "ownership" by which the exploiters live. The productive laborers form the vast majority of any society. Most of them own little or nothing. They, like the intellectuals, live on wages paid them by the exploiters.

These three classes have been known in the vocabulary of revolutionists by a great variety of names at different periods of history. Today exploiters are called "absentee owners," "capitalists," or "the bourgeoisie." Productive laborers are known as "workingmen," "wage slaves," or "the proletariat." Non-productive laborers go by the name "the intellectuals," "the intelligentsia," or "the highbrows."

None of these names is accurate. It is perhaps better to say that in a society in which there is unrest and a "sense" of repression, the repressors, the repressed, and the publicists correspond to the exploiters, the exploited, and the intellectuals, respectively.

The small minority of "repressors" can maintain the system of repression only so long as they have the willing support of the publicists. The repressed class, in a society that is ripe for revolution, always outnumbers both of the other classes combined. They can dominate either or both of the other classes whenever they have become sufficiently class conscious and sufficiently organized and disciplined to act collectively. The position of both repressors and publicists is therefore precarious unless the publicists maintain sufficient confidence in the existing régime to give it their loyal support.

No system of repression begins as such. Every system starts as an improvement over the previous system. It commends itself as socially advantageous — otherwise it would not be adopted. But any social system, no matter how excellent at the time of its adoption, is likely to become repressive with the lapse of time and the progress of civilization. A given institution, proving itself to be good, is "sold" to the society by the publicists and becomes an integral part of the social structure. It is sanctioned by law and custom, by religion and ethics. When the institution becomes repressive, the inarticulate masses feel the repression first but do not understand the causes of it. An interval, generally a long one, occurs between the time any institution is first felt to be repressive and the time the publicists lose their faith in it. During such intervals (which cover most of the years of recorded history) the publicists support repressive institutions. But sooner or later the publicists become infected with the prevailing unrest and begin to sympathize with the repressed class. Frequently, after a time the publicists feel the repression themselves. In that case they bestir themselves energetically to discover the cause of the existing unrest. The repressors neither feel the repression nor, except in rare cases, understand its causes. When the publicists are sure that an institution, which they had supposed to be good, is really repressive, they attack that institution with a zeal proportionate to their anger at having been deluded as to its nature. In other words, they desert the cause of the existing institution and support the cause of the institution that is, as they hope and believe, to replace it.

It is to be noted in the discussion of the present-day class conflict that the word "idle" applied to the dominant class means not only inactive but, what is more important, it means the practice of forms of activity conceived to be useless or harmful by a given society at a given time. Similarly, and with the same qualifications, the term "working people" or "working class" embraces not only mechanics and manual laborers, but all persons, except the publicists, engaged in activities considered to be socially useful.

In the case of the Protestant Reformation the stages in the "transfer" are clear. From John of Paris, D'Ailly, and Gerson through Colet, More, and Erasmus to Luther, Calvin, and Knox the change is evident. First is the desire for administrative reform, then the demand for thoroughgoing reconstruction, and finally the determination to destroy the ancient church altogether. An identical transition of publicists' opinions can be traced in every country that became Protestant.

In the case of the Puritan Revolution in England, even the most careless reader of history cannot help perceiving that the attitude of such publicists as Eliot, Pym, and Hampden foreshadowed the coming of Cromwell and the commonwealth.

In France, in the year 1700, publicists of the most eminent character and ability — men like Bossuet and Fenelon — upheld the doctrine of the divine right of kings. Two generations later there was not a man of intellectual distinction in the kingdom who did not attack that doctrine as false and ridiculous. The importance of the encyclopedists and philosophers as the harbingers of the coming revolution is one of the commonplaces of history.

Adams, Otis, Lee, Franklin, and many other leaders in the American Revolution attained eminence by their support of the cause of liberty at least ten years before the Declaration of Independence. Pitt, Burke, and numerous others in England supported the American publicists. This antagonistic attitude of the publicists portended revolution as early as 1765, if not earlier. If the government of George III had had any reasonable degree of perspicacity it would have recognized the danger signal.

The gradual transfer of the allegiance of the Russian intellectuals can be traced readily for three generations. Gogol and Puskin were more moderate critics of the czardom than Dostoievsky and Tolstoi, who in turn were moderates compared to Kropotkin and Gorki. For decades before its final overthrow, the government of the czars was without a public apologist of even second-rate ability. Had it not been hopelessly blind, it would have perceived in this fact the certainty of its own destruction.

An institution of any size or importance always has enemies. A certain amount of criticism is to be expected, and is no sign of revolution — or of anything else of moment. Then there are the occasional and sporadic outbursts of small groups of intellectuals. These, also, are without importance. But a change of front by the majority of publicists, kept up through a period of years, is a matter of the very first importance. It is both the most easily recognized symptom of coming upheaval and the most potent cause of the upheaval which it portends.

When the publicists once decide to support the repressed class rather than the repressors, there is a decided quickening in the *tempo* of the revolutionary movement though everyone is still ignorant that any revolution is to take place.

One of the first results of the publicists' change of front is a loss of faith in the individuals who at the time have control of the society. The intellectuals, though aware of repression, are not yet aware of its cause. Being angry and ignorant — to some degree angry because ignorant — they strike out, childlike, at the most conspicuous persons in sight. The persons who have control, being the most conspicuous persons, naturally become the objects of the publicists' wrath. All and several are attacked under the impression that all are, or may be, repressors.

The conspicuous individuals under stress of this attack speedily lose the respect of the public. They are contemned as dull and uninspiring. Idealism and enthusiasm are no longer engendered by their purposes or actions. Whatever they do is esteemed wrong. In more extreme cases these individuals, without regard to personal character and merit, become objects of popular odium and may be mobbed or even assassinated.

The publicists and public alike at this stage become victims of the "goodman" fallacy. They have the idea that everything will come out all right if only good men are placed at the head of affairs. Everybody pins his faith on the good pope, the good king, or the good ruler of some sort. This fallacy is natural. Institutions that are essentially sound will work well if good men are placed in control of them. The whole point about a prerevolutionary society is that its institutions, or some of them, are essentially unsound, and will not work well no matter who is in control of them. But the publicists do not immediately recognize that this is the condition of their society. They demand the removal of obnoxious, conspicuous persons and their replacement by good men. Sometimes the replacement occurs, sometimes not. The result is the same in either case. The repression, not being due to the faults of individuals, remains in spite of any substitution of good individuals for bad ones. The only result is that the good individuals lose their popularity. Leo X was succeeded by Adrian VI, a good man if there ever was one, but the revolt against the papacy went on just the same. Strafford and Laud were replaced by Falkland and Hyde. The change did no more to save the head of Charles I than the similar substitution of Turgot and Necker for Brienne and Calonne did to save that of Louis XVI.

But in any society in which the majority of the publicists are really in revolt against the existing conditions, the good-man fallacy does not persist very long. It is only a passing phase and generally a short one.

The publicists presently discover that the real cause of the unrest is to be found in certain archaic elements of the social order. The archaism generally, perhaps always, is embodied in some group or order of men, who are forthwith brought into prominence and then into condemnation as representatives of the archaic institutions. The publicists, having ascertained the identity of the delinquent institutions, start what is essentially an "advertising offensive" against them. The technique is in general the same as that of a political campaign. Often it begins as a political campaign, though it does not end as one. A political campaign is in some respects a sort of small-bore, blank-cartridge imitation of a revolution. The people in a political campaign do not really care how it comes out. Both sides agree beforehand to abide the issue no matter which side wins, because the issue is esssentially unimportant and does not involve their elemental wishes. A revolution is like a political campaign in which no such previous agreement is made. People really do care how it comes out because their elemental wishes are involved. A revolution therefore contains an important psychological ingredient lacking in a political campaign, but within fairly wide limits the operative technique at this stage is the same.

An essential step in the development of revolution is the gradual concentration of public dissatisfaction upon some one institution and the persons representing it. Before any institution can become either very popular or very unpopular public attention must be fixed on it — and must stay fixed. In the earlier stages of a revolutionary movement the dissatisfaction is diffused and dissipated. All sorts of institutions — the political government, the educational system, the church, the economic organization, and many others — are growled about and criticized. Because the discontent is directed against too many and too diverse objects, it is rendered both feeble and futile. One great service which the publicists render to the revolutionary movement is that of concentrating the general irritation which is spending itself thus wastefully. They focus the discontent against some one institution or class and keep it focused there. The institution or class in question becomes the object of popular antagonism to the exclusion of all other institutions or classes.

The real test of the intellect of the intellectuals comes at just this point. They may make a mistake. They may concentrate public anger on the wrong institution or class — on a class or institution not really the cause of the repression. In such a case revolutionary effort runs up a blind alley, reaction follows this futility, and the whole movement must be redirected at great cost of time and effort.

At this point, similarly, there occurs one of the best opportunities of the repressors to avert, or at least postpone, revolution. If they can succeed in diverting the attention of the repressed classes to some other group or institution which is not to blame for the repression, and if they can arouse sufficient animosity against this other institution so that an attack is made upon it, they can save their class and the institution they represent for a long time — at least two or three generations. In cases where there are still able publicists in the service of the threatened institution, and in cases where the intellectuals are still uncertain as to what is the cause of repression, these tactics are likely to prove successful.

King James I had [an] opportunity to divert the Puritan Revolution when Parliament urged him to raise a powerful army and intervene in support of the Protestants in the Thirty Years' War. Had he done so — and had he been victorious — as might well have happened, the Stuart dream of an absolute monarchy would very likely have been achieved. The Puritan Revolution might have been nearly contemporary with that of France.

To divert popular attention from domestic repressions by starting a foreign war is one of the oldest tricks of statecraft. There is some reason to believe that the Russian czardom may have had this ancient trick in mind when it entered the late war. But they may have forgotten that for the trick to succeed it is essential that the war be successful. Defeat in foreign war hastens revolution, as it did in this case.

Orgiastic excitement — dances, festivals, and religious movements — are sometimes substitutes for foreign war, as the outlet for popular discontent. Emotional energy and mental energy have this in common. There is only so much of them. If they are exhausted in one way they are not available in another — at least not until there has been time for recuperation. If the late czardom, instead of abolishing vodka, had made it very plentiful and very cheap — if, in addition, they had stimulated to the utmost those forms of religious frenzy and excitement to which the Russian populace appear to be so susceptible — then it is at least possible that the people would have been so exhausted mentally, emotionally, and financially by their alcoholic and religious orgies that they would not have had sufficient energy left to carry out a successful revolution.

All of this may seem very theoretical, as indeed it is. But with the development of the technique of government propaganda, some such orgiastic substitution for revolution may well come within the range of the practical politics of the not distant future.

The manner in which the publicists focus the public attention on the repressive class is worth noticing; by and large, the method is that of popularizing scandal. If the newspapers of the world are any evidence, the public seems to have an insatiable appetite for scandal. It is easiest to concentrate public interest on that class in society that is most conspicuous. The repressors are that class. Social unrest makes news for the same reason that it makes politics. It is out of the general discontent that political issues arise. The publicists have a "flair for news." A flair for news includes the ability to discover scandal. The dominant class is inevitably a shining mark if for no other reason than merely because it is conspicuous. A due regard for the increase of their own influence, prestige, power, and emolument naturally leads the intelligentsia to concentrate their efforts upon the "exposure" of that class.

The repressive class is thereupon subjected to the most pitiless investigation and publicity. It becomes the object of the most pervading and merciless gossip. Its weakness and its failures, its ignorance and stupidities, its sins and its shames, its vices and its crimes, its heartlessness and its frivolity, are dwelt upon — not once or twice but a hundred and a thousand times. No class of people is ever subjected to such complete exposure and such terrific attack as the dominant class in a pre-revolutionary society. There is naturally in such exposures a large element of truth uncovered. But every scandal substantiated by facts is enlarged and exaggerated through constant repetition. Every publicist seeks to outdo his colleagues in the quantity and quality of his "muck-raking." The more startling and exciting the conditions exposed, the more eagerly it is seized upon by the public and the greater is the author's prestige. This is true not only of the publicists as a class but of all the individuals who retail the scandals throughout the society. It comes about, therefore, that in addition to the scandals that are true, and to those that are exaggerated, others are added which have no basis in fact at all. Rumors of the wildest kind are readily circulated and as readily believed. There is nothing unnatural or unusual about this. The growth of scandal and rumor is a most ordinary phenomenon observable in all societies at all times. Under ordinary circumstances it is a matter of small importance. The persons and institutions attacked are so numerous and so heterogeneous, the succession of them is so rapid, that the result is negligible. In a pre-revolutionary society the importance of scandal and rumor arises from the fact that the same class is subjected to them over a long period. As a result of sheer repetition, exaggerated scandals and baseless rumors come to be believed as facts, and these have an influence on public opinion much greater than that of the simple truth.

The attacks on the dominant classes by the publicists often attain a high level of literary and forensic excellence — as might be expected when able and eloquent men are deeply stirred by manifest wrongs. This "literature of exposure" is one of the most characteristic symptoms of a coming revolution, and naturally it continues in ever increasing volume during the course of the revolution until the position of the obnoxious class and the institutions they represent is completely undermined.

It is not necessary to do more than mention one or two examples of these attacks. In the Puritan Revolution, the Marprelate tracts and the Grand Remonstrance are two illustrations among thousands. The American Declaration of Independence is a summary of numerous "declarations" and "resolutions" put out in all the colonies from the time of the famous "Five Resolutions" of Patrick Henry in 1765 onward. The collection of speeches, pamphlets, sermons, articles, poems, dialogues, plays, and literature of all sorts attacking the royal government that were published before the outbreak of the Revolution makes a considerable library. For some reason the attacks made upon religious repressors are especially numerous and voluminous. The attacks of the publicists upon the church and the priesthood go back for centuries before the Reformation, and are of a most appalling bulk. They comprise tens of thousands, if not hundreds of thousands, of separate publications. The attacks of the early Christians upon the pagan religion and pagan society have, in great part, perished in the course of the centuries. Enough remains, however, to fill a goodly number of stout volumes.

When the publicists launch this attack upon the repressive class an enormous amount of discussion ensues. Many of the so-called "repressors" are personally men of kindly and benevolent character. They have their relatives, friends, and dependents who rally to their defense. Much of the scandal published, being either false or exaggerated, is refuted by those attacked and those in a position to know the facts. But there is not at this time any sharp division into two parties or factions. Instead, there are a great number of ill-defined, inchoate groups not very certain as to the extent of their own agreement. Everybody considers that reform is desirable, or at least necessary. As to the kind and degree of reform there are numerous gradations of opinion — as there are also over the question of how the reform can be best accomplished. It is to be noted that the only idea is reform. There is no purpose, or even thought, of revolution. That idea is entirely absent, or very remote, from the minds of the persons engaged in discussion. It never even comes up for discussion, except, possibly, when suggested by a very few extreme radicals who are too far in advance of public sentiment to be of importance. As the discussion continues and so many different points of view are disclosed, the persons holding the most divergent opinions sometimes go beyond the stage of verbal conflict. Social and economic antagonisms begin to show themselves. Friendships are broken. Business boycotts are instituted. Even family disunion appears. The repressive classes and their supporters are subject to various kinds of social pressure — even ostracism.

The deluge of pamphlets, poems, plays, and literary productions of all sorts is only the most visible part of the attack on the repressive class. It is by no means all of it, nor perhaps the most important part of it. Discussion takes place also among the great "unprinting masses" — the people who form their opinions from conversation instead of from reading. These people are commonly forgotten, but their influence, especially in the crises of revolution, is important. The attack of the publicists causes the repressors to defend themselves as best they can. They reply both by writing and by word of mouth. It is soon evident that their defense is feeble. Even when, as at first, they and their supporters may be in a numerical majority, they are weak because they are held together only by a traditional, unthinking loyalty to existing institutions. In the course of the discussion on reform this loyalty suffers great attrition until in great numbers of men only a shell of custom remains — though they frequently are unaware of the fact.

It is needless to give any extensive examples of the reformist discussions which go on for months and years in every pre-revolutionary society after the publicists concentrate popular attention on the evils of that society. Luther and Eck hold a great disputation about the Catholic church — the sign and symbol of the innumerable religious discussions which characterized the whole of Western civilization at the time. So many thousands of argumentative pamphlets were issued during the period preceding the Puritan Revolution that, in the words of Green, they "turned England at large into a school of political discussion."[1] The arguments and debates about colonial liberty, both in England and America, for years before the American Revolution are chronicled in every schoolbook of American history. If Johnson's *Taxation No Tyranny* is not so well known as Burke's *Plea for Conciliation*, it only proves that even the greatest arguer could do little for such a bad cause. Even under the extreme repression of the czardom a notable period of discussion followed the attacks of the great publicists on the autocracy. The Duma, established after the abortive uprising of 1905, was chiefly useful as a discussion club. But the discussions of reform in the Duma were by no means isolated phenomena. Similar discussions both in print and verbally went on during a dozen years all over Russia, and indeed all over the civilized world. Reformist discussion is, in short, a symptom discoverable in every pre-revolutionary society.

During this long period of discussion an important psychological change takes place in the repressed classes. This change is an enormous development of what Miller calls the "oppression psychosis," which is the obsession that there is nothing much in the world except oppression; that the only object of life is to fight oppression. It is an attitude of mind that is always looking for trouble. Groups dominated by it always "have a chip on the shoulder." They are always expecting slights, disparagements, and injustices. They see oppression even where there is none. They become violently self-assertive at the least opportunity. Th oppression psychosis is important in the revolutionary process because it turns the previous more or less passive discontent of the repressed group into the active emotion of hate of the repressors. Hatred of a common enemy is the most powerful known agency for producing group unity. The publicists, by their previous attack, have pointed out the repressors as the common enemy. The discontent of the repressed at their lot turns into hatred of the repressors, because the discussion of reform, which goes on for a long time, gets nowhere. It is, in the nature of the case, impossible that it should get anywhere. The case is one in which a large group of socially useful people are deprived of due honor, wealth, dignity, prestige, social rank, political power, ease, comfort, luxury, and all the other good things of this life, while a small group of socially useless people possess a superabundance of all these good things. The only solution is to deprive the socially useless people of all their good things and bestow them upon the socially useful people. This cannot be done by discussion, voting, or any other sort of parliamentary procedure. Neither party will abide the issue of the parliamentary process. If those who possess all the good things are outdiscussed or outvoted, they will fight to keep their possessions. If those who are deprived of the good things are outdiscussed or outvoted, they will fight to get possession of them. The long pre-revolutionary discussion is thus predestined to failure.

But the failure of the discussion is the failure of the repressed class. This failure generates in their minds the oppression psychosis. They have the better of the discussion, but no matter how completely they triumph in argument, the repressors continue in possession of the good things. During the discussion the repressed class prove the fact that they are suffering injustice. But they obtain no redress. Obtaining no redress they naturally come to hate those who profit by the injustice from which they suffer. They consider the repressors to be the authors of the injustice — though the injustice, as a matter of fact, is due to archaic social arrangements.

All repressed groups in pre-revolutionary societies develop this oppression psychosis, its concomitant hatred of the repressors, and group solidarity.

The growth of the oppression psychosis in the opponents of the papacy during the pre-reformation period is familiar to all students of church history. Illustrations are to be found in *The Ship of Fools,* in *The Letters of Obscure Men,* and in many of the writings of Erasmus. In the period preceding the Puritan Revolution the famous *Histriomastix* is only an outstanding example of the psychology of the whole Puritan group. The authorization of innocent and healthy outdoor games after church on Sunday was considered to be a wicked plot to destroy all true religion. The touchiness and irritability of Voltaire and so many other French philosophers is at least in part due to the oppression psychosis. The numerous hindrances and delays to which the various Parliaments subjected the edicts of Louis XVI can be largely ascribed to the same cause. The fantastic legends of the Parc-aux-Cerfs and the baths of children's blood show, at a still earlier time, the grotesque and horrible development of this psychosis among the masses of the people.

In the thirteen American colonies before the Revolution, the psychosis is well illustrated in Dickinson's *Letters of a Farmer.* The enormous popularity of these *Letters* proves how accurately they reflected the mood of the people. The growing irritation and sensitiveness of the colonial assemblies to any exercise of the royal prerogative without their approval is another instance of the same disposition. Dr. Johnson, in his *Taxation No Tyranny,* proposed that the negro slaves be freed and provided with agricultural implements to enable them to earn their living as farmers. The proposal, in itself, was humane and possibly intelligent. It was construed to be an advocacy of a negro rebellion and the massacre of the plantation owners by their slaves.

Another technique employed by the publicists in the course of the pre-revolutionary discussion greatly aids the growth of the oppression psychosis. This technique consists in putting a very great stress upon the worth and value of the repressed class. Their importance is brought out in the clearest light. History is ransacked to provide them with an illustrious background. Their cause is linked up with the famous popular revolutions of all ages. The events of past time are interpreted as a preparation for their advent to power. Their virtues are exaggerated. Their faults are minimized or entirely overlooked. They are provided with a common body of tradition and a long list of heroes, largely manufactured *ad hoc.* However apocryphal this common body of tradition may be, it serves to give the repressed class a feeling of dignity and self-respect. It is an important factor in promoting their unity, and of reinforcing the solidarity produced by the more powerful emotion of hatred of the repressors. The more their sense of their own importance increases the greater appears the wickedness of their repression and the more keenly they resent any sign of that repression.

During this discussion period the repressors gradually lose faith in themselves and in their cause. They continue to hold possession of all the good things of life, but they come to question the justice of their title to them. The case for the repressed class is a strong one. It is ably presented by the publicists. It is argued at great length and in minute detail, and it produces its effect despite the continuance of the repressors in power. Those of the repressors who are intelligent and open minded admit that the existing conditions are unjust and intolerable. They do not wish them to continue, even though they may be opposed to violent or sudden change. Others, though they still defend the system of repression, do so half-heartedly and with no great enthusiasm or self-confidence. A certain number of repressors, the most narrow-minded and least-intelligent ones, react the other way. They become more convinced than ever of the indefeasible righteousness of the repressive régime. These defenders of abuses are mentally incapable of a rational defense of their opinions. But this bothers them not at all, since they commonly rest their case on some super-rational ground such as the "divine right" of kings or the "sacredness" of property. They become reactionary, and get so out of touch with contemporary ideas that they lose all influence except with the most ignorant and superstitious sections of the population, such as the peasantry of remote districts.

So long as the entire body of repressors believe firmly in themselves and in the righteousness of their actions, they cannot be overthrown by revolution. They possess all the power of government and law, all the prestige of authority and position, and all the sanction of religion and morals. These advantages are sufficient to enable them to retain their position for some time even after their morale has become low. When their morale is high these same advantages are decisive in making their position secure. Being confident of their own right, they possess all the agencies for begetting a like confidence in the rest of society. Under such conditions their rule is firm. They make decisions promptly and carry them out vigorously. They are courageous, both in war and in the conduct of civil government. The army respects and obeys them because they exhibit both military ability and personal bravery. They are the most capable people in the society, and bear rule because of that fact. Their rule is to a serious degree repressive of the legitimate elemental wishes of the lower classes, yet it seems certain that, on the whole, their social usefulness is still sufficient to justify their retention of power. All ruling classes pass through this period when they are both repressive and self-confident. Such a period is generally seen at its best about halfway between the beginning and the end of the domination of the class concerned.

The Albigenses certainly had as good cause to revolt against the papacy as had the Protestants of a later time. But the Catholic church of the thirteenth century believed in itself. It was firm in its theological doctrines, and its clergy were proudly conscious of their great function as the upholders of justice and the maintainers of social order. The pope, Innocent III, was the most able ruler then alive. He was firm, intelligent, and shrewd. He had plenty of confidence both in himself and in his cause, and he was able to inspire like confidence in others. The result was that he had no great difficulty in putting down the revolt. The crusade against the Albigenses was exceedingly cruel and bloody, but it was short, and it ended in the total destruction of the heretical movement.

Bacon's Rebellion in Virginia in 1667 was as much justified by tyranny and misgovernment as was the American Revolution of one hundred years later. Bacon was a popular and skillful leader. Great numbers of the colonists sympathized with his cause, which was identically the same as that of 1776. He was for a time successful. Yet Governor Berkeley, in spite of his personal unpopularity and that of his government, was able very quickly to stamp out the rebellion with the aid of troops from England.

The fact is that until 1763 the royal governors maintained their authority, arbitrary as it often was, with relatively little trouble. When necessary they sent for British troops to maintain their authority, and this met with only very slight complaint from the colonists. This reason, of course, was that until 1763 royal governors and British troops were useful and even necessary people. The colonists were in constant danger of attack from the Indians and from the French. Royal governors with real power and able to summon the aid of British troops in time of danger were essential to the peace and welfare, if not to the very existence of the colonies. The governors and their soldiers knew this, and to their credit be it said they did their job well, if roughly. The Indians were driven back, the French colonies in Canada were conquered, and all danger of external attack removed. Until the time this task was accomplished the royal governors with the aid of British soldiers were able to put down revolt with great ease.

Since no revolution against a ruling class can be successful so long as they have confidence in themselves and faith in what they stand for, it is important to note the method employed by the publicists in destroying their faith and self-confidence. The fact is that the repressors, no less than the repressed, depend upon the intellectuals for their ideas. The intellectuals are the professional custodians of education, morality, and religion. It is their job to make and unmake right and wrong, good and bad, vice and virtue, morality and immorality, nobleness and depravity, orthodoxy and heresy, sense and foolishness. They are limited in this great task by the state of economic development in the society concerned, and by the extent of the social unrest that for any reason exists at the time. But within this limit they can do very much as they please, provided they are willing to work hard enough and long enough.

No sooner do the publicists espouse the cause of the repressed class than they proceed to put forth, and to popularize by discussion, a new body of knowledge and a new code of morals, including new standards of wisdom and foolishness. This new teaching is designed, among other things, to make the repressors ridiculous in their own eyes as well as in the eyes of everyone else. Unless it succeeds in doing this, the revolution is likely to be postponed. If it is not postponed, it will be abortive. A ruling class can survive even though it knows itself to be tyrannical. It cannot survive if it is made to appear foolish in its own sight. Repressors, in order to retain power, will continue to do conscious evil for a long time. They will not long continue to do things they know to be silly. The most effective argument against any form of repression is not that it is wicked or even sinful, but that it is foolish and ridiculous. This argument will "get under the skin" of the repressors when all others fail. The condition of repression which exists in any society before a great revolution really is stupid and silly when looked at rationally, just as it is tyrannical and unjust when regarded emotionally. Nothing undermines authority so completely as making it ridiculous — particularly to itself. Since both the repressors and their system of repression actually are ridiculous it is a relatively easy matter to show them to be so, and the intellectuals have a fine time doing it.

The Ship of Fools, The Letters of Obscure Men, and similar satires did more to undermine respect for the medieval church than all the solemn tomes setting forth its iniquities. It is not a mere coincidence that the Reformation began in the pontificate of Leo X, who declared that Christianity was a profitable superstition for ecclesiastics. The very words "hocus-pocus" (for *Hoc est Corpus* — the most sacred words in the mass) show how ridicule succeeded in undermining a whole religious system. The word "dunce" is another proof of the same thing. It is derived from Duns Scotus; Duns was a theologian of the highest repute in the medieval church.

Even a casual examination of the enormous pamphlet literature which preceded the Puritan Revolution will convince anyone that the Puritans, in spite of their reputation for extreme solemnity, were by no means lacking in wit, shrewdness, and the power of making their opponents ridiculous. They seem to have recognized and exposed the absurdity of every form of superstition except their own. In the light of their robust common sense the doctrine of the divine right of kings came to appear incredible and fantastic. The Cavaliers, brave and gallant as they were, bear to this day the brand put upon them by the Puritans — the brand of being roistering and foppish spendthrifts, unfit for the administration of important business. The current American concept of aristocracy comes by direct descent from the Puritans. According to this concept, aristocracy, in addition to being intrinsically inequitable, is intrinsically irrational and ludicrous. By this simple process of making the then-ruling class appear foolish and frivolous, the Puritans did more to weaken the Stuart despotism than by all their solemn declarations about royal tyranny.

The American colonies might, perhaps, have tolerated the government of an autocrat who was a capable ruler. They could not tolerate the government of an autocrat who was a blockhead. The great point made by the publicists, both in England and America, was that the British government, in its dealings with the colonies, was perverse and foolish. The verdict of these famous publicists has been upheld by history. That verdict is that George III was not so much cruel as stupid. He was more a dunce than a tyrant. A long series of actions, at once provocative and puerile, destroyed all respect for regal authority. The Americans finally overthrew it, as much because of its hopeless lack of intelligence as because of its actual misdeeds. Even if the American Revolution had not put an end to George III's silly attempt at autocratic government, the English people themselves would presently have done so. But it was the public's belief in its folly rather than in its wickedness which destroyed it.

In the pre-revolutionary societies of France and Russia the process of undermining the self-confidence of the ruling classes was so similar that both countries can be considered together. In both we see a feeble autocrat, a decadent nobility, and an un-Christlike church exploiting a great and powerful people. The situation was such, in each case, as to offer unlimited scope for satire and ridicule. In each case a whole succession of clever and able publicists took full advantage of the extraordinary opportunity. In both countries the effect was the same. The more enlightened and capable members of the ruling class openly scoffed at the absurdity of the institutions to which they owed their own eminence. The conviction of the essential silliness of the ancient system of repression prevented its intelligent beneficiaries in either nation from making any real effort to prevent its overthrow. The unintelligent beneficiaries could do nothing. Louis XV uttered the prophetic words: "Après moi, le déluge." Nicholas II was too stupid to say anything.

---

[1] *History of the English People*, Book VII, chap. viii.

6. The Anatomy of Revolution

CRANE BRINTON

When all necessary concessions are made to those who insist that events in history are unique, it remains true that the four revolutions we have studied do display some striking uniformities. Our conceptual scheme of the fever can be worked out so as to bring these uniformities clearly to mind. We shall find it worth while, in attempting to summarize the work of these revolutions, to recapitulate briefly the main points of comparison on which our uniformities are based.

We must be very tentative about the prodromal symptoms of revolution. Even retrospectively, diagnosis of the four societies we studied was very difficult, and there is little ground for belief that anyone today has enough knowledge and skill to apply formal methods of diagnosis to a contemporary society and say, in this case revolution will or will not occur shortly. But some uniformities do emerge from a study of the old regimes in England, America, France, and Russia.

First, these were all societies on the whole on the upgrade economically before the revolution came, and the revolutionary movements seem to originate in the discontents of not unprosperous people who feel restraint, cramp, annoyance, rather than downright crushing oppression. Certainly these revolutions are not started by down-and-outers, by starving, miserable people. These revolutionists are not worms turning, not children of despair. These revolutions are born of hope, and their philosophies are formally optimistic.

Second, we find in our prerevolutionary society definite and indeed very bitter class antagonisms, though these antagonisms seem rather more complicated than the cruder Marxists will allow. It is not a case of feudal nobility against bourgeoisie in 1640, 1776, and 1789, or of bourgeoisie against proletariat in 1917. The strongest feelings seem generated in the bosoms of men — and women — who have made money, or at least who have enough to live on, and who contemplate bitterly the imperfections of a socially privileged aristocracy. Strong feelings, too, as James C. Davies suggests, are roused in those who find an intolerable gap between what they have come to want — their "needs" — and what they actually get. Revolutions seem more likely when social classes are fairly close together than when they are far apart. "Untouchables" very rarely revolt against a God-given aristocracy, and Haiti gives one of the few examples of successful slave revolutions. But rich merchants whose daughters can marry aristocrats are likely to feel that God is at least as interested in merchants as in aristocrats. It is difficult to say why the bitterness of feeling between classes *almost* equal socially seems so much stronger in some societies than others — why, for instance, a Marie Antoinette should be so much more hated in eighteenth-century France than a rich, idle, much publicized heiress in contemporary America; but at any rate the existence of such bitterness can be observed in our prerevolutionary societies, which is, clinically speaking, enough for the moment.

Third, there is what we have called the transfer of allegiance of the intellectuals. This is in some respects the most reliable of the symptoms we are likely to meet. Here again we need not try to explain all the hows and whys, need not try to tie up this transfer of allegiance with a grand and complete sociology of revolutions. We need state simply that it can be observed in all four of our societies.

Fourth, the governmental machinery is clearly inefficient, partly through neglect, through a failure to make changes in old institutions, partly because new conditions — in the societies we have studied, pretty specifically conditions attendant on economic expansion and the growth of new monied classes, new ways of transportation, new business methods — these new conditions laid an intolerable strain on governmental machinery adapted to simpler, more primitive, conditions.

Fifth, the old ruling class — or rather, many individuals of the old ruling class — come to distrust themselves, or lose faith in the traditions and habits of their class, grow intellectual, humanitarian, or go over to the attacking groups. Perhaps a larger number of them than usual lead lives we shall have to call immoral, dissolute, though one cannot by any means be as sure about this as a symptom as about the loss of habits and traditions of command effective among a ruling class. At any rate, the ruling class becomes politically inept.

The dramatic events that start things moving, that bring on the fever of revolution, are in three of our four revolutions intimately connected with the financial administration of the state. In the fourth, Russia, the breakdown of administration under the burdens of an unsuccessful war is only in part financial. But in all our societies the inefficiency and inadequacy of the governmental structure of the society come out clearly in the very first stages of the revolution. There is a time — the first few weeks or months — when it looks as if a determined use of force on the part of the government might prevent the mounting excitement from culminating in an overthrow of the government. These governments attempted such a use of force in all four instances, and in all four their attempt was a failure. This failure indeed proved a turning point during the first stages, and set up the revolutionists in power.

Yet one is impressed in all four instances more with the ineptitude of the governments' use of force than with the skill of their opponents' use of force. We are here speaking of the situation wholly from a military and police point of view. It may be that the majority of the people are discontented, loathe the existing government, wish it overthrown. Nobody knows. They don't commonly take plebiscites just *before* revolutions. In the actual clash — even Bastille Day, Concord, or the February Days in Petrograd — only a minority of the people is actively engaged. But the government hold over its own troops is poor, its troops fight halfheartedly or desert, its commanders are stupid, its enemies acquire a nucleus of the deserting troops or of a previous militia, and the old gives place to the new. Yet, such is the conservative and routine-loving nature of the bulk of human beings, so strong are habits of obedience in most of them, that it is almost safe to say that no government is likely to be overthrown from within its territory until it loses the ability to make adequate use of its military and police powers. That loss of ability may show itself in the actual desertion of soldiers and police to the revolutionists, or in the stupidity with which the government manages its soldiers and police, or in both ways.

The events we have grouped under the names of first stages do not of course unroll themselves in exactly the same order in time, or with exactly the same content, in all four of our revolutions. But we have listed the major elements — and they fall into a pattern of uniformities — financial breakdown, organization of the discontented to remedy this breakdown (or threatened breakdown), revolutionary demands on the part of these organized discontented, demands which if granted would mean the virtual abdication of those governing, attempted use of force by the government, its failure, and the attainment of power by the revolutionists. These revolutionists have hitherto been acting as an organized and nearly unanimous group, but with the attainment of power it is clear that they are not united. The group which dominates these first stages we call the moderates, though to emotional supporters of the old regime they look most immoderate. They are not always in a numerical majority in this stage — indeed it is pretty clear that if you limit the moderates to the Kadets they were not in a majority in Russia in February, 1917. But they seem the natural heirs of the old government, and they have their chance. In three of our revolutions they are sooner or later driven from office to death or exile. Certainly there is to be seen in England, France, and Russia a process in which a series of crises — some involving violence, street fighting, and the like — deposes one set of men and puts in power another and more radical set. In these revolutions power passes by violent or at least extralegal methods from Right to Left, until at the crisis period the extreme radicals, the complete revolutionists, are in power. There are, as a matter of fact, usually a few even wilder and more lunatic fringes of the triumphant extremists — but these are not numerous or strong and are usually suppressed or otherwise made harmless by the dominant radicals. It is therefore approximately true to say that power passes on from Right to Left until it reaches a limit usually short of the most extreme or lunatic Left.

The rule of the extremists we have called the crisis period. This period was not reached in the American Revolution, though in the treatment of Loyalists, in the pressure to support the army, in some of the phases of social life, you can discern in America many of the phenomena of the Terror as it is seen in our three other societies. We cannot here attempt to go into the complicated question as to why the American Revolution stopped short of a true crisis period, why the moderates were never ousted in this country, or at least ousted only in 1800. We must repeat that we are simply trying to establish certain uniformities of description, and are not attempting a complete sociology of revolutions.

The extremists are helped to power no doubt by the existence of a powerful pressure toward centralized strong government, something which in general the moderates are not capable of providing, while the extremists, with their discipline, their contempt for half measures, their willingness to make firm decisions, their freedom from libertarian qualms, are quite able and willing to centralize. Especially in France and Russia, where powerful foreign enemies threatened the very existence of the nation, the machinery of government during the crisis period was in part constructed to serve as a government of national defense. Yet though modern wars, as we know in this country, demand a centralization of authority, war alone does not seem to account for all that happened in the crisis period in those countries.

What does happen may be a bit oversimply summarized as follows: emergency centralization of power in an administration, usually a council or commission, and more or less dominated by a "strong man" — Cromwell, Robespierre, Lenin; government without any effective protection for the normal civil rights of the individual — or if this sounds unrealistic, especially for Russia, let us say the normal private life of the individual; setting up of extraordinary courts and a special revolutionary police to carry out the decrees of the government and to suppress all dissenting individuals or groups; all this machinery ultimately built up from a relatively small group — Independents, Jacobins, Bolsheviks — which has a monopoly on all governmental action. Finally, governmental action becomes a much greater part of all human action than in these societies in their normal condition: this apparatus of government is set to work indifferently on the mountains and molehills of human life — it is used to pry into and poke about corners normally reserved for priest or physician, or friend, and it is used to regulate, control, and plan the production and distribution of economic wealth on a national scale.

This pervasiveness of the Reign of Terror in the crisis period is partly explicable in terms of the pressure of war necessities and of economic struggles as well as of other variables: but it must probably also be explained as in part the manifestation of an effort to achieve intensely moral and religious ends here on earth. The little band of violent revolutionists who form the nucleus of all action during the Terror behave as men have been observed to behave before when under the influence of active religious faith. Independents, Jacobins, Bolsheviks, all sought to make all human activity here on earth conform to an ideal pattern, which, like all such patterns, seems deeply rooted in their sentiments. A striking uniformity in all these patterns is their asceticism, or if you prefer, their condemnation of what we may call the minor as well as the major vices. Essentially, however, these patterns are a good deal alike, and all resemble closely what we may call conventional Christian ethics. Independents, Jacobins, and Bolsheviks, at least during the crisis period, really make an effort to enforce behavior in literal conformity with these codes or patterns. Such an effort means stern repression of much that many men have been used to regarding as normal; it means a kind of universal tension in which the ordinary individual can never feel protected by the humble routines to which he has been formed: it means that the intricate prerevolutionary network of customary interactions among individuals — a network which is still to the few men devoted to its intelligent study almost a complete mystery — this network is temporarily all torn apart. John Jones, the man in the street, the ordinary man, is left floundering.

We are almost at the point of being carried away into the belief that our conceptual scheme is something more than a mere convenience, that it does somehow describe "reality." At the crisis, the collective patient does seem helpless, thrashing his way through a delirium. But we must try to avoid the emotional, metaphorical appeal, and concentrate on making clear what seems to be the really important point here. Most of us are familiar with the favorite old Tory metaphor: the violent revolutionist tears down the noble edifice society lives in, or burns it down, and then fails to build up another, and poor human beings are left naked to the skies. That is not a good metaphor, save perhaps for purposes of Tory propaganda. Even at the height of a revolutionary crisis period, more of the old building is left standing than is destroyed. But the whole metaphor of the building is bad. We may take instead an analogy from the human nervous system, or think of an immensely complicated gridwork of electrical communications. Society then appears as a kind of network of interactions among individuals, interactions for the most part fixed by habit, hardened and perhaps adorned as ritual, dignified into meaning and beauty by the elaborately interwoven strands of interaction we know as law, theology, metaphysics, and similar noble beliefs. Now sometimes many of these interwoven strands of noble beliefs, some even of those of habit and tradition, can be cut out, and others inserted. During the crisis period of our revolutions some such process seems to have taken place; but the whole network itself seems so far never to have been altered suddenly and radically, and even the noble beliefs tend to fit into the network in the same places. If you kill off *all* the people who live within the network, you don't so much change the network of course as destroy it. This type of destruction is as yet rare in human history. Certainly in none of our revolutions was there even a very close approach to it.

What did happen, under the pressure of class struggle, war, religious idealism, and a lot more, was that the hidden and obscure courses which many of the interactions in the network follow were suddenly exposed, and passage along them made difficult in the unusual publicity and, so to speak, self-consciousness. The courses of other interactions were blocked, and the interactions went on with the greatest of difficulties by all sorts of detours. The courses of still other interactions were confused, short-circuited, paired off in strange ways. Finally, the pretensions of the fanatical leaders of the revolution involved the attempted creation of a vast number of new interactions. Now though for the most part these new interactions affected chiefly those strands we have called the noble beliefs — law, theology, metaphysics, mythology, folklore, high-power abstractions in general — still some of them did penetrate at an experimental level into the obscurer and less dignified part of the network of interactions among human beings and put a further strain on it. Surely it is no wonder that under these conditions men and women in the crisis period should behave as they would not normally behave, that in the crisis period nothing should seem as it used to seem, that, indeed, a famous passage from Thucydides, written two thousand years before our revolutions, should seem like a clinical report:

> When troubles had once begun in the cities, those who followed carried the revolutionary spirit further and further, and determined to outdo the report of all who had preceded them by the ingenuity of the enterprises and the atrocity of their revenges. The meaning of words had no longer the same relation to things, but was changed by them as they thought proper. Reckless daring was held to be loyal courage; prudent delay was the excuse of a coward; moderation was the disguise of unmanly weakness; to know everything was to do nothing. Frantic energy was the true quality of a man. A conspirator who wanted to be safe was a recreant in disguise. The lover of violence was always trusted, and his opponent suspected. He who succeeded in a plot was deemed knowing, but a still greater master in craft was he who detected one. On the other hand, he who plotted from the first to have nothing to do with plots was a breaker up of parties and a poltroon who was afraid of the enemy. In a word, he who could outstrip another in a bad action was applauded, and so was he who encouraged to evil one who had no idea of it. . . . The tie of party was stronger than the tie of blood, because a partisan was more ready to dare without asking why.

With this we may put a quotation from a much humbler source, an obscure Siberian co-operative leader protesting against Red and White Terror alike. Mr. Chamberlin quotes:

> And we ask and appeal to society, to the contending political groups and parties: When will our much-suffering Russia outlive the nightmare that is throttling it, when will deaths by violence cease? Doesn't horror seize you at the sight of the uninterrupted flow of human blood? Doesn't horror seize you at the consciousness that the deepest, most elementary bases of the existence of human society are perishing: the feeling of humanity, the consciousness of the value of life, of human personality, the feeling and consciousness of the necessity of legal order in the state? . . . Hear our cry and despair: we return to prehistoric times of the existence of the human race; we are on the verge of the death of civilization and culture; we destroy the great cause of human progress, for which many generations of our worthier ancestors labored.

Certainly, however, none of our revolutions quite ended in the death of civilization and culture. The network was stronger than the forces trying to destroy or alter it, and in all of our societies the crisis period was followed by a convalescence, by a return to most of the simpler and more fundamental courses taken by interactions in the old network. More especially, the religious lust for perfection, the crusade for the Republic of Virtue, died out, save among a tiny minority whose actions could no longer take place directly in politics. An active, proselyting, intolerant, ascetic, chiliastic faith became fairly rapidly an inactive, conformist, worldly ritualistic faith.

The equilibrium has been restored and the revolution is over. But this does not mean that nothing has been changed. Some new and useful tracks or courses in the network of interations that makes society have been established, some old and inconvenient ones — you may call them unjust if you like — have been eliminated. There is something heartless in saying that it took the French Revolution to produce the metric system and to destroy *lods et ventes* and similar feudal inconveniences, or the Russian Revolution to bring Russia to use the modern calendar and to eliminate a few useless letters in the Russian alphabet. These tangible and useful results look rather petty as measured by the brotherhood of man and the achievement of justice on this earth. The blood of the martyrs seems hardly necessary to establish decimal coinage.

Yet those who feel that revolution is heroic need not despair. The revolutionary tradition is an heroic one, and the noble beliefs which seem necessary to all societies are in our Western democracies in part a product of the revolutions we have been studying. They were initiated, even in Russia, by Peter Gay's "part of humanity." Our revolutions made tremendous and valuable additions to those strands in the network of human interactions which can be isolated as law, theology, metaphysics and, in the abstract sense, ethics. Had these revolutions never occurred, you and I might still beat our wives or cheat at cards or avoid walking under ladders, but we might not be able to rejoice in our possession of certain inalienable rights to life, liberty, and the pursuit of happiness, or in the comforting assurance that one more push will bring the classless society.

When one compares the whole course of these revolutions, certain tentative uniformities suggest themselves. If the Russian Revolution at the end of our series is compared with the English at its beginning, there seems to be a development of conscious revolutionary technique. This is of course especially clear since Marx made the history of revolutionary movements of the past a necessary preparation for revolutionists of the present. Lenin and his collaborators had a training in the technique of insurrection which Independents and Jacobins lacked. Robespierre seems almost a political innocent when his revolutionary training is compared with that of any good Bolshevik leader. Sam Adams, it must be admitted, seems a good deal less innocent. All in all, it is probable that this difference in the explicitness of self-conscious preparation for revolution, this growth of a copious literature of revolution, this increasing familiarity of revolutionary ideas, is not one of the very important uniformities we have to record. It is a conspicuous uniformity, but not an important one. Revolutions are still not a form of logical action. The Bolsheviks do not seem to have guided their actions by the "scientific" study of revolutions to an appreciably greater degree than the Independents or the Jacobins. They simply adapted an old technique to the days of the telegraph and railroad trains.

This last suggests another conspicuous but not very important tendency in our four revolutions. They took place in societies increasingly influenced by the "Industrial Revolution," increasingly subject to those changes in scale which our modern conquests of time and space have brought to societies. Thus the Russian Revolution directly affected more people and more square miles of territory than any previous revolution; its sequence of events compresses into a few months what in England in the seventeenth century had taken years to achieve; in its use of the printing press, telegraph, radio, airplanes and the rest it seems, as compared with our other revolutions, definitely a streamlined affair. But again we may well doubt whether such changes of scale are in themselves really important factors. Men's desires are the same, whether they ride toward their achievement in airplanes or on horseback. Revolutions may be bigger nowadays, but surely not better. Our prophets of doom to the contrary notwithstanding, the loudspeaker does not change the words.

Finally, at the risk of being tedious, we must come back to some of the problems of methods in the social sciences which were suggested in our first chapter. We must admit that the theorems, the uniformities, which we have been able to put forward in terms of our conceptual scheme, are vague and undramatic. They are by no means as interesting or as alarming as the ideas of revolution held by the late George Orwell, who really believed that totalitarian revolutionary leaders have learned how to change human beings into something wholly different from their immediate predecessors. On the contrary, even Communist Russians begin to look more and more like — Russians. Our uniformities cannot be stated in quantitative terms, cannot be used for purposes of prediction or control. But at the very outset we warned the reader not to expect too much. Even such vague theorems as that of the transfer of allegiance of the intellectuals, that of the role of force in the first stages of revolution, that of the part played by "religious" enthusiasm in the period of crisis, that of the pursuit of pleasure during

Thermidor, are, one hopes, not without value for the study of men in society. In themselves they amount to little, but they suggest certain possibilities in further work.

In the first place, by their very inadequacies they point to the necessity for a more rigorous treatment of the problems involved, challenging those who find them incomplete and unsatisfactory to do a better job. In the second place, they will serve the purpose of all first approximations in scientific work — they will suggest further study of the *facts,* especially in those fields where the attempt to make first approximations has uncovered an insufficient supply of the necessary facts. Notably here the facts for a study of class antagonisms are woefully inadequate. So, too, are the facts for a study of the circulation of the elite in prerevolutionary societies. But there are a hundred such holes, some of which can surely be filled. Our first approximations will then lead the way to another's second approximations. No scientist should ask more, even though the public does.

Wider uniformities will, to judge by the past of science, someday emerge from more complete studies of the sociology of revolutions. Here we dare not hazard much that we have not already brought out in the course of our analysis of four specific revolutions. After all, these are but four revolutions of what seems to be the same type, revolutions in what may be not too uncritically called the democratic tradition. So precious a word is "revolution" to many in that tradition, and especially to Marxists, that they indignantly refuse to apply it to such movements as the relatively bloodless but certainly violent and illegal assumption of power by Mussolini or Hitler. These movements, we are told, were not revolutions because they did not take power from one class and give it to another. Obviously with a word in some ways as imprecise as "revolution" you can play all sorts of tricks like this. But for the scientific study of social change it seems wise to apply the word revolution to the overthrow of an established and legal parliamentary government by Fascists. If this is so, then our four revolutions are but one kind of revolution, and we must not attempt to make them bear the strain of generalizations meant to apply to all revolutions.

We need not, however, end on a note of blank skepticism. It would seem that there are, from the study of these revolutions, three major conclusions to be drawn: first, that, in spite of their undeniable and dramatic differences, they do present certain simple uniformities of the kind we have tried to bring together under our conceptual scheme of the fever; second, that they point sharply to the necessity of studying men's deeds and men's words without assuming that there is always a simple and logical connection between the two, since throughout their courses, and especially at their crises, they frequently exhibit men saying one thing and doing another;

third, that they indicate that in general many things men do, many human habits, sentiments, dispositions, cannot be changed at all rapidly, that the attempt made by the extremists to change them by law, terror, and exhortation fails, that the convalescence brings them back not greatly altered.

Yet one hesitant major generalization binding all four of these revolutions together may here be made from many anticipations earlier in this book. These four revolutions exhibit an increasing scale of promises to the "common man" — promises as vague as that of complete "happiness" and as concrete as that of full satisfaction of all material wants, with all sorts of pleasant revenges on the way. Communism is but the present limit of this increasing set of promises. It is not for us here to rail or protest, but simply to record. So far, these promises in their extreme form have been fulfilled nowhere. That they are made at all offends the traditional Christian, the humanist, perhaps even the man of common sense. But they are made, more vigorously perhaps today in China, in Southeast Asia, in the Near East, wherever Communism is still a young, fresh, and active faith. It is not enough for us Americans to repeat that the promises are impossible of fulfillment, and ought not to be made. It would be folly for us to tell the world that we Americans can fill these promises, especially since we have not filled them at home. Revolution is not a fever that will yield to such innocent and deceptive remedies. For a time, at least, we must accept it as being as incurable as cancer.

As to what the experience of a great revolution does to the society that experiences it, we cannot conclude here too widely without trespassing on wider fields of history and sociology. Yet it does seem that the patient emerges stronger in some respects from the conquered fever, immunized in this way and that from attacks that might be more serious. It is an observable fact that in all our societies there was a flourishing, a peak of varied cultural achievements, after the revolutions. Certainly we may not moralize too much about the stupidities and cruelties of revolutions, may not lift up our hands in horror. It is quite possible that wider study would show that feeble and decadent societies do not undergo revolutions, that revolutions are, perversely, a sign of strength and youth in societies.

One quiet person emerges from his study, not indeed untouched by a good deal of horror and disgust, but moved also with admiration for a deep and unfathomable strength in men which, because of the softer connotations of the word, he is reluctant to call spiritual. Montaigne saw and felt it long ago:

> I see not one action, or three, or a hundred, but a commonly accepted state of morality so unnatural, especially as regards inhumanity and treachery, which are to me the worst of all sins, that I have not the

heart to think of them without horror; and they excite my wonder almost as much as my detestation. *The practice of these egregious villainies has as much the mark of strength and vigor of soul as of error and disorder.*

Berkman the anarchist, who loathed the Russian Revolution, tells a story which may represent merely his own bias, but which may nonetheless serve as a brief symbolical conclusion to this study. Berkman says he asked a good Bolshevik acquaintance during the period of attempted complete communization under Lenin why the famous Moscow cabmen, the *izvoschiks,* who continued in diminished numbers to flit about Moscow and to get enormous sums in paper roubles for their services, were not nationalized like practically everything else. The Bolshevik replied, "We found that if you don't feed human beings they continue to live somehow. But if you don't feed the horses, the stupid beasts die. That's why we don't nationalize the cabmen." That is not an altogether cheerful story, and in some ways one may regret the human capacity to live without eating. But clearly if we were as stupid — or as sensible — as horses we should have no revolutions.

7. Causes of Revolution

LOUIS GOTTSCHALK

The author of this article is a specialist in the history of the French Revolution. It is as that kind of specialist that he proposes to discuss the causes of revolutionary change. That does not mean, however, that after asking himself, "What are the causes of the French Revolution?" he has been content to assume that the answers to that question hold good also for all other revolutions. On the contrary, the method adopted has been posited on a series of questions and answers.

To begin with, an analysis of the nature of historical causes seems necessary. "Cause" may be defined as "that from which something known as the result proceeds and without which the thing known as the result cannot happen." From that definition it follows that there are at least four attributes of the concept "cause." In the first place, cause must be *antecedent* to result in chronological order. In the second place, that antecedence must be logically interrelated or *concurrent* with the result. In the third place, cause must be *sufficient* to bring about the result. Where a single antecedent suffices to explain the cause-result relationship, it alone is the cause. When several antecedents have to be considered, no one of which is alone sufficient to explain the phenomenon and all of which play an interrelated or concurrent part, the phenomenon has multiple causes. All but the simplest forms of historical causal relationships show multiple causes, since single causes usually are insufficient to account for complex results.

The problem of multiple causes raises the question of the fourth attribute of historical causation — that of *necessity*. No result can appear without a cause or causes. But need the cause or causes always be the same? Let us take a simple example. A headache may be "caused" by a blow, indigestion, eyestrain, etc. But none of these is the immediate cause of the headache. They only cause that which, in fact, makes the headache — excitation of the pain nerves in the head. They are, in other words, *remote* or *secondary* or *contributory causes*. Conceivably, any one of them could occur without resulting in a headache. The excitation of the pain nerves is the *immediate* or *primary* or *main cause* of the headache.

The immediate cause is always part of the definition of the result. "Headache" means, at least partly, "excitation of the pain nerves in the head." Similarly, the immediate cause of "war" is "the outbreak of hostilities between two or more countries," and that is also part of the definition of war. Other examples would be easy to give. We shall soon see how the immediate cause of "revolution" helps to define the concept "revolution."

The immediate cause of any historical result is a single event and not a set of conditions. Hence, it is convenient and proper to refer to it as the *occasion* of that result. Similar results always have a similar immediate cause or occasion, which, however, may itself be explicable by variant circumstances. The immediate cause is seldom a sufficient explanation of the result that follows without an understanding of its own remoter causes. In fact, without such an understanding, immediate causes of single episodes are likely to appear both accidental and trivial — like the loss of the proverbial kingdom "for the want of a nail."

Remote causes, in turn, need explanation. Hence, in history — as, indeed, in the natural sciences — the quest for causes is likely to reach further and further into space toward an all-inclusive cause or to recede further and further into time toward a first-cause. To avoid such a dissipation of attention, the historian must assume the constancy or irrelevance of certain tangentials, like gravitation or sunspots, and must limit each inquiry to a more or less arbitrary geographical and chronological area. While such assumptions and limitations leave room for subjective judgments, without them discussion of causation is not likely to be fruitful to the historian.

Causes may be circumvented or aborted. A headache need not occur, though all the causes are at work, if certain nerves are anesthetized; and the outbreak of hostilities may be mediated without bringing about a real war. In consequence, it is impossible in human affairs — as in physical nature also, though to a lesser degree — to be sure, when something that resembles a known cause is found to have occurred, that the result must follow. The historian, however, has an advantage over the natural scientist in this regard, in that he works backward into time — from the present to the past. Hence, he always knows the results and from them can work back to causes that he knows have not been circumvented.

That logical process is not peculiar to history. The natural sciences also proceed that way sometimes. Franklin knew the results of lightning before he conducted his experiments to find the cause. Physiologists often know the results of a disease before they carry on experiments to find its causes. The difference between the natural sciences and history in that regard is that history has no other way of proceeding. Whereas natural scientists can produce causes in their laboratories and with them obtain results, historians can proceed only by discerning from the result what the cause or causes must have been.

In effect, that means that the historian uses analogy more than any other logical process. He derives his generalizations from his own experience and from the experiences of others which vicariously have become his own. He has learned from his own past and studies and from the past and studies of others that similar results usually come from similar causes; and he argues that, therefore, the results which interest him as a student of history must have had causes like those that in his real or vicarious experience brought similar results. This is another way of stating Hume's well-known dictum: "All our reasonings concerning causes and effects are derived from nothing but custom."

Since that is so, any historian's discussion of revolutionary causation must be based upon an examination of contemporary, as well as remote, revolutions. His derivation of causes of revolution must come not merely from a study of the French Revolution and other remote revolutions but also from his experience of revolutions in his own time. His task would be rendered much easier if he dared to assume that under the same circumstances people must act in the same way, regardless of their times, training, or environment. But that is not altogether true. In human affairs a causal generalization derived entirely from a set of analogous events is undependable, for the simple reason that human beings sometimes profit from experience. The fact that present circumstances are similar to past circumstances may be the very reason why the same causes will not lead to the same results. Unfortunately, we dare not count upon human beings to profit from experience. If we could, we would be able to say that the same causes would certainly not lead to the same results unless they were desirable results. The chief trouble for the historian interested in causation comes from the fact that human beings are perverse: they cannot be counted upon *not* to profit from experience. And so it is sometimes possible that apparently similar causes may lead to dissimilar results, that the expected results may be avoided if they are undesirable. The historian must be constantly on his guard against the introduction of variables through the ability of human beings to learn.

So in the following examination of the causal relationship between old regimes and revolutions it is not necessary to insist that the causes set forth will necessarily lead to revolution if they should occur again. All that is claimed is that, if this set of causes should occur again, one of the possible results — one of the several things that may be anticipated — is a revolution. That sort of anticipation (rather than prediction) is all that social scientists should dare to claim with regard to any causal generalization derived from human experience. Setting forth a certain number of conditions that have in the past led to certain events, he can only maintain that those conditions *may* again lead to the same results in the future. He cannot be absolutely sure that they will, because of the variability of human behavior.

The logical process just described explains the method whereby the present theory of revolutionary causation has been derived. The results of revolution are more or less well known to historians — the Dutch, English, American, French, German, Russian, Chinese, and other revolutions. About them many generalizations derived *inter alia* from common sense, personal experience, and scholarly observation are available. The historian, picking one of those revolutions and applying his definition of revolution, finds its immediate cause or occasion. Then, using the (to him) most applicable of the available generalizations, he tries to discover among the infinity of antecedents that remoter cause or those remoter causes which are concurrent and sufficient to account for the occasion. This is not only in large part a subjective operation, since definitions and the selections of generalizations may differ; but it is also repetitive, since it has to be done over again for each revolution and, in fact, for each change within each revolution. Hence, if a causal pattern can be devised, it might simplify the task of students of revolutions. To draw such a general pattern, it has seemed desirable to check the causal design derived from a single set of revolutionary antecedents against the antecedents of other revolutions, modifying it as seemed necessary and possible. Wherever scholarly or philosophical generalizations were known and considered helpful in this comparative process, they were applied.

Hence, the theory of revolutionary causation here presented is based upon the answers to the questions: How can revolution be defined? How does that definition apply to the French Revolution? What, by that definition, was the immediate cause or occasion of the French Revolution? What were the antecedents of that occasion which were logically concurrent and sufficient to explain it? (Here a set of generalizations had to be used.) How far does the design formed by those concurrent and sufficient antecedents (or causes) fit into the causal designs antecedent to other revolutions? (Here the same or other generaliations proved useful.) How far could these separate designs be modified so as to conform to each other and thus be made into a pattern of revolutionary causes? The results of this inquiry and not the separate answers, are presented below. The author recognizes the subjective element in his answers but does not believe that that subjectivity is sufficiently unique or isolated to invalidate his theory for the use of others.

An examination of the several movements that generations of historians have called "revolutions" leads to the definition that a revolution is a popular movement whereby a significant change in the structure of a nation or a society is effected. Usually an overthrow of the existing government and the substitution of another comes early in such a movement, and significant social and economic changes follow. Palace coups that have no popular backing and mere riots or rebellions that produce no significant change are not revolutions. Counterrevolutions are properly designated "revolutions" — at least to the extent that the revolutions they counter are so designated.

In the past, several prominent and in many ways significant monistic explanations of revolutionary changes have been advanced. The most prominent is that of the Marxists, who maintain that revolutionary change is due to the conflict between the methods of production and "the legal and psychological institutions of property" (i.e., the laws and thought patterns resulting from the control of the propertied classes). That conflict leads to class struggles, which in turn lead to shifts of power among the classes — hence revolutions. Another monistic theory is often given as an explanation particularly of the French Revolution. It has been designated "the conspiracy theory": Revolutions come about because some groups — intellectuals of one kind or another, or Jews, or Masons — for reasons of their own (generally selfish), have persuaded the people to follow along paths which the historians who hold this "conspiracy theory" usually consider bad. Sorokin believes that all social change (revolution included) results from epistemological or ethical causes, or what he calls "'meaningful-causal interdependence." Change thus comes from conflicts of values.

Needless to say, there is much of truth in these monistic theories. The thing that makes it difficult to accept any of them as a complete explanation is that, in general, such a variable result as a revolution, even a revolution primarily political, has many social, economic, and intellectual implications and can hardly come from a single cause, whether it be socioeconomic, like the Marxist theory, or biographical-psychological, like the conspiracy theory, or ethical-epistemological, like the Sorokin theory.

For a more satisfactory explanation of revolutionary change, one has to look to multiple causation. A study of the causes of the French Revolution and of other revolutions of recent centuries leads to the conclusion that there is a combination of five causes which, together, give a more satisfactory explanation of important revolutions than any other theory. This conclusion regarding revolutionary causation has been checked against several works which deal with the nature of revolution — particularly Leon Trotsky's *History of the Russian Revolution* (New York, 1937), the article by Alfred Meusel in the *Encyclopaedia of the Social Sciences* on "Revolution and Counter-revolution," Lyford P. Edwards' *The Natural History of Revolution* (Chicago, 1927), and Crane Brinton's *The Anatomy of Revolutions* (New York, 1938). While none of these studies sets forth this theory in the same bold terms as here advanced, Trotsky's work contains it by implication and the others permit its formulation — or at least do not directly contradict it. Even Pitirim A. Sorokin's *Social and Cultural Dynamics* (4 vols.; New York, 1937–41), despite his emphasis upon the epistemological interpretation of history, would apparently permit it (IV, 599–620 and 694–99), though he would seem to doubt its utility or completeness.

The first two of the five causes of revolution here advanced may be placed in a single category. That category may be called "demand." As W. F. Ogburn has pointed out, there is always to be found sufficient demand or necessity for any social change. The kind of demand that helps to create a revolution consists of two parts. It is not mere discontent or despair. Discontent is personal and subjective. Nearly all historians and sociologists probably would agree that mere personal discontent leads so definitely to an intensification of the struggle for personal existence or for personal improvement that the discontented do not have time to think in terms of social betterment. Such discontent may play a part in the creation of individual leaders of revolutions (and we shall return to it in that connection in a moment). But as a factor in creating social change, something is required more general than individual discontent or despair. That more general feeling is found in the social dissatisfaction that comes from widespread provocation.

The first cause of revolution, therefore, may be called "provocation" if it results in dissatisfaction sufficiently general to create not merely a certain slough of subjective despair but an epidemic desire for action. Such provocation came in the American Revolution, the French Revolution, and the Russian Revolution from such things as land hunger; taxation; high fees for services rendered or for services not rendered; exclusion from certain kinds of prestige or from certain kinds of office; misgovernment; bad roads; commercial restrictions; corruption; military or diplomatic defeat; famine; high prices; low wages and unemployment. Such provocations are to be found antecedent to every revolution. Where they are sufficiently intense, they create not only strength for the revolutionaries but also, as we shall see, weakness for the conservatives. Since these provocations often are of an economic nature, the economic interpretation of history finds a partial support here.

But provocations alone do not create revolutions. If they did, we should always be having revolutions, for some of them are constantly to be found in human society — often many of them in the same region at the same time. As has been said, provocations, to cause revolution, must be such that there is a widespread awareness of them. Therefore, a second factor in creating that kind of demand for change which leads to revolutions is a *solidified public opinion*. The fact that I am discontented will not lead me to revolution unless I am aware that quite a number of other people are equally discontented and are likely to unite with me in the expression of my discontent. General awareness of resentment against the provocations, together with the provocations themselves, creates that kind of demand for change which becomes effective in making revolutions.

Demand alone, however, as everyone knows, does not create supply. In order to have a revolution, there must be not merely a demand for revolution but also a certain hopefulness of success. *Hopefulness,* therefore, constitutes a second category of revolutionary causes. Hopefulness also may be broken down into two parts. Hopefulness of revolutionary success comes first from the fact that there exists a *program of reform*. Sometimes there are several conflicting programs. In that case (as in the English, the French, and the Russian revolutions) revolutionary waves, in each of which one of the conflicting programs is dominant, are likely to follow each other in fairly rapid succession. The Lockes, the Franklins, the Otises, the Henrys, and the Adamses furnished programs for the American Revolution; the Montesquieus, the Voltaires, the Rousseaus, for the French Revolution; the Marxes, the Kropotkins, the Milyukovs, for the Russian Revolution.

In providing programs the intellectuals play their major role. To be sure, they also help to create that general awareness of dissatisfaction, that solidified public opinion, which was described above as necessary to create effective demand for revolutionary change. They are aided in that regard, however, by many factors not exclusively intellectual, such as law courts, pulpits, schools and colleges, newspapers, political rallies, salons, and theaters. And they may sometimes also furnish or educate a small part of the leadership to be mentioned below, though the history of the French and Russian revolutions seems to indicate that that is true only for the early stages. But in propounding programs they stand largely alone, or at least in the forefront.

A popular program does not by itself guarantee revolutionary success. It will not even make people hopeful unless they also feel that someone whom they trust is going to lead them to the achievement of that program.

That trusted leader must not only take the first step, must not only serve as the spearhead in the attack upon the existing regime, but must also assume responsibility for the next step, should the first one succeed. Without such leaders, movements that bade fair by glorious beginnings to become major revolutions ended with the first concessions to the revolutionaries. (Witness Lafayette embracing Louis Philippe on the balcony of the Hôtel de Ville in 1830.) Thus *leadership* is another important factor in creating that kind of hopefulness which makes for successful revolution.

Leaders are themselves the result of many factors — social and biographical. Until the psychologists learn more about personality and human motivation than they now know, the biographer must flounder around among many possible explanations — youthful frustration, Freudian complexes, social conditions, dominant thought patterns, adolescent imitation, "circulation of the élite," etc. — in the endeavor to discover what makes leaders. Undoubtedly there are, here too, many economic factors at play, as the Marxists would insist. But self-interest, which is not necessarily economic, is often counterbalanced by altruism; and both are sometimes overshadowed by idealism.

That conflict of motives helps to explain why leaders of lower-class movements frequently come from the upper classes. The English Revolution, for example, had its Lord Fairfax; the French Revolution, Lafayette, Mirabeau, and Talleyrand; the American Revolution, Washington and Lord Stirling; the Russian Revolution, Prince Lvov and Lenin. Although such upper-class leaders do not provide all leadership, they frequently provide so important a part that it is incorrect to say that they are only the exceptions that prove the rule. The exceptions are so many collectively and so important singly that they raise doubt as to whether any rule about the lower-class origin of leaders does in fact exist.

Leaders are, of course, also created *after* the revolution has got well under way. If that were always and exclusively the case, we should have to conclude that leadership was neither logically concurrent with nor antecedent to revolution — in other words, that revolutions produced leaders rather than leaders revolutions. That leadership is logically concurrent with revolution, however, can be argued from the fact that there have been revolutions that failed because *inter alia* they had no adequate leadership. The revolutions of 1830 and 1848 provide good examples. To be sure, there have been incipient revolutionary movements that have failed to materialize despite conspicuous leadership. That was because the other causes of successful revolution were lacking. The careers of John Hus in the Bohemian religious movement of the fifteenth century, of Robespierre in the effort to achieve the Republic of Virtue during the French Terror, and of General Robert E. Lee in the revolutionary attempt of the Confederate States of America illustrate that good leadership alone is an insufficient, though concurrent, cause of revolution. What was missing to make the revolutionary causes in those cases insufficient for success?

So far it has been argued that revolutions occur because of (1) a demand for change, which is itself the result of (a) widespread provocation and (b) solidified public opinion; and (2) a hopefulness of change, which is itself the result of (a) a popular program and (b) trusted leadership. All these four factors, however, even when they act together, cannot by themselves create revolution. They are only the remote causes of revolution. There are several examples of popular movement in which all four have been operative and yet successful revolutions have not occurred; or in which, if the initial revolutionary steps were taken, they failed to effect significant change, as in the case of the Hussite movement, the Republic of Virtue, and the Confederacy.

Another most revealing example here is the Revolution of 1905 in Russia. In that instance nearly the same causes operated as in 1917. The provocations were remarkably similar in 1905 and in 1917; the same parties existed in 1905 and promoted nearly as high a degree of solidified public opinion as in 1917; they had the same programs — Constitutional, Revolutionary Socialist, Menshevik, and Bolshevik. They had the same leaders — Milyukov, Kerensky, Trotsky, Lenin. Yet the revolution failed in 1905 and succeeded in 1917. Why?

The answer leads to the last and the most important of the five causes of revolution under discussion — *the weakness of the conservative forces*. This is the necessary *immediate cause* of revolution. Despite the universal demand for revolutionary change, despite intense hopefulness of success, unless those who wish to maintain the status quo are so weak that they cannot maintain themselves, there is little likelihood of a successful revolution. That is why the many revolutionary outbreaks against Louis XV of France failed but one finally succeeded against Louis XVI in 1789. Louis XV had the support of the army, the clergy, and a great number of the nobility and therefore was able to maintain himself against practically the same kind of revolutionary spirit as that of 1789. But in 1789 Louis XVI could not count on a unified army, clergy, or nobility and, as a consequence, was obliged to yield to a revolutionary spirit that differed, if at all, in degree rather than in kind. In 1848, because Prussia was on the side of the conservative forces, the revolution in Germany failed. But in 1866, because Prussia was on the side of the revolutionary forces, the unification of Germany was effected. In 1848–49, likewise, Russia was on the side of Austria and so Hungary could not establish her independence. But seventy years later foreign intervention was on the side of Hungary and she could do so. In 1905 the Russian army and the Russian aristocracy were firm, and the revolution failed. But in 1917, because the army and the aristocracy were disrupted, the Russian Revolution succeeded.

As these illustrations show, many factors help to create conservative weakness. The decisive factor may be conflict within one of the conservative classes or disagreement among them. (In the French Revolution, for example, not only were the clergy and the nobility divided within themselves, but the nobility also were in conflict with the king.) Or it may be the disaffection of the army, as was true of both the French and the Russian revolutions. Or it may be a shift in international alliance (which would explain why the so-called Holy Alliance, despite its success in suppressing revolution before 1830, failed in the Greek War of Independence and the French and Belgian revolutions of 1830). Poverty, inflation, and bankruptcy, corruption and treachery, military reversal or diplomatic defeat, are also obvious factors contributing to the weakness of governments and dominant classes. These factors (often, as was pointed out above, economic in nature) are usually the same as those that created the *provocations* necessary toward a demand for revolution.

Whatever the factors contributing to their weakness, where the conservative groups are weak, revolution is likely to succeed. That is almost a truism. It is a part of the definition of revolution — as the immediate cause always is of its result. It is almost tantamount to saying that, if the revolutionaries are strong enough, there will be a revolution, and, if they are weak enough, there will not be a revolution. But it is not quite the same. The weakness of the conservatives is not necsesarily due to the strength of the revolutionaries. A good example of that is again the history of the revolutionary movement in Russia. What effected that revolution was not so much that the revolutionaries got stronger as it was that the conservatives got weaker as time went on. That difference is important. If it were not so, the four factors explained above would by themselves be sufficient as causes of revolution, since they would show why revolutionaries grow stronger. But the fact has been illustrated time and again that, until the dominant groups become weak, the rising or ascendant groups cannot oust them.

Lenin himself recognized that fact. All that has been said above in analyzing the five causes of revolution is well summed up (except for the emphasis on "classes") in a statement attributed to him: "A revolution occurs when the upper class cannot and the lower class will not continue the old system" (Meusel, *loc. cit.*, p. 368). The four remote causes of revolution, here divided into the two categories *demand* and *hopefulness*, explain why the so-called "ascendant groups" (those who are rising to power and wish to overthrow the status quo) are not *willing* to preserve the existing regime. The fifth (the immediate) cause indicates why the dominant groups *are not able* to preserve the existing regime.

The identification of the immediate cause — that is, the occasion — of any particular revolution thus becomes simple. It is that event which demonstrates clearly that the conservative forces are no longer able to resist the revolutionary tide. It was the absence of such an occasion that made revolution impossible in the Western nations during the depression of 1929–37, though there were provocations, solidified public opinion, programs, and potential leadership aplenty. And, because conservative middle-class groups were weakened by military defeat, inflation, international humiliation, and other contributing factors, revolution (or, if you like, counterrevolution) came to Germany at the moment that control passed to popular leaders who offered a program sufficiently attractive to win a public already provoked toward solidified action by the same contributing factors.

8. The International
Civil War

SIGMUND NEUMANN

This is the age of revolutions. No longer are they the domain of the theorizer or the peripheral plotter. They have moved into the center of the average man's daily thought. They are on everybody's mind and in every newspaper's headline.[1]

No continent is exempted. The whole of Europe is in upheaval. Her political parties are aligned in the name of, or in opposition to, revolution. China's four decades of civil war, India's final attainment of independence, the awakening nationalism of the Near East and South Eastern Asia spell not only the end of historical empires, but also call into action socio-revolutionary forces that break the frame of established society. Even those areas that are not engulfed by revolution are confronted with its threat. Fascism and National Socialism, though they proved in the test of history to be mere pseudo-revolts, were nourished by grievances of modern society that are not overcome by military defeat and—as long as they remain unanswered—still represent a challenge to our democratic world. Revolution has gained a new momentum, direction, and urgency by the drive of contemporary Bolshevism. It is not only the greater frequency and wider spread but the new quality and intensity of revolution that makes it penetrate the whole fiber of today's international, national, and personal existence.

Revolution—commonly regarded as a mere internal upheaval—has become a world phenomenon. The international character of the revolution

110

is of the very essence.[2] Wherever its effect remains isolated (as in historical Spanish pronunciamentos, in South American coups d'états and in shifting ruling cliques of palace revolts) it may be discounted as a significant movement. Radical upheavals, as all great revolutions are, must now be played on an international scene. In fact, they constitute the dynamic element of world affairs today. Even our wars are fundamentally revolutions and the interwar periods merely an uneasy armistice between drastic, sweeping transformations.

This "global" era has made every region sensitive to the developments of far-distant lands; moreover its "popular" base has changed the decisive forces in the conduct of international affairs. The time-honored concept, since Ranke's day, of the "primacy of foreign affairs," defining the internal nature and needs of the nations, has been increasingly replaced by the "preponderance of domestic forces," pushing into world domains and circumscribing international actions. The frontiers between internal affairs and world politics — despite neat differentiations by the academicians — are irreparably blurred. This change calls for a new "international relations," the outer contours of which are only dimly recognized. All fundamental concepts such as nationalism, sovereignty, intervention must be redefined.

This holds equally true of the concept of revolution. In fact, the clear recognition of its changed character, structure and strategy has become a *conditio sine qua non* for more adequate directives in contemporary international politics. We are still living with an outdated reality, specifically that of 1848. The centennial of this year of revolutions has recently given us the opportunity to evaluate afresh its meaning for the mid-twentieth century. It was a "romantic" revolution, and if we retain this romantic model as our stereotype for interpreting today's revolution, we shall surely be defeated in the international civil war, the form in which the revolution of our time finds expression.

CONCEPTUAL CHANGES AND CONTEMPORARY COMPLEXITIES

"Revolution" as a concept in the social sciences has undergone fundamental changes. Three distinct stages can be observed in the development of the idea. They may be characterized as the natural, romantic, and realistic concepts of revolution.

The term as originally used by Dante, Copernicus, and Galileo connoted a *natural* phenomenon outside of human control (and it still does in the terminology of the natural sciences). In astronomy it referred to "the rotation of the celestial bodies around an axis or center following the iron laws of the spheres." In transferring this "scientific" observation into the field of human history, the Renaissance meant to recognize in revolution "the power of the stars," *i.e.*, the interference of super-human forces within world affairs. *Rivoluzioni*, thus defined, was a fundamental, total, objective transformation. It was *rerum commutatio* and this concept prevailed until the French Revolution. When the courtier Duc de Liancourt informed Louis XVI of the storming of the Bastille (July 14, 1789), the King exclaimed "But good god that is revolt!" "No, Sire," answered the Duc, "C'est la révolution"[3] — which meant that this force of nature could not be controlled by human power.

It is during the French Revolution that this "objective" natural concept of radical transformation changes its meaning to that of a "subjective" *romantic* deed. Now, the individual hero becomes the main actor of the revolution. Robespierre, *révolutionnaire sans phrase*, makes himself its declared spokesman. In fact, this underlying conceptual development is foreshadowed in the writings of the Enlightenment, as when Voltaire discusses "la révolution dans les esprits" and Condorcet speaks of the revolutionary who makes liberty the object of his attack and defense.[4] This new concept not only reflects the reality of "la grande révolution" but characterizes the structure and strategy of the whole nineteenth century, especially the upheavals of 1848. Individual action can overthrow the normal "course of history." It is the age of the barricades where the romantic revolutionary may do his heroic deed. It is this romantic concept of revolution which is still foremost in the people's mind even in this twentieth century.

Yet, our age has reached a new stage of the revolutionary process: the *realistic* phase. On this third level, the two preceding views have been dialectically raised to a higher plane. No longer is the revolution simply the result of unpredictable super-human forces nor the whim of individual action. The revolution comes when the time is "ripe" for it. In this sense it is dependent on objective sociological constellations. It occurs in the "revolutionary situation," but in order to become effective a decided leadership must recognize, articulate, and direct the revolutionary forces of the time. The modern revolution is a calculated, planned, long-range process and not an unexpected, uncontrollable, sudden event. It builds on the preceding upheavals and gives them new life and meaning. The whole nineteenth century is interpreted as an articulation of the French Revolution. Revolution changes from a unique phenomenon to a series of consecutive turning-points in an extended, historical process. Such a conscious recovery of historical experience may lead the contemporary to become the prisoner of past revolutions. This is exactly the peril that threatens today's strategy of revolution. Oriented on an outmoded reality the revolution as well as its democratic response may miss the real challenge of our time.

Barriers to understanding the contemporary crisis result not only from the conceptual changes in the idea of revolution but also from the complex co-existence of different types of revolution in the same historical period as Bolshevism, Fascism, and the revolt of the backward nations today. They cannot be isolated in neat separate compartments. They fight, they influence, they imitate each other. Cultural borrowing goes on in war as well as in peace. The contemporary revolutions are interwoven and inextricably mixed in structure and strategy, patterns and politics. Still every era has its predominant type. The stronger revolution sets the style.

Three outstanding types in modern history may be identified: the democratic, the national, and the social revolution. While the first and the second kind have been the characteristic revolutionary expression of the Great World in the nineteenth century, they are now finally evolving in the erstwhile colonial areas. Yet, their belated appearance in China, Southeast Asia, the Near East, and Southeast Europe makes them contemporaries of the twentieth century social revolution. And, as in earlier upheavals, a stronger nationalism had penetrated and conquered the weaker liberal forces, so today the dynamic social revolutions easily take command of the budding democratic-national movements and direct them into the stream of the "coming world revolution." This may not be surprising in view of the difficult plight of these newcomers among nations (the effect of long-lasting foreign political and economic domination, of "imported" revolutions, of inexperienced leadership and of a weak middle class basis), and in view of the master strategists of the Soviet Revolution who, in accordance with Lenin's threefold slogan — peace for the masses, land for the peasants and control over the factories by the victorious proletariat — have succeeded in uniting different revolutions under the banner of Bolshevism.

The Leninist-Stalinist theory of imperialism, indeed, represents an attempt at the coordination of social and colonial liberation and therewith a claim to revolutionary world leadership. It has not been without success in the areas of awakening nationalism. And this despite the fact that the drive for Westernization has been the clarion call for the "undeveloped peoples," the U.S.S.R. included. In fact, Bolshevism itself has directed from the very beginning a twofold revolution: Russia's catching up with the West while at the same time challenging it with a new expansive social order. The often conflicting drives for national self-assertion and world revolution no doubt have created tremendous tensions, internal and international, for the Soviet system. At times even the most circumspect observers of the Soviet scene could not be sure which of the two drives would prevail. And though the earlier hopes for an eventual rapprochement have been fading of late, the attainments of the Western World still stir Soviet ambitions for a richer "fatherland." "The U. S. too was born of revolution." Agents of unsettlement and change, the Americans are "presiding at a general reorganization of the ways of living throughout the entire world."[5]

The American example has certainly aroused world-wide expectations though this nation may hardly be aware of its appeal and attraction. President Truman's Inaugural Address is a first call to mobilize the imagination of the colonial world and of the American public too. It may be late in this great competition for the support of the new protagonists, just passing the threshold of their conscious history. Yet these very choices before the "awakening peoples" reflect the confluence of different streams of revolution and their consequent confusion. It also indicates the widespread uncertainties as to the true nature and direction of the revolution in our time.

PATTERNS OF THE TWENTIETH CENTURY REVOLUTION

While the aims, spread, and directions of the contemporary revolution are still ambiguous and confusing — proud pronunciamentos of the revolutionaries notwithstanding — its patterns seem to be more clearly drawn by now. Their full recognition can make possible an up-to-date analysis of the structure and strategy of revolution. Such a recognition may also lay open the raw material of contemporary society, its fundamental drives and desires, its hopes and fears. What should properly start as a mere "anatomy of the revolution" may well be suggestive of a better understanding of its life-stream and purposes.

What are the patterns of the twentieth century revolution? For one, they are fundamentally different from those of their historic forerunners. A study in contrasts may serve as a fruitful approach to a realistic appraisal, and may best convey the specific nature of the contemporary upheaval.

Gone are the individual exploits, the spontaneity of action, the romantic hero, the intimacy of localized encounters — those familiar stereotypes of the revolution of story books and more learned texts. Today's spasm reflects a different atmosphere and attitude altogether — cold, calculated, coordinated. Four basic features seem to characterize the new movements. They are totalitarian and institutionalized; they command mass support based upon a militant myth of unlimited expansion.

1. Totalitarianism

The all-embracing revolution is first of all totalitarian. It extends into all spheres of life (politics, economics, education, religion, family). This is the end of any privacy, of fundamental and inalienable rights, of individuality. *Gleichschaltung*, in other words, the enforcement of conformity, takes the place of the free interplay of competing parties and spontaneous social agencies. Nothing is left to chance, not even the surprise of romantic deeds. There is no place for the individual hero — for a poet like Ferdinand

Freiligrath or an artist like George Sand or Chopin — to become the spokesman of the revolution. The dictator alone and his elite can express the will of the whole and give the marching orders.

Discipline becomes the password of the movement. Said Lenin in 1900: "We must train men and women who will devote to the revolution not merely their spare evenings, but the whole of their life." His call for professional revolutionaries indicated the new stern political climate. The father of the modern totalitarian party defined it as the revolutionary vanguard of the future state. His fight at the turn of the century for a small centralized revolutionary Bolshevist elite, as opposed to the Menshevists' idea of a loose democratic mass organization, laid the foundations for such a disciplined totalitarian party. It never mustered more than 30,000 members before it seized the power of state. Lenin thus anticipated what revolutionary parties a generation later experienced when they had to choose between thoroughly revolutionary policies and mass followings and, in their wavering attempts "to steer between sectarianism and opportunism," lost many a battle.

Only in a "revolutionary situation," that is, at a time when complete victory brings a rush of adherents to the revolutionary cause, it is possible for a radical party to win and hold the masses. Revolutionary parties reckoning with a long struggle can count only on a small elite of unrelenting fighters who do not care for rewards today and who are ready to make the revolution their life's calling. The young Bolshevist party comprised, above all, those professional revolutionaries who took their orders from the central party organization. With such reliable cadres at hand the Bolshevist Revolution could reach for power — when the time was "ripe."

The machine character of the revolution has been even more strengthened since the days of Lenin and the establishment of the regime. In fact, one may detect in this Stalinist age a change in the personal quality of leadership, national and international, even on the top level. In its progression from the humanitarian Rosa Luxemburg to the unscrupulous Ana Pauker the movement has lost its once appealing warmth and has become a stranger to its original protagonists.

Two major factors may account for this change. First, the revolution has found a "fatherland"; it has been transformed from a mere myth to a political reality. Fulfilled is the dream of one of its romantic forerunners, Blanqui: "The revolution is an idea that has found bayonets to support it." Yet, having finally found them, it has attained a *raison d'état*, vested interests, national ambitions. Moscow's dual role as the center of Russian politics and as the fountain of the world revolution begins to play havoc with the party lines and national loyalties of the revolutionary leaders all over the world. It calls for bound satraps ready to take orders from above, not for revolutionary free-lances who take fate into their own hands. The rules of selection and rejection of leadership have changed under the centralized direction of the Kremlin.

There is a second reason for the transformation in the ruling elite. The revolution has ceased to be a unique act and has become an extended process in time and space. No longer can it trust to the appearance of the dynamic dilettante whom the spirit moves to enter meteorlike and to disappear when the excitement of the heroic battle is over; he has to make room for the sober rationality of the patient professional. Settling down to the prosaic order of married life, the revolution has no more use for the perpetual honeymooners. It expels a Trotsky from its ranks ruthlessly and without thanks. It now depends for its fulfillment on a "reliable" staff of lieutenants. They reflect the "daily life" of the revolution, the persistence of its efforts, the peculiarities of its national environment, the differentiations of its manifold functions. The specific types, called into action by the supreme command of the World Revolution, correspond to the composite elements of the national dictator's henchmen. They are bureaucratic, feudal, quasi-democratic, and militant. All key men of the satellite states have spent an extended period of indoctrination and schooling in the science of revolution at Moscow and in this sense have proved their trustworthiness — at least until they fall prey to the sin of defection — as executors of the central authority's will. Dimitrov of Bulgaria, the grand old man of the late Comintern, stands out as a reliable bureaucrat of the international order. Ana Pauker, unchallenged chief of the Rumanian party, put into power by the victorious Red Army, derives her commanding position from her direct liaison with the Kremlin as Stalin's "truest paladin." Gottwald, operating within the apparent democratic framework of Czechoslovakia, endeavors to bring this rich industrial prize into the Soviet orbit. Tito's Yugoslavia of traditional fighters is the only satellite nation born out of its own efforts. The partisan state, loyal to its condottiere leader, guards its proud independence, insured by a safe geographic distance from the commanding center. Its own Politburo unites a carefully balanced leadership, among them Serbian General Rankovic in control of the Ministry of Interior, Montenegrin General Djilas, chief of Propaganda, and Slovene Eduard Kardelj in charge of Foreign Affairs and second only to Tito. Tito himself stands in the limelight today — the object of envy, loathing, and vituperation in the Red Empire's circle of number two men, the deep concern of the authorities of the Cominform, and the secret hope of the world revolution's foes. Yet the fights among the satellite lieutenants, like the bitter quarrels between a Goering and Goebbels, do not spell the end of the revolution. They only indicate that it has reached international dimensions and is suffering the strains of the overgrown Leviathan.

Base all this on
Russian Revolution and
spread of communism

The International Civil War   117

2. *Institutionalization*

The institutionalization of modern revolution is closely tied up with its totalitarianism. Paradoxical though it may seem to put a revolution on a permanent basis, this is exactly the purpose for which is created a complex pyramid, from the leader and his henchmen, down through the party and an all-inclusive net of mass organizations, to the lowest level of society. The fully institutionalized dictatorship promises the perpetuation of the revolutionary regime beyond the dictator's life. No further revolutions are to be tolerated. The new masters play for keeps, even if this calls for continuous purges and eternal vigilance. Welcome justification though these threats are for "totalitarian control," they hardly hit the core of its power. Despite significant daily tensions among the lieutenants, a revolution from within is well-nigh impossible. Monopoly over military power of highly mechanized weapons spells the end of the barricades and of the romantic revolution.[6] Military defeat from without becomes almost the only chance for the dictator's fall. Benes realistically understood that all too well; after Munich he welcomed the coming of the war as the only opportunity of liberating his country.

To expect in our time the sudden rise of a militant underground behind the Iron Curtain, answering the far away and tender "Voice of America," is to misunderstand the character of modern dictatorship and to persist in an image of revolution appropriate only to a bygone era. The disappointed bystanders 4000 miles away can easily decry the cowardice of the people under totalitarianism.

There has been no lack of quiet courage and moral integrity even in the darkest of dictatorships. Yet such individual heroism, symbolic though it may be of human stamina and greatness, cannot break the Leviathan machine. If the present-day patterns were not clearly known before, the demise of Fascist dictatorships leaves no excuse for misunderstanding their real nature and that of their opposition too. The flood of first-hand documents on the German underground in the Third Reich affords a full picture of its desperate existence, its fatal limitations, and its eventual futility. The only agency able to bring about a revolutionary upheaval in the modern police state is the army — an institution, however, whose constitutional weakness in policy-making and political courage has been evidenced not only in Fascist dictatorships.[7]

The modern revolutionary has learned his lesson long before. To win and to hold the revolution he must seize and control the key positions of political society — the ministries of Interior, Defense, and Popular Information. These were exactly the three offices that the Czech Communists took over in the first postwar coalition cabinet of the "National Front." The conquest of the whole state proceeded from this vantage position and the consolidation of power after the coup was based on control of the army, the police and the media of mass communication. This important strategy of infiltration was no less successfully applied in all eastern European countries.[8] On the other hand, the exclusion of the Communists from the French and Italian governments signalized the revolutionaries' loss in power and prestige in the West — for the moment at least — and even the prospects of irresponsible opposition could hardly console them.

3.   Mass Basis and the International Civil War

Modern dictatorship, despite popular misconceptions, is utterly unlike the earlier autocratic regimes; it cannot afford to neglect the masses. They are awakened now. They have experienced some kind of democracy. The people can no longer be forced back under an "unpopular" autocracy. It may deceive them, but it cannot neglect them. The post-democratic dictator knows that he must counteract this "democratic memory." Whenever he can, he seizes power legally by adroit use of democratic institutions, thus re-inforcing himself with the help of the prevailing myth of the time. After he has won power he debunks democracy's decadent deeds and then proceeds to establish an "ennobled democracy" of his own.

The formation of a mass basis is a primary concern of twentieth century revolutionary regimes. They capitalize on the failures of rational and democratic leadership and on its inability to satisfy and integrate large segments of society. Their propaganda derives its successes from the grievances it finds in society and from the promises it holds out. Modern industrialization, rapid urbanization, and total war have brought forth major groups of discontent: the frustrated middle class, the rootless unemployed, and the militant irregulars who have made fighting their life's calling. In agrarian societies, especially where feudalism rules, a discontented peasantry longing for liberation may also become a staunch supporter of the revolution, even if used only temporarily by the astute strategists of the movement.

It is in the plight of these social forces that one finds an important key to understanding the appeal, strength, and persistence of the twentieth century revolutionary pattern. China, Southeast Asia and Southeastern Europe are its natural field of operations today and democracy has already lost critical battles on these fronts.[9]

Czechoslovakia does not so obviously fit into the pattern, and yet it was here that in 1948 a model in contemporary upheavals was unfolded — a shocking illustration of the international impact of revolutions and a supreme warning to a world that still does not recognize the character of modern revolution and the strategy of its leaders.

What was the social basis of the Czech revolution? No doubt, the trade unions played an important role. The conquest of the unions, this mass arm of industrial society, became the first aim of the power-conscious, revolutionary strategists. The chaos of Hitler's New Order and the ensuing turmoil of the war years had disrupted the established power of the old-line trade union leaders. Control over the loyal proletarian masses had slipped out of their hands. The power vacuum, here as in international affairs, gave the alert strategists of the revolution a chance at gaining wide support from depressed, confused, leaderless masses.

In many lands the entering wedge was the resistance movement where after some somersaults and tight-rope walking on the "party line," the Communists soon won respect and repute as daring fighters. Militant activism and underground operations had been their *métier*. No wonder they often proved superior to the peaceful middle class and the stodgy Social Democrats. They made good use of their wartime appeal. To the surprise of Europe, awakening from the stupor of the Nazi "millennium," the Communists emerged in the dawn of victory as possessors of the precious trade union organizations in a number of nations. Since then they have been partly dislodged from this power position in Belgium. In France and Italy, their predominance has been increasingly challenged.

In Czechoslovakia, however, the Communists were from the beginning well entrenched. Their strong position was partly based on historical circumstances. That country's traumatic experience at the time of Munich fundamentally altered what originally had been a western-oriented attitude. Russia had not been a partner to this vivisection and mutilation of Czechoslovakia. Thus, it was as early as 1938 that the first bastion was won by the Communists and their international "protector," Soviet Russia. When finally, in 1945, the Russians and not General Patton's Third Army "liberated" the country, it was easy to establish the myth of the U.S.S.R.'s commanding victory and trustworthy friendship. True, it did not take long for the myth to fade. The behavior of the Russian troops and the generous UNRRA help from the United States changed the political balance and undoubtedly led to a decline in the influence of the Communists who were dreading the forthcoming election of 1948.

Revolutionaries usually strike, not when their opponents seem to be weakest, but on the contrary, when they show first signs of recovery — signs which are not yet strong enough to re-establish confidence in the existing "order" but sufficiently visible to indicate the passing of the revolutionary situation. This was the hour of Mussolini's march on Rome in 1922, of Hitler's "gentlemen's agreement" with his arch-enemies Papen and Hugenberg in 1933. The danger point may be most acute when recovery of strength is looming.

It was at such a strategic point that the Czech revolutionaries had to strike; yet they could do so successfully because they were fully entrenched in their complete internal control of labor and party organizations and in their international connections with the Slavic big brother and "good neighbor" Russia. Their political opponents on the other hand were divided, disorganized and without any substantial hold over mass organizations. Moreover, their international allies in no way made their influence felt. They could not meet the revolution because they had not recognized its storm signs in time.

The most promising and positive move to meet and counteract the revolutionary assault is to destroy its mass basis. What is imperative in order for a long-run strategy to encounter the revolutionary assault of our time is to help create the conditions — economic, political, psychological — for the reintegration of the uprooted masses. The social basis of Europe can no longer be restored by national action alone. International support is essential to spread the revolutionary pattern; and international action, from another quarter, will be necessary to check its spread and to achieve the rehabilitation of strife-torn nations. This, in fact, is the original and fundamental meaning of E.R.P. Its success or failure will define the future and the frontiers of the contemporary revolution. The U.S.S.R. knows that too. The fight against E.R.P., therefore, has become the front line of the international civil war.

Czechoslovakia, which proudly had called itself the bridge between East and West, became the first victim of their split. The in-between nation was forced into the Soviet camp on June 4, 1947, when the Marshall Plan was proclaimed. While even Moscow-trained Premier Gottwald wanted to join the E.R.P., the Czech government — hurriedly ordered to Moscow — had to accept the revolutionary fatherland's command to stay out and to join instead the Cominform front of the international civil war.

The Communist Information Bureau (Cominform) of September 1947 is not a simple revival of the Comintern, disbanded opportunely at the height of Allied war coalition in 1943. International Communism has learned some lessons from its failures during the inter-war period. It tries to avoid the mistakes of the rigid Comintern strategy and to mobilize instead, if only for short-run tactical purposes (as it behooves a system of permanent revolution), all elements of unrest within the nations on the road of the revolutionary drive. Now a shrewd and realistic appraisal of the dynamics of modern society calls for more than a mere proletarian base of recruitment. While still insisting on the fundamental Lenin formula of "class loyalty above national loyalty," the party appeals to powerful national ambitions. The strategists of the revolution had done so before in the Europe and China of the twenties;[10] but these peripheral trials with esoteric groups of national Bolshevism were soon discarded by the Politburo, which was pursuing its policy of "socialism in one country." Still, in the light of the Second World War's aftermath, these feelers two decades back can well be detected as dress rehearsals of portentous policies. Mao Tsetung and Pieck may take their line from Borodin and Radek. Revolutionary activists of the war resistance,[11] and awakened peasantry in the shadow of feudal Southeast Europe, China and Southeast Asia, even a deeply disillusioned middle class all over the map, can be steered into a new "Fatherland Front," united by the militant appeal of a grass-roots, partisan nationalism and by the fear of American "imperialism." The Cominform's line of attack can be detected in the title of its official semi-monthly publication, *For a Lasting Peace and for a People's Democracy*. But while the new Communist combine of the U.S.S.R. with the six satellites and two prospective candidates (France and Italy), as compared with the old Comintern, allows for greater national autonomy and a more decentralized system of Red Internationalism, its main purpose still remains the establishment of a strong arm of Soviet foreign policy in a definitely polarized world.[12] Wherever the new nationalism comes into conflict with Russian interests, it must be denounced, in the name of the revolution, as a nationalist deviation.[13] It must be crushed the more so as this may well be the first battle with the centrifugal forces, threatening the far-flung Red Empire. Central command must be guaranteed if the advantages of the strategies of the international civil war are to be preserved.

In the age of the international civil war it is not always necessary to move armies across national frontiers in order to win major battles. A central revolutionary authority, enforced by the new weapons of psychological warfare, can direct its orders by remote control through the well-established revolutionary pipeline of the disciplined party within the border.

One may wonder whether a Marshall Plan, had it followed immediately upon the end of hostilities, might have prevented the spread of the revolution through positive measures in time. Timing is of the essence in great periods of transition. When help rendered is too little and too late it cannot turn the tide. By then the revolutionary forces may be too well entrenched ever to be dislodged. The great decisions of social alliances must be made early in the struggle of the international civil war. They can be fatal if the democracies merely let themselves be pushed into a tardy defense of the *status quo* and an alliance with the forces of reaction.

Moreover, a Marshall Plan and a Western Defense Alliance will not suffice. Arms and economics are not enough to combat the deep-seated defeatism of a world torn by war and revolution. If democracy does not want to go under it has to restore in itself and in the world at large the confidence in its ability eventually to bring about lasting peace, to guarantee security, and to establish an integrated community that can meet the challenge of the revolution.

In order to do that successfully, a realistic appraisal of a nation's promising forces is as important on the social battle line as is the proper evaluation of its war potential for military conflict. In both cases the outcome is often decided long before the actual declaration of hostilities. In fact, the well-planned modern revolution is all over but for the shouting at the time of its official outbreak. By February 1948, Gottwald's party had already won control over Czechoslovakia. All Gottwald had to do was to call the workers into the street for a demonstration of power. The workers' militia and the Communist Action Committees were geared for the final push. Democracy had gone under long before.

To attribute the destruction of the once model democracy to Benes' serious illness or to the indecision of U. S. Ambassador Steinhardt at the moment of the coup is as totally inadequate an explanation as to credit the communist victory to former Soviet Ambassador Zorin's presence in Prague. This is still seeing the carefully planned, long-range revolution with the eyes of the dreamy romantic who expects heroes or villains like miracle men to determine suddenly the fate of nations. This is not the pattern of the twentieth century revolution. It is totalitarian and institutionalized, operating from a powerful mass basis and militantly organized to play its role in the international civil war.

---

[1] The term revolution, as used in this paper, is defined as a sweeping, fundamental change in political organization, social structure, economic property control and the predominant myth of a social order, thus indicating a major break in the continuity of development.

It is significant for the spiritual climate of our time that the concept of revolution has been used frequently, loosely and often contradictorily. While the 19th century applied it almost exclusively in respect to spectacular political change, it is now-a-days widely referred to in other fields by the suffix of a qualifying adjective such as industrial, managerial, colonial, cultural, scientific, technological, etc., in which case not so much a sudden upheaval as a long-range process is emphasized together with the far-reaching change caused by the "revolution" in this specific field. As a matter of fact, any significant evolutionary process will appear as a revolutionary change provided that this transformation is observed over a sufficiently prolonged period as to present a fundamental shift. True, the violent outburst is usually preceded in all great historical revolutions by an extended preliminary period that initiates and largely accomplishes the change long before the actual seizure of power through revolution sets the final stage by openly breaking outmoded institutions, power relations and social usages. In this sense revolutions represent only an acceleration and crystallization of the evolutionary process.

Hazy though the border lines may be, drawn between revolution and evolution, it is still imperative not only for a much-needed conceptual housecleaning, but even more so for appropriate policies, meeting the contemporary revolution, to distinguish between radical breaks in the continuity of development and persistent transformations that are accomplished within the framework of existing institutions, flexible enough to make the necessary adjustments, to integrate rising strata into the ruling system, and to relinquish outmoded forms and groups. The effective prevention of the revolution will depend on the existence and cultivation of certain prerequisites for peaceful change. On the other hand, the attempt to forestall the revolution by declaring the *status quo* as a desirable aim is probably one of the surest shortcuts to the very revolution which the "forces of stability" are eager to prevent. It is a fatal fallacy to identify significant change with revolution. Every living society must allow for far-reaching change. The study of the processes and channels through which it is effected constitute the key problem of constructive politics. It has been correctly stated that the warning signal for any society, internal and international, is the petrification of its controlling powers. Thus, promising forces are frustrated from joining in the "circulation of elites" and are finally pushed into revolution, breaking the natural fluctuation within society.

2 "All revolutions start in principle as world revolutions. . . . Their symbols and principles must, in the opinion of their initiators, become universal or nothing." Quincy Wright, *A Study of War*, 2 vols., Chicago, University of Chicago Press, 1942, II, 1110.

3 Egon Friedell, *A Cultural History of the Modern Age*, 3 vols., New York, A. A. Knopf, 1930–1932, II, 368.

4 "Sur le sens du mot révolutionnaire," Condorcet, *Oeuvres complètes*, 12 vols., Paris, 1847, XII, 516.

5 Isabel C. Lundberg, "World Revolution, American Plan," *Harpers Magazine*, December, 1948, pp. 38–46.

6 Friedrich Engels already testified to the necessary changes of revolutionary strategy in the introduction of the newly edited *Class Struggles in France, 1848–1850*, London, 1895, reprinted under the title *The Revolutionary Act*, New York, New York Labor News, 1922. "The fighting methods of 1848 are obsolete today in every respect. . . . The barricade had lost its charm; the soldier saw behind it no longer the people but rebels . . . the officer . . . had become familiar with the tactical forms of street battles." See also Sigmund Neumann, "Engels and Marx: Military Concepts of the Social Revolutionaries," in Edward M. Earle, ed., *Makers of Modern Strategy*, Princeton, Princeton University Press, 1943.

7 See Allen W. Dulles, *Germany's Underground*, New York, Macmillan, 1947; Hans B. Gisevius, *To the Bitter End*, Boston, Houghton Mifflin, 1947; *The Von Hassell Diaries*, Garden City, Doubleday, 1947; Rudolph Pechel, *Deutscher Widerstand*, Erlenbach-Zurich, 1947; Fabian von Schlabbrendorff, *Offiziere Gegen Hitler*, Zurich, 1946; Hans Rothfels, *The German Opposition to Hitler*, Hinsdale, Ill., H. Regenery, 1948; Ruth Andreas-Friedrich, *Berlin Underground, 1938–1945*, New York, Henry Holt, 1947; H. R. Trevor-Roper, *The Last Days of Hitler*, New York, Macmillan, 1947.

8 Andrew Gyorgy, "Political Trends in Eastern Europe," *Foreign Policy Reports*, Vol. XXIX, No. 3 (November 15, 1948).

9 John K. Fairbank, *The United States and China*, Cambridge, Mass., Harvard University Press, 1948; Andrew Gyorgy, *Governments of Danubian Europe*, to be published in 1949; Charles Wolf, *The Indonesian Story*, New York, John Day, 1948; Rupert Emerson, "The Indonesian Case," *World Politics*, Vol. I, No. 1 (October, 1948), pp. 59–81.

10 Sigmund Neumann, *The Future in Perspective*, New York, G. P. Putnam's Sons, 1946, pp. 96 ff. and pp. 170 ff.

11 Gabriel A. Almond, "The Resistance and the Political Parties of Western Europe," *Political Science Quarterly*, Vol. XLII, No. 1 (March, 1947), pp. 27–61.

12 Andrei Zhdanov, *The International Situation*, Moscow, 1947.

13 *The Soviet-Yugoslav Dispute* (Text of the published correspondence), Royal Institute of International Affairs, London, 1948.

9. On the Etiology of Internal Wars

HARRY ECKSTEIN

THE CONCEPT "INTERNAL WAR"

The term "internal war" denotes any resort to violence within a political order to change its constitution, rulers, or policies. It is not a new concept; distinctions between external and internal war (*guerre extérieure* and *guerre intérieure*) were made already in the nineteenth century by writers on political violence.[1] Nor does it mean quite the same thing as certain more commonly used terms, such as revolution, civil war, revolt, rebellion, uprising, guerrilla warfare, mutiny, *jacquerie, coup d'état,* terrorism, or insurrection. It stands for the genus of which the others are species.

Using the generic concept alongside, or even in place of, the more specific terms is justifiable on several grounds. Most obviously, all cases of internal war do have common features, however much they differ in detail. All involve the use of violence to achieve purposes which can also be achieved without violence. All indicate a breakdown of some dimension in legitimate political order as well as the existence of collective frustration and aggression in a population. All presuppose certain capabilities for violence by those who make the internal war and a certain incapacity for preventing violence among those on whom it is made. All tend to scar societies deeply and to prevent the formation of consensus indefinitely. There is, consequently, at least a possibility that general theories about internal war may be discovered — general theories which may also help to solve problems posed by specific instances.

Another justification for grouping internal wars in a single universe is that actual instances of internal war often combine different types of violence, in space and time. Guerrilla warfare in one area may be combined with terrorism in another; it may be preceded by insurrections and develop into full-scale civil war, or culminate in a mere *coup d'état*. Indeed the large-scale and prolonged instances of internal war that we generally call revolutions are notable chiefly for the fact that they combine, in strikingly similar sequences, many different types of violence.[2] To focus analysis from the outset on particular species of internal war therefore makes it necessary to abstract from actual internal wars occurrences which may not in fact be strictly separable. This may be fine for working out abstract theories, but will not do for developing theories closely relevant to historical (i.e., concrete) cases in all their complexity.

A third justification for studying internal wars generically is furnished by the very limited results so far obtained in comparative historical studies of revolutions, particularly the pre-war studies of L. P. Edwards, Crane Brinton, and George S. Pettee, and the more recent study of Hannah Arendt.[3] These studies deal only with the so-called Great Revolutions of history — conspicuous and much-studied disturbances that occurred in relatively advanced, mildly autocratic, western societies, between 1640 and 1917. Consequently, they seem to say little that is reliable about, or even relevant to, much of the political violence of our more far-flung and variegated world, or of pre-modern times, or, for that matter, of the period they cover. They draw mammoth inferences from very few cases; and they ignore not only the vast spectrum of *coups, Putsches,* uprisings, riots, and so forth, but also Mr. Hobsbawm's hero, the "primitive rebel," once so important, and again come to the center of affairs.[4] Thus, they are neither very "scientific" nor very historical. A more extensive view of the subject should yield not only knowledge more relevant to many particular cases but generalizations more trustworthy, by sheer weight of numbers, for the cases covered in the classic comparative histories. Pettee does say that by studying the more egregious cases he intends to illuminate all the rest — but he never does, and one doubts that he can.

Finally, the terminologies presently used to distinguish types of internal war vary greatly, are generally ambiguous, often define overlapping phenomena or phenomena difficult to distinguish in practice, and are rarely based on clearly discernible analytical needs. For few phenomena do social science, history, and conventional language offer so various and vague a vocabulary. Consider a few examples — a mere small sample of what there is to consider. Lasswell and Kaplan divide internal wars into palace revolutions, political revolutions, and social revolutions. Palace revolutions, as they define the term, are changes in rulers contrary to the "political formulas" of governments (that is, their formal constitutions), are usually effected by members of the ruling group themselves, and rarely lead to important changes in policy; political revolutions are changes in "authority structures" (formal power structures), and social revolutions changes in the overall "control structures" (effective power structures) of society, usually effected by men not already in ruling positions. A conventional distinction often made is that between revolutions and rebellions, the former being something broader in purpose and more tightly organized, as well as longer in duration and more violent, than the latter. Gabriel Bonnet, perhaps the most illustrious exponent of the French military doctrine of "revolutionary warfare," distinguishes between civil wars of liberation, and revolutionary wars, with civil wars further divided into riots, insurrections, pronunciamentos, and revolutions — terms which perhaps speak sufficiently for themselves.[5] Huntington talks about revolutionary wars and *coups d'état*, the key distinctions between them being their duration (*coups* are decided quickly, revolutions not) and the extent to which the insurgents already participate in the existing system of power (they do in *coups*, but not in revolutionary wars); *coups* are then further distinguished into governmental *coups*, which lead to no significant changes in social or political institutions; revolutionary *coups*, which do attempt to achieve such changes; and reform *coups*, which fall somewhere between the other two.[6] George Blanksten speaks of "real" revolutions, "near" revolutions, and mere non-constitutional changes of government in Latin America,[7] and Stokes uses a still more complicated typology to characterize Latin American political violence: *machetismo, cuartelazo, golpe de estado,* and *revolución.*[8]

One can derive from these and similar classificatory schemes a sort of composite typology, distinguishing between relatively unorganized and spontaneous *riots* by crowds with low capabilities for violence and modest aims, *coups d'état* by members of an elite against other members of the elite, full-scale *political revolutions* to achieve important constitutional changes, *social revolutions* to achieve large-scale socio-economic as well as constitutional changes, and *wars of independence* to achieve sovereignty in a previously dependent territory. But this typology is not necessarily better than the others. It does relate the various typologies by including most of the terms of the complicated schemes and adding more terms to the simple ones; but this alone does not make it more precise, easier to apply or more suited to the substantive tasks of study.

For all of these reasons it can do no harm and might do much good to consider internal wars as all of a piece at the beginning of inquiry and to introduce distinctions only as they become necessary or advisable. In this way, the possibilities of developing general theories are increased, as is the likelihood that the distinctions made will be important and precise. In any event, that is how I shall proceed here, showing at the end how a general theory about the genus "internal war" can be adapted to give an account of special cases.

"PRECONDITIONS" OR "PRECIPITANTS"?

Perhaps the first thing that becomes apparent when one tries to classify causal explanations . . . is that many of the explanations do not really require a choice to be made by the analyst. The propositions do not always contradict one another; often, in fact, they are complementary, differing only because they refer to different points in the time-sequence leading to revolution, or because they refer to different kinds of causality, or because they single out one factor among many of equal significance.

The most important distinction to make in this connection is between preconditions and precipitants of internal wars. A "precipitant" of internal war is an event which actually starts the war ("occasions" it), much as turning the flintwheel of a cigarette lighter ignites a flame. "Preconditions" of internal war, on the other hand, are those circumstances which make it possible for the precipitants to bring about political violence, as the general structure of a lighter makes it possible to produce a flame by turning the flintwheel. . . . Between explanations singling out precipitants and explanations emphasizing preconditions of internal war there obviously is no genuine contradiction. The distinction between precipitants and preconditions can therefore prevent much pointless argument between those who stress short-run setbacks and those who emphasize long-term trends in the etiology of civil strife. Clearly no internal war can occur without precipitant events to set it off; and clearly no precipitants can set off internal war unless the condition of society makes it possible for them to do so.

The greatest service that the distinction between precipitants and preconditions of internal war can render, however, is to shift attention from aspects of internal war which defy analysis to those which are amenable to systematic inquiry. Phenomena which precipitate internal war are almost always unique and ephemeral in character. A bad harvest, a stupid or careless ruler, moral indiscretion in high places, an ill-advised policy: how could such data be incorporated into general theories? They are results of the vagaries of personality, of forces external to the determinate interrelations of society, of all those unique and fortuitous aspects of concrete life which are the despair of social scientists and the meat and drink of narrative historians.

Closely related, the distinction between precipitants and preconditions of internal wars will also help one to avoid what is perhaps the most misleading theory about their causes: an unqualified conspiracy theory of internal war.

To be sure, conspiracy seems to play an essential role in certain types of internal war, particularly those previously referred to as *coups* and palace revolutions. As well, one undoubtedly finds conspiratorial organizations in every internal war of any consequence — in one case Jacobins, in others fascists, in still others communists. This is precisely what tempts so many to attribute internal wars solely or mainly to conspirators, and thus to regard them, in the manner of Malaparte, essentially as matters of technique — plotting on one hand and intelligence and suppression on the other. In many cases, however, the conspirators seem to do little more than turn the flintwheel in volatile situations, or indeed not even as much as that; sometimes they merely turn the revolutionary conflagration to their own purposes. Internal wars do not always have a clear aim, a tight organization, a distinct shape and tendency from the outset. Many seem to be characterized in their early stages by nothing so much as amorphousness. They are formless matter waiting to be shaped, and if there is an art of revolution, it involves, largely at least, not making or subduing it, but capitalizing on the unallocated political resources it provides.

This reference to techniques of revolution leads to another point. If one leaves precipitants aside and focuses solely on data the social scientist can handle, one does not even leave out of consideration anything that matters from a practical standpoint. Preconditions are the crucial concern of men of affairs, revolutionaries or anti-revolutionaries, no less than of social scientists. After all, they have an interest in the etiology of internal wars in order to anticipate such wars in good time, prevent them when they are preventable, further their actual occurrence, or otherwise prepare for them. But unique and ephemeral phenomena cannot, by their very nature, be anticipated; they simply happen. The vital knowledge to have concerns those conditions under which almost any setback or vagary, any misguided policy or indiscretion, can set society aflame.

Certain kinds of precipitants of internal war have a special importance of their own, however, in what one might call "practical etiology" — the anticipation of internal wars for policy purposes. A precipitant may be found so frequently on the eve of internal wars that its existence can be treated as a particularly urgent danger signal, particularly if its effects are delayed sufficiently to allow some adaptation to the danger. As far as we know, both of these conditions are satisfied by economic precipitants of internal war. The point deserves some elaboration, particularly in view of the persistent emphasis on economic conditions in writings on internal war.

It now seems generally agreed that persistent poverty in a society rarely leads to political violence. Quite the contrary. As Edwards points out, following an argument already developed by de Tocqueville, economic oppression, indeed all kinds of oppression, seems to wane rather than increase in pre-revolutionary periods.[9] Brinton makes the same point. While not underestimating the amount of poverty in the societies he analyzes in *The Anatomy of Revolution,* he does point out that all of these societies were economically progressive rather than retrograde. He points out also that revolutionary literature, at any rate in the pre-Marxist period, hardly ever dwelt on economic misery and exploitation — one hears about economic grievances, to be sure, but not the sort of grievances which arise out of "immiseration." [10] Even some Marxists seem to share this view. Trotsky, for example, once remarked that if poverty and oppression were a precipitant of revolution the lower classes would always be in revolt, and obviously he had a point.

It is equally difficult to establish a close link between economic improvement and internal war. Pre-revolutionary periods may often be economically progressive, but economic progress is not always (or even often) connected with internal war. From this, however, one need not conclude that economic tendencies are simply irrelevant to the occurrence of political violence. Only the long-term tendencies seem, in fact, to be irrelvant. The moment one focuses on short-term tendencies, a fairly frequently repeated pattern emerges — and one which tells us why it is that some writers adhere stubbornly to the immiseration theory of internal war and others, with just as much conviction, to the economic progress theory. It so happens that before many internal wars, one finds both economic improvement and immiseration; more precisely, many internal wars are preceded by long-term improvements followed by serious short-term setbacks.[11] The bad harvests and unfavorable weather conditions in pre-revolutionary France, the American recession of 1774–1775, the bad Russian winter of 1916–1917 (not to mention the economic impact of the war on Russia) and the marked rise of unemployment in Egypt before Naguib's *coup* are cases in point. All dealt serious short-term blows to economic life and all followed long periods of economic progress, especially for those previously "repressed."

It is this dual pattern which really seems to be lethal, and it is not difficult to see why. In times of prolonged and marked economic progress, people become accustomed to new economic standards and form new economic expectations, which previously they could scarcely imagine. Confidently expecting continuous progress, they also tend to take risks (like accumulating debts) which they might not take otherwise. All this greatly exaggerates the impact of serious temporary setbacks; both psychologically and economically the costs of such setbacks are bound to be greater than if they occurred after long periods of stagnation or very gradual progress.

Occasionally, perhaps, the study of precipitants of internal war may play a minor role in "theoretical" as well as "practical etiology." It could conceivably shed some light on the preconditions themselves in that there might be a connection between revolutionary conditions and how internal wars are actually brought about. For example, someone may blame internal war on dissatisfactions in the rural population of a society; but if we find peasants playing no role in the fomenting of violence, then we have good reason to doubt the interpretation. Precipitants may not directly tell us what the preconditions of internal war are, but they can sometimes indicate what they are not — be useful for falsifying hypotheses, or at least shedding doubt on them. But this does not alter the basic point: that the task of an etiology of internal wars is to discover their preconditions.

COMMON HYPOTHESES ABOUT THE PRECONDITIONS OF INTERNAL WAR

We can profitably relegate to a secondary role most of those greatly varying, unique, and largely fortuitous events which occasion the outbreak of internal wars. But even if we do, a great variety of hypotheses remains — great enough if we confine ourselves to general treatments of internal war, and greater still if we deal with hypotheses formulated to deal with particular cases. In this connection, it might be useful to supplement the explanations of particular revolutions listed above with a sample of propositions frequently found in the more general literature on internal war. These include:[12]

a) *Hypotheses emphasizing "intellectual" factors:*
1. Internal wars result from the failure of a regime to perform adequately the function of political socialization.
2. Internal wars are due to the coexistence in a society of conflicting social "myths."
3. Internal wars result from the existence in a society of unrealizable values or corrosive social philosophies.
4. Internal wars are caused by the alienation (desertion, transfer of allegiance) of the intellectuals.

b) *Hypotheses emphasizing economic factors:*
1. Internal wars are generated by growing poverty.
2. Internal wars result from rapid economic progress.
3. Internal wars are due to severe imbalances between the production and distribution of goods.
4. Internal wars are caused by a combination of long-term economic improvement and short-term setbacks.

c) *Hypotheses emphasizing aspects of social structure:*
   1. Internal wars are due to the inadequate circulation of elites (that is, inadequate recruitment into the elite of the able and powerful members of the non-elite).
   2. Internal wars result from too much recruitment of members of the non-elite into the elite, breaking down the internal cohesion of the elite.
   3. Internal war is a reflection of *anomie* resulting from great social mobility.
   4. Internal war is a reflection of frustration arising from little general social mobility — from general social stagnation.
   5. Internal wars result from the appearance in societies of new social classes.

d) *Hypotheses emphasizing political factors:*
   1. Internal wars are due to the estrangement of rulers from the societies they rule.
   2. Internal war is simply a response to bad government (government which performs inadequately the function of goal-attainment).
   3. Internal wars are due, not to the attacks of the governed on those who govern, but to divisions among the governing classes.
   4. Internal wars are responses to oppressive government.
   5. Internal wars are due to excessive toleration of alienated groups.

e) *Hypotheses emphasizing no particular aspects of societies, but general characteristics of social process:*
   1. Political violence is generated by rapid social change.
   2. Political violence results from erratic and/or uneven rates of social change, whether rapid or not.
   3. Internal war occurs when a state is somehow "out of adjustment" to society.

From this sample of propositions, all of them at least plausible, we can get some idea of the overwhelming ambiguities that general studies of the preconditions of internal war have created to supplement those originating in case studies. These ambiguities arise most obviously from the fact that many of the propositions are manifestly contradictory; less obviously, from the sheer variety and disparity of factors included, not all of which, surely, can be equally significant, or necessary, in the etiology of internal wars. For this reason, even when precipitants are subtracted, a considerable range of choices between theories remains to be made.

INSURGENTS OR INCUMBENTS?

One crucial choice that needs to be made is whether to put emphasis upon characteristics of the insurgents or incumbents, upon the side that rebels or the side that is rebelled against. Not surprisingly, the existing literature concentrates very largely on the rebels, treating internal war as due mainly to changes in the non-elite strata of society to which no adequate adjustment is made by the elite. This would seem to be only natural; after all, it is the rebels who rebel. At least some writings suggest, however, that characteristics of the incumbents and the classes that are usually their props must be considered jointly with characteristics of the insurgents, indeed perhaps even emphasized more strongly. Pareto, for example, while attributing revolution partly to blockages in a society's social mobility patterns, considered it equally necessary that certain internal changes should occur in an elite if revolution was to be possible; in essence, he felt that no elite which had preserved its capacity for timely and effective violence, or for effective manipulation, could be successfully assailed, or perhaps assailed at all. One must, according to this view, seek the origins of internal war not only in a gain of strength by the non-elite, but also in the loss of it on the part of the elite. Brinton makes the same point: revolutions, in his view, follow the loss of common values, of internal cohesion, of a sure sense of destiny and superiority and, not least, of political efficiency in elites, and thus must be considered results as much as causes of their disintegration. And in Edwards's and Pettee's studies as well, revolutions emerge as affairs of the elites (if not always directly of the actual rulers): the crucial roles in them are played by intellectuals, by men rich and powerful but "cramped" by their lack of status or other perquisites, and by the gross inefficiency of the ruling apparatus.

Significantly enough, this view is stated perhaps more often in the writings of actual revolutionaries than in those of students of revolution. Trotsky, for example, believed that revolution requires three elements: the political consciousness of a revolutionary class, the discontent of the "intermediate layers" of society, and, just as important, a ruling class which has "lost faith in itself," which is torn by the conflicts of groups and cliques, which has lost its capacity for practical action and rests its hopes in "miracles or miracle workers." [13]

The joint consideration of insurgent and incumbent patterns thus would seem to be the logical way to proceed in the early stages of inquiry into the causes of revolution. But one should not overlook the possibility that sufficient explanations of the occurrence of many internal wars might be found in elite characteristics alone. A ruling elite may decay, may become torn by severe conflict, may be reluctant to use power, may come to lack vital political skills— and thus make it perfectly possible for a relatively weak, even disorganized, opposition of a sort that may exist in any political system to rise against it and destroy it. Indeed, there are theories which maintain that internal wars are always caused solely or primarily by changes in elite characteristics, and that one can practically ignore the insurgents in attempting to account for the occurrence of internal wars.

One such theory is propounded in Mosca's *The Ruling Class*. If the elementary needs of human life are satisfied, argued Mosca, one thing above all will cause men to rebel against their rulers, and that is their feeling that the rulers live in a totally different environment, that they are "separated" from their subjects in some profound sense. In other words, the estrangement of the elite from the non-elite is inseparable from the alienation of the latter; only the elite itself, consequently, can undermine its political position. In this regard Mosca made much of the feudal societies of Poland, Ireland, England, and Russia. The Polish nobles of the Middle Ages, for example, practiced extreme economic extortion, taking in levies almost all the peasant produced; they were ruthless and violent; they scrupulously extracted the *droit du seigneur;* and despite all that, and more, the peasants never rebelled — as long as the nobles "lived among them, spoke their language, swore the same oaths, ate the same kind of food, wore the same style of clothes, exhibited the same manners or lack of them, had the same rustic superstitions." [14] But a drastic change occurred when the nobility acquired French manners and tastes, "gave luxurious balls after the manner of Versailles and tried to dance the minuet." Despite more humane treatment, vicious and frequent revolts attended the estrangement of the nobles from their people.

This interpretation certainly makes sense in light of French experience: the French Revolution was far more an attack upon the refined and parasitic court nobility than upon the coarse, and little less parasitic, provinicial nobility. It makes sense also in the case of Britain, for the British nobility (in the main) always preserved close ties to the soil and to the manner and morals of its tenantry; Squire Western is the embodiment of that fact. That is why it was for so long the butt of jokes among the more sophisticated, and shorter-lived, continental aristocracies.

Perhaps the most prolonged period of civil unrest in American history, the late nineteenth century, can be, and has been, interpreted in much the same manner — not only by political sociologists like De Grazia, but also by acute literary observers like Mark Twain and historians like Miriam Beard.[15] One of the more conspicuous features of that period was the compulsive attempt of the American plutocracy to imitate European "society." At no other time in American history was the elite so profoundly estranged from American life. Mark Twain gave this period a name which fits it exactly and has stuck to it ever since. It was the Gilded Age, the age of English clothes and accents, Roman orgies, continental travel, title-mongering, art-collecting, butlers and footmen, conspicuous consumption of every sort — the age which invented those now much more Americanized institutions, the debutante and the society page. Not until the American plutocracy had returned to its old habits of thrift and earthiness, of being plain Americans, was there a return to relative civil calm in the United States.[16]

It is worth noting that in the postwar period internal wars have been relatively rare in two kinds of societies: either thoroughly modernized countries or very underdeveloped countries whose elites have remained tied closely to the traditional ways and structures of life.[17] Of course, a generalization of this kind is becoming increasingly harder to test, since the number of societies without a gulf between highly modernized elites and much less modernized masses seems to be rapidly shrinking. Nevertheless the notion is given credibility by the fact that, while transitional societies seem to suffer more from internal wars than either traditional or modern societies — as one would expect upon many hypotheses — a very few seem to have strikingly low rates of violence compared to the rest. Egypt is one example, and Pakistan another. These societies seem to differ from the rest in one main respect. They have had "secondary" revolutions, so to speak, in which men of rather humble origins and popular ways (colonels' regimes) have unseated previously victorious transitional elites.

All this is not meant to validate the idea that elite estrangement is the main cause of internal war but only to show why it should be taken very seriously. The possible consequences of elite estrangement are not, however, the only reason for emphasizing studies of the incumbents at least as much as studies of insurgents in the etiology of internal wars. Another is the fact that internal wars are almost invariably preceded by important functional failures on the part of elites. Above all is this true of difficulties in financial administration — perhaps because finance impinges on the ability of governments to perform all their functions. And finally, insurgent groups seem rarely to come even to the point of fighting without some support from alienated members of incumbent elites. On this point, agreement in the literature on internal war is practically unanimous.

STRUCTURAL OR BEHAVIORAL HYPOTHESES?

A second strategic choice to be made in constructing an etiology of internal wars is between structural and behavioral hypotheses. A structural hypothesis singles out, so to speak, "objective" social conditions as crucial for the occurrence of internal war: aspects of a society's "setting," such as economic conditions, social stratification and mobility, or geographic and demographic factors. A behavioral hypothesis, on the other hand, emphasizes attitudes and their formation — not setting, but "orientations" (such as degrees of strain and *anomie* in societies, the processes by which tension and aggression are generated, and the processes by which human beings are "socialized" into their communities). The great majority of propositions regarding the causes of internal war are, on the basis of these definitions, structural in character. But, in concentrating upon structural explanations have writers on internal war taken the more promising tack?

At first glance, there would seem to be little to choose between structural and behavioral approaches. Since most human action is motivated, not reflexive, one always wants to know, if one can, about attitudes underlying men's actions. At the same time, there can be little doubt that attitudes are always formed somehow in response to external conditions. The difference between structural and behavioral theories would therefore seem to be, at best, one of emphasis or point of view. Yet emphasis can make a difference. Certain research results do seem to be associated with one point of view or the other. Behavioral approaches, for instance, may lead to theories stressing "intellectual" and voluntaristic factors in the etiology of political violence, or to theories attributing internal war mainly to efficient revolutionary indoctrination or inadequate value-formation by the incumbents. Structural explanations may lead to theories of mechanical imbalance in society, or to theories attributing internal war mainly to specific situational conditions, attitudes being treated as mechanical responses to such conditions.

Which approach is preferable? Despite the fact that there is a danger that the behavioral approach might lead to naive conspiracy theory (the belief that internal wars are always the results of insidious indoctrination by subversive elements, and could therefore always occur or always be avoided) the arguments against a primary emphasis on structural theories are very strong.

One such argument derives from the general experience of modern social science. Purely structural theories have generally been found difficult to sustain wherever they have been applied, and one fundamental reason for this is that patterns of attitudes, while responsive to the settings in which men are placed, seem also to be, to an extent, autonomous of objective conditions, able to survive changes in these conditions or to change without clearly corresponding objective changes. This is one of the basic insights underlying the sociological theory of action, which, to be sure, assigns an important role to the situations in which human action occurs, but treats "culture" largely as a separate variable and attaches particularly great significance to agencies of socialization and acculturation. It underlies as well the relatively successful use of mediational models, rather than simple S-R models, in behavioral psychology.

No doubt this point should be much elaborated. But one can make a cogent case for stressing behavioral theories of the causes of internal wars without going lengthily into the general nature and past experiences of social science.

The most obvious case for behavioral theories of internal war derives from the very fact that so many different objective social conditions seem capable of generating it. We may have available many interpretative accounts of internal wars simply because an enormous variety of objective conditions can create internal-war potential. Certain internal wars do seem to have followed economic improvement, others seem to have followed closely the Marxist model of internal wars, however many more have followed some combination of the two. Some internal wars have in fact been preceded by great, others by little social mobility; some regimes have been more oppressive and others more liberal in the immediate pre-revolutionary period, some both and some neither. Is it not reasonable to conclude that one should not seek explanations of the occurrence of internal wars in specific social conditions, but rather in the ways in which social conditions may be perceived? Instead of looking for direct connections between social conditions and internal war, should one not look rather for the ways in which an existing cognitive and value system may change, so that conditions perceived as tolerable at one point are perceived as intolerable at another; or, concomitantly, look for the ways in which old systems of orientation are in some cases maintained rather than adapted in the face of social change, so that changes which one society absorbs without trouble create profound difficulties in another?

The point is not that objective conditions are unrelated to internal war. Rather it is that orientations mediate between social setting and political behavior, and — because they are not simply mirrors of environment — so that different objective conditions may lead to similar political activities, or similar conditions to different activities in different contexts; that in a single context a considerable change in political activity may occur without significant changes in objective conditions or changes in objective conditions without changes in activity. What should be avoided is linking aspects of social setting *directly* to internal war or *mechanically* to orientations. Internal wars are best conceived as responses to political disorientation (such as "cognitive dissonance," *anomie,* and strains in the definition of political roles), particularly in regard to a society's norms of legitimacy; and political disorientation may follow from a considerable variety of conditions, due to the variable nature of the orientations themselves and of the agencies that implant them in different societies.

One conspicuous point of agreement in comparative studies of revolution gives further credence to this argument. This is that revolutions are invariably preceded by the "transfer of allegiance" of a society's intellectuals and the development by them of a new political "myth." If intellectuals have any obvious social "functions," in the sense social scientists understand the term function, they are surely these: to socialize the members of a society outside of the domestic context, in schools and adult learning situations; to reinforce and rationalize attitudes acquired in all social contexts; and to provide meaning to life and guidelines to behavior by means of conscious doctrines where events have robbed men of their less conscious bearings. Intellectuals are particularly important in the education of adolescents and young people, and it has been shown quite definitely that political socialization occurs (or fails) mainly in the years between early childhood and full maturity.[18] It could also be shown that among revolutionaries the young tend to predominate, sometimes quite remarkably. Together these points go far to explain why the alienation of intellectuals is, in Edwards's language, a "master-symptom" of revolution: a condition that makes revolutionary momentum irreversible.

Another point that speaks for behavioral propositions is that internal wars can, and often do, become chronic. In some societies, the most manifest cause of internal war seems to be internal war itself, one instance following another, often without a recurrence of the conditions that led to the original event. This means that political disorientation may be followed by the formation of a new set of orientations, establishing a predisposition toward violence that is inculcated by the experience of violence itself. In such cases, internal wars result not from specifiable objective conditions, and not even from the loss of legitimacy by a particular regime, but from a general lack of receptivity to legitimacy of any kind. Violence becomes a political style that is self-perpetuating, unless itself "disoriented."

The very fact that elite estrangement so often precedes acute political unrest itself fits the case for behavioral propositions. It fits in part because the Establishment of any society includes its intellectuals, but also for a more important, rather technical, reason. Orientations, particularly as treated in action theory, are not purely internal and self-sufficient, as it were, but involve expectations from others ("alters") — mutualities or complementarities in behavior. Hence men are likely to become disoriented and alienated when those with whom they interact become aliens to them, even if the alien ways involve, from abstract moral standpoints, a change for the better. The Polish peasant probably did not positively like to be beaten, but he *expected* to be, and he himself undoubtedly committed a good deal of institutionalized mayhem on anyone subordinated to his authority. A liberal aristocrat would appear to him not only to act strangely but arbitrarily, and, in a way, as a constant personal reproach.

To give still more support to the argument for behavioral theories there is the object lesson provided by the sad history of Marxist theory. Marxism singles out certain objective social conditions as underlying internal wars. It also singles out certain social groups as indispensable to the making of internal war. But Marxist revolutions themselves have been made neither under the social conditions nor by the groups emphasized in the theory. What is more, these revolutions have been made in a large variety of conditions, with a large variety of means, by organizations constituted in a large variety of ways. This is true even if one can show that the appeal of Marxism is greatest in transitional societies, for the term transition, in its very nature, denotes not a particular social state but a great many different points on whatever continuum social development may involve.

PARTICULAR CONDITIONS OR GENERAL PROCESSES?

This argument has a close bearing upon a third strategic choice to be made in analyzing the causes of internal war. Even if one emphasizes behavioral characteristics in theories of internal wars, one must, as I have said, always relate these characteristics to the social setting. The question is how to do this. Should one, in the manner of most of the hypotheses listed above, develop propositions emphasizing particular social conditions or, in the manner of a few of them, select propositions about general characteristics of social process? In the first case, one would relate internal war to particular socio-economic changes, in the second to characteristics of the general phenomenon of social change itself, such as rapid change or erratic change in any sectors of society, or conditions that may result from any social change whatever, such as imbalances between social segments (e.g., between elites of wealth and elites of status) or incongruities among the authority patterns of a society.

The proper choice between these alternatives is already implied in the arguments of the previous section. If many particular social conditions may be connected with internal wars, then clearly one should stress broad propositions about social processes and balances that can comprehend a variety of such conditions. The same position results if disorientation is conceived, in large part, as a breakdown in mutualities and complementarities of behavior. Not least, there is overwhelming evidence to show that *"anomie,"* the feeling that one lacks guidelines to behavior, is increased by rapidity of change in any direction (for example, by rapid economic betterment no less than rapid economic deterioration) and that "strain," the feeling that one's roles make inconsistent demands, is aggravated by uneven or incongruent changes in different social sectors (for example, when the economic sector of society becomes significantly modern while the political remains largely traditional).

What has been said about economic conditions preceding internal wars fits the argument particularly well. It is not just that cases can be found to support both immiseration and improvement theories of revolution, hence the view that internal wars are related to economic changes as such, not to change in any particular direction; more suggestive still is the fact that internal wars most frequently follow an irregular — an anomalous — course of economic change, long-term trends being interrupted by abrupt and short-lived reversals. Such a course exhibits at least two of the general characteristics of social processes that would, upon earlier arguments, seem to be related to the occurrence of internal wars: rapidity of change and eccentricity of change.

From this standpoint it would be most interesting to investigate whether *any* rapid and eccentric course of economic development tends to be related to internal war, perhaps even one involving long-term stagnation or deterioration followed by abrupt short-term improvement. This idea is not as far-fetched as may seem; after all has not Durkheim fully documented the argument that *"fortunate crises, the effect of which is abruptly to enhance a country's prosperity, affect suicide like economic disasters"*?[19]

Undoubtedly there is a danger that broad formulations concerning general social processes will turn into empty and untestable generalizations, trivialities like the much-repeated proposition that political violence tends to accompany social or economic change. But this danger is avoidable; one can, after all, be specific and informative about general social processes as well as about their substantive content.

OBSTACLES TO INTERNAL WAR

So far I have tried to make two related points. The first is that one is most likely to gain understanding of the forces impelling societies toward internal war if one avoids preoccupation with the more visible precipitants of internal wars, including conspiracies, and directs one's efforts to the analysis of their preconditions, stressing disorientative general social processes and particularly taking into account elite behavior, performance, and cohesion. The second point is in a sense the converse of this: that existing etiologies of internal wars are chaotic and inadequate precisely because studies have so far concentrated on precipitants rather than preconditions, insurgents rather than incumbents, and particular aspects of social structure rather than the effects on orientations of general social processes.

An important point must now be added. Even if we had better knowledge of the forces which push societies toward political violence, a crucial problem relating to the etiology of internal wars would remain, one that is generally ignored in the studies available to us. This problem concerns forces that might countervail those previously discussed: "obstacles" to internal war, as against forces which propel societies toward violence.

In the real world of phenomena, events occur not only because forces leading toward them are strong, but also because forces tending to inhibit, or obstruct, them are weak or absent. An automobile may generate a great deal of force, but if driven up a steep incline is unlikely to go very fast. A government may have the desire and technical capacity for rapid industrialization, but if faced by the rapid growth of an already too great population may simply find it impossible to channel sufficient resources into capital goods to achieve a certain rate of development. So also internal wars may fail to occur solely or mainly because of certain hindrances to their occurrence.

Some of these hindrances may be absolute in character, in that wherever they exist internal war fails to materialize; hence their obverse may be considered "requisites" of internal war (necessary, but not sufficient, conditions). In the main, however, obstacles to internal war, like forces making for internal war, are better conceived as factors making such wars more or less likely, rather than either inevitable or impossible — their actual significance depending, at least in part, on the strength of forces pulling in a contrary direction. It certainly seems unlikely that we shall ever find a condition that makes internal war quite inevitable under any circumstances, and equally unlikely that we could discover conditions that always rule it out (except perhaps purely definitional ones: e.g., the absence of any perceived frustrations). In real life, internal war, like other concrete events, results from the interplay of forces and counterforces, from a balance of probabilities pulling toward internal war and internal peace.

Repression. The most obvious obstacle to internal war is, of course, the incumbent regime. It goes almost without saying that by using repression the established authorities can lessen the chances of violent attack upon themselves, or even reduce them to nil. Internal wars, after all, are not made by impersonal forces working in impersonal ways, but by men acting under the stress of external forces. This much at least there is in the conspiracy theory of revolution: wholly spontaneous riots by wholly unstructured and undirected mobs may occur, but hardly very frequently or with much effect. Actual cases of internal war generally contain some element of subversion, some structure for forming political will and acting upon decisions, however primitive and changeable. On this point, if no other, the great enemies of revolution (Burke, Chateaubriand, Taine) are at one with the great revolutionaries (Lenin, Trotsky); it is also this point, rather than some more subtle idea, which underlies Pareto's and Brinton's argument that revolutions are due to elites as much as non-elites. And anything with a structure can of course be detected and repressed, though not always very easily.

The matter, however, is not quite so simple. Repression can be a two-edged sword. Unless it is based upon extremely good intelligence, and unless its application is sensible, ruthless, and continuous, its effects may be quite opposite to those intended. Incompetent repression leads to a combination of disaffection and contempt for the elite. Also, repression may only make the enemies of a regime more competent in the arts of conspiracy; certainly it tends to make them more experienced in the skills of clandestine organization and *sub rosa* communication. No wonder that botched and bungled repression is often a characteristic of pre-revolutionary societies.

The worst situation of all seems to arise when a regime, having driven its opponents underground, inflamed their enmity, heightened their contempt, and cemented their organization, suddenly relaxes its repression and attempts a liberal policy. The relaxation of authority is a part of the pre-revolutionary syndrome, no less than other forms of social amelioration; in that sense, repression in societies with high internal war potential is little more than a narcotic, intensifying the conditions it seeks to check and requiring ever larger doses to keep affairs in balance — if other things are equal. We can see this dynamic at work in the development of totalitarian rule, particularly if we remember that blood-letting, while certainly the ultimate in repression, is only one form that coercion can take.

From this standpoint, repression may be both an obstacle to and precipitant of internal war. Repression is of course least likely to prevent internal war in societies which, unlike totalitarian regimes, have a low capacity for coercion. In such societies, adjustive and diversionary mechanisms seem to check revolutionary potential far better. Indeed, they may in any society.

Diversions and Concessions. Diversionary mechanisms are all those social patterns and practices which channel psychic energies away from revolutionary objectives — which provide other outlets for aggressions or otherwise absorb emotional tensions. If Elie Halévy's theory is correct, then English non-conformist evangelicalism, especially the Methodist movement, furnishes an excellent case in point.[20] Halévy, being French, was deeply puzzled by the fact that England did not have any serious revolution in the early nineteenth century, despite conditions which, on their face, seem to have contained very great revolutionary potential — conditions resulting from the industrial revolution and from the fact of endemic revolution throughout the Western world. His solution was that English evangelicalism, more than anything else, performed a series of functions which greatly lowered the revolutionary level of British politics. Among these functions were the provision of outlets for emotional expression and the inculcation of a philosophy which reconciled the lower classes to their condition, made that condition seem inevitable, and made patient submission to it a sacred obligation. In England, at least at the time in question, religion seems indeed to have been the opiate of the people, as Marx and Engels, no less than later and different-minded historians, seem to have realized.

England may have been spared major political violence since the seventeenth century for other reasons too: for example, because at least twice in English history, just when she seemed to be on the very brink of civil war, external war opportunely occurred, unifying the country as external wars will: at the time of the Napoleonic wars, and again in 1914 after the mutiny in the Curragh threatened to develop into something much more serious. Indeed, diverting popular attention from domestic troubles by starting foreign wars is one of the most venerable dodges of statecraft. This too, however, is a weapon that cuts two ways. Military adventures are excellent diversions, and military successes can marvelouslly cement disjoined societies, but military failure, on the evidence, can hardly fail to hasten revolution in such cases. Russia may well have entered the first World War to distract domestic unrest, but, if so, the outcome was revolution rather than the contrary.

Totalitarian regimes seem to be shrewder about such matters, as well as being more coercive. The massive sports programs which are a feature of every totalitarian regime (German, Russian, or Chinese) may have a variety of purposes — physical fitness as preparation for war, or the inculcation of discipline — but one of them assuredly is to absorb the energies of the young and the interest of the not-so-young. No less than eschatological ideology, sport is the opiate of the masses in totalitarian countries, and not in these alone.

Adjustive mechanisms reduce, or manage, tensions, rather than providing for them surrogate outlets. Concessions are perhaps the most obvious of such mechanisms. It is banal, but probably true, to say that timely concessions have been the most effective weapons in the arsenal of the British ruling class, and one of Halévy's more cogent points about the pacific effects of evangelicalism on nineteenth-century England is that it made the elite extraordinarily willing to ameliorate the lot of the masses. It enjoined upon them philanthropy as a sacred duty and educated them in the trusteeship theory of wealth — remember Wesley's counsel "gain all you can, save all you can, give all you can" — at the same time as it made the masses extraordinarily willing to suffer their burdens in peace. (For this reason, we can of course regard all functioning institutions for adjusting conflict as barriers to internal war.) But concessions too may work in two directions, no less than repression and certain diversionary tactics. They may only lead to further and greater demands, further and greater expectations of success, and must therefore, like repression, be continuous, and continuously greater, to succeed.

Facilities for Violence. A final set of obstacles to internal war are conditions that affect the capacities of alienated groups to use violence at all, or, more often in real life, to use it with fair prospects of success. These conditions do not always prevent violence. But they can prevent its success. For this very reason, they help determine the likelihood of decisions to use violence at all. What are some of these conditions?

Perhaps the first to come to mind is terrain. While practically all kinds of terrain can be used, in different ways, for purposes of rebellion, not all can be used to equal advantage. The ideal, from the viewpoint of the insurgents, seems to be an area which is relatively isolated, mountainous, overgrown, criss-crossed by natural obstacles (hedges, ditches, etc.), and near the sea or other sources of external supply — terrain which affords secure bases to the insurgents in their own territory, gives them the advantage of familiarity with local conditions, and allows ready access to them of external supporters.

The communications facilities of a society are another relevant condition. Marx, among many others, seems to have realized this when he argued that urbanization increases the likelihood of revolution, if only in that it makes men accessible to one another and thus makes revolutionary organization easier to achieve. "Since the collective revolutionary mentality is formed by conversation and propaganda," writes the French historian Lefebvre, "all means that bring men together favor it." [21] In this one case, a condition which may heighten the chances of successful internal war (bad communications) may also discourage its outbreak. There may be nothing more mysterious to the celebrated peaceability of peasants, as compared to city-dwellers, than the physical difficulty in rural life, especially if fairly primitive, to form a "collective revolutionary mentality."

Terrain and communications are physical obstacles to (or facilities for) internal war. There are human obstacles as well. For example, internal wars seem rarely to occur, even if other conditions favor them, if a regime's instruments of violence remain loyal. This applies above all to the armed forces. Trotsky for one, and Lenin for another, considered the attitude of the army absolutely decisive for any revolution;[22] so also did Le Bon.[23] Pettee, on the other hand, dissents, but for a rather subtle reason: not because he considers the attitude of the armed forces insignificant, but because he feels that armies never fail to join revolutions when all other causes of revolution are present, and that they never fail to oppose them when this is not the case.[24] We could enlarge this point to read that internal wars are unlikely wherever the cohesion of an elite is intact, for the simple reason that insurgent formations require leadership and other skills, and are unlikely to obtain them on a large scale without some significant break in the ranks of an elite. Even if elites do not always "cause" their own downfall by becoming rigid or foreign to their people, they can certainly hasten their own demise by being internally at odds. From this standpoint, if not from that of Mosca's theory, elite cohesion is a factor which should be classified among the obstacles to internal war, as well as among their causes.

A final human obstacle to internal war — perhaps the greatest of all — is lack of wide popular support for rebellion. It seems generally accepted among modern writers on internal war, indeed it is the chief dogma of modern revolutionaries, that without great popular support the insurgents in an internal war can hardly hope to win (and with it are hardly likely to lose) — unless by means of a *coup d'état*. So vital is this factor that some writers think that the distinctive characteristic of internal war is the combination of violent techniques with psychological warfare, the latter designed, of course, to win the active support of the non-combatants; this is asserted in the much repeated pseudo-formula of the French theorists of *guerre révolutionnaire*: revolutionary warfare = partisan war + psychological warfare.[25] To be sure, psychological warfare occurs nowadays also in international wars. Its role in these, however, is not nearly so crucial as in internal war; it is incidental in one case but seems to be decisive in the other.

One reason for this is that in internal wars, unlike international wars, there is generally a great disparity in capacity for military effort between the incumbents and insurgents. The former tend to be in a much stronger position — not always, of course, for this is where the loyalties of the established instrumentalities of violence enter the picture, but more often than not. The insurgents are therefore forced, in the normal case, to supplement their capabilities by taking what advantage they can of terrain and the cooperation of the non-combatant population. Like terrain itself, a well-disposed population affords a secure base of operations to rebels, as well as providing them with indispensable logistical support. Rebels who can count on popular support can lose themselves in the population (according to Mao "the populace is for revolutionaries what water is for fish"), count on the population for secrecy (in wars in which intelligence is practically the whole art of defense), and reconstitute their forces by easy recruitment; if they can do all of these things, they can be practically certain of victory, short of a resort to genocide by the incumbents.

Great popular support is necessary also because internal wars, precisely because the common disparity of forces rules out quick victory by the insurgents (except by *coup*), tend to be long drawn out wars of attrition — perhaps better, either very prolonged or very quickly settled. In such wars, when victory always seems remote, when, at times, impasse is the best that can be hoped for, when the disruption of normal life is greater even than in external war, the morale of the revolutionaries, their ultimate trump card against their opponents, can hardly be sustained if they feel themselves isolated from their own people.

TOWARD AN ETIOLOGY OF INTERNAL WARS

Needless to say, these arguments do not amount to anything like a finished etiology of internal wars. My concern here has been with preliminary, but fundamental and neglected, questions of strategy in theory-building, no more. Nevertheless, taking it all in all, this study does imply something more than that certain lines of inquiry are more promising than others in internal-war studies. When its arguments are added up, there emerges at least a considerable clue to the *form* that an adequate etiology of internal wars should take, even if little of a very specific nature can as yet be said about content. We have arrived at a paradigm, if not a fully-fledged theory.

Two points can serve as summary, as well as to spell out the nature of the paradigm I have in mind. One is that internal-war potential (the likelihood that internal war in some form will be precipitated)[26] should be conceived formally as a ratio between positive forces making for internal war and negative forces working against it — with the *possibility* that internal war of some kind may be fomented existing no matter what the overall potential, and the *probability* of its occurrence increasing as internal-war potential rises. This is certainly elementary, but it is in fact far more usual, in both general theories and specific interpretations of internal war, to speak of revolutionary or pacifying forces alone, and to depict rebelliousness as either absolutely present or absolutely lacking in societies. The other, and more important point, is that the forces involved should be conceived in both cases as functions of four factors. The positive forces are produced by the *inefficacy of elites* (lack of cohesion and of expected performance), *disorienting social processes* (delegitimization), *subversion* (attempts deliberately to activate disorientation, to form new political orientations and to impede the efficacy of elites), and the *facilities* available to potential insurgents. Countervailing these factors are four others: the *facilities* of incumbents, *effective repression* (not any kind of repression), *adjustive concessions* and *diversionary mechanisms* — the first referring to the incumbents' perceived capacity to fight if internal war occurs, the others to preventative actions.

This summation provides at least the minimum that one expects from paradigms: a formal approach to study and a checklist of factors that should be particularly considered whether one is interpreting specific cases or constructing general theory. But a minimum is not much. It is necessary to go further, particularly in the direction of determining the relative values of the factors and their relations to one another. After being stated, the variables must be ordered. Consequently, to conclude, I should like to add some suggestions that indicate how one might proceed from the mere cataloguing of promising variables toward their systematization.

In the first place, it seems, from what has been said about possible obstacles to internal war, that the negative forces vary within a much smaller range than the positive ones, so that beyond a point, internal-war potential can be reduced only with geometrically decreasing effectiveness, if at all. Take, for example, adjustive concessions. These cannot be indefinitely increased, for in the end, they would be tantamount to surrender, and long before that point, would only serve to increase the insurgents' capabilities (not to mention the probable effects on the insurgents' demands and the incumbents' cohesion). Repression is intrinsically limited as well, among other reasons because it requires repressors and because its use will tend to intensify alienation; as in the case of concessions there may be an optimum of repression, but a maximum of it is as bad as none at all. And one can doubt the efficacy of diversions where disorientation is very widespread and goes very deep; besides, intrinsic limitations operate in the case of this factor too, for a society that lives on diversions to the extent of, say, the Roman Empire is for that very reason in decay. The factors that make for internal-war potential clearly are less inherently circumscribed. More clearly still, certain of them, like the crucial facility of popular support, belong to the realm of zero-sums, so that an increase of forces on the positive side implies a concomitant decrease on the other. In this sense, the variables involved in internal-war potential have a certain hierarchical order (an order of "potency"): one set is more significant than the other.

Such an order seems to exist within each set as well. For example, no one rebels simply because he has appropriate facilities — otherwise, the military and police would be everywhere and constantly in rebellion. At the very least, internal war presupposes some degree of subversion as well as brute capabilities. Subversion in turn, however, presupposes something that can be subverted — disorientations to activate and to reshape toward new legitimizations. And much evidence suggests that, whatever forces may be at work in a society, in whatever fashion, disorientation and subversion are both unlikely where the elite performs well, is highly cohesive, and is deeply enough attuned to the general spirit of social life to provide the mutualities and complementarities that settled social orientations require — granted that certain social processes make this extremely improbable. Per contra, elite inefficacy in itself always invites challenge, from within or without, no matter what other forces may be at work in the non-elite; in one form (incohesion), it implies the likelihood of internecine elite conflict, in others the probability of alienation of the non-elite. If disorientation arising from other sources is added, the brew obviously becomes more lethal (and its explosion tends to take a different form), with or without much concerted subversion. The latter, and insurgent facilities, are essentially extra additives, the more so since insurgents can hardly lack facilities on some scale where elite inefficacy and political disorientation are great; these factors may intensify internal-war potential, but do not create it.

The factors that reduce internal-war potential can be arranged (with rather more ambiguity, to be sure) in a similar order of potency. The essential criterion that establishes their weight is the extent to which they are intrinsically limited, either because they can become self-defeating or because they are zero-sums that do not allow increases on the positive side to be balanced by increases on the other. Diversions, while certainly not unlimited, are probably the most potent of the factors, for they can apparently be carried very far before they thoroughly devitalize societies. Repression and concessions seem to have a much lower optimum point. It is difficult at present to say which of them is the less potent; in all probability, however, it is repression — if only because concessions may increase the legitimation of authority among potential dissidents (that is, serve as surrogates for other kinds of elite "performance") while acts of repression, as well as being inherently self-denials of legitimacy, are well-tailored to cope only with the less potent factor of subversion. Incumbent facilities, finally, while being by all odds the most ambiguous factor, seem to belong somewhere between diversions on one hand and concessions on the other. The reasons for this are three: First, since the most vital of them are zero-sums, they can be, in a sense, either very weak or very potent, a decrease in them implying a corresponding increase in insurgent facilities and the reverse holding as well (a sort of inherent limitation different from that operating in the case of the other factors). Secondly, it seems, on the evidence, more difficult for incumbents to regain lost facilities (especially lost loyalties) than for insurgents to multiply their stock of them, even if "logical" reasons for this are not readily apparent. And thirdly, while an increase in incumbent facilities most clearly reduces one of the positive factors, that factor happens to be least potent of the four.

The catalogue of forces making for internal-war potentials thus takes on a certain preliminary order — even if this order is as yet far from precise.

A further element of order can be introduced into the list of variables by noting that, to an extent, they can be paired with one another, specific negative and positive forces being particularly closely related. This is manifest in the case of insurgent and incumbent facilities — clearest of all where the facilities in question are zero-sums. All else being equal, it is obviously not the absolute value of facilities on either side that matters, but the ratio of the facilities concerned. Just as obviously, as already stated, there is a special relation between subversion and repression. Disorientation or elite inefficacy can hardly be repressed; only subversion can.[27] Less manifestly, but pretty clearly still, adjustive concessions bear a particular relation to certain elite failures, particularly in performance, and diversions can, to an extent, provide gratifications that alleviate the psychic stresses of disorientation; but neither is likely to counteract anything else.

One final point that bears more indirectly upon the ordering of the variables listed above requires consideration. It is an appropriate theme on which to conclude, for it is the point with which we started. Throughout the discussion, no distinction has been made between types of internal war, and this not without reasons. The fact remains, however, that internal wars, although in some ways similar, are in most respects greatly various. An adequate etiology of internal wars should therefore be able to tell one more than whether internal war in some form will occur in a society. It should also enable one to account for the specific forms internal wars take in different circumstances.

Any discussion of this matter is at present greatly handicapped by the lack of a settled, well-constructed typology of internal wars — and constructing such a typology is a task great enough to require another, and rather extensive, study. This much can be said, however, without settling on specific typological categories: Approaching the etiological study of internal wars in the manner suggested here makes it possible to deal with the many different phenomena covered by the term internal war within a single theoretical framework, yet in a way that yields quite different accounts of clearly disparate events. And this is surely desirable where phenomena that differ in many respects have also much in common.

The point is that two things can be done with the paradigm I have sketched. By weighing the general balance of positive and negative forces, one can arrive at an assessment of the overall degree of internal-war potential in a society. By considering the *particular* forces, combinations of forces, and ratios of forces that are strong or weak — the forces that are especially instrumental in determining the overall result — one can arrive at definite ideas of what kinds of internal war are likely to occur (quite apart from the possibility that the general degree of internal-war potential may itself set limits to the varieties that internal war can take). For example, where elite inefficacy, especially incohesion, greatly predominates among the positive forces, something like what many have called palace revolution is a very likely result. Where disorientation is very great but other positive factors are negligible, one might expect relatively unorganized, sporadic rioting as the normal response. Where subversion looms large relative to other factors, *coups, Putsches* or terrorism are more likely. Where incumbent and insurgent facilities are rather equally matched and elite cohesion is particularly tenuous, the stage is probably set for full-scale civil war. One could, in fact, contrive a useful, although very complex, typology of internal wars by working out probable results for the various possible constellations of factors included in the paradigm; and one could similarly take any typology otherwise worked out and produce for it a set of appropriately corresponding combinations of the factors.

The signal advantage of this procedure is that it avoids what defaces the whole corpus of historical studies of internal war available to us, the *ad hoc* piling up of unrelated theories, and prevents also the most conspicuous flaw of unhistorical, abstract models of revolutionary processes, the disregarding of special forces in particular cases. As well, the procedure I suggest can deal coherently with another eminently historical and theoretical matter, the transformation of many internal wars in the course of their development — the revolutionary "process." It can do so simply by applying typological theories dynamically. For the constellations of forces that provide initial impetus to internal wars are likely to undergo constant transformation in their course, much as such constellations may vary in the pre-revolutionary period. Subversion may become more intense, more purposeful; the balance of facilities may shift; incumbent elites may become more cohesive or disunited under fire; mild disorientation may become severe as authority is challenged and society disrupted by violence; the insurgents may win power, but at the cost of their own cohesion and without being able to provide effective new legitimations — and thus internal wars may proceed from stage to stage, from type to type, in unique or characteristic, continuous or spasmodic, dynamic patterns.

---

1 For example, in Pierre Kropotkin, *Paroles d'un révolté*, ed. by Elisée Reclus (Paris, not dated, but circa 1885). The term was used by Count Fersen as early as 1790 and occurs also in the writings of Sismondi and the Federalist Papers.

2 "The [French] Revolution is a series of shocks, each shock displacing power from Right to Left, from larger groups, to smaller and more determined groups, each shock taking on more and more the aspect of a *coup d'état*, less and less that of a widespread, spontaneous outbreak of the people, until finally, in a commonplace *coup d'état* hardly worthy of a good operetta, power comes to rest in the hands of the dictator Bonaparte." Crane Brinton, *A Decade of Revolution, 1789–1799* (New York, 1934), 1. This inspired characterization of the French Revolution might well serve as a rudimentary developmental model for any internal war that begins in large-scale, mainly spontaneous, popular violence.

3 L. P. Edwards, *The Natural History of Revolutions* (Chicago, 1927); Crane Brinton, *The Anatomy of Revolution* (New York, 1958 — first published 1938); George S. Pettee, *The Process of Revolution* (New York, 1938); Hannah Arendt, *On Revolution* (New York, 1963).

4 E. J. Hobsbawm, *Primitive Rebels* (London, 1960).

5 Gabriel Bonnet, *Les guerres insurrectionelles et révolutionnaires* (Paris, 1958), 34 ff.

⁶ S. P. Huntington, ed., *Changing Patterns of Military Politics* (New York, 1962), 22 ff.

⁷ George I. Blanksten, "Revolutions," in Harold Eugene Davis, *Government and Politics in Latin America* (New York, 1958), Chapter 5.

⁸ W. S. Stokes, "Violence as a Power Factor in Latin American Politics," *Western Political Quarterly*, Summer 1952, 445–68.

⁹ Edwards, *The Natural History of Revolutions*, 33.

¹⁰ Brinton, *The Anatomy of Revolution*, 29–37.

¹¹ See James C. Davies, "Toward a Theory of Revolution," *American Sociological Review*, 27 (1962), 5–19.

¹² The hypotheses come from a large variety of sources, including: Lasswell and Kaplan, *Power and Society* (New Haven, 1950); the works of Edwards, Pettee, and Brinton cited above; Rudé, *The Crowd in the French Revolution* (Oxford, 1959); Trotsky, *The History of the Russian Revolution* (Ann Arbor, Michigan, 1957); De Grazia, *The Political Community* (Chicago, 1948); Gaetano Mosca, *The Ruling Class* (New York, 1939); and Vilfredo Pareto, *The Mind and Society* (New York, 1935).

¹³ Trotsky, *The Russian Revolution*, 311.

¹⁴ De Grazia, *The Political Community*, 74–75.

¹⁵ De Grazia, *The Political Community*, esp. 117 ff. and Miriam Beard, *A History of the Business Man* (New York, 1938).

¹⁶ For evidence of acute unrest in the United States in this period, see De Grazia, *The Political Community*.

¹⁷ Cases in point are the stable, highly developed democracies on the one hand, and countries like Ethiopia and Somalia on the other.

¹⁸ For evidence, see Herbert H. Hyman, *Political Socialization* (Glencoe, Illinois, 1959).

¹⁹ Emile Durkheim, *Suicide* (London, 1952), 243 (author's italics).

²⁰ Elie Halévy, *A History of the English People*, 6 vols. (London, 1960), vol. 1.

²¹ G. Lefebvre, "Foules Révolutionnaires," *Annales Historiques de la Révolution Française*, 1934, 23.

²² Trotsky, *The Russian Revolution*, 116.

²³ Gustave Le Bon, *The Psychology of Revolution* (New York, 1913), 29.

²⁴ G. S. Pettee, *The Process of Revolution*, 105.

²⁵ G. Bonnet, *Les guerres insurrectionelles* (Paris, 1958), 60. The point that in guerrilla warfare almost everything turns on popular support is argued in many sources, most strongly perhaps in C. A. Johnson, "Civilian Loyalties and Guerrilla Conflict," *World Politics*, July 1962.

²⁶ I stress internal-war *potential* because this is all one can assess if the actual occurrence of internal wars depends on precipitants beyond the scope of systematic analysis or even the predictive capacities engendered by practical wisdom. Needless to say, however, the actual occurrence of internal wars gives the best assurance that the societies concerned indeed had great internal war potential.

²⁷ To avoid misunderstanding, it should be clearly understood that repression here refers not to puting down rebels in internal wars but preventative actions by the incumbents.

10. A Psychological Theory of Revolutions

CHARLES A. ELLWOOD

Among the phenomena of social evolution there are none more striking to the student of history and sociology than those commonly called revolutions. I do not use the word in a loose sense, to designate any sudden political or social change from *coups d'état* or "palace revolutions" to reversions in fashions and industrial changes due to great inventions; but I refer to those convulsive movements in the history of societies in which the form of government, or, it may be, the type of the industrial and social order, is suddenly transformed. Such movements always imply a shifting of the center of social control from one class to another, and inwardly are often marked by a change in the psychical basis of social control; that is, a change in the leading ideas, beliefs, and sentiments upon which the social order rests. Outwardly such movements are characterized by bloody struggles between the privileged and the unprivileged classes, which not infrequently issue in social confusion and anarchy. Revolutions in this sense are best typified in modern history, perhaps, by the Puritan Revolution in England and by the French Revolution. Less typical, but still in some sense revolutions, were our War for Independence and our Civil War.

The objective explanations of revolutions which have usually been offered by historians and economists — that is, explanations in terms of economic, governmental, and other factors largely external — have been far from satisfactory, inasmuch as they have lacked that universal element which is the essential of all true science. These explanations have, to be

151

sure, pointed out true causes operating in particular revolutions, but they have failed to reveal the universal mechanism through which all revolutions must take place. In the mind of the sociologist, therefore, there has arisen the further question: Is there any explanation of revolutions in general? What is their significance in the social life-process? Have they any universal form or method of development, and is that method capable of scientific formulation?

To have even asked these questions a score of years ago would probably have called forth a storm of ridicule. But such has been the progress of science that today many, if not most, social investigators would admit the possibility of finding universal forms in social occurrences, and so in revotions. If a digression may be permitted, I would say that this change of attitude on the part of scientific students of society is due largely to the progress of the science of psychology. The new functional psychology has proposed to interpret all mental life in terms of habit and adaptation; and the new psychological sociology, which is building itself up on the basis of the new psychology, proposes to do the same thing for the social life. Thus the possibility of finding universal forms for social occurrences on the subjective side, if not on the side of objective, environmental factors, is today more widely accepted than ever before. The reasons for the failure of the objective method of explaining social events are, indeed, now quite obvious. It is now seen that nearly all social occurrences are in the nature of responses to external stimuli. But these responses are not related, psychology tells us, to their stimuli as effects are to causes, as sociologists have so often assumed. The same response or similar responses may be called forth by very different stimuli, since the stimulus is only the opportunity for the discharge of energy. Consequently, any explanation of social occurrences in terms of external causes or stimuli is in a sense foredoomed to failure, since such an explanation will fall short of that universality which science demands. Hence the demands for a subjective or psychological explanation of social phenomena, a demand which is being met today by the new psychological sociology. It is in accordance with this demand that I venture to offer a psychological theory of revolutions.

The theory of revolutions here presented was first formulated by the writer in 1898, and first published in brief outline in an article of this *Journal*[1] in May, 1899. The purpose of this paper is merely to expand and restate the theory there presented. It is not an attempt, however, to give the theory anything more than a tentative form; its details must necessarily be left to be worked out through the further development of psychology and sociology. Moreover, it is not claimed that this theory of revolutions is anything absolutely new; foreshadowings of it are to be found in many historical and sociological writers.[2] The essence of the theory is this: that revolutions are disturbances in the social order due to the sudden breakdown of social habits under conditions which make difficult the reconstruction of those habits, that is, the formation of a new social order. In other words, revolutions arise through certain interferences or disturbances in the normal process of the readjustment of social habits.

The merit which is claimed for this theory is that it is in harmony with the new psychology and attempts to explain revolutions in terms of habit and adaptation. Habit and adaptation have their social consequences, not less than their individual mental consequences. The institutions and customs of society are but social expressions of habit; while the normal changes in the social order may be looked upon as social adaptations. Habit and adaptation are, therefore, fundamental categories for the interpretation of the social life-process not less than of the individual life-process; and the theory of revolutions here presented attempts to bring their phenomena within these categories.

Normally social habits are continually changing; old habits are gradually replaced by new ones as the life-conditions change. Normally the breakdown of a social habit is so gradual that by the time the old habit disappears a new habit has been constructed to take its place. Thus the process of social change, of continuous readjustment in society, goes on under normal conditions without shock or disturbance; new habits, or institutions, adapted to the new life-conditions replace the old habits and institutions which are no longer adapted. This transition from one habit to another is effected under ordinary conditions in society by such peaceful means as public criticism, discussion, the formation of a public opinion, and the selection of individuals to carry out the line of action socially determined upon. But where these normal means of effecting readjustments in the social life are lacking, social habits and institutions become relatively fixed and immobile, and a conservative organization of society results. Now, societies, like individuals, are in danger when their habits for any reason become inflexible. In the world of life, with its constant change and ceaseless struggle, only those organisms can survive which maintain a high degree of flexibilty or adaptability. It is even so in the world of societies. As Professor Ward says: "When a society makes for itself a procrustean bed, it is simply preparing the way for its own destruction by the on-moving agencies of social dynamics."[3] It is evident, then, that a society whose habits become inflexible for any reason is liable to disaster. That disaster may come in two forms: it may come in the form of conquest or subjugation by a foreign foe; or it may come in the form of internal disruption or revolution, when the conditions of life have sufficiently changed to make old habits and institutions no longer workable. It is with this latter case that we are concerned.

The conditions under which social habits become inflexible, hard and fast, are many, and I shall attempt no specific enumeration of them. In a general way they have already been indicated by saying that the mechanism by which the transition from one social habit to another is effected — namely, public criticism, free discussion, public opinion — has been destroyed. This has occurred most frequently no doubt, under despotic forms of government; and hence the connection in popular thought between tyranny and revolution. Not only absolute monarchies, but aristocracies and oligarchies also, have frequently created types of social organization which were relatively inflexible. Despotic governments, however, are only one of many conditions favorable to social immobility. Authoritative religions which have glorified a past and put under ban all progress have also had much to do with creating social inflexibility. Again, the mental character of a race or people has much to do with the adaptability and progressiveness of the social groups which it forms, and some writers would make this the chief factor. Finally, it is well known that in societies without any of the impediments of despotic government, authoritative ecclesiasticism, or inferior racial character, public sentiment, prejudice, fanaticism, and class interest can and do suppress free thought and free speech, and produce a relatively inflexible type of society.

Whatever the cause of their immobility, societies with inflexible habits and institutions are bound to have trouble. The conditions of social life rapidly change, and opposing forces accumulate until, sooner or later, the old habit is overwhelmed. Under these conditions the breakdown of the old habit is sharp and sudden; and the society, being unused to the process of readjustment, and largely lacking the machinery therefor, is unable for a greater or less length of time to reconstruct its habits. There ensues, in consequence, a period of confusion and uncertainty in which competing interests in the society strive for the mastery. If the breakdown under these conditions be that of a habit which affects the whole social life-process, and especially the system of social control, we have a revolution. It is consequent upon such a breakdown of social habit, then, that the phenomena of revolutions arise.

But before considering some of these phenomena in detail, let us note somewhat more concretely how the old habits and institutions are overthrown. Of course, the opposing forces must embody themselves in a party of opposition or revolt. This party is composed, on the whole, of those individuals whom the changed conditions of social life most affect, those on whom the old social habits set least easily. The psychology of the revolt of large numbers of men to an established social order is, at bottom, a simple matter. It is simply a case of the breakdown of a social habit at its weakest point, that is, among those individuals with whom the habit is least workable, or, in other words, whose interest lies in another direction.[4] From these the attitude of revolt spreads by imitation, first among those to whom the old social habits are ill-adapted, and finally among all who are susceptible to the influence of suggestion. Thus the party of opposition grows until it comes to embody all of the influences and interests which make the old habits and institutions ill-adapted or even unworkable. If these forces continue to grow, it is evident that there is possible to the ruling classes only two alternatives: either they must make concessions, that is, attempt themselves the readjustment of institutions; or they must face actual conflict with the party of opposition. As a matter of fact, historically the former alternative has much more often been chosen, thus open conflict avoided, and so-called "peaceful revolutions" effected. If, however, no concessions are made by the ruling classes, or only such as are insufficient to bring about the readjustments demanded by the life-conditions; if, in other words, the relative inflexibility of the social order is maintained, then the antagonism between the old social habits and the new life-conditions can be resolved only by open conflict between the ruling classes and the party of revolt. And when this conflict results in the success of the party of revolt, we call it a "revolution."

Thus the old social order is overthrown, violently, suddenly, and sometimes almost completely. Now in the transition from one habit to another in the individual there is frequently to be observed a period of confusion and uncertainty; and this confusion is intensified if the breakdown of the old habit has been sudden or violent. We should expect, therefore, an analogous confusion in society upon the breakdown of social habits; and this is exactly what we find. The so-called anarchy of revolutionary periods is not due simply to the absence of efficient governmental machinery, but to the general breakdown of the social habits of the population. The anarchy is, of course, proportionate to the violence and completeness with which the old habits and institutions are overthrown. Again, in such periods of confusion in the individual consequent upon the entire breakdown of a habit, we observe a tendency to atavism or reversion in his activities; that is, the simpler and more animal activities tend to come to expression. This tendency not only manifests itself in revolutions, but is of course greatly intensified by the struggle between the classes; for fighting, as one of the simplest and most primitive activities of man greatly stimulates all the lower centers of action. Hence the reversionary character of many revolutionary periods. They appear to us, and truly are, epochs in which the brute and the savage in man reassert themselves and dominate many phases of the social life. The methods of acting, of attaining ends, in revolutions are, indeed, often characteristic of much lower stages of culture. These methods, as a rule, are unreflective, extremely direct and crude. Thus resort to brute force is constant, and when attempts are made at psychical control, it is usually through appeal to the lower emotions, especially fear. Hence the terrorism which is sometimes a feature of revolutions, and which conspicuously marked the French Revolution.

Here another striking phenomenon of revolutionary epochs must be noted; and that is the part played at such times by mobs and other crowds. Le Bon has worked over this matter so thoroughly that only a word on this phase of our subject is necessary. It is evident that in the confusion and excitement of revolutionary times the most favorable conditions exist for the formation of crowds and the doing of their work. There is an absence, on the one hand, of those controlling habits, ideas, and sentiments which secure order in a population; and, on the other hand, there is the reversion to the unreflective type of mental activities. Under such conditions crowds are easily formed, and a suggestion suffices to incite them to the most extreme deeds. Thus much of the bloodiest work of revolutions is done by crowds. But it is a mistake to think that true revolutions can be initiated by mobs, or carried through by a series of them. Revolutions simply afford opportunities for mobs to manifest themselves to a much greater degree than they can in normal social life.

The duration of the period of confusion, anarchy, and mob-rule in a revolution is dependent upon a number of factors. If the party of revolt is united upon a program, and if the population generally has not lost its power of readjustment, the period of confusion may be so short as to be practically negligible. Under such circumstances the reconstruction of new social habits and institutions goes on rapidly under the guidance of the revolutionary party. As an illustration of this particular type of revolution with a happy outcome we may take our War of Independence. In this case the relative unity of the revolutionary party, the incompleteness of the destruction of the old social order, the vigorous power of readjustment in a relatively free population, all favored the speedy reconstruction of social institutions.

Unfortunately, this speedy reconstruction of social habits is not the outcome of all revolutions. Too often the revolutionary party is unified in nothing except its opposition to the old régime. It can find no principle or interest upon which a new social order can be reconstructed. Moreover, through a long period of social immobility the population seems often to have lost in great degree its power of readaptation. Indeed, in rare cases, peoples seem to have lost all power of making stable readjustments for themselves. Under any or all of these conditions it is evident that the period of confusion, anarchy, and mob-rule in a revolution must continue for a relatively long time. During this time frequent attempts may be made at the reconstruction of the social order without success. These attempts are continued until some adequate stimulus is found, either in an ideal principle or in the personality of some hero, to reconstruct the social habits of the population. Or, if no basis for the reconstruction of the social order can be found, revolution may become chronic; and the period of relative anarchy and mob-rule may last for years, only to be ended perhaps by the subjugation and government of the population by an external power.

A more usual outcome, however, to the chronic revolutionary condition is the "dictatorship." How this can arise from the conditions in revolutionary times is not difficult to understand. The labors of ethnologists have shown us that democracy in some shape is the natural and primitive form of government among all races of mankind; that despotism has arisen everywhere through social stresses and strains, usually those accompanying prolonged war, when a strong centralized system of social control becomes necessary, if the group is to survive. Now, in that internal war which we call a revolution, if it is prolonged, it is evident that we have all the conditions favorable to the rise of despotism. When the party of revolt are unable to agree among themselves, and can offer to the population no adequate stimulus for the reconstruction of the social order, nothing is more natural than that that stimulus should be found in the personality of some hero; for social organization is primitively based upon sentiments of personal attachment and loyalty far more than upon abstract principles of social justice and expediency. The personality of a military hero affords, then, the most natural stimulus around which a new social order can, so to speak, crystallize itself, when other means of reconstructing social institutions have failed, and when continued social danger demands a strong centralized social control. The dictatorship, in other words, does not arise because some superior man hypnotizes his social group by his brilliant exploits, but because such a man is "selected" by his society to reconstruct the social order. Cæsar, Cromwell, and Napoleon, these typical dictators of revolutionary eras, would probably have had their places filled by other, though perhaps inferior, men, had they themselves never existed.

Here may be briefly explained, finally, the reaction which frequently follows revolutions. No revolution is, of course, complete; it is never more than a partial destruction of old habits and institutions. Now new habits, psychology tells us, have to be erected on the basis of old habits. What remains of the old social habits after a revolution must serve, therefore, as the foundation for the new institutions, since no other foundation is possible. After repeated attempts at reconstruction of the social order which have failed, it is the easiest thing to copy the old institutions, and this is often the only successful means of restoring social stability. Hence the reversion to pre-revolutionary conditions. But, in the nature of things, such a reaction is usually only temporary. The population has learned that the social order can be changed, and at some later time is quite sure to attempt it again.

If the theory of revolutions here outlined is in any degree correct, it is evident that they are regular phenomena conforming to the laws of the mental life. It is possible, therefore, to predict their occurrence in the sense that the conditions favorable to their development can be stated. This has already been done in the discussion of our theory, but it may be worth our while to consider these conditions more critically, in order to see how far social prevision is possible in this matter and in social science in general.

It is evident that, according to our theory, revolution is impossible in a perfectly flexible and adaptable type of social organization. On the other hand, revolution is inevitable, barring foreign conquest, in those types of social and political organization which do not change with changing life-conditions. Thus from a purely theoretical point of view everything seems clear. But when we apply these principles to concrete societies, we experience difficulties. It is easy to predict, in the case of extremely inflexible societies like China and Russia, that revolution is, sooner or later, inevitable, unless conditions greatly change. Even in this easiest instance, however, our foresight is qualified by a great "if." But we cannot say with even as much assurance that our democratic societies are free from the danger of revolution. They may have the forms of freedom without the substance. Our own American society, for example, may be relatively inflexible in certain matters which are of vital importance to the life of our group. A tyrannical public sentiment or class interest may induce even in a democracy such an inflexibility or stagnation in institutions that only a revolution can sweep away the obstructing social structure. This is what actually occurred in the case of slavery in our country, which institution required a war of essentially revolutionary character for its overthrow. This can happen again in the future; for example, in the relations of the capitalistic and wage-earning classes. Whenever, in fact, an institution or a condition of society is set above public criticism, and freedom of discussion and thought is suppressed concerning it, we have a condition of social inflexibility and a loss of the power of adaptation which may breed revolution. Thus the most that can be said in the way of predicting revolutions must be in very general terms. All that we can say is that some societies are more liable to revolutions than others, while no society can safely be judged to be entirely free from the danger of revolution. In other words, no one can say where revolutions will occur, and much less when.

But this negative conclusion regarding the predictability of revolutions is not valueless. If the social sciences cannot foretell social events, they nevertheless can so define the conditions under which they occur that social development can be controlled. Thus it is of value to society to know the general conditions under which revolutions occur; for such knowledge points out the way by which revolutions can be avoided. Surely it cannot be valueless for a society to know that by encouraging intelligent public criticism, free discussion, and free thought about social conditions and institutions, by keeping itself adaptable, flexible, alert for betterment, it is pursuing the surest way to avoid future disaster. Social science, if it cannot foretell the future, can nevertheless indicate the way of social health and security.

The important practical truth, then, brought out by this study of revolutions, is that which has been so well expressed by Professor Ward when he says of societies:

Only the labile is truly stable, just as in the domain of living things only the plastic is enduring. For lability is not an exact synonym of instability, but embodies besides the idea of flexibilty and susceptibility to change without destruction or loss. It is that quality in institutions which enables them to change and still persist, which converts their equilibrium into a moving equilibrium, and which makes possible their adaptation to both internal and eternal modification, to changes in both individual character and the environment.[5]

[1] *American Journal of Sociology*, Vol. IV, pp. 817, 818.

[2] Among historical writers Carlyle might be mentioned (cf. his *French Revolution*, Vol. I, p. 38); among sociologists, Ward especially has approximated the above views (cf. his *Pure Sociology*, pp. 222–31).

[3] *Pure Sociology*, p. 230.

[4] Of course, the whole process of social differentiation and the resulting antagonism of social interests are closely connected with the phenomena of revolutions; but the psychology of this process has been so fully worked out by Ratzenhofer, Tarde, Simmel, Ward, and others, that it is only necessary for the details of this aspect of revolutions to refer to those writers.

[5] *Pure Sociology*, p. 230.

11. The Psychology of Revolutions

GUSTAVE LE BON

The knowledge of a people at any given moment of its history involves an understanding of its environment and above all of its past. Theoretically one may deny that past, as did the men of the Revolution, as many men of the present day have done, but its influence remains indestructible.

In the past, built up by slow accumulations of centuries, was formed the aggregation of thoughts, sentiments, traditions, and prejudices constituting the national mind which makes the strength of a race. Without it no progress is possible. Each generation would necessitate a fresh beginning.

The aggregate composing the soul of a people is solidly established only if it possesses a certain rigidity, but this rigidity must not pass a certain limit, or there would be no such thing as malleability.

Without rigidity the ancestral soul would have no fixity, and without malleability it could not adapt itself to the changes of environment resulting from the progress of civilisation.

Excessive malleability of the national mind impels a people to incessant revolutions. Excess of rigidity leads it to decadence. Living species, like the races of humanity, disappear when, too fixedly established by a long past, they become incapable of adapting themselves to new conditions of existence.

Few peoples have succeeded in effecting a just equilibrium between these two contrary qualities of stability and malleability. The Romans in antiquity and the English in modern times may be cited among those who have best attained it.

The peoples whose mind is most fixed and established often effect the most violent revolutions. Not having succeeded in evolving progressively, in adapting themselves to changes of environment, they are forced to adapt themselves violently when such adaptation becomes indispensable.

Stability is only acquired very slowly. The history of a race is above all the story of its long efforts to establish its mind. So long as it has not succeeded it forms a horde of barbarians without cohesion and strength. After the invasions of the end of the Roman Empire France took several centuries to form a national soul.

She finally achieved one; but in the course of centuries this soul finally became too rigid. With a little more malleability, the ancient monarchy would have been slowly transformed as it was elsewhere, and we should have avoided, together with the Revolution and its consequences, the heavy task of remaking a national soul.

The preceding considerations show us the part of race in the genesis of revolutions, and explain why the same revolutions will produce such different effects in different countries; why, for example, the ideas of the French Revolution, welcomed with such enthusiasm by some peoples, were rejected by others.

The influence of race in the destiny of the peoples appears plainly in the history of the perpetual revolutions of the Spanish republics of South America. Composed of half-castes, that is to say, of individuals whose diverse heredities have dissociated their ancestral characteristics, these populations have no national soul and therefore no stability. A people of half-castes is always ungovernable.

If we would learn more of the differences of political capacity which the racial factor creates we must examine the same nation as governed by two races successively.

The event is not rare in history. It has been manifested in a striking manner of late in Cuba and the Philippines, which passed suddenly from the rule of Spain to that of the United States.

We know in what anarchy and poverty Cuba existed under Spanish rule; we know, too, to what a degree of prosperity the island was brought in a few years when it fell into the hands of the United States.

The same experience was repeated in the Philippines, which for centuries had been governed by Spain. Finally the country was no more than a vast jungle, the home of epidemics of every kind, where a miserable population vegetated without commerce or industry. After a few years of American rule the country was entirely transformed: malaria, yellow fever, plague and cholera had entirely disappeared. The swamps were drained;

the country was covered with railways, factories and schools. In thirteen years the mortality was reduced by two-thirds.

It is to such examples that we must refer the theorist who has not yet grasped the profound significance of the word race, and how far the ancestral soul of a people rules over its destiny.

The part of the people has been the same in all revolutions. It is never the people that conceives them nor directs them. Its activity is released by means of leaders.

Revolution is easy when the leaders are very influential. But new ideas penetrate the people very slowly indeed. Generally it accepts a revolution without knowing why, and when by chance it does succeed in understanding why, the revolution is over long ago.

The people will create a revolution because it is persuaded to do so, but it does not understand very much of the ideas of its leaders; it interprets them in its own fashion, and this fashion is by no means that of the true authors of the revolution. The French Revolution furnished a striking example of this fact.

The Revolution of 1789 had as its real object the substitution of the power of the nobility by that of the *bourgeoisie;* that is, an old *élite* which had become incapable was to be replaced by a new *élite* which did possess capacity.

There was little question of the people in this first phase of the Revolution. The sovereignty of the people was proclaimed, but it amounted only to the right of electing its representatives.

Extremely illiterate, not hoping, like the middle classes, to ascend the social scale, not in any way feeling itself the equal of the nobles, and not aspiring ever to become their equal, the people had views and interests very different to those of the upper classes of society.

The struggles of the assembly with the royal power led it to call for the intervention of the people in these struggles. It intervened more and more, and the bourgeois revolution rapidly became a popular revolution.

An idea having no force of its own, and acting only by virtue of possessing an affective and mystic substratum which supports it, the theoretical ideas of the *bourgeoisie,* before they could act on the people, had to be transformed into a new and very definite faith, springing from obvious practical interests.

This transformation was rapidly effected when the people heard the men envisaged by it as the Government assuring it that it was the equal of its former masters. It began to regard itself as a victim, and proceeded to pillage, burn, and massacre, imagining that in so doing it was exercising a right.

The great strength of the revolutionary principles was that they gave a free course to the instincts of primitive barbarity which had been restrained by the secular and inhibitory action of environment, tradition, and law.

All the social bonds that formerly contained the multitude were day by day dissolving, so that it conceived a notion of unlimited power, and the joy of seeing its ancient masters ferreted out and despoiled. Having become the sovereign people, were not all things permissible to it?

The motto of Liberty, Equality, Fraternity, a true manifestation of hope and faith at the beginning of the Revolution, soon merely served to cover a legal justification of the sentiments of jealousy, cupidity, and hatred of superiors, the true motives of crowds unrestrained by discipline. This is why the Revolution so soon ended in disorder, violence, and anarchy.

The laws of the psychology of crowds show us that the people never acts without leaders, and that although it plays a considerable part in revolutions by following and exaggerating the impulses received, it never directs its own movements.

In all political revolutions we discover the action of leaders. They do not create the ideas which serve as the basis of revolutions, but they utilise them as a means of action. Ideas, leaders, armies, and crowds constitute four elements which all have their part to play in revolutions.

The crowd, roused by the leaders, acts especially by means of its mass. Its action is comparable to that of the shell which perforates an armour-plate by the momentum of a force it did not create. Rarely does the crowd understand anything of the revolutions accomplished with its assistance. It obediently follows its leaders without even trying to find out what they want.

In order to answer to certain theoretical conceptions the people was erected into a mystic entity, endowed with all the powers and all the virtues, incessantly praised by the politicians, and overwhelmed with flattery. We shall see what we are to make of this conception of the part played by the people in the French Revolution.

To the Jacobins of this epoch, as to those of our own days, this popular entity constitutes a superior personality possessing the attributes, peculiar to divinities, of never having to answer for its actions and never making a mistake. Its wishes must be humbly acceded. The people may kill, burn, ravage, commit the most frightful cruelties, glorify its hero to-day and throw him into the gutter to-morrow; it is all one; the politicians will not cease to vaunt its virtues, its high wisdom, and to bow to its every decision.

Now in what does this entity really consist, this mysterious fetich which revolutionists have revered for more than a century?

It may be decomposed into two distinct categories. The first includes the peasants, traders, and workers of all sorts who need tranquility and order that they may exercise their calling. This people forms the majority, but a majority which never caused a revolution. Living in laborious silence, it is ignored by the historians.

The second category, which plays a capital part in all national disturbances, consists of a subversive social residue dominated by a criminal mentality. Degenerates of alcoholism and poverty, thieves, beggars, destitute "casuals," indifferent workers without employment — these constitute the dangerous bulk of the armies of insurrection.

The fear of punishment prevents many of them from becoming criminals at ordinary times, but they do become criminals as soon as they can exercise their evil instincts without danger.

To this sinister substratum are due the massacres which stain all revolutions.

To the elements recruited from the lowest dregs of the populace are added, by way of contagion, a host of idle and indifferent persons who are simply drawn into the movement. They shout because there are men shouting, and revolt because there is a revolt, without having the vaguest idea of the cause of shouting or revolution. The suggestive power of their environment absolutely hypnotises them, and impels them to action.

These noisy and maleficent crowds, the kernel of all insurrections, from antiquity to our own times, are the only crowds known to the orator. To the orator they are the sovereign people. As a matter of fact this sovereign people is principally composed of the lower populace.

At no period of history was the *rôle* of the lowest elements of the population exercised in such a lasting fashion as in the French Revolution.

The massacres began as soon as the beast was unchained — that is, from 1789, long before the Convention. They were carried out with all possible refinements of cruelty. During the killing of September the prisoners were slowly chopped to bits by sabre-cuts in order to prolong their agonies and amuse the spectators, who experienced the greatest delight before the spectacle of the convulsions of the victims and their shrieks of agony.

Similar scenes were observed all over France, even in the early days of the Revolution, although the foreign war did not excuse them then, nor any other pretext.

Such is the behaviour of the base populace so soon as imprudent hands have broken the network of constraints which binds its ancestral savagery. It meets with every indulgence because it is in the interests of the politicians to flatter it. But let us for a moment suppose the thousands of beings who constitute it condensed into one single being. The personality thus formed would appear as a cruel and narrow and abominable monster, more horrible than the bloodiest tyrants of history.

This impulsive and ferocious people has always been easily dominated so soon as a strong power has opposed it. If its violence is unlimited, so is its servility. All the despotisms have had it for their servant. The Cæsars are certain of being acclaimed by it, whether they are named Caligula, Nero, Marat, Robespierre, or Boulanger.

Beside these destructive hordes whose action during revolution is capital, there exists, as we have already remarked, the mass of the true people, which asks only the right to labour. It sometimes benefits by revolutions, but never causes them. The revolutionary theorists know little of it and distrust it, aware of its traditional and conservative basis. The resistant nucleus of a country, it makes the strength and continuity of the latter. Extremely docile through fear, easily influenced by its leaders, it will momentarily commit every excess while under their influence, but the ancestral inertia of the race will soon take charge again, which is the reason why it so quickly tires of revolution. Its traditional soul quickly incites it to oppose itself to anarchy when the latter goes too far. At such times it seeks the leader who will restore order.

This people, resigned and peaceable, has evidently no very lofty nor complicated political conceptions. Its governmental ideal is always very simple, is something very like dictatorship. This is why, from the times of the Greeks to our own, dictatorship has always followed anarchy. It followed it after the first Revolution, when Bonaparte was acclaimed, and again when, despite opposition, four successive plebiscites raised Louis Napoleon to the head of the republic, ratified his *coup d'État,* re-established the Empire, and in 1870, before the war, approved of his rule.

Doubtless in these last instances the people was deceived. But without the revolutionary conspiracies which led to disorder, it would not have been impelled to seek the means of escape therefrom.

INDIVIDUAL VARIATIONS OF CHARACTER IN TIME OF REVOLUTION

I have dwelt at length elsewhere upon a certain theory of character, without which it is absolutely impossible to understand divers transformations or inconsistencies of conduct which occur at certain moments, notably in time of revolution. Here are the principal points of this theory.

Every individual possesses, besides his habitual mentality, which, when the environment does not alter, is almost constant, various possibilities of character which may be evoked by passing events.

The people who surround us are the creatures of certain circumstances, but not of all circumstances. Our ego consists of the association of innumerable cellular egos, the residues of ancestral personalities. By their combination they form an equilibrium which is fairly permanent when the social environment does not vary. As soon as this environment is considerably modified, as in time of insurrection, this equilibrium is broken, and the dissociated elements constitute, by a fresh aggregation, a new personality, which is manifested by ideas, feelings, and actions very different from those formerly observed in the same individual. Thus it is that during the Terror we see honest *bourgeois* and peaceful magistrates who were noted for their kindness turned into bloodthirsty fanatics.

Under the influence of environment the old personality may therefore give place to one entirely new. For this reason the actors in great religious and political crises often seem of a different essence to ourselves; yet they do not differ from us; the repetition of the same events would bring back the same men.

When the normal personality has been disaggregated under the influence of certain events, how does the new personality form itself? By several means, the most active of which is the acquisition of a strong belief. This orientates all the elements of the understanding, as the magnet collects into regular curves the filings of a magnetic metal.

Thus were formed the personalities observed in times of great crises: the Crusades, the Reformation, the Revolution notably.

At normal times the environment varies little, so that as a rule we see only a single personality in the individuals that surround us. Sometimes, however, it happens that we observe several, which in certain circumstances may replace one another.

These personalities may be contradictory and even inimical. This phenomenon, exceptional under normal conditions, is considerably accentuated in certain pathological conditions.

In all these variations of personality it is not the intelligence which is modified, but the feelings, whose association forms the character.

During revolution we see several sentiments developed which are commonly repressed, but to which the destruction of social constraints gives a free vent.

These constraints, consisting of the law, morality, and tradition, are not always completely broken. Some survive the upheaval and serve to some extent to damp the explosion of dangerous sentiments.

The most powerful of these restraints is the soul of the race. This determines a manner of seeing, feeling, and willing common to the majority of the individuals of the same people; it constitutes a hereditary custom, and nothing is more powerful than the ties of custom.

This racial influence limits the variations of a people and determines its destiny within certain limits in spite of all superficial changes.

For example, to take only the instances of history, it would seem that the mentality of France must have varied enormously during a single century. In a few years it passed from the Revolution to Cæsarism, returned to the monarchy, effected another Revolution, and then summoned a new Cæsar. In reality only the outsides of things had changed.

We cannot insist further here on the limits of national variability, but must now consider the influence of certain affective elements, whose development during revolution contributes to modify individual or collective personalities. In particular I will mention hatred, fear, ambition, jealousy or envy, vanity, and enthusiasm. We observe their influence during several of the upheavals of history, notably during the course of the French Revolution, which will furnish us with most of our examples.

Hatred. — The hatred of persons, institutions, and things which animated the men of the Revolution is one of these affective phenomena which are the more striking the more one studies their psychology. They detested, not only their enemies, but the members of their own party. "If one were to accept unreservedly," said a recent writer, "the judgments which they expressed of one another, we should have to conclude that they were all traitors and boasters, all incapable and corrupt, all assassins or tyrants." We know with what hatred, scarcely appeased by the death of their enemies, men persecuted the Girondists, Dantonists, Hébertists, Robespierrists, &c.

One of the chief causes of this feeling resided in the fact that these furious sectaries, being apostles in possession of the absolute verity, were unable, like all believers, to tolerate the sight of infidels. A mystic or sentimental certitude is always accompanied by the need of forcing itself on others, is never convinced, and does not shrink from wholesale slaughter when it has the power to commit it.

If the hatreds that divided the men of the Revolution had been of rational origin they would not have lasted long, but, arising from affective and mystic factors, men could neither forget nor forgive. Their sources being identical in the different parties, they manifested themselves on every hand with identical violence.

The hatreds of the Revolution did not arise entirely from divergence of belief. Other sentiments — envy, ambition, and self-love — also engendered them. The rivalry of individuals aspiring to power led the chiefs of the various groups in succession to the scaffold.

As man has only recently entered upon the age of knowledge, and has always hitherto been guided by sentiments and beliefs, we may conceive the vast importance of hatred as a factor of his history.

Commandant Colin, professor at the College of War, remarks in the following terms on the importance of this feeling during certain wars: —

"In war more than at any other time there is no better inspiring force than hatred; it was hatred that made Blücher victorious over Napoleon.

Analyse the most wonderful manœuvres, the most decisive operations, and if they are not the work of an exceptional man, a Frederick or a Napoleon, you will find they are inspired by passion more than by calculation. What would the war of 1870 have been without the hatred which we bore the Germans?"

Fear. — Fear plays almost as large a part in revolutions as hatred. During the French Revolution there were many examples of great individual courage and many exhibitions of collective cowardice.

All the forms of fear were observed at this period. One of the most widespread was the fear of appearing moderate. Members of the Assemblies, public prosecutors, representatives "on mission," judges of the revolutionary tribunals, &c., all sought to appear more advanced than their rivals. Fear was one of the principal elements of the crimes committed at this period. If by some miracle it could have been eliminated from the revolutionary Assemblies, their conduct would have been quite other than it was, and the Revolution itself would have taken a very different direction.

Ambition, Envy, Vanity, &c. — In normal times the influence of these various affective elements is forcibly contained by social necessities. Ambition, for instance, is necessarily limited in a hierarchical form of society. Although the soldier does sometimes become a general, it is only after a long term of service. In time of revolution, on the other hand, there is no need to wait. Everyone may reach the upper ranks almost immediately, so that all ambitions are violently aroused. The humblest man believes himself fitted for the highest employments, and by this very fact his vanity grows out of all measure.

All the passions being more or less aroused, including ambition and vanity, we see the development of jealousy and envy of those who have succeeded more quickly than others.

The effect of jealousy, always important in times of revolution, was especially so during the great French Revolution. Jealousy of the nobility constituted one of its most important factors. The middle classes had increased in capacity and wealth, to the point of surpassing the nobility. Although they mingled with the nobles more and more, they felt, none the less, that they were held at a distance, and this they keenly resented. This frame of mind had unconsciously made the *bourgeoisie* keen supporters of the philosophic doctrine of equality.

The philosopher Rivarol has very well described in the following passage, already cited by Taine, the influence of wounded self-love and jealousy upon the revolutionary hatreds: —

"It is not," he writes, "the taxes, nor the *letters de cachet,* nor any of the other abuses of authority; it is not the sins of the intendants, nor the long and ruinous delays of justice, that has most angered the nation; it is the prejudices of the nobility for which it has exhibited the greatest hatred. What proves this clearly is the fact that it is the *bourgeois*, the men of letters, the men of money, in fact all those who are jealous of the nobility, who have raised the poorer inhabitants of the cities against them, and the peasants in the country districts."

This very true statement partly justifies the saying of Napoleon: "Vanity made the Revolution; liberty was only the pretext."

Enthusiasm. — The enthusiasm of the founders of the Revolution equalled that of the apostles of the faith of Mohammed. And it was really a religion that the *bourgeois* of the first Assembly thought to found. They thought to have destroyed an old world, and to have built a new one upon its ruins. Never did illusion more seductive fire the hearts of men. Equality and fraternity, proclaimed by the new dogmas, were to bring the reign of eternal happiness to all the peoples. Man had broken for ever with a past of barbarity and darkness. The regenerated world would in future be illuminated by the lucid radiance of pure reason. On all hands the most brilliant oratorical formulæ saluted the expected dawn.

That this enthusiasm was so soon replaced by violence was due to the fact that the awakening was speedy and terrible. One can readily conceive the indignant fury with which the apostles of the Revolution attacked the daily obstacles opposed to the realisation of their dreams. They had sought to reject the past, to forget tradition, to make men over again. But the past reappeared incessantly, and men refused to change. The reformers, checked in their onward march, would not give in. They sought to impose by force a dictatorship which speedily made men regret the system abolished, and finally led to its return.

THE MYSTIC MENTALITY AND THE JACOBIN MENTALITY

To create broad distinctions between the various mentalities observable in time of revolution, as we are about to do, is obviously to separate elements which encroach upon one another, which are fused or superimposed. We must resign ourselves to losing a little in exactitude in order to gain in lucidity. The fundamental types which we are about to describe synthetise groups which would escape analysis were we to attempt to study them in all their complexity.

We have shown that man is influenced by different logics, which under normal conditions exist in juxtaposition, without mutually influencing one another. Under the action of various events they enter into mutual conflict, and the irreducible differences which divide them are visibly manifested, involving considerable individual and social upheavals.

Mystic logic, which we shall presently consider as it appears in the Jacobin mind, plays a very important part. But it is not alone in its action. The other forms of logic — affective logic, collective logic, and rational logic — may predominate according to circumstances.

Leaving aside for the moment the influence of affective, rational, and collective logic, we will occupy ourselves solely with the considerable part played by the mystic elements which have prevailed in so many revolutions, and notably in the French Revolution.

The chief characteristic of the mystic temperament consists in the attribution of a mysterious power to superior beings or forces, which are incarnated in the form of idols, fetiches, words, or formulæ.

The mystic spirit is at the bottom of all the religious and most political beliefs. These latter would often vanish could we deprive them of the mystic elements which are their chief support.

Grafted on the sentiments and passionate impulses which it directs, mystic logic constitutes the might of the great popular movements. Men who would be by no means ready to allow themselves to be killed for the best of reasons will readily sacrifice their lives to a mystic ideal which has become an object of adoration.

The principles of the Revolution speedily inspired a wave of mystic enthusiasm analogous to those provoked by the various religious beliefs which had preceded it. All they did was to change the orientation of a mental ancestry which the centuries had solidified.

So there is nothing astonishing in the savage zeal of the men of the Convention. Their mystic mentality was the same as that of the Protestants at the time of the Reformation. The principal heroes of the Terror — Couthon, Saint-Just, Robespierre, &c. — were Apostles. Like Polyeuctes, destroying the altars of the false gods to propagate his faith, they dreamed of converting the globe. Their enthusiasm spilled itself over the earth. Persuaded that their magnificent formulæ were sufficient to overturn thrones, they did not hesitate to declare war upon kings. And as a strong faith is always superior to a doubtful faith, they victoriously faced all Europe.

The mystic spirit of the leaders of the Revolution was betrayed in the least details of their public life. Robespierre, convinced that he was supported by the Almighty, assured his hearers in a speech that the Supreme Being had "decreed the Republic since the beginning of time." In his quality of High Pontiff of a State religion he made the Convention vote a decree declaring that "the French People recognises the existence of the Supreme Being and the immortality of the soul." At the festival of this Supreme Being, seated on a kind of throne, he preached a lengthy sermon.

All the heretics who criticised the Jacobin orthodoxy were excommunicated — that is, were sent to the Revolutionary Tribunal, which they left for the scaffold.

The mystic mentality of which Robespierre was the most celebrated representative did not die with him. Always ready to kill if killing would spread their faith, the mystics of all ages have employed the same means of persuasion as soon as they have become the masters.

It is therefore quite natural that Robespierre should still have many admirers. Minds moulded like his are to be met with in their thousands. His conceptions were not guillotined with him. Old as humanity, they will only disappear with the last believer.

Movements are never comprehended by those who imagine that their origin is rational. Political or religious, the beliefs which have moved the world possess a common origin and follow the same laws. They are formed, not by the reason, but more often contrary to reason. Buddhism, Christianity, Islamism, the Reformation, sorcery, Jacobinism, socialism, spiritualism, &c., seem very different forms of belief, but they have, I repeat, identical mystic and affective bases, and obey forms of logic which have no affinity with rational logic. Their might resides precisely in the fact that reason has as little power to create them as to transform them.

Given the silent power of reason over mystic beliefs, it is quite useless to seek to discuss, as is so often done, the rational value of revolutionary or political ideas. Only their influence can interest us. It matters little that the theories of the supposed equality of men, the original goodness of mankind, the possibility of re-making society by means of laws, have been given the lie by observation and experience. These empty illusions must be counted among the most potent motives of action that humanity has known.

Although the term "Jacobin mentality" does not really belong to any true classification, I employ it here because it sums up a clearly defined combination which constitutes a veritable psychological species.

This mentality dominates the men of the French Revolution, but is not peculiar to them, as it still represents one of the most active elements in our politics.

The mystic mentality which we have already considered is an essential factor of the Jacobin mind, but it is not in itself enough to constitute that mind. Other elements, which we shall now examine, must be added.

The Jacobins do not in the least suspect their mysticism. On the contrary, they profess to be guided solely by pure reason. During the Revolution they invoked reason incessantly, and considered it as their only guide to conduct.

The mind of the true Jacobin, at the time of the Revolution as now, was composed of elements which we must analyse if we are to understand its function.

This analysis will show in the first place that the Jacobin is not a rationalist, but a believer. Far from building his belief on reason, he moulds reason to his belief, and although his speeches are steeped in rationalism he employs it very little in his thoughts and his conduct.

A Jacobin who reasoned as much as he is accused of reasoning would be sometimes accessible to the voice of reason. Now, observation proves, from the time of the Revolution to our own days, that the Jacobin is never influenced by reasoning, however just, and it is precisely here that his strength resides.

And why is he not accessible to reason? Simply because his vision of things, always extremely limited, does not permit of his resisting the powerful and passionate impulses which guide him.

These two elements, feeble reason and strong passions, would not of themselves constitute the Jacobin mind. There is another.

Passion supports convictions, but hardly ever creates them. Now, the true Jacobin has forcible convictions. What is to sustain them? Here the mystic elements whose action we have already studied come into play. The Jacobin is a mystic who has replaced the old divinities by new gods. Imbued with the power of words and formulæ, he attributes to these a mysterious power. To serve these exigent divinities he does not shrink from the most violent measures.

The Jacobin mentality is found especially in narrow and passionate characters. It implies, in fact, a narrow and rigid mind, inaccessible to all criticism and to all considerations but those of faith.

The mystic and affective elements which dominate the mind of the Jacobin condemn him to an extreme simplicity. Grasping only the superficial relations of things, nothing prevents him from taking for realities the chimerical images which are born of his imagination. The sequence of phenomena and their results escape him. He never raises his eyes from his dream.

As we may see, it is not by the development of his logical reason that the Jacobin exceeds. He possesses very little logic of this kind, and therefore he often becomes dangerous. Where a superior man would hesitate or halt the Jacobin, who has placed his feeble reason at the service of his impulses, goes forward with certainty.

So that although the Jacobin is a great reasoner, this does not mean that he is in the least guided by reason. When he imagines he is being led by reason it is really his passions and his mysticism that lead him. Like all those who are convinced and hemmed in by the walls of faith, he can never escape therefrom.

A true aggressive theologian, he is astonishingly like the disciples of Calvin. Hypnotised by their faith, nothing could deter them from their object. All those who contradicted their articles of faith were considered worthy of death. They too seemed to be powerful reasoners. Ignorant, like the Jacobins, of the secret forces that led them, they believed that reason was their sole guide, while in reality they were the slaves of mysticism and passion.

The truly rationalistic Jacobin would be incomprehensible, and would merely make reason despair. The passionate and mystical Jacobin is, on the contrary, easily intelligible.

With these three elements — a very weak reasoning power, very strong passions, and an intense mysticism — we have the true psychological components of the mind of the Jacobin.

THE REVOLUTIONARY AND CRIMINAL MENTALITIES

We have just seen that the mystic elements are one of the components of the Jacobin mentality. We shall now see that they enter into another form of mentality which is also clearly defined, the revolutionary mentality.

In all ages societies have contained a certain number of restless spirits, unstable and discontented, ready to rebel against any established order of affairs. They are actuated by the mere love of revolt, and if some magic power could realise all their desires they would simply revolt again.

This special mentality often results from a faulty adaptation of the individual to his surroundings, or from an excess of mysticism, but it may also be merely a question of temperament or arise from pathological disturbances.

The need of revolt presents very different degrees of intensity, from simple discontent expressed in words directed against men and things to the need of destroying them. Sometimes the individual turns upon himself the revolutionary frenzy that he cannot otherwise exercise.

These perpetual rebels are generally highly suggestible beings, whose mystic mentality is obsessed by fixed ideas. Despite the apparent energy indicated by their actions they are really weak characters, and are incapable of mastering themselves sufficiently to resist the impulses that rule them. The mystic spirit which animates them furnishes pretexts for their violence, and enables them to regard themselves as great reformers.

In normal times the rebels which every society contains are restrained by the laws, by their environment — in short, by all the usual social constraints, and therefore remain undetected. But as soon as a time of disturbance begins these constraints grow weaker, and the rebel can give a free reign to his instincts. He then becomes the accredited leader of a movement. The motive of the revolution matters little to him; he will give his life indifferently for the red flag or the white, or for the liberation of a country which he has heard vaguely mentioned.

The revolutionary spirit is not always pushed to the extremes which render it dangerous. When, instead of deriving from affective or mystic impulses, it has an intellectual origin, it may become a source of progress. It is thanks to those spirits who are sufficiently independent to be intellectually revolutionary that a civilisation is able to escape from the yoke of tradition and habit when this becomes too heavy. The sciences, arts, and industries especially have progressed by the aid of such men. Galileo, Lavoisier, Darwin, and Pasteur were such revolutionaries.

Although it is not necessary that a nation should possess any large number of such spirits, it is very necessary that it should possess some. Without them men would still be living in caves.

The revolutionary audacity which results in discoveries implies very rare faculties. It necessitates notably an independence of mind sufficient to escape from the influence of current opinions, and a judgement that can grasp, under superficial analogies, the hidden realities. This form of revolutionary spirit is creative, while that examined above is destructive.

The revolutionary mentality may, therefore, be compared to certain physiological states in the life of the individual which are normally useful, but which, when exaggerated, take a pathological form which is always hurtful.

All the civilised societies inevitably drag behind them a residue of degenerates, of the unadapted, of persons affected by various taints. Vagabonds, beggars, fugitives from justice, thieves, assassins, and starving creatures that live from day to day, may constitute the criminal population of the great cities. In ordinary times these waste products of civilisation are more or less restrained by the police. During revolution nothing restrains them, and they can easily gratify their instincts to murder and plunder. In the dregs of society the revolutionaries of all times are sure of finding recruits. Eager only to kill and to plunder, little matters to them the cause they are sworn to defend. If the chances of murder and pillage are better in the party attacked, they will promptly change their colours.

To these criminals, properly so called, the incurable plague of all societies, we must add the class of semi-criminals. Wrongdoers on occasion, they never rebel so long as the fear of the established order restrains them, but as soon as it weakens they enrol themselves in the army of revolution.

These two categories — habitual and occasional criminals — form an army of disorder which is fit for nothing but the creation of disorder. All the revolutionaries, all the founders of religious or political leagues, have constantly counted on their support.

We have already stated that this population, with its criminal mentality, exercised a considerable influence during the French Revolution. It always figured in the front ranks of the riots which occurred almost daily. Certain historians have spoken with respect and emotion of the way in which the sovereign people enforced its will upon the Convention, invading the hall armed with pikes, the points of which were sometimes decorated with newly severed heads. If we analyse the elements composing the pretended delegations of the sovereign people, we shall find that, apart from a small number of simple souls who submitted to the impulses of the leaders, the mass was almost entirely formed of the bandits of whom I have been speaking. To them were due the innumerable murders of which the massacres of September and the killing of the Princesse de Lamballe were merely typical.

They terrorised all the great Assemblies, from the Constituent Assembly to the Convention, and for ten years they helped to ravage France. If by some miracle this army of criminals could have been eliminated, the progress of the Revolution would have been very different. They stained it with blood from its dawn to its decline. Reason could do nothing with them, but they could do much against reason.

THE PSYCHOLOGY OF REVOLUTIONARY CROWDS

Whatever their origin, revolutions do not produce their full effects until they have penetrated the soul of the multitude. They therefore represent a consquence of the psychology of crowds.

Man, as part of a multitude, is a very different being from the same man as an isolated individual. His conscious individuality vanishes in the unconscious personality of the crowd.

Material contact is not absolutely necessary to produce in the individual the mentality of the crowd. Common passions and sentiments, provoked by certain events, are often sufficient to create it.

The collective mind, momentarily formed, represents a very special kind of aggregate. Its chief peculiarity is that it is entirely dominated by unconscious elements, and is subject to a peculiar collective logic.

Among the other characteristics of crowds, we must note their infinite credulity and exaggerated sensibility, their short-sightedness, and their incapacity to respond to the influences of reason. Affirmation, contagion, repetition, and prestige constitute almost the only means of persuading them. Reality and experience have no effect upon them. The multitude will admit anything; nothing is impossible in the eyes of the crowd.

By reason of the extreme sensibility of crowds, their sentiments, good or bad, are always exaggerated. This exaggeration increases still further in times of revolution. The least excitement will then lead the multitude to act with the utmost fury. Their credulity, so great even in the normal state, is still further increased; the most improbable statements are accepted.

These various characteristics show that man in the crowd descends to a very low degree in the scale of civilisation. He becomes a savage, with all a savage's faults and qualities, with all his momentary violence, enthusiasm, and heroism. In the intellectual domain a crowd is always inferior to the isolated unit. In the moral and sentimental domain it may be his superior. A crowd will commit a crime as readily as an act of abnegation.

Personal characteristics vanish in the crowd, which exerts an extraordinary influence upon the individuals which form it. The miser becomes generous, the sceptic a believer, the honest man a criminal, the coward a hero. Examples of such transformations abounded during the great Revolution.

As part of a jury or a parliament, the collective man renders verdicts or passes laws of which he would never have dreamed in his isolated condition.

One of the most notable consequences of the influence of a collectivity upon the individuals who compose it is the unification of their sentiments and wills. This psychological unity confers a remarkable force upon crowds.

The formation of such a mental unity results chiefly from the fact that in a crowd gestures and actions are extremely contagious. Acclamations of hatred, fury, or love are immediately approved and repeated.

What is the origin of these common sentiments, this common will? They are propagated by contagion, but a point of departure is necessary before this contagion can take effect. Without a leader the crowd is an amorphous entity incapable of action.

A knowledge of the laws relating to the psychology of crowds is indispensable to the interpretation of the elements of our Revolution, and to a comprehension of the conduct of revolutionary assemblies, and the singular transformations of the individuals who form part of them. Pushed by the unconscious forces of the collective soul, they more often than not say what they did not intend, and vote what they would not have wished to vote.

Although the laws of collective psychology have sometimes been divined instinctively by superior statesmen, the majority of Governments have not understood and do not understand them. It is because they do not understand them that so many of them have fallen so easily.

12. Toward a Theory of Revolution

JAMES C. DAVIES

In exhorting proletarians of all nations to unite in revolution, because they had nothing to lose but their chains, Marx and Engels most succinctly presented that theory of revolution which is recognized as their brain child. But this most famed thesis, that progressive degradation of the industrial working class would finally reach the point of despair and inevitable revolt, is not the only one that Marx fathered. In at least one essay he gave life to a quite antithetical idea. He described, as a precondition of widespread unrest, not progressive degradation of the proletariat but rather an improvement in workers' economic condition which did not keep pace with the growing welfare of capitalists and therefore produced social tension.

> A noticeable increase in wages presupposes a rapid growth of productive capital. The rapid growth of productive capital brings about an equally rapid growth of wealth, luxury, social wants, social enjoyments. Thus, although the enjoyments of the workers have risen, the social satisfaction that they give has fallen in comparison with the increased enjoyments of the capitalist, which are inaccessible to the worker, in comparison with the state of development of society in general. Our desires and pleasures spring from society; we measure them, therefore, by society and not by the objects which serve for their satisfaction. Because they are of a social nature, they are of a relative nature.[1]

Marx's qualification here of his more frequent belief that degradation produces revolution is expressed as the main thesis by de Tocqueville in his study of the French Revolution. After a long review of economic and social decline in the seventeenth century and dynamic grow in the eighteenth, de Tocqueville concludes:

> So it would appear that the French found their condition the more unsupportable in proportion to its improvement. . . . Revolutions are not always brought about by a gradual decline from bad to worse. Nations that have endured patiently and almost unconsciously the most overwhelming oppression often burst into rebellion against the yoke the moment it begins to grow lighter. The regime which is destroyed by a revolution is almost always an improvement on its immediate predecessor. . . . Evils which are patiently endured when they seem inevitable become intolerable when once the idea of escape from them is suggested.[2]

On the basis of de Tocqueville and Marx, we can choose one of these ideas or the other, which makes it hard to decide just when revolutions are likely to occur — when there has been social and economic progress or when there has been regress. It appears that both ideas have explanatory and possibly predictive value, if they are juxtaposed and put in the proper time sequence.

Revolutions are most likely to occur when a prolonged period of objective

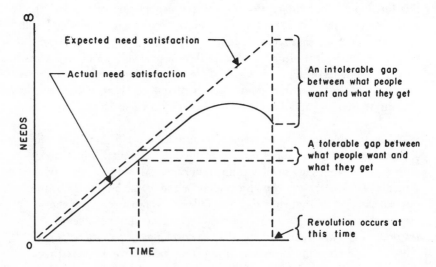

FIGURE 1. NEED SATISFACTION AND REVOLUTION

economic and social development is followed by a short period of sharp reversal.[3] The all-important effect on the minds of people in a particular society is to produce, during the former period, an expectation of continued ability to satisfy needs — which continue to rise — and, during the latter, a mental state of anxiety and frustration when manifest reality breaks away from anticipated reality. The actual state of socio-economic development is less significant than the expectation that past progress, now blocked, can and must continue in the future.

Political stability and instability are ultimately dependent on a state of mind, a mood, in a society. Satisfied or apathetic people who are poor in goods, status, and power can remain politically quiet and their opposites can revolt, just as, correlatively and more probably, dissatisfied poor can revolt and satisfied rich oppose revolution. It is the dissatisfied state of mind rather than the tangible provision of "adequate" or "inadequate" supplies of food, equality, or liberty which produces the revolution. In actuality, there must be a joining of forces between dissatisfied, frustrated people who differ in their degree of objective, tangible welfare and status. Well-fed, well-educated, high-status individuals who rebel in the face of apathy among the objectively deprived can accomplish at most a coup d'état. The objectively deprived, when faced with solid opposition of people of wealth, status, and power, will be smashed in their rebellion as were peasants and Anabaptists by German noblemen in 1525 and East Germans by the Communist élite in 1953.

Before appraising this general notion in light of a series of revolutions, a word is in order as to why revolutions ordinarily do not occur when a society is generally impoverished — when, as deTocqueville put it, evils that seem inevitable are patiently endured. They are endured in the extreme case because the physical and mental energies of people are totally employed in the process of merely staying alive. The Minnesota starvation studies conducted during World War II[4] indicate clearly the constant pre-occupation of very hungry individuals with fantasies and thoughts of food. In extremis, as the Minnesota research poignantly demonstrates, the individual withdraws into a life of his own, withdraws from society, withdraws from any significant kind of activity unrelated to staying alive. Reports of behavior in Nazi concentration camps indicate the same preoccupation.[5] In less extreme and barbarous circumstances, where minimal survival is possible but little more, the preoccupation of individuals with staying alive is only mitigated. Social action takes place for the most part on a local, face-to-face basis. In such circumstances the family is a — perhaps the major — solidary unit[6] and even the local community exists primarily to the extent families need to act together to secure their separate survival. Such was life on the American frontier in the sixteenth through nineteenth centuries. In very much attenuated form, but with a substantial degree of social isolation persisting, such evidently is rural life even today. This is clearly related to a relatively low level of political participation in elections.[7] As Zawadzki and Lazarsfeld have indicated,[8] preoccupation with physical survival, even in industrial areas, is a force strongly militating against the establishment of the community-sense and consensus on joint political action which are necessary to induce a revolutionary state of mind. Far from making people into revolutionaries, enduring poverty makes for concern with one's solitary self or solitary family at best and resignation or mute despair at worst. When it is a choice between losing their chains or their lives, people will mostly choose to keep their chains, a fact which Marx seems to have over-looked.[9]

It is when the chains have been loosened somewhat, so that they can be cast off without a high probability of losing life, that people are put in a condition of proto-rebelliousness. I use the term proto-rebelliousness because the mood of discontent may be dissipated before a violent outbreak occurs. The causes for such dissipation may be natural or social (including economic and political). A bad crop year that threatens a return to chronic hunger may be succeeded by a year of natural abundance. Recovery from sharp economic dislocation may take the steam from the boiler of rebellion.[10] The slow, grudging grant of reforms, which has been the political history of England since at least the Industrial Revolution, may effectively and continuously prevent the degree of frustration that produces revolt.

A revolutionary state of mind requires the continued, even habitual but dynamic expectation of greater opportunity to satisfy basic needs, which may range from merely physical (food, clothing, shelter, health, and safety from bodily harm) to social (the affectional ties of family and friends) to the need for equal dignity and justice. But the necessary additional ingredient is a persistent, unrelenting threat to the satisfaction of these needs: not a threat which actually returns people to a state of sheer survival but which puts them in the mental state where they believe they will not be able to satisfy one or more basic needs. Although physical deprivation in some degree may be threatened on the eve of all revolutions, it need not be the prime factor, as it surely was not in the American Revolution in 1775. The crucial factor is the vague or specific fear that ground gained over a long period of time will be quickly lost. This fear does not generate if there is continued opportunity to satisfy continually emerging needs; it generates when the existing government suppresses or is blamed for suppressing such opportunity.

Three rebellions or revolutions are given considerable attention in the sections that follow: Dorr's Rebellion of 1842, the Russian Revolution of 1917, and the Egyptian Revolution of 1952. Brief mention is then made of several other major civil disturbances, all of which appear to fit the J-curve pattern.[11] After considering these specific disturbances, some general theoretical and research problems are discussed.

No claim is made that all rebellions follow the pattern, but just that the ones here presented do. All of these are "progressive" revolutions in behalf of greater equality and liberty. The question is open whether the pattern occurs in such markedly retrogressive revolutions as Nazism in Germany or the 1861 Southern rebellion in the United States. It will surely be necessary to examine other progressive revolutions before one can judge how universal the J-curve is. And it will be necessary, in the interests of scientific validation, to examine cases of serious civil disturbance that fell short of producing profound revolution — such as the Sepoy Rebellion of 1857 in India, the Pullman Strike of 1894 in America, the Boxer Rebellion of 1900 in China, and the Great Depression of the 1920s and 1930s as it was experienced in Austria, France, Great Britain, and the United States. The explanation for such still-born rebellions — for revolutions that might have occurred — is inevitably more complicated than for those that come to term in the "normal" course of political gestation.

DORR'S REBELLION OF 1842

Dorr's Rebellion[12] in nineteenth-century America was perhaps the first of many civil disturbances to occur in America as a consequence, in part, of the Industrial Revolution. It followed by three years an outbreak in England that had similar roots and a similar program — the Chartist agitation. A machine-operated textile industry was first established in Rhode Island in 1790 and grew rapidly as a consequence of domestic and international demand, notably during the Napoleonic Wars. Jefferson's Embargo Act of 1807, the War of 1812, and a high tariff in 1816 further stimulated American industry.

Rapid industrial growth meant the movement of people from farms to cities. In Massachusetts the practice developed of hiring mainly the wives and daughters of farmers, whose income was thereby supplemented but not displaced by wages. In Rhode Island whole families moved to the cities and became committed to the factory system. When times were good, industrialized families earned two or three times what they got from the soil; when the mills were idle, there was not enough money for bread.[13] From 1807 to 1815 textiles enjoyed great prosperity; from 1834 to 1842 they suffered depression, most severely from 1835 to 1840. Prosperity raised expectations and depression frustrated them, particularly when accompanied by stubborn resistance to suffrage demands that first stirred in 1790 and recurred in a wave-like pattern in 1811 and then in 1818 and 1820 following suffrage extension in Connecticut and Massachusetts. The final crest was reached in 1841, when suffrage associations met and called for a constitutional convention.[14]

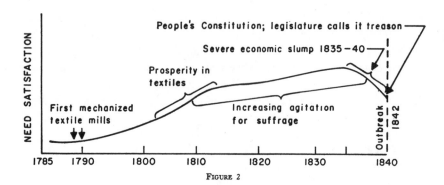

FIGURE 2

Against the will of the government, the suffragists held an election in which all adult males were eligible to vote, held a constitutional convention composed of delegates so elected and in December 1841 submitted the People's Constitution to the same electorate, which approved it and the call for an election of state officers the following April, to form a new government under this unconstitutional constitution.[15]

These actions joined the conflict with the established government. When asked — by the dissidents — the state supreme court rendered its private judgment in March 1842 that the new constitution was "of no binding force whatever" and any act "to carry it into effect by force will be treason against the state." The legislature passed what became known as the Algerian law, making it an offense punishable by a year in jail to vote in the April election, and by life imprisonment to hold office under the People's Constitution.

The rebels went stoutly ahead with the election, and on May 3, 1842 inaugurated the new government. The next day the People's legislature met and respectfully requested the sheriff to take possession of state buildings, which he failed to do. Violence broke out on the 17th of May in an attempt to take over a state arsenal with two British cannon left over from the Revolutionary War. When the cannon misfired, the People's government resigned. Sporadic violence continued for another month, resulting in the arrest of over 500 men, mostly textile workers, mechanics, and laborers. The official legislature called for a new constitutional convention, chosen by universal manhood suffrage, and a new constitution went into effect in January, 1843. Altogether only one person was killed in this little revolution, which experienced violence, failure, and then success within the space of nine months.

It is impossible altogether to separate the experience of rising expectations among people in Rhode Island from that among Americans generally. They all shared historically the struggle against a stubborn but ultimately rewarding frontier where their self-confidence gained strength not only in the daily process of tilling the soil and harvesting the crops but also by improving their skill at self-government. Winning their war of independence, Americans continued to press for more goods and more democracy. The pursuit of economic expectations was greatly facilitated by the growth of domestic and foreign trade and the gradual establishment of industry. Equalitarian expectations in politics were satisfied and without severe struggle — in most Northern states — by suffrage reforms.

In Rhode Island, these rising expectations — more goods, more equality, more self-rule — were countered by a series of containing forces which built up such a head of steam that the boiler cracked a little in 1842. The textile depression hit hard in 1835 and its consequences were aggravated by the Panic of 1837. In addition to the frustration of seeing their peers get the right to vote in other states, poor people in Rhode Island were now beset by industrial dislocation in which the machines that brought them prosperity they had never before enjoyed now were bringing economic disaster. The machines could not be converted to produce food and in Rhode Island the machine tenders could not go back to the farm.

When they had recovered from the pre-occupation with staying alive, they turned in earnest to their demands for constitutional reform. But these were met first with indifference and then by a growing intransigence on the part of the government representing the propertied class. Hostile action by the state supreme court and then the legislature with its Algerian law proved just enough to break briefly the constitutional structure which in stable societies has the measure of power and resilience necessary to absorb social tension.

THE RUSSIAN REVOLUTION OF 1917

In Russia's tangled history it is hard to decide when began the final upsurge of expectations that, when frustrated, produced the cataclysmic events of 1917. One can truly say that the real beginning was the slow modernization process begun by Peter the Great over two hundred years before the revolution. And surely the rationalist currents from France that slowly penetrated Russian intellectual life during the reign of Catherine the Great a hundred years before the revolution were necssary, lineal antecedents of the 1917 revolution.

Without denying that there was an accumulation of forces over at least a 200-year period,[16] we may nonetheless date the final upsurge as beginning with the 1861 emancipation of serfs and reaching a crest in the 1905 revolution.

The chronic and growing unrest of serfs before their emancipation in 1861 is an ironic commentary on the Marxian notion that human beings are what social institutions make them. Although serfdom had been shaping their personality since 1647, peasants became increasingly restive in the second quarter of the nineteenth century.[17] The continued discontent of peasants after emancipation is an equally ironic commentary on the belief that relieving one profound frustration produces enduring contentment. Peasants rather quickly got over their joy at being untied from the soil after two hundred years. Instead of declining, rural violence increased.[18] Having gained freedom but not much free land, peasants now had to rent or buy land to survive: virtual personal slavery was exchanged for financial servitude. Land pressure grew, reflected in a doubling of land prices between 1868 and 1897.

It is hard thus to tell whether the economic plight of peasants was much lessened after emancipation. A 1903 government study indicated that even with a normal harvest, average food intake per peasant was 30 per cent below the minimum for health. The only sure contrary item of evidence is that the peasant population grew, indicating at least increased ability of the land to support life, as the following table shows.

The land-population pressure pushed people into towns and cities, where

TABLE 1. POPULATION OF EUROPEAN RUSSIA (1480–1895)

	Population in Millions	Increase in Millions	Average Annual Rate of Increase*
1480	2.1	. .	. .
1580	4.3	2.2	1.05%
1680	12.6	8.3	1.93%
1780	26.8	14.2	1.13%
1880	84.5	57.7	2.15%
1895	110.0	25.5	2.02%

* Computed as follows: dividing the increase by the number of years and then dividing this hypothetical annual increase by the population at the end of the preceding 100-year period.

Source for gross population data: *Entsiklopedicheskii Slovar*, St. Petersburg, 1897, vol. 40, p. 631. Russia's population was about 97% rural in 1784, 91% in 1878, and 87% in 1897. See Masaryk, *op. cit.*, p. 162n.

the rapid growth of industry truly afforded the chance for economic betterment. One estimate of net annual income for a peasant family of five in
the rich blackearth area in the late nineteenth century was 82 rubles. In
contrast, a "good" wage for a male factory worker was about 168 rubles per
year. It was this difference in the degree of poverty that produced almost
a doubling of the urban population between 1878 and 1897. The number
of industrial workers increased almost as rapidly. The city and the factory
gave new hope. Strikes in the 1880s were met with brutal suppression but
also with the beginning of factory legislation, including the requirement
that wages be paid regularly and the abolition of child labor. The burgeoning proletariat remained comparatively contented until the eve of the 1905
revolution.[19]

There is additional, non-economic evidence to support the view that 1861
to 1905 was the period of rising expectations that preceded the 1917 revolution. The administration of justice before the emancipation had largely
been carried out by noblemen and landowners who embodied the law for
their peasants. In 1864 justice was in principle no longer delegated to such
private individuals. Trials became public, the jury system was introduced,
and judges got tenure. Corporal punishment was alleviated by the elimination of running the gauntlet, lashing, and branding; caning persisted until
1904. Public joy at these reforms was widespread. For the intelligentsia,
there was increased opportunity to think and write and to criticize established institutions, even sacrosanct absolutism itself.

But Tsarist autocracy had not quite abandoned the scene. Having inclined but not bowed, in granting the inevitable emancipation as an act
not of justice but grace, it sought to maintain its absolutist principle by
conceding reform without accepting anything like democratic authority.
Radical political and economic criticism surged higher. Some strong efforts
to raise the somewhat lowered floodgates began as early as 1866, after an
unsuccessful attempt was made on the life of Alexander II, in whose name
serfs had just gained emancipation. When the attempt succeeded fifteen
years later, there was increasing state action under Alexander III to limit
constantly rising expectations. By suppression and concession, the last Alexander succeeded in dying naturally in 1894.

When it became apparent that Nicholas II shared his father's ideas but not
his forcefulness, opposition of the intelligentsia to absolutism joined with
the demands of peasants and workers, who remained loyal to the Tsar but
demanded economic reforms. Starting in 1904, there developed a "League
of Deliverance" that coordinated efforts of at least seventeen other revolutionary, proletarian, or nationalist groups within the empire. Consensus on
the need for drastic reform, both political and economic, established a many-
ringed circus of groups sharing the same tent. These groups were geographi-

cally distributed from Finland to Armenia and ideologically from liberal constitutionalists to revolutionaries made prudent by the contrast between their own small forces and the power of Tsardom.

Events of 1904–5 mark the general downward turning point of expectations, which people increasingly saw as frustrated by the continuation of Tsardom. Two major and related occurrences made 1905 the point of no return. The first took place on the Bloody Sunday of January 22, 1905, when peaceful proletarian petitioners marched on the St. Petersburg palace and were killed by the hundreds. The myth that the Tsar was the gracious protector of his subjects, however surrounded he might be by malicious advisers, was quite shattered. The reaction was immediate, bitter, and prolonged and was not at all confined to the working class. Employers, merchants, and white-collar officials joined in the burgeoning of strikes which brought the economy to a virtual standstill in October. Some employers even continued to pay wages to strikers. University students and faculties joined the revolution. After the great October strike, the peasants ominously sided with the workers and engaged in riots and assaults on landowners. Until peasants became involved, even some landowners had sided with the revolution.

The other major occurrence was the disastrous defeat of the Russian army and navy in the 1904–5 war with Japan. Fundamentally an imperialist venture aspiring to hegemony over the people of Asia, the war was not regarded as a people's but as a Tsar's war, to save and spread absolutism. The military defeat itself probably had less portent than the return of shattered soldiers from a fight that was not for them. Hundreds of thousands, wounded or not, returned from the war as a visible, vocal, and ugly reminder to the entire populace of the weakness and selfishness of Tsarist absolutism.

The years from 1905 to 1917 formed an almost relentless procession of increasing misery and despair. Promising at last a constitutional government, the Tsar, in October, 1905, issued from on high a proclamation renouncing absolutism, granting law-making power to a duma, and guaranteeing freedom of speech, assembly, and association. The first two dumas, of 1906 and 1907, were dissolved for recalcitrance. The third was made pliant by reduced representation of workers and peasants and by the prosecution and conviction of protestants in the first two. The brief period of a free press was succeeded in 1907 by a reinstatement of censorship and confiscation of prohibited publications. Trial of offenders against the Tsar was now conducted by courts martial. Whereas there had been only 26 executions of the death sentence, in the 13 years of Alexander II's firm rule (1881–94), there were 4,449 in the years 1905–10, in six years of Nicholas II's soft regimen.[20]

But this "white terror," which caused despair among the workers and intelligentsia in the cities, was not the only face of misery. For the peasants, there was a bad harvest in 1906 followed by continued crop failures in several areas in 1907. To forestall action by the dumas, Stolypin decreed a series of agrarian reforms designed to break up the power of the rural communes by individualizing land ownership. Between these acts of God and government, peasants were so preoccupied with hunger or self-aggrandizement as to be dulled in their sensitivity to the revolutionary appeals of radical organizers.

After more than five years of degrading terror and misery, in 1910 the country appeared to have reached a condition of exhaustion. Political strikes had fallen off to a new low. As the economy recovered, the insouciance of hopelessness set in. Amongst the intelligentsia the mood was hedonism, or despair that often ended in suicide. Industrialists aligned themselves with the government. Workers worked. But an upturn of expectations, inadequately quashed by the police, was evidenced by a recrudescence of political strikes which, in the first half of 1914 — on the eve of war — approached the peak of 1905. They sharply diminished during 1915 but grew again in 1916 and became a general strike in February 1917.[21]

Figure 3 indicates the lesser waves in the tidal wave whose first trough is at the end of serfdom in 1861 and whose second is at the end of Tsardom in 1917. This fifty-six year period appears to constitute a single long phase in which popular gratification at the termination of one institution (serfdom) rather quickly was replaced with rising expectations which resulted from intensified industrialization and which were incompatible with the continuation of the inequitable and capricious power structure of Tsarist society. The small trough of frustration during the repression that followed

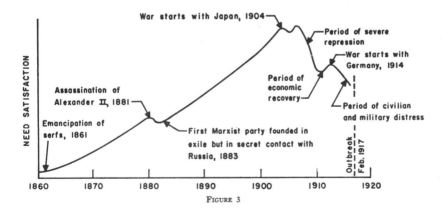

FIGURE 3

the assassination of Alexander II seems to have only briefly interrupted the rise in popular demand for more goods and more power. The trough in 1904 indicates the consequences of war with Japan. The 1905–6 trough reflects the repression of January 22, and after, and is followed by economic recovery. The final downturn, after the first year of war, was a consequence of the dislocations of the German attack on all kinds of concerted activities other than production for the prosecution of the war. Patriotism and governmental repression for a time smothered discontent. The inflation that developed in 1916 when goods, including food, became severely scarce began to make workers self-consciously discontented. The conduct of the war, including the growing brutality against reluctant, ill-provisioned troops, and the enormous loss of life, produced the same bitter frustration in the army.[22] When civilian discontent reached the breaking point in February, 1917, it did not take long for it to spread rapidly into the armed forces. Thus began the second phase of the revolution that really started in 1905 and ended in death to the Tsar and Tsardom — but not to absolutism — when the Bolsheviks gained ascendency over the moderates in October. A centuries-long history of absolutism appears to have made this post-Tsarist phase of it tragically inevitable.

THE EGYPTIAN REVOLUTION OF 1952

The final slow upsurge of expectations in Egypt that culminated in the revolution began when that society became a nation in 1922, with the British grant of limited independence. British troops remained in Egypt to protect not only the Suez Canal but also, ostensibly, to prevent foreign aggression. The presence of foreign troops served only to heighten nationalist expectations, which were excited by the Wafd, the political organization that formed public opinion on national rather than religious grounds and helped establish a fairly unified community — in striking contrast to late-nineteenth century Russia.

But nationalist aspirations were not the only rising expectations in Egypt of the 1920s and 1930s. World War I had spurred industrialization, which opened opportunities for peasants to improve, somewhat, their way of life by working for wages in the cities and also opened great opportunities for entrepreneurs to get rich. The moderately wealthy got immoderately so in commodity market speculation, finance, and manufacture, and the uprooted peasants who were now employed, or at any rate living, in cities were relieved of at least the notion that poverty and boredom must be the will of Allah. But the incongruity of a money-based modern semi-feudality that was like a chariot with a gasoline engine evidently escaped the attention of ordinary people. The generation of the 1930s could see more rapid progress, even for themselves, than their parents had even envisioned. If conditions remained poor, they could always be blamed on the British, whose economic and military power remained visible and strong.

Economic progress continued, though unevenly, during World War II. Conventional exports, mostly cotton, actually declined, not even reaching depression levels until 1945, but direct employment by Allied military forces reached a peak of over 200,000 during the most intense part of the African war. Exports after the war rose steadily until 1948, dipped, and then rose sharply to a peak in 1951 as a consequence of the Korean war. But in 1945 over 250,000 wage earners[23] — probably over a third of the working force — became jobless. The cost of living by 1945 had risen to three times the index of 1937.[24] Manual laborers were hit by unemployment; white collar workers and professionals probably more by inflation than unemployment. Meanwhile the number of millionaires in pounds sterling had increased eight times during the war.[25]

Frustrations, exacerbated during the war by German and thereafter by Soviet propaganda, were at first deflected against the British[26] but gradually shifted closer to home. Egyptian agitators began quoting the Koran in favor of a just, equalitarian society and against great differences in individual wealth. There was an ominous series of strikes, mostly in the textile mills, from 1946–8.

At least two factors stand out in the postponement of revolution. The first was the insatiable postwar world demand for cotton and textiles and the second was the surge of solidarity with king and country that followed the 1948 invasion of the new state of Israel. Israel now supplemented England as an object of deflected frustration. The disastrous defeat a year later, by a new nation with but a fifteenth of Egypt's population, was the beginning of the end. This little war had struck the peasant at his hearth, when a shortage of wheat and of oil for stoves provided a daily reminder of a weak and corrupt government. The defeat frustrated popular hopes for national glory and — with even more portent — humiliated the army and solidified it against the bureaucracy and the palace which had profiteered at the expense of national honor. In 1950 began for the first time a direct and open propaganda attack against the king himself. A series of peasant uprisings, even on the lands of the king, took place in 1951 along with some 49 strikes in the cities. The skyrocketing demand for cotton after the start of the Korean War in June, 1950 was followed by a collapse in March, 1952. The uncontrollable or uncontrolled riots in Cairo, on January 26, 1952, marked the fiery start of the revolution. The officers' coup in the early morning of July 23 only made it official.

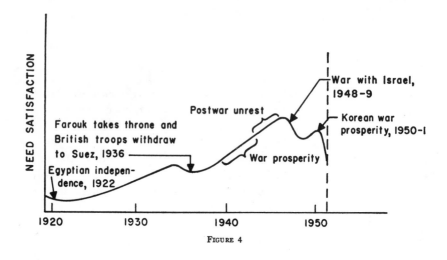

FIGURE 4

OTHER CIVIL DISTURBANCES

The J-curve of rising expectations followed by their effective frustration is applicable to other revolutions and rebellions than just the three already considered. Leisler's Rebellion in the royal colony of New York in 1689 was a brief dress-rehearsal for the American Revolution eighty-six years later. In an effort to make the colony serve the crown better, duties had been raised and were being vigorously collected. The tanning of hides in the colony was forbidden, as was the distillation of liquor. An embargo was placed on unmilled grain, which hurt the farmers. After a long period of economic growth and substantial political autonomy, these new and burdensome regulations produced a popular rebellion that for a year displaced British sovereignty.[27]

The American Revolution itself fits the J-curve and deserves more than the brief mention here given. Again prolonged economic growth and political autonomy produced continually rising expectations. They became acutely frustrated when, following the French and Indian War (which had cost England so much and the colonies so little), England began a series of largely economic regulations having the same purpose as those directed against New York in the preceding century. From the 1763 Proclamation (closing to settlement land west of the Appalachians) to the Coercive Acts of April, 1774 (which among other things, in response to the December, 1773 Boston Tea Party, closed tight the port of Boston), Americans were beset with unaccustomed manifestations of British power and began to resist forcibly in 1775, on the Lexington-Concord road. A significant decline in trade with England in 1772[28] may have hastened the maturation of colonial rebelliousness.

The curve also fits the French Revolution, which again merits more mention than space here permits. Growing rural prosperity, marked by steadily rising land values in the eighteenth century, had progressed to the point where a third of French land was owned by peasant-proprietors. There were the beginnings of large-scale manufacture in the factory system. Constant pressure by the bourgeoisie against the state for reforms was met with considerable hospitality by a government already shifting from its old landed-aristocratic and clerical base to the growing middle class. Counter to these trends, which would *per se* avoid revolution, was the feudal reaction of the mid-eighteenth century, in which the dying nobility sought in numerous nagging ways to retain and reactivate its perquisites against a resentful peasantry and importunate bourgeoisie.

But expectations apparently continued rising until the growing opportunities and prosperity rather abruptly halted, about 1787. The fiscal crisis of the government is well known, much of it a consequence of a 1.5 billion livre deficit following intervention against Britain in the American war of independence. The threat to tax the nobility severely — after its virtual tax immunity — and the bourgeoisie more severely may indeed be said to have precipitated the revolution. But less well-known is the fact that 1787 was a bad harvest year and 1788 even worse; that by July, 1789 bread prices were higher than they had been in over 70 years; that an ill-timed trade treaty with England depressed the prices of French textiles; that a concurrent bumper grape crop depressed wine prices — all with the result of making desperate the plight of the large segment of the population now dependent on other producers for food. They had little money to buy even less bread. Nobles and bourgeoisie were alienated from the government by the threat of taxation; workers and some peasants by the threat of starvation. A long period of halting but real progress for virtually all segments of the population was now abruptly ended in consequence of the government's efforts to meet its deficit and of economic crisis resulting from poor crops and poor tariff policy.[29]

The draft riots that turned the city of New York upside down for five days in July, 1863 also follow the J-curve. This severe local disturbance began when conscription threatened the lives and fortunes of workingmen whose enjoyment of wartime prosperity was now frustrated not only by military service (which could be avoided by paying $300 or furnishing a substitute — neither means being available to poor people) but also by inflation.[30]

Even the riots in Nyasaland, in February and March, 1959, appear to follow the pattern of a period of frustration after expectations and satisfactions have risen. Nyasaland workers who had enjoyed the high wages they were paid during the construction of the Kariba dam in Rhodesia returned to their homes and to unemployment, or to jobs paying $5 per month at a time when $15 was considered a bare minimum wage.[31]

One negative case — of a revolution that did not occur — is the depression of the 1930s in the United States. It was severe enough, at least on economic grounds, to have produced a revolution. Total national private production income in 1932 reverted to what it had been in 1916. Farm income in the same year was as low as in 1900; manufacturing as low as in 1913. Construction had not been as low since 1908. Mining and quarrying was back at the 1909 level.[32] For much of the population, two decades of economic progress had been wiped out. There were more than sporadic demonstrations of unemployed, hunger marchers, and veterans. In New York City, at least 29 people died of starvation. Poor people could vividly contrast their own past condition with the present — and their own present condition with that of those who were not seriously suffering. There were clearly audible rumbles of revolt. Why, then, no revolution?

Several forces worked strongly against it. Among the most depressed, the mood was one of apathy and despair, like that observed in Austria by Zawadzki and Lazarsfeld. It was not until the 1936 election that there was an increased turnout in the national election. The great majority of the public shared a set of values which since 1776 had been official dogma — not the dissident program of an alienated intelligentsia. People by and large were in agreement, whether or not they had succeeded economically, in a belief in individual hard work, self-reliance, and the promise of success. (Among workers, this non-class orientation had greatly impeded the establishment of trade unions, for example.) Those least hit by the depression — the upper-middle class businessmen, clergymen, lawyers, and intellectuals — remained rather solidly committed not only to equalitarian values and to the established economic system but also to constitutional processes. There was no such widespread or profound alienation as that which had cracked the loyalty of the nobility, clergy, bourgeoisie, armed forces, and intelligentsia in Russia. And the national political leadership that emerged had constitutionalism almost bred in its bones. The major threat to constitutionalism came in Louisiana; this leadership was unable to capture a national party organization, in part because Huey Long's arbitrariness and demagogy were mistrusted.

The major reason that revolution did not nonetheless develop probably remains the vigor with which the national government attacked the depression in 1933, when it became no longer possible to blame the government. The ambivalent popular hostility to the business community was contained by both the action of government against the depression and the government's practice of publicly and successfully eliciting the cooperation of businessmen during the crucial months of 1933. A failure then of cooperation could have intensified rather than lessened popular hostility to business. There was no longer an economic or a political class that could be the object of widespread intense hatred because of its indifference or hostility to the downtrodden. Had Roosevelt adopted a demogogic stance in the 1932 campaign and gained the loyalty to himself personally of the Army and the F.B.I., there might have been a Nazi-type "revolution," with a potpourri of equalitarian reform, nationalism, imperialism, and domestic scapegoats. Because of a conservatism in America stemming from strong and long attachment to a value system shared by all classes, an anti-capitalist, leftist revolution in the 1930s is very difficult to imagine.

SOME CONCLUSIONS

The notion that revolutions need both a period of rising expectations and a succeeding period in which they are frustrated qualifies substantially the main Marxian notion that revolutions occur after progressive degradation and the de Tocqueville notion that they occur when conditions are improving. By putting de Tocqueville before Marx but without abandoning either theory, we are better able to plot the antecedents of at least the disturbances here described.

Half of the general, if not common, sense of this revised notion lies in the utter improbability of a revolution occurring in a society where there is the continued, unimpeded opportunity to satisfy new needs, new hopes, new expectations. Would Dorr's rebellion have become such if the established electorate and government had readily acceded to the suffrage demands of the unpropertied? Would the Russian Revolution have taken place if the Tsarist autocracy had, quite out of character, truly granted the popular demands for constitutional democracy in 1905? Would the Cairo riots of January, 1952 and the subsequent coup actually have occurred if Britain had departed from Egypt and if the Egyptian monarchy had established an equitable tax system and in other ways alleviated the poverty of urban masses and the shame of the military?

The other half of the sense of the notion has to do with the improbability of revolution taking place where there has been no hope, no period in which expectations have risen. Such a stability of expectations presupposes a static state of human aspirations that sometimes exists but is rare. Stability of expectations is not a stable social condition. Such was the case of American Indians (at least from our perspective) and perhaps Africans before white men with Bibles, guns, and other goods interrupted the stability of

African society. Egypt was in such a condition, vis-à-vis modern aspirations, before Europe became interested in building a canal. Such stasis was the case in Nazi concentration camps, where conformism reached the point of inmates cooperating with guards even when the inmates were told to lie down so that they could be shot.[33] But in the latter case there was a society with eternally induced complete despair, and even in these camps there were occasional rebellions of sheer desperation. It is of course true that in a society less regimented than concentration camps, the rise of expectations can be frustrated successfully, thereby defeating rebellion just as the satisfaction of expectations does. This, however, requires the uninhibited exercise of brute force as it was used in suppressing the Hungarian rebellion of 1956. Failing the continued ability and persistent will of a ruling power to use such force, there appears to be no sure way to avoid revolution short of an effective, affirmative, and continuous response on the part of established governments to the almost continuously emerging needs of the governed.

To be predictive, my notion requires the assessment of the state of mind — or more precisely, the mood — of a people. This is always difficult, even by techniques of systematic public opinion analysis. Respondents interviewed in a country with a repressive government are not likely to be responsive. But there has been considerable progress in gathering first-hand data about the state of mind of peoples in politically unstable circumstances. One instance of this involved interviewing in West Berlin, during and after the 1948 blockade, as reported by Buchanan and Cantril. They were able to ascertain, however crudely, the sense of security that people in Berlin felt. There was a significant increase in security after the blockade.[34]

Another instance comes out of the Middle Eastern study conducted by the Columbia University Bureau of Applied Social Research and reported by Lerner.[35] By directly asking respondents whether they were happy or unhappy with the way things had turned out in their life, the interviewers turned up data indicating marked differences in the frequency of a sense of unhappiness between countries and between "traditional," "transitional," and "modern" individuals in these countries.[36] There is no technical reason why such comparisons could not be made chronologically as well as they have been geographically.

Other than interview data are available with which we can, from past experience, make reasonable inferences about the mood of a people. It was surely the sense for the relevance of such data that led Thomas Masaryk before the first World War to gather facts about peasant uprisings and industrial strikes and about the writings and actions of the intelligentsia in nineteenth-century Russia. In the present report, I have used not only such data — in the collection of which other social scientists have been less assiduous than Masaryk — but also such indexes as comparative size of vote as between Rhode Island and the United States, employment, exports, and cost of living. Some such indexes, like strikes and cost of living, may be rather closely related to the mood of a people; others, like value of exports, are much cruder indications. Lest we shy away from the gathering of crude data, we should bear in mind that Durkheim developed his remarkable insights into modern society in large part by his analysis of suicide rates. He was unable to rely on the interviewing technique. We need not always ask people whether they are grievously frustrated by their government; their actions can tell us as well and sometimes better.

In his *Anatomy of Revolution,* Crane Brinton describes "some tentative uniformities" that he discovered in the Puritan, American, French, and Russian revolutions.[37] The uniformities were: an economically advancing society, class antagonism, desertion of intellectuals, inefficient government, a ruling class that has lost self-confidence, financial failure of government, and the inept use of force against rebels. All but the last two of these are long-range phenomena that lend themselves to studies over extended time periods. The first two lend themselves to statistical analysis. If they serve the purpose, techniques of content analysis could be used to ascertain trends in alienation of intellectuals. Less rigorous methods would perhaps serve better to ascertain the effectiveness of government and the self-confidence of rulers. Because tensions and frustrations are present at all times in every society, what is most seriously needed are data that cover an extended time period in a particular society, so that one can say there is evidence that tension is greater or less than it was N years or months previously.

We need also to know how long is a long cycle of rising expectations and how long is a brief cycle of frustration. We noted a brief period of frustration in Russia after the 1881 assassination of Alexander II and a longer period after the 1904 beginning of the Russo-Japanese War. Why did not the revolution occur at either of these times rather than in 1917? Had expectations before these two times not risen high enough? Had the subsequent decline not been sufficiently sharp and deep? Measuring techniques have not yet been devised to answer these questions. But their unavailability now does not forecast their eternal inaccessibility. Physicists devised useful temperature scales long before they came as close to absolute zero as they have recently in laboratory conditions. The far more complex problems of scaling in social science inescapably are harder to solve.

We therefore are still not at the point of being able to predict revolution, but the closer we can get to data indicating by inference the prevailing mood in a society, the closer we will be to understanding the change from gratification to frustration in people's minds. That is the part of the anatomy, we are forever being told with truth and futility, in which wars and revolutions always start. We should eventually be able to escape the embarrassment that may have come to Lenin six weeks after he made the statement in Switzerland, in January, 1917, that he doubted whether "we, the old [will] live to see the decisive battles of the coming revolution." [38]

[1] The *Communist Manifesto* of 1848 evidently antedates the opposing idea by about a year. See Edmund Wilson, *To the Finland Station* (Anchor Books edition), New York: Doubleday & Co. (n.d.), p. 157; Lewis S. Feuer, *Karl Marx and Friedrich Engels: Basic Writings on Politics and Philosophy*, N. Y.: Doubleday & Co., Inc., 1959, p. 1. The above quotation is from Karl Marx and Frederick Engels, "Wage Labour and Capital," *Selected Works in Two Volumes*, Moscow: Foreign Languages Publishing House, 1955, vol. 1, p. 94.

[2] A. de Tocqueville, *The Old Regime and the French Revolution* (trans. by John Bonner), N. Y.: Harper & Bros., 1856, p. 214. The Stuart Gilbert translation, Garden City: Doubleday & Co., Inc., 1955, pp. 176–177, gives a somewhat less pungent version of the same comment. *L'Ancien régime* was first published in 1856.

[3] Revolutions are here defined as violent civil disturbances that cause the displacement of one ruling group by another that has a broader popular basis for support.

[4] The full report is Ancel Keys et al., *The Biology of Human Starvation*, Minneapolis: University of Minnesota Press, 1950. See J. Brozek, "Semi-starvation and Nutritional Rehabilitation," *Journal of Clinical Nutrition*, 1, (January, 1953), pp. 107–118 for a brief analysis.

[5] E. A. Cohen, *Human Behavior in the Concentration Camp*, New York: W. W. Norton & Co., 1953, pp. 123–125, 131–140.

[6] For community life in such poverty, in Mezzogiorno Italy, see E. C. Banfield, *The Moral Basis of a Backward Society*, Glencoe, Ill.: The Free Press, 1958. The author emphasizes that the nuclear family is a solidary, consensual, moral unit (see p. 85) but even within it, consensus appears to break down, in outbreaks of pure, individual amorality — notably between parents and children (see p. 117).

[7] See Angus Campbell et al., *The American Voter*, New York: John Wiley & Sons, 1960, Chap. 15, "Agrarian Political Behavior."

[8] B. Zawadzki and P. F. Lazarsfeld, "The Psychological Consequences of Unemployment," *Journal of Social Psychology*, 6 (May, 1935), pp. 224–251.

[9] A remarkable and awesome exception to this phenomenon occurred occasionally in some Nazi concentration camps, e.g., in a Buchenwald revolt against capricious rule by criminal prisoners. During this revolt, one hundred criminal prisoners were killed by political prisoners. See Cohen, *op. cit.*, p. 200.

[10] See W. W. Rostow, "Business Cycles, Harvests, and Politics: 1790–1850," *Journal of Economic History*, 1 (November, 1941), pp. 206–221 for the relation between economic fluctuation and the activities of the Chartists in the 1830s and 1840s.

[11] This curve is of course not to be confused with its prior and altogether different use by Floyd Allport in his study of social conformity. See F. H. Allport, "The J-Curve Hypothesis of Conforming Behavior," *Journal of Social Psychology*, 5 (May, 1934), pp. 141–183, reprinted in T. H. Newcomb & E. L. Hartley, *Readings in Social Psychology*, N. Y.: Henry Holt & Co., 1947, pp. 55–67.

[12] I am indebted to Beryl L. Crowe for his extensive research on Dorr's Rebellion while he was a participant in my political behavior seminar at the University of California, Berkeley, Spring 1960.

[13] Joseph Brennan, *Social Conditions in Industrial Rhode Island: 1820–1860*, Washington, D. C.: Catholic University of America, 1940, p. 33.

[14] The persistant demand for suffrage may be understood in light of election data for 1828 and 1840. In the former year, only 3600 votes were cast in Rhode Island, whose total population was about 94,000. (Of these votes, 23 per cent were cast for Jackson and 77 per cent for Adams, in contrast to a total national division of 56 per cent for Jackson and 44 per cent for Adams.) All votes cast in the 1828 election amount to 4 per cent of the total Rhode Island population and 11 per cent of the total U. S. population excluding slaves. In 1840, with a total population of 109,000 only 8300 votes — 8 per cent — were cast in Rhode Island, in contrast to 17 per cent of the national population excluding slaves.

[15] A. M. Mowry, *The Dorr War*, Providence, R. I.: Preston & Rounds Co., 1901, p. 114.

[16] There is an excellent summary in B. Brutzkus, "The Historical Peculiarities of the Social and Economic Development of Russia," in R. Bendix and S. M. Lipset, *Class, Status, and Power*, Glencoe, Ill.: The Free Press, 1953, pp. 517–540.

[17] Jacqueries rose from an average of 8 per year in 1826–30 to 34 per year in 1845–49. T. G. Masaryk, *The Spirit of Russia*, London: Allen and Unwin, Ltd., 1919, Vol. 1, p. 130. This long, careful, and rather neglected analysis was first published in German in 1913 under the title *Zur Russischen Geschichts — und Religionsphilosophie*.

[18] Jacqueries averaged 350 per year for the first three years after emancipation. *Ibid.,* pp. 140–141.

[19] The proportion of workers who struck from 1895 through 1902 varied between 1.7 per cent and 4.0 per cent per year. In 1903 the proportion rose to 5.1 per cent but dropped a year later to 1.5 per cent. In 1905 the proportion rose to 163.8 per cent, indicating that the total working force struck, on the average, closer to twice than to once during that portentous year. In 1906 the proportion dropped to 65.8 per cent; in 1907 to 41.9 per cent; and by 1909 was down to a "normal" 3.5 per cent. *Ibid.,* p. 175n.

[20] *Ibid.,* p. 189n.

[21] In his *History of the Russian Revolution*, Leon Trotsky presents data on political strikes from 1903 to 1917. In his *Spirit of Russia*, Masaryk presents comparable data from 1905 through 1912. The figures are not identical but the reported yearly trends are consistent. Masaryk's figures are somewhat lower, except for 1912. Cf. Trotsky, *op. cit.,* Doubleday Anchor Books ed., 1959, p. 32 and Masaryk, *op. cit. supra,* p. 197n.

[22] See Trotsky, *op. cit.,* pp. 18–21 for a vivid picture of rising discontent in the army.

[23] C. Issawi, *Egypt at Mid-Century: An Economic Survey*, London: Oxford University Press, 1954, p. 262. J. & S. Lacouture in their *Egypt in Transition*, New York: Criterion Books, 1958, p. 100, give a figure of over 300,000. Sir R. Bullard, editor, *The Middle East: A Political and Economic Survey*, London: Oxford University Press, 1958, p. 221 estimates total employment in industry, transport, and commerce in 1957 to have been about 750,000.

[24] International Monetary Fund, *International Financial Statistics*, Washington, D. C. See monthly issues of this report, 1950–53.

[25] J. and S. Lacouture, *op. cit.,* p. 99.

[26] England threatened to depose Farouk in February 1942, by force if necessary, if Egypt did not support the Allies. Capitulation by the government and the Wafd caused widespread popular disaffection. When Egypt finally declared war on the Axis in 1945, the prime minister was assassinated. See J. & S. Lacouture, *op. cit.,* pp. 97–98 and Issawi, *op. cit.,* p. 268.

[27] See J. R. Reich, *Leisler's Rebellion*, Chicago: University of Chicago Press, 1953.

[28] See U. S. Bureau of the Census, *Historical Statistics of the United States, Colonial Times to 1957*, Washington, D. C., 1960, p. 757.

[29] See G. Lefebvre, *The Coming of the French Revolution*, Princeton: Princeton University Press, 1947, pp. 101–109, 145–148, 196. G. Le Bon, *The Psychology of Revolution*, New York: G. Putnam's Sons, 1913, p. 143.

[30] The account by Irving Werstein, *July 1863*, New York: Julian Messner, Inc., 1957, is journalistic but to my knowledge the fullest yet available.

[31] E. S. Munger, "The Tragedy of Nyasaland," American Universities Field Staff Reports Service, vol. 7, no. 4 (August 1, 1959), p. 9.

[32] See U. S. Bureau of the Census, *Historical Statistics of the United States: 1789–1945*, Washington, D. C.: 1949, p. 14.

[33] Eugen Kogon, *The Theory and Practice of Hell*, New York: Farrar, Straus & Co., 1950, pp. 284–286.

[34] W. Buchanan, "Mass Communication in Reverse," *International Social Science Bulletin*, 5 (1953), pp. 577–583, at p. 578. The full study is W. Buchanan and H. Cantril, *How Nations See Each Other*, Urbana: University of Illinois Press, 1953, esp. pp. 85–90.

[35] Daniel Lerner, *The Passing of Traditional Society*, Glencoe, Ill.: Free Press, 1958.

[36] *Ibid.*, pp. 101–103. See also F. P. Kilpatrick & H. Cantril, "Self-Anchoring Scaling, A Measure of Individuals' Unique Reality Words," *Journal of Individual Psychology*, 16 (November, 1960), pp. 158–173.

[37] See the revised edition of 1952 as reprinted by Vintage Books, Inc., 1957, pp. 264–275.

[38] Quoted in E. H. Carr, *A History of Soviet Russia*, vol. 1, *The Bolshevik Revolution: 1917–23*, London: Macmillan, 1950, p. 69.

13. Revolution and the Social System

CHALMERS JOHNSON

Students of politics have long been interested in revolutions, for they concern the very heart of politics. Revolutions transfer the locus of authority within political systems (occasionally transforming the sources of authority themselves), and they are also evidence of the failure of politics — instances of social change pursued by other than normal means. But when the student of politics undertakes the systematic analysis of revolutionary behavior, he can only conclude that the malady of begged questions flourishes endemically in this subdiscipline. He may find the distinction between political and social revolution flatly stated;[1] he may find the category of "great revolutions" proposed as a species of incipient typology;[2] and he will discover that many writers view revolution as the product of psychological pressures — of frustrated expectations,[3] of the contribution of "undesirables" to human affairs,[4] or of the persistence of millenarist responses to social catastrophe.[5] No less an authority than Hannah Arendt leaves the student with the impression that constitution making, strictly defined, is the essence of revolutionary behavior,[6] and she also leaves him wondering whether all instances other than the American and French revolutions are "mere" rebellions. One can get lost in this forest without ever entering the jungle of distinctions among social, industrial, technological, and cultural revolutions.

So great a tradition of confusion is not lightly ignored. Revolutions offer data for the social scientist that appear to defy generalizations, to say nothing of other dangers. Historians lie crouching in their stacks waiting to pounce upon the juicy suggestion of comparability between, say, the events in the Vendée (1789–96) and the Mau Mau uprisings. While the student may sympathize with this impatience at comparisons that slight significant differences, he can only smile when these same historians occasionally feast themselves on bellestristic comparisons wholly devoid of conceptual rigor. These remarks are by way of indicating that I hope to open a dialogue concerning the sociology of revolution, but that I do not propose to, or imagine that I can, finish it here.

Half the battle will lie in answering the question, "What is revolution?"; but the constructing of definitions at the outset is a sterile and often tautological balancing of many different impressions. The phenomenon of revolution must first be placed within and related to the social system in which it occurs, and it must be considered in the light of what is known about social change and political development. However, the word "revolution" as understood here must be differentiated from its use in such phrases as "industrial revolution," "America — the permanent revolution," and so forth. The invention of the cotton gin does not constitute an instance of revolution for present purposes. In order to make this distinction, we require a working definition of revolution upon which many political scientists might agree for the sake of discussion. There are many from which we might choose; Sigmund Neumann's is standard. Revolution to him is "a sweeping, fundamental change in political organization, social structure, economic property control and the predominant myth of a social order, thus indicating a major break in the continuity of development." [7] That will do as a starter, subject to later qualification.

There are two general types of questions to be raised concerning revolutions as defined above: (a) the analytic question, or what causes revolution — any revolution?; and (b) the synthetic question, or, given the genus "revolution," what are its species and how are they related? Although it is useful for purposes of research to distinguish these two questions, they are inseparable parts of the general question, "What is revolution?" Therefore, it is suggested that the reader reserve judgment on the attempt at answering the former question until the second has been considered.

THE CAUSES OF REVOLUTION

When Hannah Arendt writes in the first paragraph of *On Revolution*, "For revolutions, however one may be tempted to define them, are not mere changes," [8] she has indicated at the outset the one thing that all revolutions are: changes. Revolution is a form of change within the social system; not *mere* change, but change nonetheless. Revolution is not a unique social phenomenon; there exist functional equivalents of revolution — namely, other forms of social change — and questions directed at discovering the causes of social change and identifying the level in the social system at which social change occurs are relevant to the problem of the causes of revolution. As a kind of social change, revolution is "the most wasteful, the most expensive, the last to be chosen; but also the most powerful, and therefore always appealed to in what men feel to be a last resort."[9]

And what causes social change? We put this question not because we hope to answer it to everyone's satisfaction, but in order to introduce the series of models and assumptions that will be most helpful as a foundation for the analysis of social change.[10] Our point of departure in analyzing social change is the model of a functionally integrated social system — a system whose members cooperate with each other by "playing" various "roles" that, taken together, permit the whole system to "function." This basic model is well known in contemporary social science; it is the primary construct upon which "structural-functional" analysis rests.[11] Within the framework of this model, we hope to show that revolution is a form of social change undertaken in response to specific conditions of the social system, and that it occurs at a particular stage in the system's efforts to resolve functional difficulties.

One notoriously misunderstood problem with this model of society is that it portrays the social system in a state of equilibrium; it is supposed that the model is useless (or worse) for analyzing social change because of its static bias.[12] Obviously, a changing system is not one in equilibrium; conversely, there is no place for change in an equilibrium system. But this is not an either/or proposition; "equilibrium" is not a real condition but a concept. An equilibrium social system is an ideal type, and the concept of equilibrium is only a reference point for measuring change. No other interpretation of a system's equilibrium, least of all a normative one, is permissible.[13] Since an equilibrium system is not a changing system, a changing system is one that is out of balance. What puts a social system (as here conceived) out of equilibrium?

We believe that society can best be understood as a functionally integrated system. In such a system, if one of the various component structures does not function in the way that it must in order to maintain equilibrium, then first the affected substructure and then, if no remedial action occurs, the entire system will move out of equilibrium. The condition that causes the disequilibrium, and that demands remedial action in order to restore or to create a new equilibrium, we call *dysfunction*. Dysfunction is a potential condition of any functionally integrated system, and dysfunctional conditions within an imbalanced social system vary in degree of severity over a broad range from slight to mortal. Dysfunctional conditions are caused by pressures (whether they are external or internal is a distinction that is relevant only in an historical case) that compel the members of a substructure to do their work, or view their roles, or imagine their potentialities differently from the way that they did under equilibrium conditions. The pressures that cause dysfunction (e.g., technological discoveries, imperialism, and many others discussed below) we call *sources* of dysfunction. In this context, *social change* is action undertaken to alter the structure of the system for the purpose of relieving the condition of dysfunction (in one or more of the system's substructures or, occasionally, throughout the entire structure).

Dysfunction is the condition that demands the response of social change — and of revolution. But what distinguishes revolutionary change from other forms of social change? Two considerations are relevant here: revolution occurs because non-violent evolution is not occurring, and revolution occurs in response to a distinct condition of the system that we call "multiple dysfunction." With regard to the first point, we note that a distinctive characteristic of revolutionary change is the employment of physical violence to relieve dysfunction. "Revolutionary" changes — in the popular sense of changes of great magnitude — that are not initiated by violent alteration of the system are instances of some other form of social change. Big changes are not necessarily revolutionary changes, or else the word merely means "big change." In specifying why revolutionary change is violent, we must refer to the fact that non-violent change has not previously taken place in the dysfunctional system.[14] Social violence is the appropriate response to intransigent resistance; it occurs because known methods of non-violent change are blocked by the ruling elite. That is to say, revolution is politics continued at the level of a violent physical showdown. It takes two to make a revolution, and one of these two is always the status quo elite. The revolutionaries — those recognizing the dysfunctional situation in the face of elite intransigence — are not necessarily the masses; they may be an intrinsic elite (say, a corps of officers) challenging the socially recognized extrinsic elite. Or they may be the masses. (Whatever damage may have to be done to Leninism or to the flamboyantly cynical "iron law of oligarchy," it is an error to suppose that the masses will never rise without guidance.)[15] Of course, if the elite is not intransigent, simple change will occur, dysfunction will be relieved, and no revolution will take place. Therefore the target elite must be blocking change in a revolutionary situation. These considerations say nothing about who will emerge victorious when the revolution occurs; that question is related to the condition of one particular subsystem — the army — which will be considered later.

In distinguishing revolutionary change from other, non-violent forms of change in terms of the failure of the latter to relieve dysfunctional conditions, we are oversimplifying actual revolutionary situations. Simple change in response to conditions of dysfunction may be occurring, but it may be an inappropriate or an insufficient response, it may be outrun by spreading dysfunctions or by an accelerator (see below), or it may itself produce other dysfunctions (which may, in turn, produce the "anarchistic" type of revolution, different from the one that simple change sought to forestall). True conservatives may attempt to maintain the continuity of a dysfunctional system (particularly of its integrating myth) by reforming and adjusting the system to changed circumstances. But if they fail to relieve dysfunction to a level at which revolution is inappropriate, or if an accelerator intervenes before such relief is completed, revolution will occur — and it will be directed against them.

It seems hardly necessary to say that dysfunction in the system of elite recruitment is an important element in hastening a revolution. In some instances, a caste-type of elite (e.g., the First and part of the Second Estate) which is no longer the intrinsic elite of the system may, by its actions, promote revolution. In other cases, the elite may be open to rising groups of representatives from the intrinsic elite (even, although rarely, in colonial situations); and such an elite may be implementing policies intended to relieve dysfunction. If only the structure of social mobility within a system is dysfunctional, this can probably be corrected by non-violent change — that is, either by redefining the criteria of the elite or by clipping its powers (e.g., the Lords' Reform). Regardless of the qualities of an elite and of the actions it is taking to relieve dysfunction, if change eventually takes a revolutionary form, the system elite will be attacked violently by the revolutionaries. Such an occurrence is, empirically, a mark of revolution.

The second criterion of revolution we call "multiple dysfunction." At the present stage of knowledge about social systems and social change, it is not possible to measure "amounts" of dysfunctions in a system. If we could, we would be able to describe distinctive conditions of the social system in response to which revolution is the appropriate mode of social change. In lieu of such precision, however, we still require a criterion of "appropriateness." There exists a level of dysfunctional conditions below which revolution (purposive political violence) is not appropriate regardless of how intransigent the elite may be in opposing efforts to relieve it. On the other hand, even if the elite is not intransigent, or is no longer intransigent after a period of initial vacillation, there are levels of dysfunctional conditions that transcend the adjustment capabilities of a system. Revolution will occur in these cases unless the elite acts first and declares its bankruptcy by abdication, resignation, or by otherwise terminating the old order non-violently.

One way to illustrate the need for a criterion of level, or size, of social ills that makes revolution appropriate is by an example. The economy of the United States was dysfunctional during the Great Depression; similarly, during the period of rapid industrialization in England there was considerable dysfunction in the system of property ownership and the supply of labor. But most of the other substructures or "planes" of the societies, including their integrative myths, remained functional, although at an impaired level of efficiency. The response to these instances of dysfunction was non-violent change: the New Deal on the one hand, and the abolition of the Corn Laws (1846) and the Enclosure Acts (1760–1830), on the other.

These examples are far from ideal — both British and American societies came very close to revolution in the periods mentioned — but they do suggest that social systems may survive extraordinary dislocations without experiencing revolutions so long as certain conditions are met. These conditions are: the existence of the social problems (dysfunctions) must be clearly recognized by the elites as well as by the ordinary members of the system; basic agreement on the need for change must exist; and the sector (substructure) in which the dysfunction prevails must be capable of being isolated within the general context of the social system. If the dysfunction cannot be identified or isolated, it will — like cancer or (as the French Army in Algeria called it) *pourrissement* — metastasize and lead to revolution. It is a people's awareness of the actual, or incipient, metastasis of social ills that causes the "loss of confidence" or "rupture of consensus" that so often presages revolutionary conditions. We suggest as a rule-of-thumb criterion of revolutionary change (in addition to the criterion of elite intransigence in the face of system dysfunction) that dysfunction must "metastasize" beyond one substructure in order for revolution to become appropriate. Generally speaking, no single condition of dysfunction (with the possible exception of agricultural production in certain types of systems) can disintegrate a social system; in a revolutionary situation, more than one of the relatively separable substructures of a system is dysfunctional and . . . dysfunction is systematic, including the integrative myth.[16] Let us emphasize that this is a rule-of-thumb criterion; we are as yet unable to describe, in the macroscopic terms of the model of the functionally integrated social system, precisely what are revolutionary conditions. This point will be explored further in our discussion of an "accelerator" — i.e., the final aggregate of pressure (source of dysfunction) on a system that leads at once to revolution.

Let us summarize the analysis of revolution to this point. Revolution is one form of social change in response to the presence of dysfunction in the social system. Revolution is the preferred method of change when (a) the level of dysfunctions exceeds the capacities of traditional or accepted methods of problem solving; and when (b) the system's elite, in effect, opposes change. (The second point is analytically necessary because it is possible to conceive of a system that is *completely* dysfunctional without being revolutionary. A natural catastrophe, such as a severe earthquake, might produce this condition.) Conversely, a system elite may resolutely oppose changes advocated by special groups within the system, but no revolutionary situation is generated because the system is basically functional. Revolution is the acceptance of violence in order to bring about change.

The practical importance of these ideas for the study of revolution lies in the usefulness of the concepts of a functionally integrated social system and of its potential for becoming dysfunctional. An investigator will need to discover the *sources* of dysfunction and to estimate the effects of these sources upon a given system. This is a formidable task, but it is also one toward which a great deal has already been accomplished by social scientists. We do not intend to stop here and offer a library-sized footnote on this point, both because that is not our primary purpose in this discussion and because identification of the sources of dysfunction is not the final step in an analysis of the causes of revolution. The sources of dysfunction are numerous. They include: cyclical pressures (hereditary kingship or single party rule without purge may produce dysfunctions), the global diffusion of industrial culture, imperialism, the discovery of new territories, the elaboration of new metaphysical beliefs, technical and scientific discoveries, and so forth.[17] For purposes of the present discussion, our procedure is to assume that such events do affect social systems and do occasionally generate conditions of dysfunction extensive enough to swamp the capacities of the system for adjustment.

If this assumption has been made, it is probably time to come down from the model to specific cases and to insert a small *sabot* into the machinery. For the fact of the matter is that the concepts of multiple dysfunctions and elite intransigence will never, by themselves, reveal what causes a revolution in a concrete case. We may observe that various dysfunction-inducing phenomena — rapid industrialization, relative deprivation, incoherence in the myth, and so forth — are affecting a social system; and we may allege that these pressures cause a given revolution. But the only way we know that these dysfunction-inducing elements cause the revolution is because the revolution has occurred. At the same time, we are frequently confronted with examples of dysfunctional systems — one in which known dysfunction-inducing elements are present and in which an effective sense of dysfunction does exist — but in which no revolution is occurring. (Note that the distinction is not that some societies are dysfunctional while the population has no subjective awareness of it. It is rather that some dysfunctional systems *with* self-conscious revolutionaries fully mobilized do not experience revolution, while other, similarly placed systems do.) The problem is to explain what triggers revolution, *given* sufficient "background" dysfunctions in the system to make revolution probable (e.g., as in contemporary South Africa, or Brazil, or Indonesia). It is usual at this point in the analysis of revolution (in either Marxist or non-Marxist studies) to resort to various metaphors of "ripeness," or "tides," or "waves," but let us try to be more specific.

Multiple dysfunction plus elite intransigence plus X equals revolution. And what is X? For X, let us substitute the concept of "accelerators of dysfunction." This is another rule-of-thumb concept adduced to help us understand the final causes of revolutions; in a truly sophisticated use of structural-functional theory, it ought not to be isolated. By X (or "accelerators of dysfunction") all we mean to identify are particularly intense *sources* of dysfunction that make their effects felt suddenly and powerfully, and that typically constitute the final aggregate in a growing burden of dysfunctional conditions. Accelerators are occurrences that catalyze or throw into relief the already existent revolutionary level of dysfunctions. They do not of themselves cause revolution; but when they do occur in a system already bearing the necessary level of dysfunctions (i.e., in more than one substructure), they will provide the sufficient cause of the immediately following revolution.

As accelerators we have in mind such events as the rise of a prophet or a messiah in a dysfunctional society, causing a revolutionary millenarian movement to develop; or the effects of organizational activities by a revolutionary party that is attempting to create a rebel infrastructure in order to launch a militarized mass insurrection; or, very commonly, the defeat in a foreign war of a system already suffering from multiple dysfunctions. The metaphor which best expresses our present understanding of accelerators is the heart patient who unexpectedly contracts pneumonia — a disease that a healthy man can normally survive — and who then succumbs from the combined effects of the two. A dysfunctional society can similarly experience a long-term gradual secular decline until some occurrence, such as defeat in war, suddenly accelerates or intensifies the burdens under which it labors. We submit that when such an accelerating event occurs the level of dysfunctions will rise dramatically, previous elite efforts (if any) to relieve dysfunctions will be rendered instantly irrelevant, and revolution will take place. Let us consider one such accelerator — defeat in war — in some detail, both because it has played a decisive part in promoting many revolutions and because it is related to one crucial determinant of the success or failure of any given revolutionary attempt — namely, the position of the army.

The intimate connection between defeat in war and the onset of revolution is obvious from many historical examples. The fall of Bonaparte and the defeat of the French Army by the Prussians in 1871 created for the first time in modern history the typical situation favorable to the revolutionary capture of political power; this situation was characterized by the neutralization or destruction of the regular army, by loss of confidence on the part of the people of France in any peaceful solution of social ills, and by the vastly increased significance of a military force of armed workers (the Paris National Guard). Defeat in war also accelerated dysfunctional conditions to the flash point in Russia (1905 by the Japanese, and 1917 by the Germans); in Hungary, Germany, and Turkey in 1918; in China and Yugoslavia during World War II; following the defeat of the Red Army in the Ukraine in 1941; in the French, British, and Dutch colonies in east Asia in 1941–42; and external war sufficiently accelerated the dysfunctions in the Irish system to bring the revolution of 1916–23 to the surface. Defeat in war, as an accelerator, shatters the myth of sovereignty, exacts sacrifices — even the supreme sacrifice — from a society's members for an unpopular system, and completes the crippling of an already creaking system; most important, it opens the doors to revolution because of its effects on the army.

The central position of armed forces in revolutions has been hinted at, but not explored, by several writers in the past. Hannah Arendt includes in her list of events that made up the occasion of the first (to her) "true" revolution "the defection of the royal troops before a popular attack." [18] Pettee asserts, in passing, that "there is general agreement that a revolution cannot commence until the army is no longer loyal to the old regime";[19] and, more analytically, that "the force of habit in the dull minds of functionaries and soldiers will keep a regime going long after it could be voted out of power if voting were possible."[20] Regarding the Bolshevik Revolution, Lichtheim notes, "That the revolution ultimately took the form that it did was not of course entirely due to Lenin. The war provided Lenin with the opportunity which, had it been postponed even for a few years, would probably not have recurred." [21] But why "of course," and what was the nature of this "opportunity"?

Lenin himself offers an answer in his *April Theses*, where he advocates seizing the moment rather than waiting for the development of capitalism, and again in Condition Four of the Twenty-one Conditions for admission to the Comintern: "The obligation to spread Communist ideas includes the special obligation to carry on systematic and energetic propaganda in the Army. Where such agitation is prevented by emergency laws, it must be carried on illegally." [22] From a Marxist point of view, Plekhanov may have thought that Lenin was an "alchemist of revolution" in 1917,[23] but Lenin and Trotsky intuitively recognized that 1917 was a year of heightened possibilities — a year in which an accelerator (defeat in war) was superimposed upon the multiple dysfunctions of Russian society. It is strange and significant that Lenin forgot these "opportunities" later when writing basic strategy for the Communist International — a failure that contributed to the Comintern's lack of success. The Chinese Communists, if they were to form a Fifth International today, would move Condition Four to first place, although they would express it differently.

Possibly the oldest and best-known comment on the relationship between the army and revolution is Napoleon's rebuke of the king for failing to use the army fully when the *sans-culottes* stormed the Tuileries (1792): "Comment a-t-on pu laisser entrer cette canaille? Il fallait en balayer quatre ou cinq cents avec du canon et le reste courrait encore." [24] The English equivalent, a "whiff of grapeshot," has since entered the language of political violence as the specific antidote to revolution. Katherine Chorley, alone among writers on revolution familiar to me, places primary stress on the position of the army in a revolutionary situation, and states this as a general principle: "Insurrections cannot be permanently won against a professional army operating its technical resources at full strength. They can be won only when the introduction of some extraneous factor cripples the striking power of the professional fighting forces for one reason or another. The part to be played by the army is, therefore, decisive in any revolution, whether social or nationalist." [25]

This is an important principle. By definition, revolution requires the use of violence by members of the system in order to cause the system to change. If the old order simply wheezes to a stop and a new system is formed on the basis of virtually unanimous agreement among conscious political participants (e.g., as with the end of the Tokugawa shogunate and its replacement by the Meiji oligarchy),[26] there has been change but not revolution. Practically speaking, revolution involves armed insurrection, and this implies a clash with professionally trained and equipped troops at the command of the extrinsic elite. Both the success or failure of armed insurrection and, in the age of committed professional revolutionary brotherhoods, commonly even the decision to attempt revolution rest, therefore, upon the attitude (or the revolutionaries' estimate of that attitude) that the armed forces will adopt toward the revolution. The application of science to warfare has created armed forces that are invincible to any force other than a similarly equipped and trained armed force. Regardless of the amount of dysfunction in a system, armed insurrection is futile against a modern army *if* the army can, or will, exploit its capabilities to the full; and to the extent that a given revolution is rationally calculated, its timing as well as its success or failure will depend upon this consideration.

Some revolutions do rest on calculation and will not be launched if there exists no chance of success; in the Sinn Fein revolution, for example, the Irish Republican Brotherhood took the decision secretly, on September 9, 1914, to open revolt against Britain during the war, and this decision led to Easter Week, 1916.[27] Therefore, the study of the determinants of success or failure is also relevant to the problem of cause. But it is equally possible for incapacitation of the army and the decision to revolt to coincide fortuitously. If they coincide, fortuitously or otherwise, the revolution has a good chance of success; if they do not coincide, it will probably fail. Thus, since the success or failure of any revolution depends upon the role of the armed forces, it is important that students of revolution know something about what causes conditions of dysfunction in the military substructure of the social system.

The first generalization to be made about the position of armies in revolutionary situations is that the officer corps and the rank-and-file have radically different attitudes toward the social system. Officers play elite roles in a social system and, as a consequence, are more commonly the targets of revolution that the participants in it. However, if officers are mobilized by one of the sources of dysfunction, they may make an elitist revolution — i.e., a coup d'état. Other things being equal, officers' revolutions will always succeed when the officers are in fact commanding the army. They need not worry about armed force being used against them when making their revolution (e.g., as in the installation of the Korean junta in May 1961). Because of this advantage, officers' revolutions are very frequent in dysfunctional societies, and they are commonly prompted by relatively insignificant accelerators.

Defeat in war, as an accelerator, has different effects on officers and on the rank-and-file. While defeat in war may serve as an accelerator of revolution within the total context of the system, it may also serve as a prime *source* of dysfunction within the specific context of the officer corps (whether or not the system is already afflicted with multiple dysfunctional conditions). There are many examples of this effect. German officers turned toward politics after the defeat of 1918; Pétain's rapid rise was directly related to the disaster of 1940; Arab military dictatorships were promoted by the debacles of 1948 in Palestine and 1956 in Sinai; and it is common to draw attention to French army defeats in Indochina and Algeria and to the surrenders in Syria, Morocco, and Tunisia as sources for army support of de Gaulle in 1958. The rebellious impulse was not wholly embryonic in the American officer corps after Korea (e.g., MacArthur), nor in the British military elite during and after Malaya and Cyprus.

Officers are military leaders, but they are never "apolitical." The "overlapping group memberships" of military officers are more extensive and encompass greater sectors of power than those of most other citizens except for the supreme elite. For this reason there are, of course, many sources of revolutionary mobilization for officers other than defeat in war. If one wishes to explore the causes of the Franco revolution in Spain, or of the coups d'état by the Japanese Army in the 1930's, or of the military governments in many of the new nations, one must investigate different sources and accelerators of dysfunctional conditions from those being considered here.[28] In any such investigation one is likely to be impressed by the high frequency of success in officers' revolutions. While the reasons for this are obvious, it calls attention to officers' revolts that fail (e.g., Rastenburg, 1944),[29] where the crucial element seems to be that the system elite possesses armed forces other than the formal system's defense forces.

The army rank-and-file, on the other hand, is characterized by having an autonomous morale to the greatest extent that any group can have in an integrated social system. And this fact is of immense relevance to an analysis of the causes of revolution. A revolutionary level of dysfunctions may exist and persist over long periods of time without ever affecting the rank-and-file of the army. Part of the logic of military organization is to cut off troops from civilian interests so that they will accept their officers' orders unquestioningly. The effectiveness of a modern army — the use of weapons, and of men as instruments — depends upon the creation of a calculable least common denominator of the men's abilities when working together. All of this is expressed by military scientists in the term "discipline." A practical policy usually adopted to further discipline is isolating the rank-and-file from the populace. Disciplined, professional troops obey their officers, including the order to suppress armed insurrection, *unless* some event disintegrates the rank-and-file. But there are actually very few occurrences which will shatter the subculture of a professional rank-and-file. One striking example of the immunity of troops to sources of dysfunction that mobilize other segments of the population (regardless of the troops' class interests or backgrounds) is found in the work of the Italian Communist theorist, Gramsci. He records a conversation between a Sardinian worker in Turin and a soldier of the Sassari (provincial capital of Sardinia) Brigade, which had been sent to Turin to suppress the insurrectionary general strike of August 1917. (The worker begins the dialogue.)

"What have you come to do in Turin?"

"We have come to fire on the gentry who are on strike."

"But it is not the gentry who are on strike, it is the poor people and the workers."

"Here they are all gentry: they wear collars and ties; they earn thirty *lire* a day. I know poor people and how they dress; at Sassari, yes, there are many poor people; all we countryfolk are poor and we earn one and a half *lire* a day."

"But I too am a worker and I am poor."

"You are poor because you are a Sardinian."

"But if I go on strike with the others, will you fire on me?"

The soldier reflected a little, then putting his hand on my shoulder, said:

"Listen, when you go on strike with the others, stay at home!" [30]

What does break the unity of the rank-and-file of an army? Fraternization with the populace may weaken unity and allow revolutionary sentiment to enter. A mutiny wholly related to internal military problems may open the door to revolution via, so to speak, a windfall.[31] But defeat in war is the one common occurrence that dissolves well-trained military formations. Chorley emphasizes the consequences of defeat above all others: "Experience proves that on the whole the rank and file will never disintegrate on their own initiative through the impact of direct political emotion. Some other and stronger solvent is required. The supreme solvent for the disintegration of the rank and file is an unsuccessful war. . . . There can be little doubt that under modern conditions the last stages of an unsuccessful war provide the surest combination of circumstances for a successful revolutionary outbreak." [32] Defeat in war of a potentially revolutionary dysfunctional system will accelerate the dysfunctions by adding telling new problems to the already burdened system, and it may destroy the ultimate weapon against revolution held by the status quo elite — the army (which may also join the revolution). If the defeated army can be reorganized by the status quo elite before the revolution is victorious, or if undefeated troops can be mobilized, then of course the revolution may still be defeated. But many of the most famous revolutions that have succeeded have occurred in the context of defeat of the status quo regime in external war.

Defeat in war as an accelerator is double-edged. The concept of accelerator itself is not intended to indicate anything necessary about the outcome of revolution; it is a device constructed to help us conceptualize the occurrence of revolution. But the accelerator of defeat in war tells us something about why some revolutions occur when they do and also why they may succeed. Not all accelerators will relate to the army, and the success or failure of some revolutions depends upon influences on the army other than the elements that brought the level of dysfunctions to the revolutionary boiling point.

Let us summarize again the causes of revolution. Multiple dysfunctions plus elite intransigence cause revolution. This is true of all types of revolution. In order to investigate actual revolutions, it is helpful to employ the *ad hoc* concept of "accelerators of dysfunction," so that we may isolate the final dysfunction-inducing element that brings a given revolution into being. One typical accelerator is defeat in war. Success or failure in revolution depends upon whether or not the status quo elite can employ modern armed forces working at their full capacities against the revolutionaries.

[1] *Encyclopedia of the Social Sciences,* XIII (1934), 367.

[2] George Sawyer Pettee, *The Process of Revolution* (New York, 1938), p. xi.

[3] James C. Davies, "Toward a Theory of Revolution," *American Sociological Review,* XXVII: 1 (February 1962), 5–19.

[4] Eric Hoffer, *The True Believer* (New York, 1951).

[5] Norman Cohn, *The Pursuit of the Millennium* (New York, 2nd ed., 1961).

[6] *On Revolution* (New York, 1963), pp. 142–43.

[7] "The International Civil War," *World Politics,* I:3 (April 1949), 333–34, n. 1.

[8] *Op. cit.,* p. 13.

[9] Pettee, p. 96.

[10] For an excellent critical summary of all the major theories of social change see J. A. Ponsioen, *The Analysis of Social Change Reconsidered* (The Hague, 1962).

[11] The standard works are Marion J. Levy, *The Structure of Society* (Princeton, 1952); Robert K. Merton, *Social Theory and Social Structure* (Glencoe, 1949); and the books of Talcott Parsons. For an early statement of the logic of the approach see A. R. Radcliffe-Brown, "On the Concept of Function in Social Science," *American Anthropologist,* N.S., XXXVII (July–September 1935), 394–402. For a recent application of structural-functional method see William C. Mitchell, *The American Polity* (New York, 1962).

[12] Cf. W. E. Moore, "A Reconsideration of Theories of Social Change," *American Sociological Review,* XXV (December 1960), 811.

[13] This point is made ably by Lewis Coser, "Social Conflict and the Theory of Social Change," *British Journal of Sociology,* VII (September 1957), 206–7, n. 22.

[14] "Non-violent change" does not imply non-forcible change. For the distinction between force and violence in political analysis see Sheldon Wolin, "Violence and the Western Political Tradition," *American Journal of Orthopsychiatry,* XXXIII: 1 (January 1963), 15–28.

[15] Many jacqueries illustrate this point; Eric Hobsbawm's remarks on the Andalusian anarchist movement offer a concrete example: "Spanish anarchism, more than any other political movement of our period, was almost exclusively elaborated and spread by peasants and small craftsmen. As Diaz del Moral points out, unlike Marxism it attracted practically no intellectuals, and produced no theorist of interest. Its adepts were hedge-preachers and village prophets; its literature, journals and pamphlets which at best popularized the theories elaborated by foreign thinkers: Bakunin, Reclus, Malatesta. With one possible exception – and he a Galician – no important Iberian theorist of anarchism exists. It was overwhelmingly a poor men's movement and it is thus not surprising that it reflectetd the interests and aspirations of the Andalusian *pueblo* with uncanny closeness." *Primitive Rebels* (Manchester, 1959), p. 83.

[16] Pettee supports the view, in different terms, that no single social grievance (dysfunction) can cause revolution. *Op. cit.,* p. 162.

[17] On this subject, cf.: G. L. Arnold, "The Imperial Impact on Backward Countries," *St. Antony's Papers,* II (1957), 104–25; Karl W. Deutsch, "Social Mobilization and Political Development," *American Political Science Review,* LV: 3 (September 1961), 493–514; George M. Foster, *Traditional Cultures: And the Impact of Technological Change* (New York, 1962); E. J. Hobsbawm, *The Age of Revolution, 1789–1848* (Cleveland and New York, 1962); John H. Kautsky, *Political Change in Underdeveloped Countries* (New York, 1962); and Arnold Toynbee, *The World and the West* (New York, 1953).

[18] *On Revolution,* p. 41.

[19] *The Process of Revolution,* p. 104.

[20] *Ibid.,* p. 103.

21 George Lichtheim, *Marxism: An Historical and Critical Study* (London, 1961), p. 349. Cf. Milovan Djilas, *The New Class* (New York, 1957), pp. 22–23.

22 In Gunther Nollau, *International Communism and World Revolution: History and Methods* (London, 1961), p. 341.

23 Samuel Baron, "Between Marx and Lenin: George Plekhanov," in *Revisionism*, p. 49.

24 Joseph Calmette, *Napoléon Ier* (Paris, 1952), p. 36.

25 Katherine C. Chorley, *Armies and the Art of Revolution* (London, 1943), p. 23.

26 I am aware that qualifications are necessary for this example, but the Meiji Restoration is more an instance of non-violent change than of revolution.

27 D. J. Goodspeed, *The Conspirators: A Study of the Coup d'Etat* (London, 1962), p. 45. See also Edgar Holt, *Protest in Arms: The Irish Troubles, 1916–1923* (New York, 1961), and Dorothy Macardle, *The Irish Republic* (London, 1938).

28 See S. E. Finer, *The Man on Horseback: The Role of the Military in Politics* (New York, 1962).

29 The anti-Hitler coup attempted by members of the German officer corps, July 20, 1944. See Goodspeed, *op. cit.*, pp. 172–207.

30 Antonio Gramsci, "The Southern Question," in *The Modern Prince and Other Writings* (London, 1957), p. 35.

31 See T. H. Wintringham, *Mutiny: Being a Survey of Mutinies from Spartacus to Invergordon* (London, 1936).

32 Chorley, *op. cit.*, pp. 108, 38–39.

14. The Marxian Revolutionary Idea

ROBERT C. TUCKER

In his parting word about Marx at Highgate Cemetery, Engels character-ized his friend as "before all else a revolutionist." This was a true summa-tion of Marx both as a man of action and as a thinker. For as a theorist Marx was before all else a theorist of revolution. The revolutionary idea was the keystone of his theoretical structure. Marxism, as he fashioned it with the assistance of Engels, was in its essence a theory and program of revolution.

Like many another powerful teaching that becomes the ideology of movements carried on in its name and dedicated to its realization, Marxism has not always reflected its original inspiration. It has tended at various times to lose its "revolutionary soul" (to borrow Lenin's phrase). This hap-pened with the revisionist Marxism of Eduard Bernstein, who forsook even the revolutionary theory of Marx in favor of a doctrine of evolutionary socialism. It was reflected too, if less obviously, in the orthodox Social Democratic Marxism of Karl Kautsky, whose fidelity to Marxist revolution-ism in theory went along with an abandonment of it in practice. A similar if less pronounced discrepancy is becoming apparent in some present-day Soviet Marxism. Its exponents rather resemble the German orthodox Marx-ists of a generation ago in their tendency to talk Marxist revolutionism while pursuing a relatively unrevolutionary policy. But all these instances of the decline of the revolutionary impulse in the Marxist movement belong to the story of what happened to Marxism after its founder's death. Our subject here is Marx's Marxism, and this was the *Weltanschauung* of a revolutionist.

It was so, moreover, from the beginning of his intellectual career. Marx's first independent act of theorizing, contained in notes to his doctoral dissertation of 1841, was an essay on the necessity of a complete revolutionary transformation of the world in the name of the "realization of philosophy," meaning the Hegelian philosophy of humanity's apotheosis in history. Marx was thus in some sense committed to the idea of world revolution prior to his conversion to the notions of socialism or communism, and he only accepted the latter a year or so later when he found a way of assimilating them into the philosophy of world revolution that he had evolved as a Young Hegelian philosopher. Marxism was born of this fusion in an intellectual process recorded in Marx's *Economic and Philosophic Manuscripts of 1844,* whose publication in the present century presaged a new era in Marxian scholarship in the West.

As a form of socialist doctrine, then, Marxism was inseparable from the idea of revolution. It conceived of socialism or communism (these two terms were always used by Marx and Engels more or less interchangeably) as a radically new state of the world, and of man in the world, which was to be achieved by revolutionary means. This, according to the *Communist Manifesto,* was what distinguished Marxism from the main currents of earlier socialist thought and most earlier socialist movements, which were essentially reformist rather than revolutionary.

The idea of revolution is present in nearly everything that Marx wrote. It is the theoretical axis of his early philosophical writings. It is the *leitmotif* of his great political pamphlets on the 1848 events, the *coup d'état* of Louis Bonaparte, and the Paris Commune. It informs almost all that he has to say on the strategy and tactics of the Communist movement. It is a favorite subject in the voluminous correspondence that he carried on with Engels and others. And his major work, *Capital,* together with his other economic writings, is essentially a political economy of revolution, an inquiry into the conditions of capitalism's revolutionary self-destruction. In a basic sense, therefore, revolution was the master theme of Marx's thought, and an exposition of the Marxian revolutionary idea in complete form would be nothing other than an exposition of Marxism itself as a theoretical system.

It follows that the Marxian revolutionary idea has as many dimensions of meaning as Marxism itself. Revolution for Marx is a social, an economic, a technological, a political, a legal, and an ideological phenomenon. It is even, in its way, a natural phenomenon, for it involves the appropriation of the man-produced world of material objects that Marx describes in his early writings as "anthropological nature" or the "nature produced by history." Furthermore, revolution means transformation of man himself. In Marx's words, "the whole of history is nothing but a continual transformation of human nature."[1] He especially looks to the future Communist revolution as the source of a radical transformation of man or "change of self," and here we touch upon the moral and religious dimensions of the Marxian revolutionary idea. Finally, revolution for Marx is a historical category. The whole of his theory of revolution is set in the frame of the materialist conception of history. His theory of society is a theory of society-in-history, and his theory of revolution is a theory of the transformations of society in history, a theory of history itself as a process of man's revolutionary evolution.

Understandably, much of the literature of and about Marxism as a revolutionary theory has a political orientation. Marxists beginning with Marx and Engels have been deeply concerned with the politics of revolution, and very many students of Marxist thought have interested themselves in this too. It is perhaps a measure, and in any event a symptom of this bias, that Lenin's principal treatise on Marxist revolutionary theory, *State and Revolution,* is almost wholly devoted to revolution as a political phenomenon. Now there is no doubt about the great importance of this aspect of the Marxian revolutionary idea. For Marx, every revolutionary transition from one social epoch to the next involves a political revolution — the overthrow of the existing state and conquest of political power by the revolutionary class. But to Marx's way of thinking this is not the core of the revolutionary process. Here, indeed, we encounter a certain difference of emphasis between the Marxism of Marx and that of Lenin, for whom the political process of revolution was of supreme importance both theoretically and practically. Without ever slighting the significance of the political dimension, Marx, on the other hand, always saw *social* revolution as the fundamental revolutionary fact. In the analogy between revolution and the birth process that recurs from time to time in his writings, the social revolution is the whole organic process by which a new society comes into being; the political revolution is merely a momentous incident occurring at the climax of the process. The principal question to be considered here, therefore, is what Marx meant by a social revolution.

In *The Social Revolution,* an influential little volume written in 1902, Kautsky answered this question in behalf of German orthodox Marxism by defining social revolution as "the conquest of political power by a previously subservient class and the transformation of the juridical and political superstructure of society, particularly in the property relations. . . ." As Kautsky himself pointed out, this was a "narrower" view than Marx's own as expressed in the well-known preface to the *Critique of Political Economy.*[2]

It also suffered from superficiality. Although the supplanting of one ruling class by another is integral to social revolution as Marx conceives it, this formula fails to convey the substance of what he means by social revolution. To arrive at a more adequate formulation, we must first consider Marx's conception of society.

Marx the sociologist is inseparable from Marx the theorist of history. The view of society presented in his own mature writings and those of Engels is governed at every point by the basic premises of the materialist conception of history. One of the expressions of this is the fact that Marx as a social theorist recognizes the existence of societies on a national scale but does not see in them the fundamental unit of society. For him the real social unit is the species, the human collectivity at a given stage of its historical growth process. Each such stage constitutes a social epoch dominated by a particular "social formation." Any national society, such as the German, English, or French, is but a concrete expression of human society as a whole in the given epoch, although it may be a case that exhibits the general pattern of the existing or emerging social formation most clearly and in most mature development. Marx, for example, saw contemporary English society as the model and most advanced form of a universally emerging "bourgeois society" of the modern epoch. This bourgeois or capitalist social formation, now becoming dominant on a world scale, had been preceded in history by feudal, antique, and Asiatic social formations, each of which represented the dominant form of human society in its time. An important implication for Marx's theory of revolution is that he always sees a social revolution as universal in scope, as an event of world history. It may express itself here and there on a national scale, as in the French Revolution of 1789, but such a happening is only a partial and local manifestation of a world revolutionary process. For Marx all social revolutions are world revolutions.

The materialist conception of history underlies all other aspects of Marx's sociology. Man being essentially a producer and his history a "history of production," society, to Marx's way of thinking, is in essence a productive system and process. The constitutive fact of society is that human productive activity, especially the material production on which all else depends, is social in nature. In other words, production, for Marx, is a process going on not simply between man and nature but also between man and man. This "social process of production" is the core of the social process per se. Human society is fundamentally a society of production, a set of "social relations" that men enter in the activity of producing. In the familiar formulation from *The Critique of Political Economy*, the social relations of production constitute the "basis" (*Basis, Grundlage*) of society, over which rises an institutional superstructure, and to which there corresponds a social mind expressed in various "ideological forms" (religion, philosophy, art, etc.).[3]

Since primitive times, according to Marx, the society of production has been a divided one. The social relations of production have been property relations between the immediate producers and those who, by virtue of their ownership and control of the means of production, have been able to appropriate the producers' surplus product as private property: slaves and slave owners in ancient society, serfs and landowning nobles in feudal society, proletarians and capitalists in modern bourgeois society. Each one of these sets of social relations of production has been, in Marx's terminology, a specific form of the division of labor (*Teilung der Arbeit*) in production. This concept has a twofold meaning in Marxist thought. First, it refers to occupational specialization in all its forms, beginning with the division between mental and physical labor and between town and country. But it also refers to what may be called the "social division of labor," meaning the division of society as a whole into a nonworking minority class of owners of the means of production and a nonowning majority class of workers. As already indicated, Marx holds that such a social division of labor has been the essential feature of human society so far in history. The prime expression of the division of labor is the class division of society. In Engels' words, "It is . . . the law of the division of labor which lies at the root of the division into classes." [4] Marx makes the same point more concretely when he writes: "In so far as millions of families live under economic conditions of existence that divide their mode of life, their interests and their culture from those of other classes, and put them in hostile contrast to the latter, they form a class." [5]

The determination of the class structure of society by the nature of the social division of labor may be expressed in Marxist terms by saying that every society is characterized by its particular "mode of production" (*Produktionsweise*). Contrary to what one might suppose, this key concept of Marx's is primarily social rather than technological in content, although it has a technological element. The mode of production is not equated with the productive techniques or material "productive powers," which are included, rather, under the heading of "means of production" (*Produktionsmittels*). What Marx means by the mode of production is the prevailing mode of labor or productive activity as conditioned by the existing state of technology or means of production. Now productive activity, as already noted, is for Marx exclusively and essentially social activity. Accordingly, the mode of production is equivalent to the social relations of production viewed, as it were, dynamically or in motion, together with the conditioning state of technology. And inasmuch as the social relations of production have, so far in history, been successive froms of the division of labor in production, the various historical modes of production may be described as forms of productive activity within the division of labor. Production within the division of labor has thus been the *general* mode of production in history. In Engels' formulation, "The basic form of all former production is the division of labor, on the one hand within society as a whole, and on the other, within each separate productive establishment." [6]

The central thesis of Marxist sociology is that every society in history has been characterized and, indeed, shaped in all its manifold aspects, by the nature of its particular mode of production as just defined. In ancient society the mode of production was slave labor, or productive activity performed within the social division of labor between master and slave. In feudal society was serf labor, or productive activity performed within the social division of labor between nobleman and serf. And in modern bourgeois society it is wage labor, or productive activity carried on within the social division of labor between capitalist and proletarian. In every instance — runs the argument of Marx and Engels — the mode of productive activity has been the definitive fact of the social epoch, the determinant of the character of society in all of its superstructural expressions: political, legal, intellectual, religious, etc. To this way of thinking, every society fundamentally *is* its mode of production. Speaking of wage labor, for example, Marx writes: "Without it there is no capital, no bourgeoisie, no bourgeois society." [7]

It follows that a social revolution in the Marxist definition is a change in the mode of production with consequent change of all subordinate elements of the social complex. The feudal revolution would be defined in these terms as the change from slave labor to serf labor resulting in the general transition to feudal society; the bourgeois revolution as the change from serf labor to wage labor resulting in the general transition to bourgeois society. Historically, argue Marx and Engels, these revolutions in the mode of production and therewith, in society as a whole, have been changes of the *specific form* of productive activity within the social division of labor. They have been revolutions within the general mode of production based upon the division of labor in society and the production process, i.e., upon the class division of society and occupational specialization.

Turning to the technological aspect of the theory, Marx holds, as pointed out above, that every historical mode of production has been conditioned by the nature of the available means of production or state of technology. As he puts it in a vivid passage, "The windmill gives you society with the feudal lord; the steam-mill, society with the industrial capitalist." [8] On this view, the rise of a new technology, a new set of material productive powers, will necessarily prove incompatible with the perpetuation of a mode of production associated with an older one. The rise of modern manufacturing technique led to the bourgeois revolution against serf labor and feudal society and to the enthronement of wage labor as the mode of production. Marx further supposes that the transition from early capitalist manufacture to "machinofacture" in the Industrial Revolution has brought into existence a new set of productive powers — modern machine industry — that must and will prove incompatible with the perpetuation of wage labor as the prevailing mode of production, since the new powers of production cannot be fully developed under the system of wage labor. The destruction of wage labor, and with it, of bourgeois society, in a proletarian and communist revolution is the predicted outcome. Reasoning in this way, Marx and Engels frequently define a social revolution as the resolution of a conflict or "contradiction" between the productive powers and the social relations of production, or as a "rebellion" of the former against the latter.

This "rebellion" is not understood in mechanistic terms. A social revolution originates in technological change but actually takes place, according to Marx, in a revolutionary social-political movement of producers as a class. It is not the material powers of production themselves, such as the machines, that rebel against the mode of production; it is the men involved. This presents no problem of inconsistency for Marx, however, because he views working man as the supreme productive power. "Of all the instruments of production," he writes, "the greatest productive power is the revolutionary class itself." [9] It is this productive power whose uprising constitutes the actual revolutionary process. The revolt of the productive powers against the existing social relations of production finds its manifestation in class warfare in the economic arena, culminating in the political act of revolutionary overthrow of the state. If revolutions are the locomotives of history, class struggles are the locomotives of revolution.

What motivates a class of producers to rise against and revolutionize a mode of production and its social superstructure? Suffering caused by material want and poverty is one of the immediate driving forces of revolutionary action, especially with the modern proletariat. But in Marx's view, material satisfaction as such is never the actual aim of the revolutionary class in its struggle to overthrow and transform an established social formation. What is fundamentally at issue in the class struggle and in social revolution, as in history as a whole, is not the consumption interest but the production interest — this, however, defined in a special Marxist way.

It is man as frustrated producer rather than man as dissatisfied consumer who makes a revolution, and the need of man as producer is freely to develop and express his manifold powers of productive activity, his creative potentialities in material life. Under this heading Marx includes both the productive powers within men and also industry, or the material productive forces employed by the human species in its productive interaction with nature. Thus in *Capital* he describes the material forces of production as "the productive organs of men in society" and compares them with "the organs of plants and animals as productive instruments utilized for the life purposes of these creatures." [10] His thesis is that the source of revolutionary energy in a class is the frustration of man in his capacity of producer, his inability to develop new powers of production to the full within the confines of an existing mode of production or socioeconomic order. The bourgeois revolution, for example, results from the inability of the rising capitalist class to develop the new productive powers inherent in manufacture within the cramping confines of feudal relationships. And he believes — wrongly as it turns out — that a proletarian revolution will be necessitated by the impossibility of fully developing the productive potentials of modern machine industry within the confines of wage labor as the mode of production. In each instance the effect of the revolution is to eliminate a set of social relations of production that has become, in Marx's Hegelian terminology, a "fetter" upon the evolving productive powers of the species, and thus to "emancipate" these powers. The goal of all social revolutions, according to Marx, is freedom. But freedom in a specifically Marxist sense: the liberation of human creativity.

The obstacle to freedom, the source of human bondage, and thus the evil in history, is the division of labor. This fundamental proposition of Marxist theory has several meanings, all closely interconnected. Not only does each successive historical form of the social division of labor between an owning and a producing class become an impediment to the free development of emergent productive powers; the social division of labor is also a force for enslavement in that it subjects the producer class to the acquisitive urge of the owning class, the insensate greed for possession and power that Marx sees as the dominant motive force of historical development up to now. (We read in Engels: ". . . it is precisely the wicked passions of man — greed and the lust for power — which, since the emergence of class antagonisms, serve as levers of historical development. . . ." [11]) Man's life in production is thereby transformed into a life of drudgery, of forced labor or "alienated labor" as Marx called it in his manuscripts of 1844, and always continued to view it. Above all is this true in modern society where the worker, although legally free to seek employment wherever he will, is bound down to wage labor, which Marx calls "wage slavery" and describes, in *Capital* and other writings, as productive activity performed in servitude to the capitalist profit mania, the "werewolf hunger" for surplus value.[12]

Finally, every social division of labor is an enemy of human freedom, for Marx, in so far as it enforces occupational specialization as a way of life. "For as soon as labor is distributed, each man has a particular, exclusive sphere of activity, which is forced upon him and from which he cannot escape. He is a hunter, a fisherman, a shepherd, or a critical critic, and must remain so if he does not want to lose his means of livelihood. . . ." [13] It is Marx's view, in other words, that a division of labor under which men are compelled by economic necessity to devote themselves throughout life to one particular form of work activity, be it a specialized economic function, or a noneconomic calling such as a profession or governmental work, or even intellectual activity, is slavery. And this is by no means a vew that Marx, as it were, "outgrew" in the later development of his system. Thus he speaks, in the famous passage of "The Critique of the Gotha Program," on the higher phase of communist society, of the disappearance there of "the *enslaving* subordination of man to the division of labor." [14]

Underlying their condemnation of the division of labor is the philosophical anthropology inherited by Marxism from earlier German philosophy, Hegelianism in particular. Marx's *Mensch* resembles Hegel's *Geist* in that both are imbued with a need for totality of life experience, for creative self-expression in all possible fields of activity. Thus Hegel speaks of Spirit as "manifesting, developing and perfecting its powers in every direction which its manifold nature can follow," adding: "What powers it inherently possesses, we learn from the variety of products and formations which it originates." [15] It is the same with the human species in Marx's image of it. And in view of the fact, noted earlier, that Marx constructed the materialist conception of history on the premise that Hegel's *Geist* was a mystified representation of man in his history of production, it is not at all surprising that the Marxist view of human nature shows this strain of Hegelian philosophical romanticism. Like Hegel's *Geist*, Marx's humanity develops and perfects its productive powers in every possible direction, and man as an individual shows this same tendency. A man's inherent bent — that is, his nature — is to become, as Marx puts it in *Capital*, "an individual with an all-round development (*total entwickelte Individuum*), one for whom various social functions are alternative modes of activity." [16] Consequently, the division of labor is unnatural and inhuman, an impediment to a human being's self-realization. A person who applies himself to one single life activity is alienated from his real nature, hence a self-estranged man. "In the division of labor," writes Engels, "man is divided. All other physical and mental faculties are sacrificed to the development of one single activity." [17] Even the division between town and country, between urban and rural labor, is on this view "a subjection which makes one man into a restricted town-animal, the other into a restricted country-animal." [18] And to be restricted to a particular kind of life or occupation is to be unfree.

The enslavement and dehumanization of man under the division of labor is a dominant theme of *Capital* and the other writings of Marx and Engels on capitalism and the proletarian revolution. They morally condemn capitalism not for being unjust as a mode of distribution (indeed, they hold that it is the only just one in terms of the sole applicable criterion of judgment), but for being inhuman as a mode of production, an unnatural way for man to carry on his productive activity. What makes it so, they maintain, is above all the hideous extreme to which it develops the division of labor. The capitalist mode of production — wage labor in the service of the drive for surplus value — is a system of division of labor within the division of labor. That is, within the social division of labor between capitalist and proletarian, which Marx calls the "despotism" or "dictatorship" of capital, the worker is subjected to an increasingly oppressive form of occupational specialization. He is reduced to a mere detail worker bound down to a single mindless operation endlessly repeated. As capitalism evolves from the stage of "simple cooperation" into that of manufacture, it brings "the lifelong annexation of the worker to a partial function," which "cuts at the very roots of the individual's life" and "transforms the worker into a cripple, a monster, by forcing him to develop some highly specialized dexterity at the cost of a world of productive impulses and faculties — much as in Argentina they slaughter a whole beast simply in order to get its hide or its tallow." [19]

Moreover, the inner dynamism or dialectic of capitalist production is such — according to Marx's argument — that the functions become increasingly subdivided, the specialization more and more minute, and hence the fragmentation of man more and more monstrous, as the employers, under relentless pressure of the competitive struggle, strive for greater and greater technical efficiency through mechanization of work processes. The total dehumanization of the worker comes about finally under modern "machinofacture," the descriptions of which in *Capital* resemble a *Modern Times* without the Chaplinesque anodyne of humor. Of this stage — which he treats as the stage in which capitalist production becomes wholly unendurable — Marx writes, for example, that here all the means for developing production "mutilate the worker into a fragment of a human being, degrade him to become a mere appurtenance of the machine, make his work such a torment that its essential meaning is destroyed; estrange from him the intellectual potentialities of the labor process in very proportion to the extent to which science is incorporated into it as an independent power. . . ." [20] Progress in technological terms thus spells regress in human terms, and man sinks to the nadir of wretchedness and self-estrangement in the production process at the very time in history when his productivity, technically speaking, reaches its peak and, providentially, brings with it the possibility of a thoroughly human way of life in production. This "slavery" and "labor torment" under the division of labor represents a major share of the ever increasing misery of the proletarian masses that drives them at length, according to Marx's argument, to revolt against their mode of production.[21]

The human history of production is thus also a history of revolution. The growth process of society is propelled by a series of revolutions that center in major changes in the mode of production as a social process. These changes have been the very substance of the social history of man. It is true that Marx speaks of an "epoch of social revolution" as something occurring when a form of society nears its end.[22] Yet in a way he believes that history has always, up to now, been a revolutionary process, that man has always been at least incipiently in revolt against his mode of production. This, after all, is the sense of the opening statement of the *Communist Manifesto* that the whole of recorded history is a history of class struggles. Why it should be so on Marx's premises has been made clear. Every mode of production in history has been a form of productive activity within the division of labor, and the division of labor is bondage. In Marx's mind, history is a succession of man's revolutionary breaks out of the prison-house of the division of labor for freedom in the life of production.

No sooner has a new mode of production within the division of labor been established by revolutionary means than it too starts to become a "fetter" upon the ever developing productive powers of the species. Such is the revolutionary dialectic of the historical process as Marx expounds it. Just as men begin to die biologically as soon as they are born, so societies embark upon their own revolutionary dissolution virtually from the time of their revolutionary "birth pangs." So we shall look in vain in Marx for a sociology in the sense of a theory of how societies work. His is a sociology of revolution, a theory of the internal dysfunctioning of the several historical societies, leading to their disintegration and downfall. Thus *Capital*, which is Marx's principal treatise on society and revolution as well as his chief work of economic theory, treats of the revolutionary rise, development, and fall of bourgeois society. And the whole thrust of the book is toward the "knell" of the proletarian revolution that it tolls in conclusion.

The proletarian revolution is described in various places in Marx and Engels as the overthrow of the bourgeois state and establishment of a proletarian dictatorship, accompanied by the forcible seizure and socialization of private property in the means of production. But this is only the external manifestation, the "phenomenal form" of the communist revolution. Like all previous social revolutions, the revolution of communism is, for Marx and Engels, essentially a change in the mode of production. And like all past revolutions again, it is both destructive, in that it does away with an old mode of production, and constructive, in that it establishes a new one in its place.

This presentation of the socialist or communist revolution, and hence of socialism or communism itself, as turning principally upon production, stands in substantial contrast with the view of most socialists, both of that time and now, that socialism is mainly concerned with the distribution problem. Marx and Engels were well aware of this difference. They often called attention to it in emphatic and even polemical terms. They argued that changes in the mode of distribution, leading to the practice of distribution according to needs in the higher phase of communist society, would only be incidental by-products of a change in the mode of production that would be the real substance of the revolution of communism. Marx, for example, attacks what he calls "vulgar socialism" for the "consideration and treatment of distribution as independent of the mode of production, and hence the presentation of socialism as turning principally on distribution." He states in the same passage that "it was in general a mistake to make a fuss about so-called *distribution* and put the principal stress on it." [23] In the same vein Engels pours scorn on Eugen Dühring for basing his "socialitarian" program on the unacceptable proposition that "the capitalist mode of *production* is quite good, and can remain in existence, but the capitalist mode of *distribution* is evil." He comments in this connection on "how puerile Herr Dühring's notions are — that society can take possession of the means of production without revolutionizing from top to bottom the old method of production and in particular putting an end to the old division of labor." [24]

If the communist revolution resembles all past revolutions in that it primarily revolutionizes the old mode of production, it also, according to Marx and Engels, differs from all other revolutions in history; and this thesis on the uniqueness of the projected world communist revolution is of the greatest importance in Marxist thought. The argument is that what undergoes revolutionizing in the communist revolution is not simply a particular form of productive activity within the division of labor (in this case wage labor), but the division of labor as such. Instead of replacing one form of productive activity within the division of labor by another, as the bourgeois revolution replaced serf labor by wage labor, the communist revolution will pave the way for a radically new mode of production that altogether abolishes and transcends the division of labor and therewith "labor" itself, in the sense in which mankind has always known it (i.e., in the sense of "alienated labor" in the terminology of the 1844 manuscripts). As the younger Marx formulated it, "In all revolutions up to now the mode of activity always remained unscathed and it was only a question of a different distribution of this activity, a new distribution of labor to other persons, whilst the communist revolution is directed against the preceding *mode* of activity, does away with *labor,* and abolishes the rule of classes with the classes themselves. . . ." [25] Over twenty years later the older Marx was saying the same thing when he wrote in *Capital* that the "revolutionary ferments" in modern capitalist society have as their aim "the abolition of the old division of labor." [26]

By the abolition of the old division of labor he and Engels mean, first, the abolition of the class division of society into owners of the means of production and nonowning workers. This will spell the abolition of wage labor after an interim during which old habits of working for a remuneration, and also the lack of full material abundance, will enforce a continuation of wage labor in a non-capitalist form, performed for social needs rather than in the service of the drive for profit. The disappearance of the latter as the motive force of production will make possible the withering away of the division of labor in all its subordinate forms—the division between mental and physical labor, between urban and rural labor, between different trades and professions, and between different functions in each. For as soon as man is no longer compelled by the imperatives of greed and need to engage in some one form of productive activity all his life, he will give rein to the natural human tendency (as Marx sees it) to become a universal man—"to do one thing today and another tomorrow, to hunt in the morning, fish in the afternoon, rear cattle in the evening, criticize after dinner, just as I have a mind, without ever becoming hunter, fisherman, shepherd or critic." [27] Within the factory the detail worker, annexed for life to a particular specialized function, will give way to the "individual of all-round development" for whom various functions in production are possible. Marx based this expectation, which may have been prophetic, upon the view that in modern machine industry, where machines themselves do highly specialized work, the technical foundation is established for liberating men from narrow specialization. "Since the integral movement of the factory does not proceed from the worker but from the machine," he reasoned in *Capital*, "there can be a continuous change of personnel without any interruption of the labor process." [28] Machine industry without the division of labor would thus be based upon rotation of jobs among highly trained and versatile machine operators, whose work would become a form of free productive activity owing to the constant variation and to the "almost artistic nature of their occupation." [29]

Since Marx and Engels believe that every form of society fundamentally *is* its mode of production, most of what they have to say about the future communist society (in its "higher phase") is naturally concerned with the anticipated new mode of productive activity. But the latter, as we see, is not analyzed in economic terms. This omission of an economics of communism from the theory of Marx and Engels is entirely logical considering that part of what they mean by communism is *the end of economics*. They assume that with the emancipation of the immensely potent productive forces inherent in modern machine industry from the "fetters" of capitalist wage labor, there will very soon be created a material abundance so great as to satisfy all proper human needs. At this point, which is the entry point into the "higher phase," the historic scarcity of goods and resources ceases, and therewith the need for economics as a theory and practice of allocation of scarce goods and resources. "And at this point," writes Engels, "man in a certain sense separates finally from the animal world, leaves the conditions of animal existence behind him, and enters conditions which are really human. . . . It is humanity's leap from the realm of necessity into the realm of freedom." [30] For Marx and Engels this "leap" is a take-off not into affluence as such, but into the authentically human higher form of existence that man's creative and artistic nature, as they see it, naturally tends toward and for which material well-being is no more than a precondition. The end of economics means the beginning of aesthetics as the keynote of the life of productive activity.[31]

In Marxist theory the communist revolution is the supreme revolution of freedom since it does away not simply with this or that specific form of the division of labor but with all forms, and so with bondage as such. By the same token, this is the last revolution. With production no longer based upon a division of labor in society, there will be no kind of social relations of production that could become a fetter upon the productive powers, and thereby precipitate a further revolutionary upheaval. Accordingly, the communist revolution will bring to an end the historical growth process of humanity — the "pre-history of human society" as Marx called it in a well-known passage.[32] It will mark the maturation of the species, the time when man finally becomes fully human. In his early manuscripts Marx used the terms "humanism" and "transcendence of human self-alienation" to express this idea. Later the German philosophical terminology was abandoned, but the idea was not. The communist revolution continued to be conceived as a revolution of human self-realization.

This self-realization is understood by Marx in both collective and individual terms. On the one hand, it means the completion of the whole historical process of self-development of the species, the becoming of human society. At this point "socialized humanity" (*vergesellschaftete Menschheit*) emerges out of what had been, all through recorded history, a self-divided and inwardly warring human collectivity.[33] The communist revolution, an act of appropriation by the vast majority of the totality of material means of production, is the means by which this final transformation is supposed to take place. The reasoning turns on Marx's view, mentioned earlier, that industry, the total complex of material instruments or powers of production, represents the "productive organs of men in society." Seen in this perspective, the communist revolution is the act by which man in the mass reappropriates his own organs of productive activity, of which he has been dispossessed in history owing to the division of labor in its various forms. By this collective act — runs Marx's argument — the individuals of whom the mass is composed regain their creative potentialities: "The appropriation of a totality of instruments of production is, for this very reason, the development of a totality of capacities in the individuals themselves." [34] This is the basis on which Marx advances the thesis that the change of material circumstances brought about by revolutionary praxis coincides with "change of self." [35]

It follows that man must realize himself on the scale of the species before he can do so as an individual, that there is no self-realization without social revolution. Before the communist revolution, no one can be truly human; afterwards, all can and will become so. Then and then only will free creativity become the characteristic human mode of production, will labor become "not only a means of life but life's prime want." [36] Then only will the human society of production become one in which "productive labor, instead of being a means to the subjection of men, will become a means to their emancipation, by giving each individual the opportunity to develop and exercise all his faculties, physical and mental, in all directions; in which, therefore, productive labor will become a pleasure instead of a burden." [37] Liberated from the acquisitive urge that has always in the past motivated the production process, and also from the slavery of specialization that this has engendered, men will finally become freely creative individuals, accomplished in a multitude of life activities, who produce without being driven to it by the forces of need and greed and who arrange their world according to the laws of beauty.

That the Marxian revolutionary idea has a moral meaning is clear enough. But this dimension would, it seems, be more accurately described as religious than as ethical in nature. Moral teachers desire man to be virtuous according to one or another understanding of virtue; religious ones — Marx among them — want him to be redeemed. In this conneciton it must be said that there is a close relation between revolution and religion. Though the founders of revolutionary movements need not be men of religion, the founders of religions tend in their way to be revolutionaries. They envisage for man a goal of supreme worth that involves his total self-transformation, the revolutionizing of himself as it were, and they give him directions concering the way to the goal. Marx does the same, and on this account may be characterized as a revolutionist of religious formation. The goal had variously been called the Kingdom of God, Paradise, Nirvana, Satori, Salvation; he called it Communism. When he wrote in his eleventh thesis that the point was to change the world, the message was that changing the world outside of man, by revolutionary praxis, was the way to change man himself, totally. There is little question about the religious quality of Marx's vision of the goal. The question that would have to be raised, in an examination of the religious aspect of his thought, is whether he offered valid directions as to the way.

1 *The Poverty of Philosophy* (Chicago: n.d.), p. 160.
2 *The Social Revolution* (1913), pp. 6, 8–9, 27.
3 Marx and Engels, *Selected Works*, Vol. I (Moscow: 1958), p. 363.
4 *Anti-Dühring* (Moscow: 1947), p. 418.
5 *The 18th Brumaire of Louis Bonaparte* (New York: n.d.), p. 109.
6 *Anti-Dühring*, p. 432.
7 Marx, *The Class Struggles in France 1848–1850* (New York, n.d.), p. 42.
8 *The Poverty of Philosophy*, p. 119.
9 *Ibid.*, p. 190.
10 *Capital*, Eden and Cedar Paul, trans. (1933), p. 392n.
11 Engels, *Ludwig Feuerbach*, in Marx and Engels, *Selected Works*, Vol. II (Moscow: 1951), pp. 345–346.
12 *Capital*, p. 269.
13 *The German Ideology* (1947), p. 22.
14 Marx and Engels, *Selected Works*, Vol. II (Moscow: 1951), p. 23. Italics added.
15 *The Philosophy of History* (1956), p. 73.
16 *Capital*, p. 527.
17 *Anti-Dühring*, p. 435.
18 *The German Ideology*, p. 44.
19 *Capital*, pp. 381, 384, 390.
20 *Ibid.*, p. 713.
21 *Ibid.*
22 "Preface to *The Critique of Political Economy*," Marx and Engels, *Selected Works*, Vol. I, p. 363.
23 "Critique of the Gotha Program," Marx and Engels, *Selected Works*, Vol. II, pp. 23–24.
24 *Anti-Dühring*, pp. 443, 445.
25 *The German Ideology*, p. 69.
26 *Capital*, p. 527.
27 *The German Ideology*, p. 22.
28 *Capital*, p. 449.
29 *Ibid.*, p. 405.
30 *Anti-Dühring*, pp. 420–421.
31 For a fuller exposition of this theme in Marxist thought, see *Philosophy and Myth in Karl Marx*, chapter XIII.
32 "Preface to *The Critique of Political Economy*," Marx and Engels, *Selected Works*, Vol. I, p. 364.
33 "Theses on Feuerbach," *The German Ideology*, p. 199.
34 *The German Ideology*, p. 66.
35 "Theses on Feuerbach," *The German Ideology*, p. 198.
36 "Critique of the Gotha Program," Marx and Engels, *Selected Works*, Vol. II, p. 23.
37 *Anti-Dühring*, p. 438.

III

STAGES OF REVOLUTION

INTRODUCTION

INTRODUCTION

Revolutions are natural to the history of man. Thomas Jefferson once wrote: "What country before ever existed a century and a half without revolution? . . . The tree of liberty must be refreshed from time to time with the blood of patriots and tyrants. It is its natural manure."[1] We tend to forget the revolutionary spirit upon which our country was founded. Our own Declaration of Independence asserts "that whenever any form of government becomes destructive of these ends [i.e., life, liberty, and the pursuit of happiness], it is the right of the people to alter or to abolish it, and to institute new government, laying its foundation on such principles and organizing its powers in such form, as to them shall seem most likely to effect their safety and happiness." In his first inaugural address Abraham Lincoln stated that "this country, with its institutions, belongs to the people who inhabit it. Whenever they shall grow weary of the existing government, they can exercise their constitutional right to amend it, or their revolutionary right to dismember or overthrow it." Revolution then is indigenous to our history as it has been to the history of most human societies. But all revolutions have not been alike, and the stages through which revolutions have passed have not been uniform.

In his book *The Revolutionary Idea in France, 1789–1871*, Godfrey Elton states his opposition to the simple periodization of history; dates and events are merely conveniences for historians. Similarly, he states that revolutions do not fit into this periodization since they are less sudden outbreaks than they are the continuation or culmination of a gradual process.[2] It is hard to disagree absolutely with Elton. Revolutions may be seen certainly as rapid or hastened evolution. However, the scholarly isolation of revolutions as distinct events and then their delineation into stages may be useful for understanding the process of revolution.

Revolutions seem to be frequently preceded by calamitous setbacks to society, such as defeat in war and natural disasters. These may be viewed as causative factors in the revolutionary process. But, the value in viewing them as such is limited. The essential value of calamitous setbacks to the revolutionary process lies in the fact that they function as accelerators and intensifiers. Public calamities undermine the loyalty of the population to the established order and may even assure their neutrality or hostility to that order in the beginning stages of a revolution. Thus, the early stages of revolution are usually marked by a growing inability of the establishment to maintain the status quo and by an increasing unwillingness at the bottom to tolerate it. Furthermore, this seems to indicate that revolutions begin somewhat spontaneously, without set plans or blueprints for courses of action. Those that begin with plans usually do not follow the prescribed course, and the plans are scrapped as unworkable once the revolution has begun.

Lenin was both an observer of and a participant in revolutions. He prescribed five rules concerning the techniques of revolution which should characterize the first stages: (1) revolution is a serious business and once begun it should be carried out ruthlessly to the end; (2) revolutionaries must gather superior forces at the right places; (3) offensive action is mandatory; defensive action does not make for a successful revolution; (4) surprise is crucial and the revolution must begin when the forces of the government are scattered; (5) the revolutionists must possess "moral superiority." [3]

In the first selection of Part III, Rex D. Hopper applies what is known as the *natural history* approach to revolutions. He analyzes four stages through which revolutionary movements pass: (1) the preliminary stage of mass (individual) excitement and unrest in which there is widespread but uncoordinated dissatisfaction; (2) the popular stage of crowd (collective) excitement and unrest in which those dissatisfied individuals begin to organize; (3) the formal stage of the formulation of issues and the formation of publics in which the actual revolution breaks out; (4) the institutional stage of legislation and societal organization in which the new government and society are established. These stages provide an elaborate frame of reference for the study of revolutions. In each of them Hopper details the characteristic conditions, the typical behavioral process, the effective mechanisms employed, the types of leaders to emerge, and the dominant social form of collective behavior.

In his brief analysis in the next selection, Heinz Lubasz contends that regardless of how complicated revolutions are, they are fundamentally political events. Nevertheless, the forces generated by a revolution may have lasting consequences that can affect any and all aspects of society. Lubasz discusses three phases into which revolutionary struggles fall — they are not necessarily separate and distinct and may in fact merge into one another: (1) the initial assault on the government; (2) the rule of the new revolutionary government; (3) the defense by the new regime against counterrevolutionary forces, both domestic and foreign. He concludes that revolution, unlike other socio-political processes, is by nature only temporary, and the result of revolution is invariably something less than the total embodiment of the new order it was intended to establish.

We have seen how the differences among men make their actions unpredictable, although we can with some precision anticipate them. Similarly, just as revolutions can be anticipated but not predicted so too can the stages through which revolutions pass. Nothing in the course of revolutions is inevitable, but much is likely. For example, all revolutions must destroy or eliminate one government and attempt, at least, to replace it or reconstruct another. Therefore, the stages outlined in the two selections in this section provide useful frameworks within which revolutions may be examined.

---

[1] Quoted in Henry M. Wriston, "The Age of Revolution," *Foreign Affairs*, 39, 4 (July 1961), 535.

[2] Godfrey Elton, *The Revolutionary Idea in France, 1789–1871* (New York: Longmans, Green and Co., Inc., 1923), pp. 1–3.

[3] D. J. Goodspeed, *The Conspirators* (New York: The Viking Press, 1961), p. 209.

15. The Revolutionary Process

REX D. HOPPER

The hypothesis discussed herein is an example of the use of what is known as the *natural history* approach to the study of human behavior. This approach when applied to revolutionary movements has yielded the postulate that such movements pass through four stages in their development: the Preliminary Stage of Mass (Individual) Excitement, the Popular Stage of Crowd (Collective) Excitement and Unrest, the Formal Stage of Formulation of Issues and Formation of Publics, and the Institutional Stage of Legalization and Societal Organization.[1]

To prevent what we are here doing from being judged as merely another in a series of clever surmises, it is important to realize that the hypothesis just formulated has a history. By collating the work of such pioneer students as Sorokin, Edwards, Gettys, Blumer, and Brinton, it is possible to draw a general picture of revolutionary behavior in which the nature and inter-relationships of the different aspects of a revolutionary movement are rather clearly indicated.[2] The full force of this remark will be lost unless it is remembered that such a generalized description is a necessary prerequisite to any attempt at control; that no such generally accepted description exists at present; that the fragmentary contributions of the works just mentioned represent research on empirical data rather than "armchair philosophizing"; and that the following outline of the natural history of revolutionary movements is a synthesis of research already done and not the personal creation of the writer.

236

Before undertaking to outline the revolutionary process, it is necessary to undergird such a description of revolutionary behavior with a brief statement of the way *human* behavior looks to contemporary students of the "science of human relationships." In answer to the question, "What is human behavior?" there is an increasing tendency to reply that *human* behavior is a function of the development of socially-acquired attitudes toward culturally-held values.[3]

What does this point of view mean when applied to the analysis of the revolutionary process? Expressed otherwise, what happens when one social order collapses and another emerges? It means, first, that any social order or society may be viewed as a sort of moving equilibrium of culturally-held values and socially-acquired attitudes. In relation to the culture, social order, then, consists of a system of relatively orderly values. From the point of view of the people living in the culture and responding to its values, a social order consists of a system of commonly held tendencies to act toward a given system of values. Thus men call the times orderly, speak of social order and organization, and believe that they live in a *cosmos* when the values deposited in their culture satisfy the attitudes in terms of which they tend to act. On the other hand, men deem the times to be out of joint, speak of social disorder and disorganization, and fear that they live in a *chaos* when the values deposited in their culture no longer satisfy their attitudes.

It means, second, that social order is disturbed and the process of social disorganization sets in when for any reason at all attitudes and values begin to diverge.

It means, third, that social change has taken place if and when social disorganization eventuates in the reorganization of attitudes and/or values.

It means, fourth, that significant social change always has to do with change on the institutional level— that is, with changes in the attitudes-values that are deemed to be basically important. Changes on this level are very disturbing and result in great disorganization and unrest until the changed attitudes and their corresponding values have been worked into the institutional structure of the culture and a new social order has been built. Therefore, an understanding of the process of social change on this level is imperative to those interested in doing something about social change.

It means, finally, that *revolutionary* change is precisely that kind of social change which occurs when the basic institutional (i.e., legally enforced) values of a social order are rejected and new values accepted.

We may now ask what a revolutionary movement looks like when historical events are re-examined in terms of the hypothesis which the events themselves have suggested to trained observers. Arranged in terms of the postulated four stages and in a fashion designed to indicate the interdependence of the various features of the movement during each stage, the answer runs as follows.

Of Mass (Individual) Excitement and Unrest

   Characteristic Conditions. In this stage socio-psychological conditions (meaning simply the traits which people tend to manifest in a society where a revolutionary movement may be getting under way) may be grouped under six headings, so arranged as to reveal a socio-psychological sequence or orderliness.

1. General restlessness which manfests itself in:
   a. Wish repression
   b. Development of a balked disposition mind-set
   c. Restless behavior of individuals
   d. Increase in crime, vice, insanity, suicide, agitation, and travel (wandering individuals of all classes, and emigration)
2. The development of class antagonisms as shown by:
   a. The increase in wealth, intelligence, and power of "repressed groups"
   b. The separation of economic power from political power and social distinction
   c. The development of a condition wherein men of ability are shut out from careers of any consequence
3. Marked governmental inefficiency
4. Reform efforts on the part of the government
5. Cultural drift in the direction of revolutionary change
6. Spread and socialization of restlessness as evidenced by:
   a. Increased tension, cramp, and irritation
   b. Increased talk of revolution
   c. Wandering of attention from one individual, object, or line of action to another

   It is suggested that this arrangement of the dominant characteristics of the preliminary stage portrays what happens as a *society* breaks up into a *mass,* a process that is necessarily preliminary to the initiation of a revolutionary movement.

   Typical Process. How may people like this be expected to behave? Or, what process is *typical* of the Preliminary Stage? They will be susceptible to the *milling* process or "circular interaction" as it is sometimes called.

   Borrowed from the language of the cattle ranch, the term is used to describe a type of interaction among people that is quite comparable to the "milling" of a herd of cattle.[4] On the human level milling results from vaguely apprehended unrest on the one hand and from confusion regarding goals on the other. When translated into the terms used in our earlier description of the nature of human behavior, this means that milling occurs in the early stages of the process by which disparity is produced between the attitudes of a group and their social values. This disparity is initially expressed by a sort of unorganized and unformulated restlessness, the causes of which are unknown, hence unrecognized. The diffused nature of the discontent makes impossible the projection of any plan of action and accounts for the random character of behavior at this stage as well as the uncertainty with reference to the ends toward which action should be directed.

Effective Mechanisms. How may people so behaving be influenced? What mechanisms or devices must be employed by those presuming to positions of leadership in the Preliminary Stage? In general terms, of course, the mechanisms employed to control people must be suited to their dominant mood. When applied to the present problem this means that people who exhibit the socio-psychological characteristics already outlined can be influenced by such devices as agitation, suggestion, imitation, propaganda, et cetera. It also means that those men will emerge as leaders who are most able and skilled in the use of such control devices. Thus it may be said that the dominant socio-psychological conditions determine both the nature of the leadership and the choice of mechanisms of social control.

Types of Leaders. What kind of leader will potential "revolutionists" follow? This stage belongs to the *agitator* and, as Blumer has shown, there are two types of agitators who correspond to the two types of situations in which they function.[5]

The first situation is one marked by abuse, unfair discrimination, and injustice, but a situation wherein people take this mode of life for granted and do not raise questions about it. Here the function of agitation is to lead people to challenge and question their mode of living. It serves to create unrest. Hence the agitator is the calm, dignified type who stirs the people not by what he does, but by what he says. Such potential leaders are always present in any society but they never exercise decisive influence unless the situation is *really* characterized by abuses, discrimination, and injustice. And such leaders function very early in the development of a revolutionary movement and are only recognized as real leaders after the fact, so to speak.

If factors — including the activities of the type of agitation just mentioned and which we need not pause to discuss — are favorable, the second type of situation may develop. It is one wherein people are already aroused, restless, and discontented, but where they either are too timid to act or do not know what to do. Here the function of the agitator is to intensify, release, and direct tensions which people already have. Hence the agitator himself is a different type. He is excitable, restless, and aggressive. Such leaders emerge much later in the Preliminary Stage and are much more familiar to us.

Dominant Social Form. In what sort of groupings do such people as we have been describing act? In other words, what is the *form* of elementary collective behavior, or the sort of behavior characteristic of the Preliminary Stage of a revolutionary movement?

It is suggested that possible participants in such a movement constitute a "psychological mass," a form of human collective behavior with the following features: first, the people composing it come from all walks and levels of life; second, the mass is made up of anonymous persons, responding to common influences but unknown to each other; third, because they are unknown to each other, there is little interaction or exchange of experience between the members of the mass; fourth, there is little or no organization on the level of mass behavior.[6]

In short, the nature of the mass is determined by what the people composing it are like. And the people behave as they do because of the characteristics they share. Thus persons who participate in mass behavior do so because the objects of interest which gain their attention lie outside of the local culture and groups and are something for which the mores of the local groups offer inadequate explanations. In consequence, the members of the mass are detached and alienated individuals, both with reference to the mores of their old culture and the new objects of attention. They are in a marginal position. A disparity of attitudes and values has developed and the process of social disorganization has set in.

THE POPULAR STAGE

Of Crowd (Collective) Excitement and Unrest

Whether a movement passes from the preliminary stage of mass (individual) excitement and unrest into this stage depends on the nature of developments in the first stage. The hypothesis under examination does not postulate an inevitable sequence of events. Quite to the contrary, it recognizes that in a variety of ways a possible movement may be indefinitely postponed or completely redirected. For example, governments sometimes use war with another nation as a device for keeping down threatened internal disturbances. Or the unrest may be drained off in non-political directions. This seems to have happened in England when the development of Methodism redirected a movement that might have had catastrophic revolutionary effects.

However, failure to deal with the underlying causes of unrest and discontent will mean that the evolution of the movement will continue. If it does, the basic socio-psychological conditions typical of the second stage will emerge and their general nature is suggested by the name given to the period. It is a time of the *popularization* of unrest and discontent; a time when the dissatisfaction of the people results in the development of *collective excitement*. It is not implied that unrest and discontent become popular in the sense that they spread to every last man in the population. Rather, popularization takes place among those psychologically prepared to share in the movement. On the part of the opposition, the very popularization of unrest and discontent serves to intensify their resistance to the spread of the movement. Thus popularization in one section of the population is paralleled by resistance in another.

This is the stage when individuals participating in the mass behavior of the preceding stage become aware of each other. Their negative reactions to the basic factors in their situation are shared and begin to spread. Unrest is no longer covert, endemic, and esoteric; it becomes overt, epidemic, and exoteric. Discontent is no longer uncoordinated and individual; it tends to become focalized and collective.

Characteristic Conditions. In consequence of all this, the socio-psychological conditions typically present in this stage can be classified under six headings.

1. The spread of discontent and the contagious extension of the several signs of unrest and discontent as manifested in:
   a. Increased activity
   b. Growing focus of attention
   c. Heightened state of expectancy
2. The transfer of allegiance of the intellectuals, including:
   a. Wish reformulation
   b. Loss of faith in their leadership on the part of the repressed classes and the loss of faith in themselves on the part of the leaders
   c. Spread of rumor and scandal and the development of a literature of exposure
   d. Emergence of the "good man fallacy"
   e. Identification of a guilty group, focusing of attention on it, and the development of an "advertising offensive" against it
   f. Development of an "oppression psychosis"
3. The fabrication of a social myth with these allied characteristics:
   a. Creation of collective illusions, myths, and doctrines
   b. Emergence of the economic incentive to revolutionary action
   c. Development of a tentative object of loyalty[7]

4. The emergence of conflict with the out-group and the resultant increase in in-group consciousness
5. The organization of the discontented for the purpose of remedying the threatened or actual breakdown of government
6. The presentation of revolutionary demands which if granted would amount to the abdication of those in power

Typical Processes. With reference to the processes functioning at this level, there is a marked intensification of milling. But it is not quite so random and aimless. People develop more definite notions of the causes of their difficulties and of what should be done to resolve them. This intensification and speeding up of the milling process results in so changing it that *social contagion* and *collective excitement* are better terms for describing what is going on. The attention is being caught and riveted and the people are becoming emotionally aroused and more likely to be carried away by impulses and feelings. Hence collective excitement serves to integrate unrest and discontent, break down old behavior patterns, and prepare the way for new patterns of behavior. Where collective excitement is intense and widespread there is also the possibility of social contagion; that is, there occurs the relatively rapid, unwitting, and non-rational dissemination of a mood, impulse, or form of conduct.

Social contagion, then, is simply an intense form of milling and collective excitement in which rapport is established. These processes serve to unite the individuals of the mass into the crowd and so lay the foundations for further development.

Effective Mechanisms. It is necessary again to remind ourselves that the four stages of a revolutionary movement are not clear-cut and mutually exclusive. No such claim has ever been made for them. The concept "stage" is simply a means of describing dominant tendencies and makes no pretense of dealing with absolutely delimited periods.

This reminder is particularly desirable when considering the processes and mechanisms of the Popular Stage. Milling continues, though there is a basic, if subtle, change. There is a focusing of attention on a tentative objective to be realized that was absent in the previous stage. Agitation, suggestion, imitation, and propaganda continue in use. But the change in the nature of the processes gives new direction to the mechanisms already in operation and calls into play certain additional devices.

Of these the effort to develop *esprit de corps* is especially important. Leaders who desire to intensify rapport as a means of transforming a mass of individuals into a psychological and/or acting crowd will employ *esprit de corps* as a means of social control. That is, they will foster it as a way of organizing and integrating loyalty to the movement — as a way of making people feel that they belong together and are identified with and engaged in a common undertaking. It is at once evident that *esprit de corps* is very necessary as a means of developing unity and solidarity in a movement. Its use prevents disintegration and permits the organization of unrest and discontent in such fashion as to forward the evolution of the movement. It is achieved through promoting the in-group relationship, the formation of informal fellowship associations, and participation in informal ceremonial behavior.

Another important mechanism that is brought into use at this stage has been called the "social" or "revolutionary" myth. In order to mobilize unrest and discontent and prepare for action, the people must be led to believe that they are on the march toward a New Order — a potential Utopia which it is their duty to help actualize.

In addition to these two major devices and as aids to their realization rumor, scandal, a literature of exposure, pamphlets, plays, protests, and many other mechanisms are also employed.

Types of Leaders. The conditions of the period and the skills requisite to the use of the necessary mechanisms determine the requirements for successful leadership. Thus the Popular Stage provides opportunity for the talents of the *prophet* and the *reformer*.

The prophet feels set apart or called to leadership; that he has a special and separate knowledge of the causes of unrest and discontent which the agitator has already brought to the attention of the people. He speaks with an air of authority, revealing a new message and a new philosophy of life, though always in general terms. He formulates and promulgates the social myth. He uses his belief in himself and his confidence in his message as a means of articulating the hopes and wishes of the people.

The reformer is a somewhat different type. He is produced by and is reacting to the same basic conditions, but the nature of the reaction is different and it is likely, too, that he appears somewhat later than the prophet, whose aims are general and vague. The reformer attacks specific evils and develops a clearly defined program; he attempts to change conditions in conformity with his own conceptions of what is good and desirable.

Dominant Social Form. The above brings us to the consideration of the social form typical of the Popular Stage. For the fact that the mass of the first stage evolves into the crowd of the second is the most obvious difference between the two.

Blumer's description of the process of crowd formation merits quotation:

The essential steps in the formation of the crowd seem to be quite clear. First, is the occurrence of some exciting event which catches the attention and arouses the interest of the people. In becoming preoccupied with this event, and stirred by its excitatory character, an individual is already likely to lose some of his ordinary self-control and to be dominated by the exciting object. Thus, a number of people stimulated by the same exciting object are disposed by that very fact to behave like a crowd. This becomes clear in the second step . . . the beginning of the milling process. . . . The most obvious effect of this milling is to disseminate a common mood, feeling, or emotional impulse, and also to increase its intensity. The third important step . . . is the emergence of a common object of attention on which the impulses, feelings, and imagery of the people become focused. With such a common objective, the crowd is in a position to act with unity, purpose, and consistency. The last step may be thought of as the stimulation and fostering of the impulses that correspond to the crowd objective, up to the point where the members are ready to act on them.[8]

It should be pointed out that there are two major types of crowds. The *psychological* crowd is formed in the first two steps of the process just outlined, is the work of the agitator and, of necessity, precedes the *acting* crowd. The acting crowd emerges in the third and fourth steps and is led by the prophet and reformer.

It remains only to remark that the evolution of the mass into the crowd is the result of the changing socio-psychological situation and the work of the leadership. Given the characteristics present, the processes operative, and effective leadership the crowd emerges as the form within which collective behavior goes on.

THE FORMAL STAGE

Of the Formulation of Issues and Formation of Publics

Transition from the Popular to the Formal Stage marks a crucial point in the development of a revolutionary movement. *Esprit de corps* must be buttressed by devices designed to develop group morale and ideology if disintegration is to be avoided. Furthermore, collective excitement and social contagion are not adequate to serve as the processual foundation for enduring social change. For this the formulation of issues and the formalization of procedures are demanded. In other words, the roots of the movement must strike deeper than sensationalism, sentimentalism, fashion, and fad. It must come to appeal to the essential desires of the people.

Characteristic Conditions. The typical characteristics found at this stage may be classified in terms of the two major developments which occur.

1. The fixation of motives (attitudes) and the definite formulation of

aims (values). This major characteristic is paralleled by these developments:

   a. A struggle between the conservative, moderate, and radical factions of the revolutionary group; the continuation of the in-group-out-group conflict, and the intensification of class antagonisms

   b. The moderate faction gains control to the accompaniment of these typical events:

      1) Release of prisoners

      2) Apparent co-operation of reformers and revolutionists

      3) Abortive attempts of the radicals to seize power

      4) Radical-conservative coalition attacks on the reformers

      5) Evidence of manifest incompetence on the part of the reformers

   c. The reformers are confronted with three typical handicaps:

      1) Fear of armed invasion

      2) Fear of internal rebellion

      3) Political inexperience

   d. The desertion of lukewarm supporters

   e. The elimination of the conservatives by the reformers

   f. A movement toward the "left," or an "uncontrollable swing of the masses toward radicalism"

   g. The emergence of the typical "perversions"

   h. The development of a set of norms formally stated in dogma and formally expressed in ritual, together with a marked increase in the use of shibboleths

   i. The fusion of patriotism and the social myth elevates the radical to power

   j. The radicals are also confronted with three typical dangers:

      1) The danger of conservative opposition and foreign invasion or intervention

      2) Domestic insurrection

      3) Political inexperience

2. The development of an organizational structure with leaders, a program, doctrines, and traditions. This is accompanied by:

   a. The increasing recognition of organizational breakdown and governmental inefficiency

   b. The development of a condition of dual sovereignty

   c. The occurrence of an immediate precipitating factor and the seizure of power by the radicals

   d. The presence of conflict within the ranks of the radicals

   e. The formation of a provisional government

    f. A "lull" between the seizure of power by the radicals and the initiation of the Reign of Terror

    g. The use of the Reign of Terror as a control technique

Typical Processes. Because of the character of the events of this stage the behavior of the participants in the movement may be described under three headings: (1) discussion and deliberation, (2) formulation, and (3) formalization.

Since the terms discussion and deliberation are self-defining they are introduced here only to show the interrelation of the different phases of a revolutionary movement. Given the typical events, interaction *must* take the form of discussion and deliberation, and the public is the social form within which such interaction must take place. In other words, this is the stage when issues emerge with reference to which there are differences of opinion. Publics form to discuss these issues. Discussion as a process is marked by the effort to interpret the issues under debate, by dispute, and by the dominance of conflict relations. This results in the participants becoming more self-conscious and critical. This, in turn, makes for opposition and disagreement and places a premium on the careful consideration of pertinent facts and produces arguments and counter-arguments.

The process of formulation may be thought of as both a continuation and a result of discussion. In the give and take of argument over and critical analysis of possible lines of action with reference to the issues under examination, policies begin to take shape and programs are formulated.

As the movement proceeds through the third stage a development occurs that may be called formalization. That is, wishes (attitudes) that have been reformulated, goals (values) that have emerged, and policies that have been developed get worked into the mores of the participants and become a formal part of their behavior in preparation for subsequent institutionalization.

Effective Mechanisms. In general, the mechanisms characteristic of this stage are those devices that are effective in developing group morale and ideology.

Morale is the device by which a developing movement is given cohesion, solidarity, and unity — just the qualities needed for its on-going. It roots in three convictions: (1) that the purposes and objectives of the movement are right and just and that victory will initiate a sort of Golden Age; (2) that these purposes will actually and ultimately be realized, with all the intense motivation deriving from this faith; and (3) that these purposes represent a sacred responsibility which must be fulfilled.

The ideology of a movement consists in a body of doctrines, beliefs, and myths which provide direction and the ability to withstand the opposition of out-groups. The following elements are usually present: (1) a statement of the objectives, purposes, and premises of the movement; (2) a body of criticism and condemnation of the existing social order which the movement is attacking and seeking to change; (3) a body of defense doctrine serving to justify the movement; (4) a body of belief dealing with policies, tactics, and practical operations; and (5) the myths of the movement. From all this it is evident that it is the function of an ideology to give an answer to the unrest and discontent of the people. Unless such an answer is provided the movement cannot move forward.

On a slightly different level propaganda — "the deliberately evoked and guided campaign to induce people to accept a given view"[9] — is also of major importance at this stage.

There is no thought of presenting here a complete list of possible mechanisms. Rather, the important point to be established is that, whatever mechanisms are employed, they serve to facilitate the process of formalization. Various types of leaders and various types of mechanisms combine to realize this end. Historians, apologists, poets, hymnologists, and propagandists use the radio, the press, pamphlets, books, the stage, the movie, the platform, the pulpit, cartoons, posters, slogans, banners, insignia, and so forth to carry the movement along its way.

Types of Leaders. As might be expected in view of the nature of the period, leadership is in the hands of statesmen. That is, the leaders are those who are able to formulate policies and will attempt to carry social policy into practice. They are those who are skilled in estimating and evaluating the nature and direction of the prevailing social forces. They are those who will try to understand and champion the beliefs and convictions that have become established in the thinking of the people. They are those who will propose the program which promises to resolve the issues and realize the objectives of which the people have become aware.

Dominant Social Form. As already intimated, all this goes on in a *public*. Because of the interdependent character of the different features of a revolutionary movement, discussion and deliberation, formulation and formalization can only occur in a public; these processes cannot function in a mass or a crowd.

A public is marked by the presence of the discussion of, and a collective opinion about, an issue. The following statement, contrasting a public and a society, gives an excellent picture of both:

> A public comes into existence because of an issue with reference to which there is no recognized procedure; a society, in contrast, is marked by rules and regulations that prescribe procedure. That is, a society possesses a culture; whereas, a public emerges precisely because the

culture has no solution to the issue which has caused the public to form. It follows from the above that a society has form and organization which a public lacks. Finally, the members of a society have fixed status roles and a well-developed we-feeling; in contrast the public is a kind of amorphous group whose size and membership varies with the issue. Instead of having its activity prescribed, it is engaged in an effort to arrive at an act and therefore forced to create its action.[10]

THE INSTITUTIONAL STAGE

Of Legalization and Societal Organization

We come now to the final stage in the development of a revolutionary movement: the period in which institutionalization takes place. If the revolutionaries are to avoid the stigma of permanent classification as "rebels" this must occur. That is, the out-group must finally be able to *legalize* or *organize* their power; they must become the in-group of the structure of political power. When the attitudes and values of the revolutionary leadership have thus become the legal and political foundation of social organization, a new *society* has been formed and the revolution has been consummated.

Characteristic Conditions. The socio-psychological conditions which indicate that a revolution is moving from the Formal into the Institutional Stage may be classified as *causal* or transitional and *resultant* or accommodative.

1. Causal characteristics:
   a. Psychological exhaustion which undermines the emotional foundations of the revolution
   b. Moral let-down and return to old habits (attitudes), including "escape recreation" and the re-emergence of graft, speculation, and corruption, become deterrents to continued revolutionary behavior
   c. Great economic distress, amounting almost to chaos, demands a settling down
2. Resultant characteristics:
   a. End of the Reign of Terror; granting of amnesty; return of exiles; repression of extremists; and search for scapegoats
   b. Increase in powers of central government, frequently resulting in dictatorship
   c. Social reconstruction along lines of the old social structure but with the new principles (values) essentially intact
   d. Dilution of the revolutionary ideal; transformation of evangelistic

fervor for social change into the desire for conquest; transformation of the "revolutionary sect" into a "political denomination"
  e. Re-accommodation of church and state
  f. "Reaction to the reaction" represented by escape recreation
  g. The revolution becomes attitudinally established and develops a permanent organization that is acceptable to the current mores; that is, it is institutionalized

Typical Processes. From a processual point of view, the movement increasingly relies on discussion and deliberation as the means for fixing policies and determining action. That is to say, the unrest and discontent, and collective excitement out of which the movement came, together with the correlative behavior, slip into the background and mechanisms and processes emerge that are appropriate to the prevailing mood of the participants. The process of *institutionalization* results: the process by which collective behavior which begins outside formal offices and without formal rules, engaged in by unconventional groups of people, in unexpected situations, or in ways contrary to use and wont, develop formal offices, organized groups, defined situations, and a new body of sanctioned use and wont.[11]

It is obvious that this description covers the entire process by which any area of behavior becomes institutionalized. It also describes the entire revolutionary process by which *mass* behavior, originating in unrest and discontent generated by the institutional inadequacies and inefficiencies of a society, becomes popularized and finds expression in the *crowd*; begins to acquire form in the *public*; and finally legalizes a new body of sanctioned use and wont. That is, a new *society* emerges, its core being a new constellation of institutions. Our present concern is with the final stage of this process.

It is also helpful to relate the revolutionary process to such basic sociological concepts as conflict, accommodation, and assimilation. In the Preliminary Stage, conflict remains covert and endemic because the causes of unrest and discontent have not yet been identified. In the Popular Stage it becomes overt and epidemic, increasing in intensity as issues emerge and are recognized. However, it is in the Formal Stage that conflict becomes violent, organized, and directed toward the realization of definite objectives.

Evidence that the movement is moving through the Formal into the Institutional Stage is found in the subsidence of conflict and the emergence of accommodative and/or assimilative processes. That is, the people involved in the movement are becoming reconciled to changed conditions of life through the formation of attitudes adequate to the changes that have occurred and they are beginning to recognize and accept a new set of values — a new set of defined relationships which fix a new status system.

The success of the entire revolutionary movement hinges on what happens at this point in its evolution. If the objectives (values) that were formulated in doctrine, written into the constitution, and expressed in ritual and ceremony, are really attitudinally accepted and become the bases for behavior, the goals of the movement have been assimilated and victory has been relatively complete.

What more frequently occurs makes for a condition in which the new values are *legally* but not *attitudinally* accepted. The legally-defined values are then held as *ideals*; the behavior of the people falls far short of them. A compromise is effected between the values of the decadent old order and the emergent new society. In short, what might be called incomplete or imperfect institutionalization results, and the movement comes to rest at a point that is short of its expressed purposes.

Effective Mechanisms. With reference to the mechanisms employed at this stage two observations are in order: (1) they are well-nigh innumerable, for, conceivably, any device by which the behavior of people can be influenced may be used at some time or another; therefore, (2) a general statement regarding such mechanisms must be concerned with the ends sought rather than with the specific devices employed.

From this point of view, it may be observed that the movement now intensifies the development of its ideology and perfects the tactics previously employed to carry people along in the desired direction. The use of established mechanisms and procedures takes precedence over "personalities" — "personal ascendancy is less essential to this stable and established order than the impersonal instruments it has forged for itself: the laws, descriptions, faiths, dogmas, and ideals." [12]

Type of Leader. Given what is going on at this stage, it follows that the movement now requires the services of the administrator-executive. This does not mean that a society does not and cannot always use agitators, prophets and reformers, as well as statesmen and administrators. On the contrary, it could be argued that sound administration would deliberately employ all these various types of leadership. The only point here being urged is that we are dealing with another aspect of the division of labor in leadership and that this function must be fulfilled if the movement is to reach full institutionalization. The policies formulated by the statesmen — in order to satisfy the demands for action voiced by the prophets and reformers in consequence of the unrest and discontent generated by the agitator — must be administered. Herein lies the functional justification for the rise of the administrative type of leadership.

Dominant Social Form. This brings us to the consideration of the prevailing social form in which behavior is channeled in the Institutional Stage. We have seen that the mass, the crowd, and the public are the dominant social forms of the first, second, and third stages. These have been called "forms of elementary collective behavior" because they "arise spontaneously and their action is not set or determined by existing cultural patterns. Each has a distinctive character and each arises under a special set of conditions." Thus from the point of view of the social forms within which collective behavior goes on, a revolutionary movement may be thought of as a development in the course of which a mass is transformed into a crowd, a crowd becomes a public, and a public evolves into a society. That is, the movement "acquires organization and form, a body of customs and traditions, established leadership, and enduring division of labor, social rules and social values; in short, a culture, a social organization, and a new scheme of life.[13]

The resultant society or social order may be said to possess the following characteristics:

1. A body of common expectations upon the basis of which people are able to co-operate and regulate their activities to one another. This procedure yields them customs, traditions, rules and norms. (It was this aspect of society that Park had in mind when he defined it as a "network of accommodative arrangements.")
2. A set of values which are attached to these expectations and which determine how important they are, and how readily people will adhere to them.
3. The conceptions which people have of themselves in relation to each other and to their groups.
4. A common subjective orientation in the form of dispositions and moods.[14]

In terms of what was said earlier about the nature of human nature and social change, this means that a destroyed equilibrium between the attitudes of the people and the values of the culture has been re-established; attitudes have been reformulated, values have been redefined, and a new social order has been built.

---

[1] As applied to all organized social movements this hypothesis was advanced first by W. E. Gettys and employed by him in the study of the development of Methodism in England. — Carl Dawson and W. E. Gettys, *Introduction to Sociology* (rev. ed., New York; Ronald Press, 1934), pp. 708–09.

[2] P. A. Sorokin, *The Sociology of Revolution* (Philadelphia: J. P. Lippincott, 1925); L. P. Edwards, *Natural History of Revolution* (Chicago: University of Chicago Press, 1927); Gettys, *op. cit.*; Herbert Blumer, "Collective Behavior" in *An Outline of the Principles of Sociology*, R. E. Park, ed. (New York: Barnes and Noble, 1939); Crane Brinton, *The Anatomy of Revolution* (New York: W. W. Norton, 1938).

[3] An attitude is any socially-acquired tendency to act. A value is any culturally-held object of interest. Attitudes-values, then, are the basic social elements.

[4] Blumer offers an excellent description of milling. See *op. cit.*, Part IV, pp. 224–28.

[5] *Op. cit.*, pp. 260–61.

[6] Blumer, *op. cit.*, pp. 241–45.

[7] The materials listed under items two and three are presented as they were derived from the writings of previous students. The present writer believes that if they are arranged as follows they reveal what might be termed the "natural history of the process of the transfer of allegiance of the intellectuals":

1. With the passage of time a social system initially considered to be socially-advantageous comes to be seen as repressive. The repression is felt first by the "inarticulate masses" who do not understand the causes of it. After a period of time, the "intellectuals" are infected with the discontent of the masses and begin to search for the causes of the repression. "The repressors neither feel the repression nor, except in rare cases, understand its causes."

2. This shift of the intellectuals leads both them and the public to become victims of the "bad-man-good-man fallacy." That is, they lose their respect for and faith in the individuals who at the time have control of the societies, and conclude that their difficulties result from the fact that their leaders are bad men. This leads to the conclusion that good men should be placed in control. So, such changes are demanded and are frequently effected with the result that the good individuals, like their "bad" predecessors, fail and lose their popularity.

3. However, in a society ripe for revolution this fallacious diagnosis does not lead men astray for long. Renewed search leads to the conclusion that "the real cause of the unrest is to be found in certain archaic elements of the social order," and these archaic elements are then seen to be associated with the activities of "some group or order of men."

4. Having identified what seems to be the real foundation of the repression, the intellectuals believe themselves to be under obligation to inform the public. So they seek to focus the dissatisfaction of the public on what they believe to be the source of the trouble.

5. The agitation of the intellectuals provokes a typical "period of discussion" which is characterized by the use of many methods and the results of which depend, of course, on who wins. If the intellectuals are correct in their analysis, and if the repressors are unsuccessful in their efforts to avert, direct, postpone, or abort the revolutionary movement, two developments typically occur: (1) The repressed group becomes afflicted with what has been called the "oppression psychosis," and (2) "the repressors gradually lose faith in themselves and in their cause."

6. If the foregoing occurs the time is ripe for a revolutionary upheaval if one more important factor is injected into the interactional situation: a "dynamic," a *raison d'etre* is necessary and this is provided by the fabrication of the social myth, the product of the minds of the intellectuals.

[8] *Op. cit.*, p. 234.

[9] Blumer, *op. cit.*, pp. 250–252.

[10] Blumer, *op. cit.*, pp. 245–46.

[11] E. C. Hughes, "Institutions," *Outline of the Principles of Sociology*, R. E. Park, ed. (New York: Barnes and Noble, 1939), Part V, p. 286.

[12] Dawson and Gettys, *op. cit.*, p. 725.

[13] Blumer, *op. cit.*, pp. 232 and 255.

[14] *Ibid.*, p. 279.

16. What Is Revolution?

HEINZ LUBASZ

Revolution is an essentially political process of combat and change. The characteristic weapons of revolutionary combat are political weapons; the characteristic instruments of revolutionary change are political instruments. Yet neither the aims of the revolutionaries nor the actual results of the process of revolution are exclusively or narrowly political. The very essence of revolution is the attempt to alter the conditions of social existence, to lay the foundations for an alternative order of society. Hence revolution is never merely the replacing of one ruling group with another;[1] nor is it a change in the system of government alone. It is generally "a sweeping, fundamental change in political organization, social structure, economic property control and the predominant myth of a social order, thus indicating a major break in the continuity of development."[2]

That the revolutionary process is fundamentally political in nature is underscored by the fact that its beginning and its end are themselves characteristically political: revolution begins with a political crisis and ends with a political settlement.

Revolution begins with a crisis in the state and the launching of an overt attack on the regime. It may be touched off by widespread strikes, mass demonstrations, riots, or armed insurrection. But it is only when and insofar as such activities seek to bring about fundamental innovation and so become part and parcel of a political assault that they constitute revolutionary activity and may precipitate revolution properly so called. It is this clearly political character that distinguishes, for example, the English Revolution of 1640–1660 from a mere civil war and the American Revolution from a mere rebellion. To say that revolution begins with a political crisis is not to deny that revolution is the product of profound, long-range, and widespread changes of many kinds — changes in social relations, in economic conditions, in ideas and attitudes, in a country's external relations. But even very dramatic and disruptive changes in economy and society, in thought and in foreign relations, may go on for a long time — perhaps indefinitely — without culminating in revolution. If they do engender revolution, they generally do so by precipitating a grave crisis in the body politic. The long- and short-range causes of this crisis may vary greatly from case to case; but the central issue is always who is to govern and how. Whether we regard revolutions as ultimately the results of class struggles, of shifts in economic relations and circumstances, of subversive ideas, conspiracies, or disappointed expectations, the fact remains that the actual outbreak of revolution is at heart a political event.

By the same token, to say that the process of revolution ends with a political *settlement* is not to deny that revolution has lasting *consequences*, or to maintain that, once the settlement has been achieved, the work of the revolution is over and change and conflict cease. Revolution generates forces and institutions — economic and social, cultural and political, military and diplomatic — which continue to be operative long after the period of overt and intensive upheaval has come to a close. But it is important to note the break between the period of upheaval and the subsequent period of more or less stable and uninterrupted development, between revolutionary upheaval and continuous transformation, between the revolution and the regime that issues from it. This break constitutes what we are calling the "revolution settlement": the point at which the old regime is restored (as it was in England in 1660, in France in 1815) or the new regime emerges safely established and triumphant (as it did in England in 1689, in Russia in 1921). Revolution ends with the victory or defeat of the revolutionary movement but, either way, it ends; and it ends, as it began, with an essentially political event.

The actual course of the revolution is a protracted struggle in which the principal weapons employed by the insurgents are weapons borrowed from the arsenal of state power: political weapons. It is of course true that armed force often plays a significant and at times a decisive role. But it is worth bearing in mind that, in a broad sense, the use of military power in revolution is itself an intrinsically political use. When the modern state, which claims a monopoly of organized military might, turns its armies against an insurgent population, and when the insurgents themselves direct such arms as they can command against their government, armed force becomes simply one of the instruments of political purpose. The fact is that military power is only one aspect — and, in modern European history at any rate, not even the preponderant aspect — of the revolutionary process.[3] In every revolution in modern European history the initial assault, the basis of revolutionary organization, and the characteristic means of combat have been pre-eminently political, in the strict sense of the word.

We may, somewhat schematically, distinguish three phases of revolutionary struggle which frequently merge into one another: the initial assault on the government; the rule of the revolutionary regime; and the defense — successful or not — of the revolutionary regime against counterrevolutionary forces, domestic and foreign.

The first phase is generally a period of increasingly sharp and widespread opposition to the existing system, which culminates in an overt political attack on the government. It sees the emergence of the three indispensable ingredients of a revolutionary movement: leadership, organization, and a program. The insurgents cannot effectively oppose the organized power of the state — government, police, army, and so on — unless they are themselves organized, possess some determined and effectual leaders, and have a more or less comprehensive and coherent program capable of attracting broad support to their cause. This is not to say that the insurgents organize themselves on the spur of the moment or for the express purpose of making a revolution. On the contrary, it has generally been a body already organized for political purposes that has become an insurgent group and has, at least initially, provided the basic leadership and the organizational focus for opposition to the regime. The English Revolutions of 1640 and 1688 were both precipitated by parliamentary groups. The French Revolution of the eighteenth century was unwittingly launched by nobles who in their *parlements* demanded the convoking of yet another political forum, the Estates General. The Russian Revolution began more nearly as a spontaneous popular outburst; but here too the role of organized bodies — the Duma, the workers' soviets, and the clandestine socialist groups — was of decisive practical importance.

When extensive popular opposition coincides with a severe crisis in the body politic, the result is apt to be rebellion. If an organized and well-led group, with a coherent and popular program of systematic change is also present and actively insurgent, the result is likely to be revolution.

The distinction between revolution and rebellion is an important one. The two processes are not unrelated, but they differ in crucial respects. Rebellion, whether by well-formed bands or unorganized masses, is overt opposition directed at particular laws, practices, or individuals. It aims at specific and limited changes. Rebels seek to put an end to intolerable conditions by replacing the personnel of government rather than by transforming the system of domination. They demand the redress of specific grievances rather than a systematic alteration in the foundations of the whole existing order. Even armed rebellion may involve nothing more systematic and fundamental than attacks on isolated individuals whom the rebels hold responsible for their ills — landlords, employers, tax-collectors, hoarders, minor government officials. Rebellion turns into revolution when the demand for particular and limited changes is replaced by a demand for general and fundamental change; when the sovereign power itself is held responsible for prevailing conditions; and when scattered rebellious elements join to form a more or less united revolutionary force. The coming of the French Revolution clearly shows all these processes at work. The separate revolts of nobility, middle classes, urban masses, and peasantry, came together to become a revolutionary movement; the government of Louis XVI was gradually made the chief object of criticism; and the disparate demands for specific reforms gave way to a demand for fundamental changes in the body politic — for a social order based on liberty and equality, for security of person and property, for constitutional government. The gradual emergence of an attack on the government, aimed at changing the constitution and thereby altering the very foundation of a whole range of objectionable conditions, turned mere rebellion into full-fledged revolution. A well-known exchange between the king and one of his courtiers suggests that at least one of them understood the difference. When the fall of the Bastille was reported to the royal court at Versailles, Louis asked the Duke de la Roche-foucauld-Liancourt: "Is this a rebellion?" "No, Sire," replied the duke, "it is a revolution."

If the initial assault on the old regime is successful, it is followed by the rule of a more or less revolutionary government. To what extent and in what directions the new government employs the instruments of combat and change now at its disposal depends on a great number of factors — on its program and its personnel, on the degree of opposition it continues to encounter, on the activities of other groups advocating other changes, and so on. In this brief outline of the nature of revolution we cannot undertake an analysis of these variables or examine the wide variety of ways in which the tools of revolution are wielded. We can simply note that the characteristic weapons which the revolutionary regime employs are precisely the weapons to which the state itself claims an exclusive right: legislation, decree, and executive order; police control, imprisonment, trial, execution, and even terror; confiscation, proscription, and exile — the list might be considerably expanded. The revolutionary regime may be thought of as a counter-government that typically employs all the instruments that are normally at the disposal of the state.

One of these instruments is dictatorship. Lest it be supposed that dictatorship is a form of rule peculiar to revolution, or to "totalitarianism," let us note that dictatorship is a very ancient political institution, devised by the Roman Republic for dealing with emergency situations, and thus originally intended to be a temporary expedient. Revolutionary dictatorship, like the "constitutional dictatorship" instituted by twentieth-century democracies in time of war, is usually conceived of by its instigators as a temporary device, as an emergency measure to tide the country over its crisis and to undertake all the most urgent steps of direction, mobilization, combat, and reform. The most famous of these revolutionary dictatorships are those of Cromwell, Robespierre, and Lenin. The first of these died of inanition; the second was overthrown by force; the third survived. Having survived three years of war and counterrevolution, Lenin's dictatorship was transformed into a permanent instrument of government which could be very dictatorial indeed without necessarily being revolutionary. As dictatorship became a permanent fixture in Russia, less and less was heard about its being a temporary expedient, though the fiction was maintained that the dictatorship was not one of government over the governed, but rather one of the victorious proletariat over the defeated counterrevolutionary classes. The Soviet dictatorship is, to be sure, the child of revolution; but that is very far from making it, half a century later, a revolutionary dictatorship.

The defense of the revolutionary regime constitutes the final phase of the revolution, and terminates in the victory or defeat of that regime. It consists in the conflict between the revolutionary forces and their opponents, domestic and foreign. Adherents and allies of the old regime may attempt to oust the revolutionary government, to reinstate those who formerly enjoyed power and privilege, and to restore the old order either *in toto* or in modified form. The struggle itself may be quite mild, as it was in England in the late 1650's. But it may also involve civil and international war at their most ferocious, as it did in France in the mid-1790's and in Russia between 1918 and 1921. Now, once again, as in the first phase, the part played by armed forces may be of great moment. By this time the revolutionary regime generally disposes of a very substantial military force. Even if it does, it can still be defeated "from without" by a combination of domestic counterrevolutionary forces and armed foreign intervention. But it may also fall victim to a *coup d'état* "from within": it may be overthrown by one of the members of the regime itself, or by one of its generals — as witness the counterrevolutionary coups of the two Nalopeons. Last but not least the revolution may simply collapse from lack of impetus and popular support and end in a peaceable restoration, like that of Charles II of England in 1660.

With the end of this third phase, the revolution itself comes to a close, to be followed by a period of comparative stability and domestic peace. The revolution that began when the monopoly of political power in the state was successfully challenged ends when that monopoly is re-established — in old hands or in new.[4] In contrast to the endless processes of social conflict and transformation, revolution as a process is terminable, temporary. What is sometimes called *permanent revolution* is in fact nothing but a process of continuous transformation under the auspices of government, a process from which the overthrow of the existing regime, which is an essential part of revolution properly so called, is conspicuously absent. This is not to deny that the process of transformation from above, of change directly engineered by government, is a very important political phenomenon, significantly different from the process of social change in which the role of government is indirect. But it is desirable, for the sake of clarity, to recognize that direct intervention by government in every aspect of social existence, no matter how dynamic it may be, is not synonymous with revolution.

Does the regime that issues from revolution actually represent the political foundation of that alternative order of society which it was the object of the revolutionary movement to establish? If the revolutionary movement is defeated, the projected alternative (together with its principal protagonists) may at first be completely suppressed in counterrevolution, reaction, and white terror. But to some degree, and in modified form, it often finds its way into the order which the restoration eventually establishes. It would seem that, though revolution may fail to triumph, once it has won at least a temporary success, its work cannot be wholly undone. Its partisans may not remain in power; but they continue to press, by other means or even in subsequent revolutions, for the changes they deem indispensable. What if the revolutionary movement is victorious? In every great revolution involving large masses of people, there is always more than one projected alternative, more than one insurgent group, more than one revolutionary program. In the course of the upheaval one or another of them may be dominant for a time. But the close of the revolution generally means defeat for all but one of these alternatives. From the point of view of the population as a whole, therefore, even the victory of the revolution is never complete, if only because it involves not merely the defeat of the old order but also the defeat of every alternative but one. Cromwell's victory, temporary as it proved to be, spelled defeat for the royalists; but it also meant defeat for the radical left wing of the revolutionary movement. Lenin's victory put an end to tsarism; but it also eliminated the democratic alternative.

The regime that issues from revolution is always a less than complete embodiment of the new and better society it was intended to establish. How much of an achievement, how much of an advance a given revolution represents has to be judged, not in absolute terms, but in terms of what was concretely possible, and by comparing the new society with the one that preceded it. For, when all is said and done, revolution itself does not spring from a theoretical interest in a wholly perfect social order so much as from an urgent desire to find some viable alternative to conditions that are felt to be intolerable.

[1] In Professor Brinton's view, revolution does consist essentially in the "drastic, sudden substitution of one group in charge of running a territorial political entity for another group" by means of violence "or some . . . kind of skullduggery." Crane Brinton, *The Anatomy of Revolution,* revised edition (New York: 1952), p. 2.

[2] Sigmund Neumann, "The International Civil War," *World Politics,* 1 (1948–49), pp. 333–350, at p. 333, n. 1.

[3] Considerable attention is given to the role of the military element by Chalmers A. Johnson, *Revolution and the Social System* (Stanford: 1964).

[4] *Cf.* Peter Amann, "Revolution: A Redefinition," *Political Science Quarterly,* 77 (1962), pp. 36–53, at p. 39: "As I define it, revolution prevails when the state's monopoly power is effectively challenged and persists until a monopoly of power is re-established."

IV

SUMMARY STATEMENT

17. Theories of Revolution

LAWRENCE STONE

In attacking the problem of revolution, as most others of major significance in history, we historians should think twice before we spurn the help offered by our colleagues in the social sciences, who have, as it happens, been particularly active in the last few years in theorizing about the typology, causes, and evolutionary patterns of this particular phenomenon. The purpose of this article is not to advance any new hypothesis, but to provide a summary view and critical examination of the work that has been going on.

The first necessity in any inquiry is a careful definition of terms: what is, and what is not, a revolution? According to one view, it is change, effected by the use of violence, in government, and/or regime, and/or society.[1] By *society* is meant the consciousness and the mechanics of communal solidarity, which may be tribal, peasant, kinship, national, and so on; by *regime* is meant the constitutional structure — democracy, oligarchy, monarchy; and by *government* is meant specific political and administrative institutions. Violence, it should be noted, is not the same as force; it is force used with unnecessary intensity, unpredictably, and usually destructively.[2] This definition of revolution is a very broad one, and two historians of the French Revolution, Crane Brinton and Louis Gottschalk, would prefer to restrict the use of the word to the major political and social upheavals with which they are familiar, the "Great Revolutions" as George S. Pettee calls them.[3]

Even the wider definition allows the historian to distinguish between

263

the seizure of power that leads to a major restructuring of government or society and the replacement of the former elite by a new one, and the coup d'état involving no more than a change of ruling personnel by violence or threat of violence. This latter is the norm in Latin America, where it occurred thirty-one times in the ten years 1945–1955. Merle Kling has arrived at a suggestive explanation of this Latin American phenomenon of chronic political instability, limited but frequent use of violence, and almost complete lack of social or institutional change. He argues that ownership of the principal economic resources, both agricultural and mineral, is concentrated in the hands of a tiny, very stable, elite of enormously wealthy monoculture landlords and mining capitalists. This elite is all-powerful and cannot be attacked by opposition groups within the country; externally, however, it is dependent on foreign interests for its markets and its capital. In this colonial situation of a foreign-supported closed plutocracy, the main avenue of rapid upward social mobility for nonmembers of the elite leads, via the army, to the capture of the government machine, which is the only accessible source of wealth and power. This political instability is permitted by the elite on the condition that its own interests are undisturbed. Instability, limited violence, and the absence of social or institutional change are therefore all the product of the contradiction between the realities of a colonial economy run by a plutocracy and the facade of political sovereignty — between the real, stable power of the economic elite and the nominal, unstable control of politicians and generals.[4]

The looser definition of revolution thus suits both historians of major social change and historians of the palace coup. It does, however, raise certain difficulties. Firstly, there is a wide range of changes of government by violence which are neither a mere substitution of personalities in positions of power nor a prelude to the restructuring of society; secondly, conservative counterrevolutions become almost impossible to fit into the model; and lastly, it remains hard to distinguish between colonial wars, civil wars, and social revolution.

To avoid these difficulties, an alternative formulation has recently been put forward by a group of social scientists working mainly at Princeton. They have dropped the word "revolution" altogether and put "internal war" in its place.[5] This is defined as any attempt to alter state policy, rulers, or institutions by the use of violence, in societies where violent competition is not the norm and where well-defined institutional patterns exist.[6] This concept seems to be a logical consequence of the preoccupation of sociologists in recent years with a model of society in a stable, self-regulating state of perpetual equipoise. In this utopian world of universal harmony, all forms of violent conflict are anomalies, to be treated alike as pathological disorders of a similar species. This is a model which, although it has its uses for analytical purposes, bears little relation to the reality familiar to the historian. It looks to a society without change, with universal consensus on values, with complete social harmony, and isolated from external threats; no approximation to such a society has ever been seen. An alternative model, which postulates that all societies are in a condition of multiple and perpetual tension held in check by social norms, ideological beliefs, and state sanctions, accords better with historical fact, as some sociologists are now beginning to realize.[7]

The first objection to the all-embracing formula of internal war is that, by covering all forms of physical conflict from strikes and terrorism to civil war, it isolates the use of violence from the normal processes of societal adjustment. Though some of the users of the term express their awareness that the use of violence for political ends is a fairly common occurrence, the definition they have established in fact excludes all times and places where it *is* common. It thus cuts out most societies the world has ever known, including Western Europe in the Middle Ages and Latin America today. Secondly, it isolates one particular means, physical violence, from the political ends that it is designed to serve. Clausewitz's famous definition of external war is equally applicable to internal war, civil war, or revolution: "War is not only a political act, but a real political instrument; a continuation of political transactions, an accomplishment of them by different means. That which remains peculiar to war relates only to the peculiar nature of its means."[8]

It is perfectly true that any means by which society exercises pressure or control, whether it is administrative organization, constitutional law, economic interest, or physical force, can be a fruitful field of study in its own right, so long as its students remain aware that they are looking at only one part of a larger whole. It is also true that there is something peculiar about violence, if only because of man's highly ambivalent attitude towards the killing of his own species. Somehow, he regards physical force as different in kind from, say, economic exploitation or psychological manipulation as a means of exercising power over others. But this distinction is not one of much concern to the historian of revolution, in which violence is a normal and natural occurrence. The concept of internal war is too broad in its comprehension of all types of violence from civil wars to strikes, too narrow in its restriction to normally nonviolent societies, too limited in its concern with one of many means, too arbitrary in its separation of this means from the ends in view, and too little concerned with the complex roots of social unrest to be of much practical value to him.

The most fruitful typology of revolution is that of Chalmers Johnson, set out in a pamphlet that deserves to be widely read.[9] He sees six types, identified by the targets selected for attack, whether the government personnel, the political regime, or the community as a social unit; by the nature of the carriers of revolution, whether a mass or an elite; and particularly by the goals and the ideologies, whether reformist, eschatological, nostalgic, nation-forming, elitist, or nationalist. The first type, the *Jacquerie,* is a spontaneous mass peasant rising, usually carried out in the name of the traditional authorities, Church and King, and with the limited aims of purging the local or national elites. Examples are the Peasant Revolt of 1381, Ket's Rebellion of 1549, and the Pugachev rebellion in Russia in 1773–1775. The second type, the *Millenarian Rebellion,* is similar to the first but with the added feature of a utopian dream, inspired by a living messiah. This type can be found at all times, in all parts of the world, from the Florentine revolution led by Savonarola in 1494, to the Anabaptist Rebellion in Münster led by John Mathijs and John Beukels in 1533–1535, to the Sioux Ghost-Dance Rebellion inspired by the Paiute prophet Wovoka in 1890. It has attracted a good deal of attention from historians in recent years, partly because the career of Hitler offered overwhelming proof of the enormous historical significance of a charismatic leader, and partly because of a growing interest in the ideas of Max Weber.[10] The third type is the *Anarchistic Rebellion,* the nostalgic reaction to progressive change, involving a romantic idealization of the old order: the Pilgrimage of Grace and the Vendée are examples.

The fourth is that very rare phenomenon, the *Jacobin Communist Revolution.* This has been defined as "a sweeping fundamental change in political organization, social structure, economic property control and the predominant myth of a social order, thus indicating a major break in the continuity of development."[11] This type of revolution can occur only in a highly centralized state with good communications and a large capital city, and its target is government, regime, and society — the lot. The result is likely to be the creation of a new national consciousness under centralized, military authority, and the erection of a more rational, and hence more efficient, social and bureaucratic order on the ruins of the old ramshackle structure of privilege, nepotism, and corruption.

The fifth type is the *Conspiratorial Coup d'État,* the planned work of a tiny elite fired by an oligarchic, sectarian ideology. This qualifies as a revolutionary type only if it in fact anticipates mass movement and inaugurates social change — for example the Nasser revolution in Egypt or the Castro revolution in Cuba; it is thus clearly distinguished from the palace revolt, assassination, dynastic succession-conflict, strike, banditry, and other forms of violence, which are all subsumed under the "internal war" rubric.

Finally, there is the *Militarized Mass Insurrection,* a new phenomenon of the twentieth century in that it is a deliberately planned mass revolutionary war, guided by a dedicated elite. The outcome of guerrilla warfare is determined by political atittudes, not military strategy or matériel, for the rebels are wholly dependent on broad popular support. In all cases on record, the ideology that attracts the mass following has been a combination of xenophobic nationalism and Marxism, with by far the greater stress on the former. This type of struggle has occurred in Yugoslavia, China, Algeria, and Vietnam.

Although, like any schematization of the historical process, this sixfold typology is concerned with ideal types, although in practice individual revolutions may sometimes display characteristics of several different types, the fact remains that this is much the most satisfactory classification we have so far; it is one that working historians can recognize and use with profit. The one obvious criticism is semantic, an objection to the use of the phrase "Jacobin Communist Revolution." Some of Johnson's examples are Communist, such as the Russian or Chinese Revolutions; others are Jacobin but not Communist, such as the French Revolution or the Turkish Revolution of 1908–1922. It would be better to revert to Pettee's category of "Great Revolutions," and treat Communist revolutions as a subcategory, one type, but not the only type, of modernizing revolutionary process.

Given this classification and definition of revolution, what are its root causes? Here everyone is agreed in making a sharp distinction between long-run, underlying causes — the preconditions, which create a potentially explosive situation and can be analyzed on a comparative basis — and immediate, incidental factors — the precipitants, which trigger the outbreak and which may be nonrecurrent, personal, and fortuitous. This effectively disposes of the objections of those historians whose antipathy to conceptual schematization takes the naïve form of asserting the uniqueness of each historical event.

One of the first in the field of model-building was Crane Brinton who, as long ago as 1938, put forward a series of uniformities common to the four great Western revolutions: English, French, American, and Russian. These included an economically advancing society, growing class and status antagonisms, an alienated intelligentsia, a psychologically insecure and politically inept ruling class, and a governmental financial crisis.[12]

The subjectivity, ambiguity, and partial self-contradiction of this and other analyses of the causes of specific revolutions — for example the French Revolution — has been cruelly shown up by Harry Eckstein.[13] He has pointed out that commonly adduced hypotheses run the spectrum of particular conditions, moving from the intellectual (inadequate political socialization, conflicting social myths, a corrosive social philosophy, alienation of the intellectuals) to the economic (increasing poverty, rapid growth, imbalance between production and distribution, long-term growth plus short-term recession) to the social (resentment due to restricted elite circulation, confusion due to excessive elite recruitment, anomie due to excessive social mobility, conflict due to the rise of new social classes) to the political (bad government, divided government, weak government, oppressive government). Finally there are explanations on the level of general process, such as rapid social change, erratic social change, or a lack of harmony between the state structure and society, the rulers and the ruled. None of these explanations are invalid in themselves, but they are often difficult or impossible to reconcile one with the other, and are so diverse in their range and variety as to be virtually impossible to fit into an ordered analytical framework. What, then, is to be done?

Fundamental to all analyses, whether by historians like Brinton and Gottschalk or by political scientists like Johnson and Eckstein, is the recognition of a lack of harmony between the social system on the one hand and the political system on the other. This situation Johnson calls *dysfunction*, a word derived from the structural-functional equilibrium model of the sociologists. This dysfunction may have many causes, some of which are merely cyclical, such as may develop because of personal weaknesses in hereditary kingships or single-party regimes. In these cases, the revolution will not take on serious proportions, and will limit itself to attacks on the governing institutions, leaving regime and society intact. In most cases, however, including all those of real importance, the dysfunction is the result of some new and developing process, as a result of which certain social subsystems find themselves in a condition of relative deprivation. Rapid economic growth, imperial conquest, new metaphysical beliefs, and important technological changes are the four commonest factors involved, in that order. If the process of change is sufficiently slow and sufficiently moderate, the dysfunction may not rise to dangerous levels. Alternatively, the elite may adjust to the new situation with sufficient rapidity and skill to ride out the storm and retain popular confidence. But if the change is both rapid and profound, it may cause the sense of deprivation, alienation, anomie to spread into many sectors of society at once, causing what Johnson calls multiple dysfunction, which may be all but incurable within the existing political system.

In either case the second vital element in creating a revolutionary situation is the condition and attitude of the entrenched elite, a factor on which Eckstein rightly lays great stress. The elite may lose its manipulative skill, or its military superiority, or its self-confidence, or its cohesion; it may become estranged from the nonelite, or overwhelmed by a financial crisis; it may be incompetent, or weak, or brutal. Any combination of two or more of these features will be dangerous. What is ultimately fatal, however, is the compounding of its errors by intransigence. If it fails to anticipate the need for reform, if it blocks all peaceful, constitutional means of social adjustment, then it unites the various deprived elements in single-minded opposition to it, and drives them down the narrow road to violence. It is this process of polarization into two coherent groups or alliances of what are naturally and normally a series of fractional and shifting tensions and conflicts within a society that both Peter Amman and Wilbert Moore see as the essential preliminary to the outbreak of a Jacobin Revolution.[14] To conclude, therefore, revolution becomes *possible* when a condition of multiple dysfunction meets an intransigent elite: just such a conjunction occurred in the decades immediately before the English, the French, and the Russian Revolutions.

Revolution only becomes *probable* (Johnson might say "certain"), however, if certain special factors intervene: the "precipitants" or "accelerators." Of these, the three most common are the emergence of an inspired leader or prophet; the formation of a secret, military, revolutionary organization; and the crushing defeat of the armed forces in foreign war. This last is of critical importance since it not only shatters the prestige of the ruling elite, but also undermines the morale and discipline of the soldiers and thus opens the way to the violent overthrow of the existing government.

The first defect of Johnson's model is that it concentrates too much on objective structural conditions, and attempts to relate conditions directly to action. In fact, however, as Eckstein points out, there is no such direct relationship; historians can point to similar activity arising from different conditions, and different activity arising from similar conditions. Standing between objective reality and action are subjective human attitudes. A behaviorist approach such as Brinton's which lays equal stress on such things as anomie, alienation of the intellectuals, frustrated popular aspirations, elite estrangement, and loss of elite self-confidence, is more likely to produce a satisfactory historical explanation than is one that sticks to the objective social reality. Secondly, Johnson leaves too little play for the operation of the unique and the personal. He seems to regard his accelerators as automatic triggers, ignoring the area of unpredictable personal choice that is always left to the ruling elite and to the revolutionary leaders, even in a situation of multiple dysfunction exacerbated by an accelerator. Revolution is never inevitable — or rather the only evidence of its inevitability is that it actually happens. Consequently the only way to prove this point is to indulge in just the kind of hypothetical argument that historians prudently try to avoid. But it is still just possible that modernization may take place in Morocco and India without revolution. The modernization and industrialization of Germany and Britain took place without revolution in the nineteenth century (though it can be argued that in the latter case the process was slow by twentieth-century standards, and that, as is now becom-

ing all too apparent, the modernization was far from complete). Some
think that a potentially revolutionary situation in the United States in the
1930's was avoided by political action.

Lastly it is difficult to fit into the Johnson model the fact that political
actions taken to remedy dysfunction often themselves precipitate change.
This produces the paradoxical hypothesis that measures designed to restore
equilibrium in fact upset equilibrium. Because he begins with his structural-functional equilibrium model, Johnson is a victim of the fallacy of
intended consequences. As often as not in history it is the *unintended*
consequences that really matter: to mention but one example, it was Louis
XVI's belated and half-hearted attempts at reform that provoked the aristocratic reaction, which in turn opened the way to the bourgeois, the peasant,
and the sans-culotte revolutions. Finally the dysfunction concept is not
altogether easy to handle in a concrete historical case. If societies are
regarded as being in a constant state of multiple tension, then some degree
of dysfunction is always present. Some group is always in a state of relative
deprivation due to the inevitable process of social change.

Recognition of this fact leads Eckstein to point out the importance of
forces working *against* revolution. Historians, particularly those formed in
the Western liberal tradition, are reluctant to admit that ruthless, efficient
repression — as opposed to bumbling, half-hearted repression — involving
the physical destruction of leading revolutionaries and effective control of
the media of communication, can crush incipent revolutionary movements.
Repression is particularly effective when governments know what to look
for, when they have before their eyes the unfortunate example of other
governments overthrown by revolutionaries elsewhere. Reaction, in fact, is
just as infectious as revolution. Moreover diversion of energy and attention
to successful — as opposed to unsuccessful — foreign war can ward off serious internal trouble. Quietist — as opposed to activist — religious movements
may serve as the opiate of the people, as Halévy suggested about Methodism
in England. Bread and circuses may distract popular attention. Timely —
as opposed to untimely — political concessions may win over moderate opinion and isolate the extremists.

Basing himself on this suggestive analysis, Eckstein produces a paradigm
for universal application. He sees four positive variables — elite inefficiency,
disorienting social process, subversion, and available rebel facilities — and
four negative variables — diversionary mechanisms, available incumbent
facilities, adjustive mechanisms, and effective repression. Each type of
internal war, and each step of each type, can, he suggests, be explained in
terms of these eight variables. While this may be true, it is fair to point
out that some of the variables are themselves the product of more deep-
seated factors, others mere questions of executive action that may be deter-

mined by the accidents of personality. Disruptive social process is a profound cause; elite inefficiency a behavior pattern; effective repression a function of will; facilities the by-product of geography. One objection to the Eckstein paradigm is therefore that it embraces different levels of explanation and fails to maintain the fundamental distinction between preconditions and precipitants. Secondly, it concentrates on the factors working for or against the successful manipulation of violence rather than on the underlying factors working to produce a revolutionary potential. This is because the paradigm is intended to apply to all forms of internal war rather than to revolution proper, and because all that the various forms of internal war have in common is the use of violence. It is impossible to tell how serious these criticisms are until the paradigm has been applied to a particular historical revolution. Only then will its value become apparent.

If we take the behaviorist approach, then a primary cause of revolutions is the emergence of an obsessive revolutionary mentality. But how closely does this relate to the objective material circumstances themselves? In every revolutionary situation one finds a group of men — fanatics, extremists, zealots — so convinced of their own righteousness and of the urgent need to create a new Jerusalem on earth (whether formally religious or secular in inspiration is irrelevant) that they are prepared to smash through the normal restraints of habit, custom, and convention. Such men were the seventeenth-century English Puritans, the eighteenth-century French Jacobins, the twentieth-century Russian Bolsheviks. But what makes such men is far from certain. What generates such ruthlessness in curbing evil, such passion for discipline and order? Rapid social mobility, both horizontal and vertical, and particularly urbanization, certainly produces a sense of rootlessness and anxiety. In highly stratified societies, even some of the newly-risen elements may find themselves under stress.[15] While some of the *arrivistes* are happily absorbed in their new strata, others remain uneasy and resentful. If they are snubbed and rebuffed by the older members of the status group to which they aspire by reason of their new wealth and position, they are likely to become acutely conscious of their social inferiority, and may be driven either to adopt a pose *plus royaliste que le Roi* or to dream of destroying the whole social order. In the latter case they may try to allay their sense of insecurity by imposing their norms and values by force upon society at large. This is especially the case if there is available a moralistic ideology like Puritanism or Marxism to which they can attach themselves, and which provides them with unshakable confidence in their own rectitude.

But why does the individual react in this particular way rather than another? Some would argue that the character of the revolutionary is formed by sudden ideological conversion in adolescence or early adult life (to Puritanism, Jacobinism, or Bolshevism) as a refuge from this anxiety state.[16] What is not acceptable is the fashionable conservative cliché that the revolutionary and the reformer are merely the chance product of unfortunate psychological difficulties in childhood. It is possible that this is the mechanism by which such feelings are generated, though there is increasing evidence of the continued plasticity of human character until at any rate post-adolescence. The main objection to this theory is that it fails to explain why these particular attitudes become common only in certain classes and age groups at certain times and in certain places. This failure strongly suggests that the cause of this state of mind lies not in the personal maladjustment of the individuals or their parents, but in the social conditions that created that maladjustment. Talcott Parsons treats disaffection or "alienation" as a generalized phenomenon that may manifest itself in crime, alcoholism, drug addiction, daytime fantasies, religious enthusiasm, or serious political agitation. To use Robert Merton's formulation, Ritualism and Retreatism are two possible psychological escape-routes; Innovation and Rebellion two others.[17]

Even if we accept this behaviorist approach (which I do), the fact remains that many of the underlying causes both of the alienation of the revolutionaries and of the weakness of the incumbent elite are economic in origin; and it is in this area that some interesting work has centered. In particular a fresh look has been taken at the contradictory models of Marx and de Tocqueville, the one claiming that popular revolution is a product of increasing misery, the other that it is a product of increasing prosperity.

Two economists, Sir Arthur Lewis and Mancur Olson, have pointed out that because of their basic social stability, both preindustrial and highly industrialized societies are relatively free from revolutionary disturbance.[18] In the former societies, people accept with little question the accepted rights and obligations of family, class, and caste. Misery, oppression, and social injustice are passively endured as inevitable features of life on earth. It is in societies experiencing rapid economic growth that the trouble usually occurs. Lewis, who is thinking mostly about the newly emerging countries, primarily of Africa, regards the sense of frustration that leads to revolution as a consequence of the dislocation of the old status patterns by the emergence of four new classes — the proletariat, the capitalist employers, the urban commercial and professional middle class, and the professional politicians — and of the disturbance of the old income patterns by the sporadic and patchy impact of economic growth, which creates new wealth and new poverty in close and conspicuous juxtaposition. Both phenomena he regards as merely transitional, since in a country fully developed economically there are strong tendencies toward the elimination of inequalities of opportunity, income, and status.

This model matches fairly well the only detailed analysis of a historical revolution in which a conscious effort has been made to apply modern sociological methods. In his recent study of the Vendée, Charles Tilly argues that a counterrevolutionary situation was the consequence of special tensions created by the immediate juxtaposition of, on one hand, parish clergy closely identified with the local communities, great absentee landlords, and old-fashioned subsistence farming, and, on the other, a large-scale textile industry on the putting-out system and increasing bourgeois competition.[19] Though the book is flawed by a tendency to take a ponderous sociological hammer to crack a simple little historical nut, it is nonetheless a suggestive example of the application of new hypotheses and techniques to historical material.

Olson has independently developed a more elaborate version of the Lewis theory. He argues that revolutionaries are déclassé and freed from the social bonds of family, profession, village or manor; and that these individuals are the product of rapid economic growth, which creates both *nouveaux riches* and *nouveaux pauvres*. The former, usually middle-class and urban artisans, are better off economically, but are disoriented, rootless, and restless; the latter may be workers whose wages have failed to keep pace with inflation, workers in technologically outdated and therefore declining industries, or the unemployed in a society in which the old cushions of the extended family and the village have gone, and in which the new cushion of social security has not yet been created. The initial growth phase may well cause a decline in the standard of living of the majority because of the need for relatively enormous forced savings for reinvestment. The result is a revolution caused by the widening gap between expectations — social and political for the new rich, economic for the new poor — and the realities of everyday life.

A sociologist [sic], James C. Davies, agrees with Olson that the fundamental impetus toward a revolutionary situation is generated by rapid economic growth but he associates such growth with a generally rising rather than a generally falling standard of living, and argues that the moment of potential revolution is reached only when the long-term phase of growth is followed by a short-term phase of economic stagnation or decline.[20] The result of this "J-curve," as he calls it, is that steadily soaring expectations, newly created by the period of growth, shoot further and further ahead of actual satisfaction of needs. Successful revolution is the work neither of the destitute or of the well-satisfied, but of those whose actual situation is improving less rapidly than they expect.

These economic models have much in common, and their differences can be explained by the fact that Lewis and Olson are primarily concerned with the long-term economic forces creating instability, and Davies with the short-term economic factors that may precipitate a crisis. Moreover their analyses apply to different kinds of economic growth, of which three have recently been identified by W. W. Rostow and Barry Supple: there is the expansion of production in a pre-industrial society, which may not cause any important technological, ideological, social, or political change; there is the phase of rapid growth, involving major changes of every kind; and there is the sustained trend toward technological maturity.[21] Historians have been quick to see that these models, particularly that of Rostow, can be applied only to a limited number of historical cases. The trouble is not so much that in any specific case the phases — particularly the last two — tend to merge into one another, but that changes in the various sectors occur at irregular and unexpected places on the time-scale in different societies. Insofar as there is any validity in the division of the stages of growth into these three basic types, the revolutionary model of Olson and Lewis is confined to the second; that of Davies is applicable to all three.

The Davies model fits the history of Western Europe quite well, for it looks as if in conditions of extreme institutional and ideological rigidity the first type of economic growth may produce frustrations of a very serious kind. Revolutions broke out all over Europe in the 1640's, twenty years after a secular growth phase had come to an end.[22] C. E. Labrousse has demonstrated the existence of a similar economic recession in France from 1778,[23] and from 1914 the Russian economy was dislocated by the war effort after many years of rapid growth. Whatever its limitations in any particular situation, the J-curve of actual satisfaction of needs is an analytical tool that historians can usefully bear in mind as they probe the violent social upheavals of the past.

As de Tocqueville pointed out, this formula of advance followed by retreat is equally applicable to other sectors. Trouble arises if a phase of liberal governmental concessions is followed by a phase of political repression; a phase of fairly open recruitment channels into the elite followed by a phase of aristocratic reaction and a closing of ranks; a phase of weakening status barriers by a phase of reassertion of privilege. The J-curve is applicable to other than purely economic satisfactions, and the apex of the curve is the point at which underlying causes, the preconditions, merge with immediate factors, the precipitants. The recipe for revolution is thus the creation of new expectations by economic improvement and some social and political reforms, followed by economic recession, governmental reaction, and aristocratic resurgence, which widen the gap between expectations and reality.

All these attempts to relate dysfunction to relative changes in economic prosperity and aspirations are hampered by two things, of which the first is the extreme difficulty in ascertaining the facts. It is never easy to discover precisely what is happening to the distribution of wealth in a given society. Even now, even in highly developed Western societies with massive bureaucratic controls and quantities of statistical data, there is no agreement about the facts. Some years ago it was confidently believed that in both Britain and the United States incomes were being levelled, and that extremes of both wealth and poverty were being steadily eliminated. Today, no one quite knows what is happening in either country.[24] And if this is true now, still more is it true of societies in the past about which the information is fragmentary and unreliable.

Secondly, even if they can be clearly demonstrated, economic trends are only one part of the problem. Historians are increasingly realizing that the psychological responses to changes in wealth and power are not only not precisely related to, but are politically more significant than, the material changes themselves. As Marx himself realized at one stage, dissatisfaction with the status quo is not determined by absolute realities but by relative expectations. "Our desires and pleasures spring from society; we measure them, therefore, by society, and not by the objects which serve for their satisfaction. Because they are of a social nature, they are of a relative nature." [25] Frustration may possibly result from a rise and subsequent relapse in real income. But it is perhaps more likely to be caused by a rise in aspirations that outstrips the rise in real income; or by a rise in the *relative* economic position in society of the group in question, followed by a period in which its real income continues to grow, but less fast than that of other groups around it. Alternatively it may represent a rise and then decline of status, largely unrelated to real income; or if status and real income are related, it may be inversely. For example, social scientists seeking to explain the rise of the radical right in the United States in the early 1950's and again in the early 1960's attribute it to a combination of great economic prosperity and an aggravated sense of insecurity of status.[26] Whether or not this is a general formula for right-wing rather than left-wing revolutionary movements is not yet clear.

Moreover the problem is further complicated by an extension of the reference-group theory.[27] Human satisfaction is related not to existing conditions but to the condition of a social group against which the individual measures his situation. In an age of mass communications and the wide distribution of cheap radio receivers even among the impoverished illiterate of the world, knowledge of high consumption standards elsewhere spreads rapidly, and as a result the reference group may be in another, more highly developed, country or even continent. Under these circumstances, revolutionary conditions may be created before industrialization has got properly under way.

The last area in which some new theoretical work has been done is in the formulation of hypotheses about the social stages of a "Great Revolution." One of the best attacks on this problem was made by Crane Brinton, who was thinking primarily about the French Revolution, but who extended his comparisons to the three other major Western revolutionary movements. He saw the first phase as dominated by moderate bourgeois elements; their supersession by the radicals; a reign of terror; a Thermidorian reaction; and the establishment of strong central authority under military rule to consolidate the limited gains of the revolution. In terms of mass psychology he compared revolution with a fever that rises in intensity, affecting nearly all parts of the body politic, and then dies away.

A much cruder and more elementary model has been advanced by an historian of the revolutions of 1848, Peter Amman.[28] He sees the modern state as an institution holding a monopoly of physical force, administration, and justice over a wide area, a monopoly dependent more on habits of obedience than on powers of coercion. Revolution may therefore be defined as a breakdown of the monopoly due to a failure of these habits of obedience. It begins with the emergence of two or more foci of power, and ends with the elimination of all but one. Amman includes the possibility of "suspended revolution," with the existence of two or more foci not yet in violent conflict.

This model admittedly avoids some of the difficulties raised by more elaborate classifications of revolution: how to distinguish a coup d'état from a revolution; how to define the degrees of social change; how to accommodate the conservative counterrevolution, and so on. It certainly offers some explanation of the progress of revolution from stage to stage as the various power blocs that emerge on the overthrow of the incumbent regime are progressively eliminated; and it explains why the greater the public participation in the revolution, the wider the break with the habits of obedience, and therefore the slower the restoration of order and centralized authority. But it throws the baby out with the bathwater. It is impossible to fit any decentralized traditional society, or any modern federal society, into the model. Moreover, even where it might be applicable, it offers no framework for analyzing the roots of revolution, no pointers for identifying the foci of power, no means of distinguishing between the various revolutionary types, and its notion of "suspended revolution" is little more than verbal evasion.

Though it is set out in a somewhat confused, overelaborate, and unnecessarily abstract form, the most convincing description of the social stages of revolution is that outlined by Rex D. Hopper.[29] He sees four stages. The first is characterized by indiscriminate, uncoordinated mass unrest and dissatisfaction, the result of dim recognition that traditional values no longer satisfy current aspirations. The next stage sees this vague unease beginning to coalesce into organized opposition with defined goals, an important characteristic being a shift of allegiance by the intellectuals from the incumbents to the dissidents, the advancement of an "evil men" theory, and its abandonment in favor of an "evil institutions" theory. At this stage there emerge two types of leaders: the prophet, who sketches the shape of the new utopia upon which men's hopes can focus, and the reformer, working methodically toward specific goals. The third, the formal stage, sees the beginning of the revolution proper. Motives and objectives are clarified, organization is built up, a statesman leader emerges. Then conflicts between the left and the right of the revolutionary movement become acute, and the radicals take over from the moderates. The fourth and last stage sees the legalization of the revolution. It is a product of psychological exhaustion as the reforming drive burns itself out, moral enthusiasm wanes, and economic distress increases. The administrators take over, strong central government is established, and society is reconstructed on lines that embody substantial elements of the old system. The result falls far short of the utopian aspirations of the early leaders, but it succeeds in meshing aspirations with values by partly modifying both, and so allows the reconsrtuction af a firm social order.

Some of the writings of contemporary social scientists are ingenious feats of verbal juggling in an esoteric language, performed around the totem pole of an abstract model, surrounded as far as the eye can see by the arid wastes of terminological definitions and mathematical formulæ. Small wonder the historian finds it hard to digest the gritty diet of this neo-scholasticism, as it has been aptly called. The more historically-minded of the social scientists, however, have a great deal to offer. The history of history, as well as of science, shows that advances depend partly on the accumulation of factual information, but rather more on the formulation of hypotheses that reveal the hidden relationships and common properties of apparently distinct phenomena. Social scientists can supply a corrective to the antiquarian fact-grubbing to which historians are so prone; they can direct attention to problems of general relevance, and away from the sterile triviality of so much historical research. They can ask new questions and suggest new ways of looking at old ones. They can supply new categories, and as a result may suggest new ideas.[30]

1 Chalmers Johnson, *Revolution and the Social System*, Hoover Institution Studies 3 (Stanford 1964).

[2] Sheldon S. Wolin, "Violence and the Western Political Tradition," *American Journal of Orthopsychiatry*, xxxiii (January 1963), 15–28.

[3] Brinton, *The Anatomy of Revolution* (New York 1938); Gottschalk, "Causes of Revolution," *American Journal of Sociology*, l (July 1944), 1–8; Pettee, *The Process of Revolution* (New York 1938).

[4] "Toward a Theory of Power and Political Instability in Latin America," *Western Political Quarterly*, ix (1956).

[5] Harry Eckstein, ed., *Internal War* (New York 1964), and "On the Etiology of Internal War," *History and Theory*, iv, No. 2 (1965), 133–63. I am grateful to Mr. Eckstein for allowing me to read this article before publication.

[6] The formula has been used by a historian, Peter Paret, in *Internal War and Pacification: The Vendée, 1793–96* (Princeton 1961).

[7] Barrington Moore, "The Strategy of the Social Sciences," in his *Political Power and Social Theory* (Cambridge, Mass., 1958); Ralph Dahrendorf, "Out of Utopia: Toward a Reorientation of Sociological Analysis," *American Journal of Sociology*, lxiv (September 1958), 115–27; C. Wright Mills, *The Sociological Imagination* (New York 1959); Wilbert E. Moore, *Social Change* (Englewood Cliffs 1963). It should be noted that both the equilibrium and the conflict views of society have very respectable ancestries. The equilibrium model goes back to Rousseau — or perhaps Aquinas; the conflict model to Hobbes, Hegel, and Marx.

[8] Quoted in Edward Mead Earle, ed., *Makers of Modern Strategy* (Princeton 1943), 104–5.

[9] *Revolution and the Social System.*

[10] N. R. C. Cohn, *Pursuit of the Millennium* (New York 1961); Eric J. Hobsbawm, *Primitive Rebels* (Manchester 1959); S. L. Thrupp, *Millennial Dreams in Action*, Supplement II, Comparative Studies in Society and History (The Hague 1962); A. J. F. Köbben, "Prophetic Movements as an Expression of Social Protest," *Internationales Archiv für Ethnographie*, xlix, No. 1 (1960), 117–64.

[11] Sigmund Neumann, quoted in Chalmers, 2.

[12] *Anatomy of Revolution.*

[13] "On the Etiology of Internal War."

[14] Amman, "Revolution: A Redefinition," *Political Science Quarterly*, lxxvii (1962).

[15] Émile Durkheim, *Suicide* (Glencoe 1951), 246–54; A. B. Hollingshead, R. Ellis, and E. Kirby, "Social Mobility and Mental Illness," *American Sociological Review*, xix (1954).

[16] Michael L. Walzer, "Puritanism as a Revolutionary Ideology," *History and Theory*, iii, No. 1 (1963), 59–90.

[17] Parsons, *The Social System* (Glencoe 1951); Merton, *Social Theory and Social Structure* (Glencoe 1957), chap. 4.

[18] W. Arthur Lewis, "Commonwealth Address," in *Conference Across a Continent* (Toronto 1963), 46–60; Olson, "Rapid Growth as a Destabilizing Force," *Journal of Economic History*, xxiii (December 1963), 529–52. I am grateful to Mr. Olson for drawing my attention to Sir Arthur Lewis's article, and for some helpful suggestions.

[19] *The Vendée* (Cambridge, Mass., 1964).

[20] "Toward a Theory of Revolution," *American Sociological Review* xxvii (February 1962), 1–19, esp. the graph on p. 6.

[21] Rostow, *The Stages of Economic Growth* (Cambridge, Mass., 1960); Supple, *The Experience of Economic Growth* (New York 1963), 11–12.

[22] Hobsbawm, "The Crisis of the Seventeenth Century," in T. H. Aston, ed., *Crisis in Europe, 1560–1660* (London 1965), 5–58.

[23] *La Crise de l'Économie française à la fin de l'Ancien Régime et au début de la Révolution* (Paris 1944).

24 Gabriel Kolko, *Wealth and Power in America* (New York 1962); Richard M. Titmuss, *Income Distribution and Social Change* (London 1962).

25 Davies, 5, quoting Marx, *Selected Works in Two Volumes* (Moscow 1955), I, 947.

26 Daniel Bell, ed., *The Radical Right* (Garden City 1963).

27 Merton, chap. 9.

28 "Revolution: A Redefinition."

29 "The Revolutionary Process," *Social Forces*, xxviii (March 1950), 270–79.

30 See Werner J. Cahnman and Alvin Boskoff, eds., *Sociology and History: Theory and Research* (New York 1964); H. Stuart Hughes, "The Historian and the Social Scientist," *American Historical Review*, lxvi, No. 1, (1960), 20–46; A. Cobban, "History and Sociology," *Historical Studies*, iii (1961), 1–8; M. G. Smith, "History and Social Anthropology," *Journal of the Royal Anthropological Institute*, xcii (1962); K. V. Thomas, "History and Anthropology," *Past and Present*, No. 24 (April 1963), 3–18.

18. Writings on Revolution

ROBERT BLACKEY

and

CLIFFORD T. PAYNTON

In the bibliography to Crane Brinton's popular and now almost classic study of *The Anatomy of Revolution* (1952, revised edition) there are thirty-four titles listed under the heading "The Sociology of Revolutions." These titles, eight of which are not in English, represent works that deal with revolutions in general and not with specific revolutions. Today, the number of works on the subject has grown enormously and there is no sign of a slackening in productivity. The purpose of this final essay is to focus the reader's attention on some of the recent (and a few not so recent) significant contributions, both books and articles, that we have not been able to include. Moreover, by summarizing and describing these works it is hoped that this essay will supplement the readings in this volume. The choices were selected somewhat arbitrarily, but hopefully as well for their relevance to the subject. They are grouped rather loosely and simply, but with each section following a particular theme.

There are a number of books that deal with the general theme of revolution, the military, and war. Since most revolutions involve armed insurrection there is invariably a clash between revolutionaries and a professional army, the latter with all the equipment of scientific warfare at their disposal. Therefore, in the last resort, the success or failure of the revolution hinges upon the way in which the army reacts. Katharine Chorley in *Armies and the Art of Revolution* analyzes the relationship among the army, the state, and the revolutionaries by studying historical examples.[1] She notes that the professional army is bound to enjoy a technical superiority to the rebel force, and, as a result, revolutions will fail against professional armed forces operating at full strength. Thus, the political position and consequent action of the regular army is pivotal. It is the factors which determine the position of the army that Chorley discusses. The effective strength of the armed forces may be crippled either by extraneous political circumstances, such as pressure of public opinion at home and in other countries, or by technical considerations, such as the geographical layout of the insurrection.

She adds that the army's attitude will also be determined by the officers and the rank and file. Since most officers come from the propertied classes of the community it is probable that they would not support a revolution from below. The rank and file soldiers have, in practice, been cut off from civilian interests and more often than not have accepted their officers' lead in breaking a revolution on whose success their own class interests depended. Grievances among the rank and file soldiers relating to their service will have some effect in promoting mutinous agitation. But it is questionable how far the discontent they feel can be turned to political ends, "unless it is very widespread and deep and is identified in the minds of the men with a particular system of government, and not merely with a particular set of governing officials."[2]

In modern times the last stages of an unsuccessful war are likely to provide the best combination of circumstances for a successful revolutionary outbreak. In such a large-scale war situation the armed forces are filled quickly from the civilian population. The new soldiers still have real ties with their civilian background and they are not yet politically emasculated. These new soldiers carry with them into military life all the political and class affiliations and sympathies of their civilian life and they are more likely to go against their officers. Thus, unsuccessful war is alone capable of disintegrating the necessary military support of the government sufficiently to make revolution practicable.

Nicholas S. Timasheff's *War and Revolution* is not only concerned with his title subjects, but their opposites — peace and order — as well.[3] As such, not all of his volume relates directly to a concern with revolutions, and only those portions which do will be discussed here. For Timasheff revolution is simply a violent conflict within the state. One party is the government and the other is a more or less organized group, and the goals of these two parties are incompatible. Revolution, therefore, becomes a challenge to the maintenance of law and order. The goal of the opposition is change in political leadership and/or change in the government's policy; in more drastic cases, change is of the total political and/or social order. All revolutions are reducible to the political phase of human co-existence. The basic problem always is: who will make the political decisions and what will those decisions be?

He says that the spread of education and information are important factors in the emergence of revolutionary movements. Uneducated masses may remain passive for a long time despite misery and oppression. But the situation can change when education makes available information about the possibility of a better life. Sometimes the rise of class consciousness or national consciousness is caused by a minority receiving education abroad and then spreading the news at home. Or sometimes the possibility of a better life is demonstrated by members of an arrogant aristocracy or by officials and businessmen of a colonial power among conquered peoples.

Timasheff views revolution as a residual phenomenon; that is, it is resorted to when other ways of overcoming tensions have failed. When such tensions mount and are not healed by reform or reaction, a revolution may erupt provided that the government has been weakened by inner divisions or sustained failure, thus giving a fair chance of victory to the revolutionary party.

In what is an apparent minimization of the motivating effects of ideology, Timasheff makes an interesting observation regarding the reward-punishment pattern. Revolutions are rare because a defeated one results in drastic sanctions against the participants. On the other hand, a successful revolution often results at worst in mass extermination of the leaders of the fallen order or at best in their demotion to the bottom of the new society. Revolutionary leaders generally think it over many times before giving the signal to go ahead. The government, despite its more favorable position, often yields to the demands of potential revolutionaries or does something to appease them in order to avoid the risk of being overthrown by violence. With this in mind, Timasheff proposes a formula for the causation of revolution: "If, within a state, a tension (or a cluster of tensions) has arisen between the government and an opposition and has reached such proportions that the symptoms of plasticity have become apparent; and if the conflict has not been resolved by reform or reaction, a revolution is most likely to follow." [4]

Urban insurrection and contemporary American society are the concerns of *The Urban Guerrilla* by Martin Oppenheimer.[5] No attempt is made to formulate a new theory of revolutions. Rather, Oppenheimer synthesizes the work of others and applies the results to urban insurrections. Collective behavior, paramilitary revolutions, and both violent and non-violent revolutions are discussed, and then several important observations are made by him. (1) Peasant-based revolutions seem historically to end in the dictatorship of the "new class" (i.e., a bureaucratic class as opposed to worker and anticapitalist classes). (2) Unaided urban insurrections, given the modern technology of counter-insurgency warfare, are doomed. (3) A protracted war cannot by itself disable society enough to create a revolutionary situation; instead, there must be sufficient strains within society to allow revolutionary activity to be reasonable. The protracted war can only add to the strain, but it cannot be responsible for the coming of a revolution. (4) in a contemporary, industrialized, urban setting the subversion of society by strain, aided by violent or non-violent guerrillas, will probably end in a right-wing, counter-revolutionary dictatorship. (5) Such a revolution, even if successful, since it represents only a minority, runs the strong risk of ending in a dictatorship of the "new class" (although Oppenheimer feels this risk is hardly a sufficient reason not to try anyway).

Revolution and society are the focus of the next three works under consideration. Max Handman, in his article "The Bureaucratic Culture Pattern and Political Revolutions," sees most of the world divided into two systems of social behavior or culture patterns.[6] There is what he calls the pecuniary-industrial pattern in which life is conceived in terms of engaging in the producing and selling of goods and services for monetary ends — as in the United States of America, England, etc. In these societies social status closely follows successful ability in producing and/or selling. The second system he calls the bureaucratic culture pattern. In it life is conceived in terms of belonging to a hierarchy entrusted with the management and administration of the affairs of the organized community — as in Latin America and parts of Asia and Africa. In these societies success in life means a continuous ascent in the hierarchy. It is with the second of these systems that Handman is concerned, specifically in their relations to political revolutions.

His concern centers on the relationship between the bureaucratic machinery and education. Under the bureaucratic culture pattern financial values are obtained through the entrance and advances into bureaucratic positions carrying monetary emoluments. Education serves the end of producing better bureaucrats, and, therefore, the educated population ultimately increases beyond the number of positions available, thus creating a ripe situation for political revolution. Efforts at expanding the size of the bureaucracy delay a conflict, but so long as the number of bureaucrats increases faster than new or vacant positions available the revolution is inevitable. Often the bureaucratic conflict will ignite other problems (e.g., agrarian) to swell the revolution into a great social upheaval. Although Handman does not say so, it is implicit in his hypothesis that unless a bureaucratic culture pattern system is rigid, fixed, and carefully controlled, the introduction of education inevitably leads to political revolution.

Revolution and Elite Access by Alexander Groth is based on the premise that all revolutionary movements are characterized by a degree of "linkage" or "cross-affiliation" with the established order they seek to overthrow.[7] For example, revolutionaries and the establishment are united by one degree or another in their values, attitudes, and outlook. Groth advances several hypotheses on the problem of revolution insofar as the nature of the linkage between those who seek political change and those who do not may be said to constitute a structuring factor in the revolutionary process. Two of these hypotheses are especially relevant for our purposes. First, the degree of the revolutionists' elite access determines the difficulty of the change that will develop in the revolution. For example, in those countries where there is maximum accessibility to the upper ranks of the status quo, the downfall of the existing regime will come about most easily. Where there is minimum elite accessibility, the downfall will be most difficult. Second, only in countries where elite access is high (i.e., revolutionary movements are elite-affiliated) can the coup d'etat technique of revolution be employed. Conversely, in countries where there is little elite access (i.e., where revolutionary movements are elite-isolated) the way to succeed to power is through a protracted civil war. To support these hypotheses Groth draws upon the experience of the Fascist, Nazi, and Communist revolutions. Still, he holds that they are applicable to all political systems which depend on large, interdependent, bureaucratic organizations for the performance of their functions.

Several other crucial points are discussed by Groth. He finds that the degree of power and influence possessed by an elite bears directly on its capability of resistance to a revolutionary attempt. At the same time the degree of power and influence possessed by an elite defecting from the government in favor of a revolutionary movement is a significant factor in determining how easy or difficult the transition from one regime to another will be. "Revolutionary movements . . . lacking in elite linkage to the powers of the *status-quo* have found it notoriously difficult to translate popular discontent, however bitter and widespread, into power for themselves." [8] A prerequisite to revolution against an established government is an initial, significant breakdown in the physical control of the geographic entity of the state by the status quo; that is, a breakdown enabling the revolutionists to mount a significant attack. But to be successful revolutionaries must also have "rootedness." In other words, revolutionists must be able to penetrate the elite structure which makes the political system work on a daily basis. Without reliable and quantitatively sufficient means of implementing policies in nearly every conceivable area of social organization, the revolutionaries at the very top of the political structure find themselves isolated and impotent. Without this "rootedness" the revolutionaries will find themselves threatened by the organized power of all the various elite survivors of the deposed regime.

"Explorations in the Theory of Social Movements and Revolutions" by James A. Geschwender takes J. C. Davies' theory of societal conditions which tend to produce revolutions (see part III, tenth selection) and goes a step further.[9] It is asserted that Davies' formulation is limited first because he restricted himself by concentrating only on "progressive" revolutions, rather than on those of either the right or left, and second, because he did not distinguish between two separate but related problems. One may either determine those factors which dispose types of people to take part in revolutions or one may determine those factors which produce a revolution at a certain time and place. These two problems, according to Geschwender, require different types of information, and his paper places Davies' theory in the more general context of analyzing conditions which produce both social movements and revolutions.

Four additional hypotheses are suggested by him to complement Davies' "rise and drop" theory. (1) The "rising expectations" hypothesis states that a period of improvement yields the expectation of and desire for further improvements — when these come too slowly rebellion may follow. (2) The "relative deprivation" hypothesis states that improvement for one group that proceeds at a slower pace than improvement for other groups creates a widening gap and increased dissatisfaction. (3) The "downward mobility" hypothesis affects a group experiencing loss of status and observing a previously inferior group closing the gap between them which could then create a revolutionary situation. (4) The "status inconsistency" hypothesis states that when a group's mobility progresses at a rate inconsistent with that group's expectations of itself other tensions are created which could produce protest activity. Geschwender's hypotheses, when taken with Davies' theory, provide a broader social-psychological theory of motivation which could assist the observer in accounting for individual predispositions toward participation in revolutions.

A great many recent works on revolution invariably deal with the interrelated subjects of power and violence. Feliks Gross in *The Seizure of Political Power in a Century of Revolutions* distinguishes between two basic types of political power transfer: violent and non-violent.[10] He focuses attention on an explanation of the action and techniques which have led to power seizures, especially to those violent kinds of seizure. Violent power transfers are divided into two kinds, he says. First, revolution from below which is a spontaneous mass movement, the result of social disorganization, long unrest, and often violent class struggle. Second, revolution from above which is a seizure of power by a group of armed men at the top, a seizure simply of the government and the instruments of power. Gross contends that other types of violent seizures of power are merely variations of these two, and they also are discussed (e.g., combined seizure, the palace revolution). The body of the volume is an examination of the Russian Revolutionary movement in the light of these kinds of power struggles.

The Cuban Revolution provides the background for the discussion of "Revolutions and Tyranny" by Calvin B. Hoover.[11] He contends that while tyrants are sometimes overthrown by revolutions, tyrants are almost always the creation of revolutions. Generally, the author finds that revolutions are fought in the name of liberty, but too often liberty fails to be a result. Thus, revolution and tryanny have often been merely two stages in the process by which liberty has been smothered. This relationship of revolutions and tyranny was known from classical times, only to be forgotten during the American Revolution. Jefferson, it will be recalled, wrote that "the tree of liberty must be refreshed from time to time by the blood of tyrants and patriots." Moreover, this view of revolution as the liberator of the people was strengthened by the Marxist doctrine of the economic and political liberation of the proletariat from the tyranny of the capitalists through revolution. This view Hoover labels a myth.

A coup d'etat is an attempt to change the government by a quick attack against the machinery of administration. Although the coup is different from the revolution in terms of its speed and the numbers involved — it is less wasteful — the causes and preconditions of the coup are similar enough to revolutions to warrant similar study. In this century the coup d'etat has become one of the most common means of seizing political power illegally. *The Conspirators* by D. J. Goodspeed is an empirical study of the coup d'etat.[12] Six examples of successful and unsuccessful coups are considered and compared, and then some general principles are arrived at by the author. For example, strategy is crucial for the success of a coup; it is even more important than tactics. Sound strategy must take into account three factors: the sympathy of the military, the state of public opinion, and the international situation. Another ingredient essential to a successful coup is the quality of leadership. By alluding to his six examples Goodspeed studies the role of leaders, and he also considers the stages through which coups pass.

P. A. R. Calvert in his paper "Revolution: The Politics of Violence" interprets revolution as an expression of the politics of violence.[13] Upon close scrutiny it becomes clear that at few times in the history of any Western country have politics been so free from violence as they are today. At the same time, however, the threat of violence both by the established government and by those who oppose it is ever present. Calvert analyzes certain kinds of activities which he calls sub-revolutionary: demonstrations, strikes, disobedience to authority, and riots. When such activities effect a transfer of power, revolution can be separated from this sub-revolutionary violence. He concludes that for a revolutionary group to be successful it must be able to deploy a sufficient amount of force over a given time in order to overcome the force at the disposal of the established government. There are times in a revolutionary situation when excessive force is employed. This creates needless social displacement and results in unnecessarily dangerous resentment. Calvert suggests that the dangers that come from the use of excessive force are greater for the revolutionary group.

A recent book by Carl Leiden and Karl M. Schmitt, *The Politics of Violence: Revolutions in the Modern World,* makes no attempt to present new theories or hypotheses.[14] It is valuable, however, as both a summary and a synthesis of some of the literature on the theory and analysis of revolutionary causation and development. The authors deal with the relation violence bears to revolution, the preconditions of revolution, the revolutionary environment, the stages of revolution, the participants, and the role of ideology. An important point noted by the authors is that the very modernity of our own times (i.e., the technology, the knowledge, and the spirit of freedom) has facilitated revolution. Four case studies of twentieth century Latin America and Middle East revolutions are examined in the light of the current literature.

Although not directly concerned with revolutions, *Political Violence: The Behavioral Process* by H. L. Nieburg is of great value and relevance to our subject.[15] It is based upon work done for the National Commission on the Causes and Prevention of Violence established by President Lyndon Johnson following the assassination of Robert F. Kennedy. Several themes pervade the volume. For example: (1) the incidence of group violence increases as groups assume semi-sovereign functions as a challenge to or substitute for the weakened legitimacy of the state and (2) beneath all the forms of polite society lies a stratum of potential violence which constitutes the ultimate test of the viability of social groups and institutions. Nieburg warns that violent political behavior cannot be dismissed as simply erratic, exceptional, or meaningless. Invariably, political legitimacy is based on violence. Violence is a natural form of political behavior and it is intrinsically related to the social process. Insofar as revolution is concerned, violent acts may be looked upon as society's early warning system.

A spokesman and a theorist for the Third World is the late Frantz Fanon. The purpose of his book *The Wretched of the Earth,* according to Jean-Paul Sartre, is to teach the subjected to beat the subjectors, at their own game.[16] This involves violence, revolt, and revolution. Fanon believes that violence is man re-creating himself. The system to be overthrown involves putting into practice the words: "The last shall be first and the first last." And this has to involve absolute violence. He feels that a virtual prerequisite for revolution or revolt is the realization on the part of the potential revolutionary that the skin of his oppressor is not of any more value than his own. "For if, in fact, my life is worth as much as the [oppressor's], his glance no longer shrivels me up nor freezes me, and his voice no longer turns me into stone. I am no longer on tenterhooks in his presence; in fact, I don't give a damn for him." [17]

Fanon is specifically addressing the oppressed colonial peoples of Africa, but his words obviously have a wider application. Colonialism and oppression, he claims, is violence in its natural state. They will only yield when confronted with greater violence. "The exploited man sees that his liberation implies the use of all means, and that of force first and foremost." [18] The colonial or oppressor regime owes its legitimacy to force and is based on strength and force. Just as the oppressor uses force on the grounds that it is all the oppressed understands, so does the oppressed use force and violence on the same grounds. Thus, "the colonized man finds his freedom in and through violence." [19] On the necessity and the use of violence Fanon concludes: "At the level of individuals, violence is a cleansing force. It frees the native from his inferiority complex and from his despair and inaction; it makes him fearless and restores his self-respect." [20]

As a balance to Fanon's belief in the necessity of violence the reader should see "On Revolution and Equilibrium" by Barbara Deming.[21] Deming is a professed admirer of Fanon, but she is not an advocate of violent revolution. Rather she would substitute non-violence in the form of radical and uncompromising action. She suggests that even Fanon would have preferred non-violence, quoting sentences such as the following: "We today can do everything, so long as we do not imitate Europe." Since European history has been preoccupied with violence, is not this an appeal to non-violence? The crux of Deming's argument is that "may those who have questioned non-violence come to see that one's right to life and happiness can only be claimed as inalienable if one grants, in action, that they belong to all men." [22]

As has been made obvious through the course of this volume the word revolution rarely means the same thing to different individuals. A survey of several works that have appeared during the last half century illustrates the subtle changes that have taken place in examinations of revolutions. It seems to us that the most significant changes have come in descriptive terminology which in turn is illustrative of an increased sophistication on the part of observers and a growing inter-dependence among the disciplines.

In "Current Definitions of Revolutions," published in 1926, Dale Yoder enumerates three conceptions prevalent in the writing of his day.[23] First is the view that revolution is a purely political phenomenon involving a change in the location of sovereignty. Second is the view that revolution includes any sudden social change, so that political revolution is but one of several types. And third is the view that revolution is such a drastic change that it involves all phases of social organization. Yoder dismisses the specific nuances given these definitions by their several adherents. To him a real revolution involves the change in the attitudes of the people toward the underlying basis of the institutions or customs which seemingly stand in the way of a tolerable life experience. In other words, it is the change in the social atittudes and values basic to the traditional institutional order that is crucial. The political, religious, economic and other changes are simply overt manifestations of the deeper change which had previously taken place. Yoder reveals how revolution can be viewed as either a threat to civilization or a vehicle towards freedom; it carries connotations which involve the deepest fears as well as the highest hopes.

Appearing in 1934, "Revolution and Counter-Revolution" by Alfred Meusel is a descriptive and analytical article defining terms and the process of revolution.[24] The recasting of the social order is said to be a more important characteristic of modern revolutions than a change of the political constitution or the use of violence in attaining this end. It is the social aspect that distinguishes revolutions from coups d'etat, rebellions, or insurrections. Further, the significance of a revolution lies in the fact that it is a major shift in the relations among social classes, to the degree where the old order is discarded and a new one erected in its place. Meusel also discusses the political, psychological, ideological, and organizational aspects of revolution.

Arthur Hatto's article, "'Revolution': An Enquiry into the Usefulness of an Historical Term," appeared in 1949.[25] Revolution is described simply and in broad terms — as the complete overthrow of the established government — so that it can cope with a wide range of examples. "Let [the word] 'revolution' continue to do good work by pointing the way to crucial events involving a shift of power in the state swifter than 'evolution.'"[26] Hatto is less interested in definition than he is in the usefulness and origins of the word. He asserts that words like "revolution" lend to history an appearance of movement and give history its sense of great drama. Where the article traces the origins of the word it provides an excellent comparison to the second selection in this volume by Karl Griewank. The latter dates the political use of the word from the scientific advances of the sixteenth and seventeenth centuries. Hatto dates its political application from fourteenth century Italy during which time the revolution of the heavens was associated with political change.

A 1967 paper by Raymond Tanter and Manus Midlarsky, entitled "A Theory of Revolution," brings our definitional examination closely up to date.[27] The authors examine some of the causes of revolution, particularly those that relate to changes in economic development and changes in levels of education. Four types of revolutions are listed on the basis of their increasing intensity: the palace revolution, the reform coup, the revolutionary coup, and the mass revolution. After studying these types the following definition is presented:

> A revolution may be said to exist when a group of insurgents illegally and/or forcefully challenges the governmental elite for the occupancy of roles in the structure of political authority. A successful revolution occurs when, as a result of a challenge to the governmental elite, insurgents are eventually able to occupy principal roles within the structure of the political authority.[28]

This definition, claim the authors, sets a minimum criterion for the existence of revolution. They further note that the number of deaths and the duration of a revolution may increase proportionally to the degree of societal change envisaged by the insurgents.

A revolution generally occurs after a period of instability, and the authors suggest that the form of a revolution is dependent upon the degree of political instability which exists prior to its occurrence. Basing some of their work on J. C. Davies' J-curve, they hypothesize that revolutionary intensity, measured by the level of domestic violence, is associated with a long-term increase in achievement, followed by a reversal in expectations immediately prior to the revolution. It is also suggested by them that the lower the level of educational attainment prior to the revolution, the greater the duration and violence of the revolution. These hypotheses are applied to recent revolutions and are found valid for Asian and Middle Eastern revolutions, but not for those in Latin America (except for Cuba) where palace revolutions are the usual kinds. The authors conclude that the causes of palace revolutions differ from those of the other forms mentioned above.

Two post-World War II articles treat the subject of revolutions in this century. In "Twentieth Century Revolutions" Hugh Seton-Watson finds that revolutionary movements of this century differ from those of the nineteenth century in that the earlier revolutions arose in culturally and economically advanced countries, while those of the twentieth century have for the most part affected backward regions and people.[29] He takes a cursory view of revolutions in this century and contends that few of these revolutionary movements have attained success solely by their own efforts.

The revolutions in Russia and China, for example, were won only because a foreign foe had crushed the state machine which the revolutionaries had previously been too weak to destroy or capture. Another of his observations is that the leadership of revolutionary movements comes mainly from the intelligentsia. To prevent revolutions, the author advises, the western nations must win the friendship of the intellectuals in the backward nations. It is also advised that economic action against revolution is not in itself enough; it is a delusion to suppose that the mere expenditure of money will make it possible to present to the people of non-communist Asia, Africa, and Latin America a magic, ready-made social justice.

In an article entitled "The Age of Revolution," Henry M. Wriston discusses the ways in which an established nation, such as the United States, which was founded on revolution, can best deal with newly emerging nations, similarly founded on revolutions.[30] Compassion for and understanding of current revolutions will come with a familiarity of past revolutions, particularly our own. (A brief summary of the American Revolution is provided.) Wriston comments that revolution is like turning a wheel. Spin a wheel and momentum takes over to some extent; it rarely stops — except in closely controlled circumstances — just where you want it to. Similarly with revolutions; they develop a dynamic of their own, and no one can predict just how far they will go. The righteousness of the initial impulse does not always govern the result.

One book which stands virtually by itself as a kind of grandiose study of the phenomenon of revolution is Hannah Arendt's *On Revolution*.[31] Concentrating on what are commonly referred to as the "great" revolutions — American, French, and Russian — Arendt analyzes revolutions in general and finds that the aim of revolution was, and always has been freedom. She points out that one of the distinguishing features of modern revolutions is their social character. But the social question, according to the author, did not become significant until the time of the American Revolution when men began to doubt that poverty was inherent in the human condition.

Another distinguishing feature of modern revolutions discussed in the book is that revolutions tend to begin history afresh. This concept, according to Arendt, was unknown prior to the American and French Revolutions when revolutions were really restorations. This idea of beginning over is found related to the conception of novelty, and only where novelty is connected to the idea of freedom are we entitled to speak of revolution. This is what distinguishes revolutions from coups or rebellions. Violence and change are not enough to constitute a revolution. Rather, only where violence and change are used to bring about a new beginning and to bring about liberation from oppression can we speak of revolution. Thus, to

Arendt, there have been few real revolutions in history, but many coups and rebellions.

Other points of interest are noted by the author. She finds that *terror* as an institutional device, consciously used to accelerate the momentum of the revolution, was unknown prior to 1917. To be sure, the French after 1789 employed terror. For the Bolsheviks terror was motivated by ideology, and that is the difference. She notes with regret that in countries founded on revolution freedom has not been as well preserved as in countries where no revolution ever broke out. In fact, Arendt believes there exists more civil liberty in countries where the revolution was defeated than in those where revolutions have been victorious. She states that a revolution is pre-determined by the type of government it overthrows; thus, the more absolute the ruler the more absolute will be the revolution which replaces him. Perhaps the greatest threat to the achievements of a revolution is the revo-lutionary spirit which has brought it about. This revolutionary spirit, says Arendt, was lost by America almost immediately. She shows how the Con-stitution, the "greatest achievement of the American people . . . eventually cheated them of their proudest possession" (i.e., their revolutionary spirit).[32]

It is appropriate and necessary in this essay to make a few comments about the writings on revolutions by the New Left in America. There has been an outpouring of books and articles lately from this source. We do not pretend to have read them all, but we have given a few careful examina-tion. Two of the most popular are *Revolution for the Hell of It* by Abbie Hoffman and *Do It!* by Jerry Rubin. Hardly theoretical or analytical, among other things, these books are symptoms of unrest and of what may be the early stages of a revolutionary process in the making. Hoffman and Rubin are agitators who are adept at image making and mood creating. Revolution may be theater in action for them, but their theatrics enable them to offer a message to society; they have learned their McLuhan well. Also provid-ing insight into the thinking of the New Left is the periodical literature scattered in magazines such as *Liberation, Ramparts, Evergreen Review, Socialist Revolution, The New Republic* and *The New York Review of Books.* Similarly relevant is the underground press: *SDS Notes, Palante, Sundance, The Liberated Guardian, Rat,* and the *Liberation News Service* are some examples.

"The Trial" by Tom Hayden is, if not representative, at least a good example of the thinking of the New Left.[33] To Hayden revolution is like birth: blood will flow, but the purpose of the act is to create life and not to glorify blood. A crucial lesson Hayden has learned from history is that ordinary people can and do make history. Given this, he sees a revolutionary strategy present in the way people move against the structures oppressing them.

Although Hayden's book is primarily concerned with the trial of the Chicago Eight (of which he was one), he does focus some attention on revolution and contemporary America and on the process of revolution. He sees in the protest movement of the sixties and seventies the seeds from which to create future institutions of government. Little hope is placed in the existing governmental machinery that has proven itself ineffective; therefore, new machinery is needed to meet the needs of all the people. Hayden sees revolutionary movements as evolving through three overlapping stages. The first is *protest*, in which people petition their government for changes. If the changes fail to come, the level of protest becomes massive and the government tries to suppress it. This drives the people toward the second stage, *resistance*, in which there is the beginning of the conflict between ruled and rulers. As the conflict sharpens resistance leads to the third phase, *liberation*, in which the ruling structure disintegrates and the "new guards" are established by the people. The *resistance* phase is the crucial one since it is the time of showdown in which the government will either crush the resistance and restore its own power or undergo continuous failure. America, Hayden believes, is presently in the beginnings of the *resistance* phase, and, as such, he outlines some new principles for organizing our society.

The final work to be mentioned in this selection is "Political Revolution, Civil Violence, and Uncivil Disobedience" by Henry Kenski, Jr.[34] It too is a bibliographical essay which samples some of the literature on revolution. However, it differs from the present paper in that it covers many more works, but in doing so it is only able to devote a sentence or two to each. It is specifically useful in that it refers to several publications on a number of recent revolutions (e.g., Cuba) and contemporary revolutionary-like activity (as in the United States of America among the Blacks and in France).

A revolution, wrote Friedrich Engels, "is certainly the most authoritarian thing there is; it is the act whereby one part of the population imposes its will upon the other part by means of rifles, bayonets, and cannon." [35] Lenin later revealed his own inclinations when he wrote that "it is more pleasant and useful to go through the 'experience of the revolution' than to write about it." [36] Revolution is a very serious business. Writing about it is safer than experiencing it, but knowing what it entails and understanding its causes is safer still.

1 Katharine Chorley, *Armies and the Art of Revolution* (London: Faber and Faber Ltd, 1943).
2 *Ibid.*, p. 244.

[3] Nicholas S. Timasheff, *War and Revolution* (New York: Sheed and Ward, 1965).
[4] *Ibid.*, p. 160.
[5] Martin Oppenheimer, *The Urban Guerrilla* (Chicago: Quadrangle Books, 1969).
[6] Max Handman, "The Bureaucratic Culture Pattern and Political Revolution," *The American Journal of Sociology*, XXXIX, 3 (November 1933), 301–313.
[7] Alexander Groth, *Revolution and Elite Access: Some Hypotheses on Aspects of Political Change* (Davis: Institute of Governmental Affairs, 1966).
[8] *Ibid.*, p. 5.
[9] James A. Geschwender, "Explorations in the Theory of Social Movements and Revolutions," *Social Forces*, 47, 2 (December 1968), 127–135.
[10] Feliks Gross, *The Seizure of Political Power in A Century of Revolutions* (New York: Philosophical Library, 1958).
[11] Calvin B. Hoover, "Revolutions and Tyranny," *The Virginia Quarterly Review*, XXXV (1960), 182–194.
[12] D. J. Goodspeed, *The Conspirators: A Study of the Coup d'Etat* (New York: The Viking Press, 1961).
[13] P. A. R. Calvert, "Revolution: The Politics of Violence," *Political Studies*, XV, 1 (February 1967), 1–11.
[14] Carl Leiden and Karl M. Schmitt, *The Politics of Violence: Revolution in the Modern World* (Englewood Cliffs: Prentice-Hall, Inc., 1968).
[15] H. L. Nieburg, *Political Violence: The Behavioral Process* (New York: St. Martin's Press, 1969).
[16] Frantz Fanon, *The Wretched of the Earth*, trans. Constance Farrington (New York: Grove Press Inc., 1968).
[17] *Ibid.*, p. 45.
[18] *Ibid.*, p. 61.
[19] *Ibid.*, p. 86.
[20] *Ibid.*, p. 94.
[21] Barbara Deming, "On Revolution and Equilibrium," *Liberation*, XII, 11 (February 1968), 10–21.
[22] *Ibid.*, p. 21.
[23] Dale Yoder, "Current Definitions of Revolution," *The American Journal of Sociology*, XXXII (1926), 433–441.
[24] Alfred Meusel, "Revolution and Counter-Revolution," in *Encyclopedia of the Social Sciences*, XIII (New York: The Macmillan Company, 1934, 1963).
[25] Arthur Hatto, " 'Revolution': An Enquiry into the Usefulness of an Historical Term," *MIND*, LVIII, 232 (October 1949), 495–517.
[26] *Ibid.*, p. 517.
[27] Raymond Tanter and Manus Midlarsky, "A Theory of Revolution," *The Journal of Conflict Resolution*, XI, 3 (September 1967), 264–280.
[28] *Ibid.*, p. 267.
[29] Hugh Seton-Watson, "Twentieth Century Revolutions," *The Political Quarterly*, XXII, 3 (July–September 1951), 251–255.
[30] Henry M. Wriston, "The Age of Revolution," *Foreign Affairs*, 39, 4 (July 1961), 533–548.
[31] Hannah Arendt, *On Revolution* (New York: The Viking Press, 1963).
[32] *Ibid.*, p. 242.
[33] Tom Hayden, "The Trial," *Ramparts*, IX, 1 (July 1970).
[34] Henry Kenski, Jr., "Political Revolution, Civil Violence, and Uncivil Disobedience," *Choice*, VI, 5–6 (July–August 1969), 619–625.
[35] Friedrick Engels, "On Authority," in Karl Marx and Friedrick Engels, *Selected Works* (Moscow: Foreign Languages Publishing House, 1958), I, p. 639.
[36] Quoted in Oppenheimer, *Urban Guerrilla*, p. 20.

BIBLIOGRAPHY

Adams, Arthur E. (ed.). *The Russian Revolution and Bolshevik Victory.* Lexington, Mass.: D. C. Heath and Company, 1960.

Adams, Brooks. *The Theory of Social Revolutions.* New York: The Macmillan Company, 1913.

Alavi, Hamza. "Peasants and Revolution," in Ralph Miliband & John Saville. (eds.). *The Socialist Register.* London: Merlin Press, 1965.

Alden, J. R. *The American Revolution, 1775–1783.* New York: Harper & Row, Publishers, 1954.

Ali, Tariq. (ed.). *New Revolutionaries: A Handbook of the International Radical Left.* New York: William Morrow & Co., Inc., 1969.

Alinsky, Saul. *Rules For Revolution.* New York: Random House, Inc., 1971.

AlRoy, Gil Carl. *The Involvement of Peasants in Internal Wars.* Princeton: Center of International Studies, Princeton University, Research Monograph No. 24, 1966.

———. "The Peasantry in the Cuban Revolution," *Review of Politics,* XIX (January 1967), 87–99.

———. "Revolutionary Conditions in Latin America," *Review of Politics,* XIX (July 1967), 417–422.

Amann, Peter (ed.). *The Eighteenth-Century Revolution.* Lexington, Mass.: D. C. Heath and Company, 1963.

———. "Revolution: A Redefinition," *Political Science Quarterly,* 77 (1962), 36–53.

Arciniega, German. "What's Behind Our Revolutions?" *Américas,* I (1949), 22–24, 48.

Arendt, Hannah. *On Revolution.* New York: The Viking Press, 1963.

———. "Reflections on Violence," *Journal of International Affairs,* XXIII, 1 (1969), 1–35.

———. "Revolution and Public Happiness," *Commentary,* XXX (November 1960), 413–422.

"Are We in the Middle of the 'Second American Revolution'?" *The New York Times Magazine* (May 17, 1970).

Aristotle. *The Politics of Aristotle.* Trans. Benjamin Jowett. Oxford: At The Clarendon Press, 1885.

Aron, Raymond. *The Elusive Revolution.* New York: Frederick A. Praeger, Inc., 1969.

———. "Student Rebellion: Vision of the Future or Echo from the Past," *Political Science Quarterly,* LXXXIV (June 1969), 289–310.

Artz, Frederick. *Reaction and Revolution, 1814–1832.* New York: Harper & Row, Publishers, 1934.

Baldwin, Roger N. (ed.). *Kroptkin's Revolutionary Pamphlets*. New York: Dover Publications, Inc., 1970.

Barbour, Floyd B. (ed.). *The Black Power Revolt*. Boston: Porter Sargent Publisher, 1968.

Barkan, Elliott R. *Edmund Burke on The American Revolution*. Gloucester, Mass.: Peter Smith, 1971.

Bascio, P. "Need for Revolution," *Catholic World*, 209 (August 1969), 207–209.

Bauer, Arthur. *Essai sur les Revolutions*. Paris: Giard & Brière, 1908.

Beals, Carleton. *The Nature of Revolution*. New York: Thomas Y. Crowell Company, 1970.

Becker, Frances Bennett. "Lenin's Application of Marx's Theory of Revolutionary Tactics," *American Sociological Review*, II (1937), 353–364.

Bell, Daniel (ed.). *The Radical Right: The New American Right Expanded and Updated*. Garden City: Doubleday & Company, Inc., 1963.

Beqiraj, Mehmet. *Peasantry in Revolution*. Ithaca: Cornell Research Papers in International Studies (V), 1966.

Berger, Peter L. & Richard J. Neuhaus. *Movement and Revolution*. Garden City: Doubleday & Company, Inc., 1970.

Berle, Adolph A. *Power*. New York: Harcourt, Brace & World, 1970.

Berrigan, Daniel. "Father Berrigan's letter to the Weathermen," *The Village Voice* (January 21, 1971).

Berrigan, Philip. *Prison Journals of a Priest Revolutionary*. New York: Holt, Rinehart & Winston, 1970.

Bienen, Henry. *Violence and Social Change: A Review of Current Literature*. Chicago: University of Chicago Press, 1969.

Binkley, Robert C. "An Anatomy of Revolution," *The Virginia Quarterly Review*, X (1934), 502–514.

Black, Cyril E. & Thomas P. Thornton (eds.). *Communism and Revolution: The Strategic Uses of Political Violence*. Princeton: Princeton University Press, 1964.

Blaiser, Cole. "Studies of Social Revolution: Origins in Mexico, Bolivia, and Cuba," *Latin American Research Review*, II (1967), 28–64.

Blanksten, G. "Revolutions," in H. E. Davis. *Government and Politics in Latin America*. New York: Ronald Press, 1958.

Bracey, Jr., John H., August Meier & Elliot Rudwick (eds.). *Black Nationalism in America*. Indianapolis: Bobbs-Merrill Company, Inc., 1970.

Brandes, Paul D. *The Rhetoric of Revolt*. Englewood Cliffs: Prentice-Hall, Inc., 1971.

Breunig, Charles. *The Age of Revolution and Reaction, 1789–1850*. New York: W. W. Norton & Company, Inc., 1970.

Brinkman, Carl. *Soziologische Theorie Der Revolution*. Göttingen: Vandenhoeck & Ruprecht, 1948.

Brinton, Crane. *The Anatomy of Revolution*. Englewood Cliffs: Prentice-Hall, Inc., 1938, 1952, 1965.

———. *A Decade of Revolution, 1789–1799*. New York: Harper & Row, Publishers, 1934.

Brisbane, Robert H. *The Black Vanguard: Origins of the Black Social Revolution, 1900–1960*. Valley Forge, Pa.: The Judson Press, 1970.

Brogan, D. W. *The Price of Revolution*. New York: Grosset & Dunlap, 1966.

Brzezinski, Zbigniew. *Between Two Ages: America's Role in the Technetronic Era.* New York: The Viking Press, 1970.
———. "Revolution and Counterrevolution," *The New Republic* (June 1, 1968), 23–25.
Buckingham, Peter. *The Limits of Protest.* Indianapolis: Bobbs-Merrill Company, Inc., 1970.
Bunzel, John H. "The Appeal of Revolution: The Liberal's Quandary," *The Antioch Review,* XXI, 3 (1961), 319–327.
Burke, Edmund. *Reflections on the Revolution in France.* Garden City: Doubleday & Company, Inc., 1961.
Burns, C. D. *The Principles of Revolution.* London: G. Allen & Unwin Ltd., 1920.

Califano, Jr., Joseph A. *Student Revolution: A Global Confrontation.* New York: W. W. Norton & Co., 1970.
———. *Revolution.* New York: Frederick A. Praeger, Inc., 1970.
Calvert, P. A. R. "Revolution: The Politics of Violence," *Political Studies,* XV, 1 (February 1967), 1–11.
Camejo, Peter. *How To Make a Revolution in the U. S.* New York: Pathfinder Press, Inc., n.d.
Cameron, Wm. Bruce. *Modern Social Movements.* New York: Random House, Inc., 1966.
Cantril, Hadley. *The Psychology of Social Movements.* New York: John Wiley & Sons, Inc., 1941.
Carr, E. H. *The Bolshevik Revolution: 1917–1923.* 3 vols. London: Macmillan & Co., Ltd., 1950–1953.
———. *Studies in Revolution.* New York: Grosset & Dunlap, 1964.
Carswell, John. *The Descent On England: A Study of the English Revolution of 1688 and its European Background.* New York: John Day Company, 1969.
Chamberlin, William Henry. *The Russian Revolution, 1917–1921.* 2 vols. New York: The Macmillan Company, 1952.
Chaplin, David. "Peru's Postponed Revolution," *World Politics,* XX (April 1968), 393–420.
Ch'en, Jerome. *Mao and the Chinese Revolution.* London: Oxford University Press, 1965.
Chilcote, Ronald H. *The Radical Left and Revolutions in Latin America.* Stanford: Hoover Institution Press, 1971.
———. *Revolution and Structural Change In Latin America, A Bibliography.* Stanford: Hoover Institution Press, 1970.
Chorley, Katharine. *Armies and the Art of Revolution.* London: Faber and Faber, Ltd, 1943.
Ciardi, John. "The New Left: Why Violence?" *Saturday Review* (January 23, 1971).
Clark, Ramsey. "On Violence, Peace and the Rule of Law," *Foreign Affairs* (October 1970), 31–39.
Cleaver, Eldridge. *Post-Prison Writings and Speeches.* New York: Random House, Inc., 1969.
———. *Soul On Ice.* New York: Dell Publishing Co., Inc., 1968.

Cobban, Alfred. "Age of Revolutionary Wars: An Historical Parallel," *Review of Politics*, XIII (1951), 131–141.
——. *The Social Interpretation of the French Revolution*. London: Cambridge University Press, 1964.
Cohen, Mitchell & Dennis Hale. (eds.). *New Student Left: An Anthology*. Boston: Beacon Press, 1967.
Cohn, Norman. *The Pursuit of the Millennium*. New York: Harper & Row, Publishers, 1961.
Cohn-Bendit, Daniel & Gabriel. *Obsolete Communism: The Left-Wing Alternative*. New York: McGraw-Hill Book Company, 1968.
Conant, Ralph W. *The Prospects For Revolution; A Study of Riots, Civil Disobedience, and Insurrection in Contemporary America*. New York: A Harper's Magazine Press Book, 1971.
Connor, James E. (ed.). *Lenin on Politics and Revolution*. New York: Pegasus, 1968.
Coser, Lewis. *The Functions of Social Conflict*. Glencoe, Ill.: Free Press, 1956.
Cowan, Paul. *The Making of an Un-American*. New York: The Viking Press, 1970.
Coyne, John R. *The Kumquat Statement; Anarchy in the Groves of Academe*. New York: Cowles Book Company, Inc., 1970.
——. (ed.). *When Men Revolt—And Why*. New York: The Macmillan Company, 1971.
Crook, W. H. "The Revolutionary Logic of the General Strike," *American Political Science Review*, XXIV (August 1934), 655–663.
Cross, James Eliot. *Conflict in the Shadows: The Nature and Politics of Guerrilla War*. Garden City: Doubleday & Company, Inc., 1963.

Dahl, Robert A. *After the Revolution: Authority in a Good Society*. New Haven: Yale University Press, 1970.
Daniels, R. R. "The Kronstadt Revolt of 1921: A Study in the Dynamics of Revolution," *American Slavic and East European Review*, X (1951), 241–254.
Daniels, Robert V. *The Conscience of the Revolution: Communist Opposition in Soviet Russia*. Cambridge, Mass.: Harvard University Press, 1960.
——. *The Nature of Communism*. New York: Random House, Inc., 1962.
——. (ed.). *The Stalin Revolution*. Lexington, Mass.: D. C. Heath and Company, 1965.
——. "The State and Revolution: A Case Study in the Genesis and Transformation of Communist Ideology," *The American Slavic and East European Review*, 12 (1953), 22–43.
Davies, James C. *Human Nature in Politics*. New York: John Wiley & Sons, Inc., 1963.
——. "Political Stability and Instability: Some Manifestations and Causes," *The Journal of Conflict Resolution*, XIII, 1 (March 1969), 1–17.
——. "Toward a Theory of Revolution," *American Sociological Review*, XXVII, 1 (February 1962), 5–19.
Debray, Regis. *Revolution in the Revolution?* New York: Grove Press, 1967.
Dellinger, David. *Revolutionary Nonviolence*. Indianapolis: Bobbs-Merrill Co., Inc., 1970.

Deming, Barbara. "On Revolution and Equilibrium," *Liberation*, XII, 11 (February 1968), 10–21.

Dennis, Lawrence. *The Dynamics of War and Revolution*. New York: Weekly Foreign Letter, 1940.

Deutscher, Isaac (ed.). *The Age of Permanent Revolution: A Trotsky Anthology*. New York: Dell Publishing Co., Inc., 1964.

———. "Marxism and Nonviolence," *Liberation*, XIV, 4 (July 1969), 10–16.

———. *The Unfinished Revolution: Russia, 1917–1967*. New York: Oxford University Press, 1967.

Dohrn, Bernardine. "Fierce Against The Man," *New Morning—Changing Weather; Weather Underground Communique* (December 1970).

Douglas, William O. *Points of Rebellion*. New York: Random House, Inc., 1970.

———. "The U.S. and the Revolutionary Spirit," *Saturday Review* (June 10, 1961).

Dowd, David L. (ed.). *The Age of Revolution, 1770–1870*. Boston: D. C. Heath and Company, 1967.

Draper, Theodore. *Castro's Revolution: Myths and Realities*. New York: Frederick A. Praeger, Inc., 1962.

———. *The Rediscovery of Black Nationalism*. New York: The Viking Press, 1970.

Duveau, Georges. *1848: The Making of a Revolution*. New York: Random House, Inc., 1967.

Eastman, Max. *Marx, Lenin and the Science of Revolution*. London: George Allen & Unwin, Ltd, 1926.

Ebony Editors, *et al*. *Black Revolution*. Chicago: Johnson Publishing Company, 1970.

Eckstein, Harry (ed.). *Internal War*. New York: Free Press of Glencoe, 1964.

———. "On the Etiology of Internal Wars," *History and Theory*, IV, 2 (1965), 133–163.

Edelmann, Alexander T. *Latin American Government and Politics: The Dynamics of a Revolutionary Society*. Homewood: The Dorsey Press, 1969.

Edwards, Harry. *Black Students*. New York: The Free Press, 1970.

Edwards, Lyford P. "The Mechanics of Revolution," *St. Stephen's College Bulletin*, LXIX, 2.

———. *The Natural History of Revolution*. Chicago: University of Chicago Press, 1927.

Ehrenreich, Barbara & John. *Long March Short Spring: The Student Uprisings At Home and Abroad*. New York: Monthly Review Press, 1969.

Eichel, Lawrence, *et al*. *The Harvard Strike*. Boston: Houghton Mifflin Company, 1970.

Eisenstadt, S. N. *Modernization: Protest and Change*. Englewood Cliffs: Prentice-Hall, Inc., 1966.

Ellwood, Charles A. "A Psychological Theory of Revolutions," *The American Journal of Sociology*, 11 (July 1905), 49–59.

Elton, Godfrey. *The Revolutionary Idea in France, 1789–1871*. New York: Longmans, Green & Co., Inc., 1923.

Engels, Friedrich. *The German Revolutions.* Chicago: University of Chicago Press, 1967.

Epstein, Jason. *The Great Conspiracy Trial; An Essay on Law, Liberty and the Constitution.* New York: Random House, Inc., 1970.

Erikson, Erik H. *Gandhi's Truth; On the Origins of Militant Nonviolence.* New York: W. W. Norton & Company, Inc., 1969.

Fall, Bernard (ed.). *Ho Chi Minh on Revolution.* New York: Signet Books, 1968.

Fanon, Frantz. *The Wretched of the Earth.* New York: Grove Press, 1966.

Fasel, George. *Europe in Upheaval: The Revolutions of 1848.* Chicago: Rand McNally & Company, 1970.

Fischer-Galati, Stephen. "The Peasants as a Revolutionary Force in the Balkans," *Journal of Central European Affairs,* XXIII (April 1963), 12–22.

Fitzgibbon, Russell H. "Revolutions: Western Hemisphere," *The South Atlantic Quarterly,* 55 (1956), 263–279.

Fogelson, Robert M. *Violence as Protest; A Study of Riots in the Ghetto.* Garden City: Doubleday & Company, Inc., 1971.

Forster, Robert & Jack P. Greene. (eds.). *Preconditions of Revolution in Early Modern Europe.* Baltimore: The Johns Hopkins Press, 1970.

———. "Whose Country Is America?" *The New York Times Magazine* (November 22, 1970).

———. *First Things, Last Things.* New York: Harper & Row, Publishers, 1971.

Fox, George. "Counterrevolution," *Playboy,* XVII, 3 (March 1970).

Friedrich, Carl J. (ed.). *Revolution (Nomos VIII).* New York: Atherton Press, 1966.

Gall, Norman. "The Chileans Have Elected A Revolution," *The New York Times Magazine* (November 1, 1970).

Gandhi, M. K. *Non-Violent Resistance.* New York: Schocken Books, 1961.

Gann, Lewis. *Guerrillas in History.* Stanford: Hoover Institution Press, 1971.

Gasset, José Ortega y. *The Revolt of the Masses.* New York: W. W. Norton & Company, Inc., 1932.

Gasster, Michael. *Chinese Intellectuals and the Revolution of 1911: The Birth of Modern Chinese Radicalism.* Seattle: University of Washington Press, 1969.

Gellner, Ernest. "Myth, Ideology and Revolution," *The Political Quarterly,* XL, 4 (October–December 1969), 472–484.

George, C. H. *Revolution: European Radicals from Hus to Lenin.* Chicago: Scott, Foresman and Company, 1971.

Gershoy, Leo. *The French Revolution, 1789–1799.* New York: Holt, Rinehart and Winston, 1932.

———. *From Despotism to Revolution, 1763–1789.* New York: Harper & Row, Publishers, 1944.

Geschwender, James A. "Explorations in the Theory of Social Movements and Revolutions," *Social Forces,* XLVII, 2 (December 1968), 127–135.

Giap, Vo Nguyen. *People's War, People's Army.* New York: Frederick A. Praeger, Inc., 1962.

Gillespie, Joan. *Algeria: Rebellion and Revolution*. New York: Frederick A. Praeger, Inc., 1961.

Gipson, Lawrence H. *The Coming of the Revolution, 1763–1775*. New York: Harper & Row, Publishers, 1954.

Glazer, Nathan. *Remembering the Answers: Essays on the American Student Revolt*. New York: Basic Books, Inc., Publishers, 1970.

Godechot, Jacques. *France and the Atlantic Revolution of the Eighteenth Century, 1770–1799*. New York: The Free Press, 1965.

Goldenberg, Boris. *The Cuban Revolution and Latin America*. New York: Frederick A. Praeger, Inc., 1965.

Goodman, Mitchell. *Movement Toward A New America: The Beginnings of a Long Revolution*. Philadelphia: Pilgrim Press, 1970.

Goodman, Paul. *New Reformation: Notes of a Neolithic Conservative*. New York: Random House, Inc., 1970.

Goodspeed, D. J. *The Conspirators: A Study of the Coup d'Etat*. New York: The Viking Press, 1961.

Gordon, Leonard A. "Portrait of a Bengal Revolutionary," *Journal of Asian Studies*, XXVII (February 1968), 197–216.

Gott, Richard. "Defeat of the Revolution?" *Evergreen Review* (February 1971).

———. *Guerrilla Movements in Latin America*. Garden City: Doubleday & Company, Inc., 1971.

Gottschalk, Louis. "Causes of Revolution," *The American Journal of Sociology*, L, 1 (July 1944), 1–8.

Goulet, Denis. "The Troubled Conscience of the Revolutionary," *The Center Magazine*, A Publication of the Center for the Study of Democratic Institutions 2, no. 3 (May 1969), 43–50.

Graham, Hugh Davis and Ted Robert Gurr. (eds.). *The History of Violence in America; Historical and Comparative Perspectives*. New York: Praeger Publishers, 1969.

Gramont, Sanche de. "How One Peasant, Scholarly Young Man From Brazil Became A Kidnapping, Gun-Toting, Bombing Revolutionary," *The New York Times Magazine* (November 15, 1970).

———. "Our Other Man In Algiers," *The New York Times Magazine* (November 1, 1970).

Granqvist, Hans. *The Red Guard: A Report on Mao's Revolution*. Trans. by Erik J. Friis. New York: Praeger Publishers, 1967.

Grayson, Jr., George W. "Latin Revolts Shift to Cities: Peasants, Radicals Don't Mix," *Los Angeles Times* (January 17, 1971).

Green, Gil. *The New Radicalism: Marxism versus Anarchism*. New York: International Publishers, 1971.

———. *Revolution Cuban Style*. New York: International Publishers, 1970.

Greenlaw, Ralph W. (ed.). *The Economic Origins of the French Revolution*. Lexington, Mass.: D. C. Heath and Company, 1958.

Griewank, Karl. *Der Neuzeitliche Revolutionsbegriff*. Frankfurt am Main: Europäische Verlagsanstalt, 1969.

Griffith, J. A. G. "Why We Need A Revolution," *The Political Quarterly*, XL, 4 (October–December 1969), 383–393.

Gross, Feliks. *The Seizure of Political Power in a Century of Revolutions*. New York: Philosophical Library, 1958.

Groth, Alexander. *Revolution and Elite Access: Some Hypotheses on Aspects of Political Change.* Davis: Institute of Governmental Affairs, 1966.

Guevara, Che. *Guerrilla Warfare.* New York: Random House, Inc., 1969.

———. *On Vietnam and World Revolution.* New York: Pathfinder Press, Inc., 1967.

———. *Reminiscences of the Cuban Revolutionary War.* New York: Grove Press, Inc., 1968.

Gurr, Ted Robert. *The Conditions of Civil Violence.* Princeton: Center of International Studies, 1967.

———. *Why Men Rebel.* Princeton: Princeton University Press, 1970.

Haddad, George M. *Revolutions and Military Rule in the Middle East.* New York: Robert Speller, 1965.

Halpern, Manfred. "A Redefinition of the Revolutionary Situation," *Journal of International Affairs,* XXIII, 1 (1969), 54–75.

Hampden-Turner, Charles. *Radical Man.* Cambridge, Mass.: Schenkman Publishing Company, 1970.

Hampson, Norman. *A Social History of the French Revolution.* Toronto: University of Toronto Press, 1963.

———. *The First European Revolution, 1776–1815.* New York: Harcourt, Brace & World, Inc., 1969.

Handal, Schafik. "Reflections on Continental Strategy for Latin American Revolutionaries," *World Marxist Review* (April 1968).

Handman, Max. "The Bureaucratic Culture Pattern and Political Revolutions," *The American Journal of Sociology,* XXXIX, 3 (November 1933), 301–313.

Hanser, Richard. *Putsch! How Hitler Made Revolution.* New York: Peter H. Wyden, 1971.

Haring, C. E. "The Chilean Revolution of 1931," *Hispanic-American Historical Review,* XIII (1933), 197–203.

Harris, Christina P. *Nationalism and Revolution in Egypt.* The Hague: Mouton and Co., 1964.

Harris, David. *Goliath.* New York: Richard W. Baron Publishing Co., Inc., 1970.

Harris, Richard. *Independence and After: Revoluton in Underdeveloped Countries.* London: Oxford University Press, 1962.

Hartogs, Renatus & E. Artzt. *Violence: Causes and Solutions.* New York: Dell Publishing Company, 1970.

Hatto, Arthur. "Revolution: An Inquiry into the Usefulness of an Historical Term," *Mind,* LVIII, 232 (October 1949), 495–517.

Hayden, Tom. *Rebellion and Repression.* New York: World Publishing Co., 1970.

———. "The Trial," *Ramparts,* IX, 1 (July 1970).

Heberle, Rudolf. *Social Movements.* New York: Appleton-Century-Crofts, 1951.

Hendin, Herbert. "A Psychoanalyst Looks at Student Revolutionaries," *The New York Times Magazine* (January 17, 1971).

Henissart, Paul. *Wolves in the City; The Death of French Algeria.* New York: Simon and Schuster, 1970.

Hill, Christopher. *Intellectual Origins of the English Revolution*. Oxford: The Clarendon Press, 1965.

————. *Puritanism and Revolution*. New York: Schocken Books, 1964.

The History of Violence in America: A Report to the National Commission on the Causes and Prevention of Violence. New York: Bantam Books, 1969.

Hobsbawm, E. J. *The Age of Revolution, 1789–1848*. New York: Mentor Books, 1962.

Hoffer, Eric. *The True Believer; Thoughts on the Nature of Mass Movements*. New York: Harper & Row, Publishers, 1951.

Hoffman, Abbie. *Revolution For The Hell Of It*. New York: The Dial Press, 1968.

————. *Woodstock Nation*. New York: Random House, Inc., 1969.

Hofstadter, Richard & Michael Wallace. (eds.). *American Violence; A Documentary History*. New York: Alfred A. Knopf, 1970.

Hooker, James R. *Black Revolutionary: George Padmore's Path from Communism to Pan-Africanism*. New York: Praeger Publishers, 1967.

Hoover, Calvin B. "Revolutions and Tyranny," *The Virginia Quarterly Review*, XXXVI (1960), 182–194.

Hopper, Rex. "The Revolutionary Process," *Social Forces*, XXVIII (1950), 270–279.

Horowitz, David. *Containment and Revolution*. Boston: Beacon Press, 1967.

————. *Empire and Revolution: A Radical Interpretation of Contemporary History*. New York: Random House, Inc., 1969.

Huberman, Leo & Paul M. Sweezy. *Cuba: Anatomy of a Revolution*. New York: Monthly Review Press, 1960.

————. (eds.). *Regis Debray and the Latin American Revolution*. New York: Monthly Review Press, 1968.

Hulse, James W. *Revolutionists in London: A Study of Five Unorthodox Socialists*. New York: Oxford University Press, 1970.

Humphrey, Robert A. & John Lynch. (eds.). *The Origins of the Latin American Revolutions, 1808–1826*. New York: Alfred A. Knopf, Inc., 1965.

Hunter, Robert. *Revolution: Why, How, When?* New York: Committee For Constitutional Government, 1943.

Hyndman, H. M. *The Evolution of Revolution*. London: G. Richard Ltd, 1920.

Issawi, Charles P. *Egypt in Revolution*. London: Oxford University Press, 1963.

James, C. L. R. *Black Jacobin: Toussaint L'Overture and the San Domingo Revolution*. New York: Random House, Inc., 1963.

Janos, Andrew C. *The Seizure of Power; A Study of Force and Popular Consent*. Princeton: Princeton University Press, 1964.

Jezer, Martin. "Revolution and the Generational Revolt," *Liberation*, XIII, 3 (July & August 1968), 22–25.

Johnson, Chalmers. *Revolution and the Social System*. Stanford: The Hoover Institution, 1964.

————. *Revolutionary Change*. Boston: Little, Brown and Company, 1966.

Johnson, Olive M. & Arnold Peterson. *Revolution.* New York: New York Labor News Company, 1935.

Kahin, George McT. *Nationalism and Revolution in Indonesia.* Ithaca: Cornell University Press, 1952.

Kahn, Roger. *The Battle For Morningside Heights: Why Students Rebel.* Clifton, N.J.: William Morrow & Company, Inc., 1970.

Kaiser, Robert B. "Lessons From Revolution," *America,* 117, 18 (October 28, 1967), 469–473.

Kaplan, Morton A. (ed.). *The Revolution in World Politics.* New York: John Wiley & Sons, 1962.

Karol, K. S. *Guerrillas in Power; The Course of the Cuban Revolution.* Trans. by Arnold Pomerans. New York: Hill & Wang, Inc., 1971.

Karpat, Kemal H. "The Military and Politics in Turkey, 1960–64; A Socio-Cultural Analysis of a Revolution," *American Historical Review,* LXXV, 6 (October 1970), 1654–1683.

Katope, Christopher & Paul Zolbrod (eds.). *The Rhetoric of Revolution.* New York: The Macmillan Company, 1970.

Kautsky, Karl. *The Social Revolution.* Chicago: Charles H. Kerr, 1913.

Kecskemeti, Paul. *The Unexpected Revolution: Social Forces in the Hungarian Uprising.* Stanford: Stanford University Press, 1961.

Kelman, Steve. *Push Comes to Shove.* Boston: Houghton Mifflin Company, 1970.

Kenski, Jr., Henry. "Political Revolution, Civil Violence, and Uncivil Disobedience," *Choice,* VI, 5–6 (July–August 1969), 619–625.

Kiernan, V. G. *The Revolution of 1854 in Spanish History.* Oxford: The Clarendon Press, 1966.

Killian, Lewis M. *The Impossible Revolution: Black Power and the American Dream.* New York: Random House, Inc., 1968.

King, Jr., Martin Luther. *Conscience For Change.* Toronto: Canadian Broadcasting Corporation, 1967.

Kirchheimer, Otto. "Confining Conditions and Revolutionary Breakthroughs," *The American Political Science Review,* LIX, 4 (December 1965), 964–974.

Knollenberg, Bernhard. *Origin of the American Revolution, 1759–1766.* New York: The Macmillan Company, 1960.

Knox, Gregory H. C. "Notes of a Young Radical," *Saturday Review* (August 15, 1970).

Koehan, Lionel. *Russia in Revolution, 1890–1921.* New York: New American Library, 1967.

Kohn, Hans. *Revolutions and Dictatorships.* Cambridge, Mass.: Harvard University Press, 1943.

Kort, Fred. "The Quantification of Aristotle's Theory of Revolution," *American Political Science Review,* LXVI (June 1952), 486–493.

Kousoulas, D. George. *Revolution and Defeat: The Story of the Greek Communist Party.* New York: Oxford University Press, 1965.

Kranzberg, Melvin (ed.). *1848.* Lexington, Mass.: D. C. Heath and Company, 1959.

Kunen, James S. *The Strawberry Statement; Notes of a College Revolutionary.* New York: Random House, Inc., 1969.

Laski, Harold. *Reflections on the Revolution of Our Time*. London: G. Allen & Unwin, Ltd, 1913.

Lasswell, Harold D., and A. Kaplan. *Power and Society: A Framework for Political Inquiry*. New Haven: Yale University Press, 1950.

———— & Daniel Lerner (eds.). *World Revolutionary Elites: Studies in Coercive Ideological Movements*. Cambridge, Mass.: M. I. T. Press, 1965.

Le Bon, Gustave. *The Psychology of Revolution*. London: T. Fisher Unwin, 1913.

Lefebvre, Georges. *The Coming of the French Revolution*. Princeton: Princeton University Press, 1947.

————. *The French Revolution from Its Origins to 1799*. 2 vols. New York: Columbia University Press, 1962, 1964.

Leiden, Carl & Karl M. Schmitt. *The Politics of Violence: Revolution in the Modern World*. Englewood Cliffs: Prentice-Hall, Inc., 1968.

Leith, James A. *Media and Revolution: Moulding A New Citizenry During the Terror*. Toronto: Canadian Broadcasting Corporation, 1968.

Lenin, V. I. *The State and Revolution*. London: Martin Lawrence Ltd, 1932.

Lester, Jules. *Revolutionary Notes*. New York: Richard W. Baron Publishing Co., Inc., 1969.

Lewis, J. D. (ed.). "Marxism, Revolution, and Democracy: 1848 and 1948," *Journal of Politics*, 11 (1949), 518–565.

Lifton, Robert Jay. *Boundaries: Psychological Man In Revolution*. New York: Random House, Inc., 1970.

————. *Revolutionary Immortality: Mao Tsê-tung and the Chinese Cultural Revolution*. New York: Random House, Inc., 1968.

Lipset, Seymour Martin & Sheldon S. Wolin (eds.). *The Berkeley Student Revolt: Facts and Interpretations*. Garden City: Doubleday & Company, Inc., 1965.

————. *Revolution and Counterrevolution*. New York: Basic Books, Inc., Publishers, 1968.

Lockwood, Lee. *Conversations with Eldridge Cleaver (Algiers)*. New York: McGraw-Hill Book Company, 1970.

Long, Priscilla (ed.). *The New Left*. Boston: Porter Sargent Publisher, 1969.

Lowenfels, Walter (ed.). *In A Time Of Revolution; Poems From Our Third World*. New York: Random House, Inc., 1970.

Lubasz, Heinz (ed.). *Revolutions in Modern European History*. New York: The Macmillan Company, 1970.

Luce, Paul A. *Road To Revolution*. San Diego: Viewpoint Books, 1967.

Lukas, J. Anthony. *The Barnyard Epithet and Other Obscenities; Notes on the Chicago Conspiracy Trial*. New York: Harper & Row, Publishers, 1970.

Lunn, Alfred. *Communism and Socialism: A Study in the Technique of Revolution*. London: Eyre & Spottiswoode, 1939.

Luttwak, Edward. *Coup D'Etat: A Practical Handbook*. New York: Alfred A. Knopf, 1969.

Luxemburg, Rosa. *Reform or Revolution*. New York: Pathfinder Press, Inc., n.d.

MacGaffey, Wyatt & Clifford Barnett. *Twentieth Century Cuba: The Background of the Castro Revolution*. Garden City: Doubleday & Company, Inc., 1965.

McAlister, Jr., John T. *Vietnam: The Origins of Revolution*. Garden City: Doubleday & Company, Inc., 1969.

McLaughlin, Barry (ed.). *Studies in Social Movements: A Social Psychological Perspective*. New York: The Free Press, 1969.

McReynolds, David. "The Revolution Is Over, Now The Struggle Begins," *The Village Voice* (July 23, 1970), 19–20.

———. *We Have Been Invaded by the 21st Century*. New York: Frederick A. Praeger, Inc., 1970.

Maguire, J. J. *The Philosophy of Modern Revolution*. Washington: Catholic University of America Press, 1943.

Malaparte, Curzio. *Coup D'Etat: The Technique of Revolution*. New York: E. P. Dutton & Co., 1932.

Mallin, Jay. (ed.). *"Che" Guevara On Revolution; A Documentary Overview*. Coral Gables, Fla.: University of Miami Press, 1970.

Malloy, James M. *Bolivia: The Uncompleted Revolution*. Pittsburgh: The University of Pittsburgh Press, 1971.

Mandel, Ernest. (ed.). *Fifty Years of World Revolution; An International Symposium*. New York: Pathfinder Press, Inc., 1970.

———. *Peaceful Coexistence and World Revolution*. New York: Pathfinder Press, Inc., n.d.

——— & George Novack. *The Revolutionary Potential of the Working Class*. New York: Pathfinder Press, Inc., n.d.

———. *Revolutionary Strategy in the Imperialist Countries*. New York: Pathfinder Press, Inc., n.d.

———. *Revolutionary Student Movement: Theory & Practice*. New York: Pathfinder Press, Inc., 1969.

Mao Tsê-tung. *On Guerrilla Warfare*. New York: Frederick A. Praeger, Inc., 1961.

———. *On Revolution and War*. Ed. M. Rejai. Garden City: Doubleday & Company, Inc., 1969.

Marcum, John. *The Angolan Revolution*. Vol. I, *The Anatomy of an Explosion (1950–1962)*. Cambridge, Mass.: M.I.T. Press, 1969.

Marcuse, Herbert. *Reason and Revolution*. Boston: Beacon Press, 1960.

Marek, Franz. *Philosophy of World Revolution*. New York: International Publishers, 1969.

Marks, Robert W. *The Meaning of Marcuse*. New York: Ballantine Books, Inc., 1969.

Martin, E. D. *Farewell to Revolution*. New York: H. Holt & Co., 1935.

Marx, Karl & Friedrich Engels. *Basic Writings on Politics and Philosophy*. Ed. Lewis S. Feuer. Garden City: Doubleday & Company, Inc., 1959.

———. *Capital*. Trans. E. & C. Paul. London: J. M. Dent & Sons, 1933.

——— & Friedrich Engels. *The Communist Manifesto*. New York: Appleton-Century-Crofts, Inc., 1955.

Masotti, Louis H. & Don R. Bowen. (eds.). *Riots and Rebellion: Civil Violence in the Urban Community*. Beverly Hills: Sage Publications, 1968.

Mathiez, Albert. *The French Revolution*. New York: Grosset & Dunlap, Inc., 1964.

Mazlish, Bruce, Arthur D. Kaledin & David B. Ralston. (eds.). *Revolution: A Reader*. New York: The Macmillan Company, 1971.

Mazour, Anatole G. *The First Russian Revolution, 1825.* Stanford: Stanford University Press, 1961.

Meisel, James. *Counterrevolution: How Revolutions Die.* New York: Atherton Press, 1966.

Merriman, Roger B. *Six Contemporaneous Revolutions.* Hamden, Conn.: Archon Books, 1963.

Mészáros, János. "On the Eve of Revolution," *Journal of Central European Affairs,* 18 (1958), 48–68.

Meusel, Alfred. "Revolution and Counter-Revolution," *Encyclopedia of Social Sciences.* XIII. New York: The Macmillan Company, 1934.

Michelet, Jules. *History of the French Revolution.* Chicago: University of Chicago Press, 1967.

Miller, John C. *Origins of the American Revolution.* Boston: Little, Brown & Co., 1943.

Mitchell, Allan. *Revolution in Bavaria, 1918–1919.* Princeton: Princeton University Press, 1965.

Molnar, Thomas. *The Counter-Revolution.* New York: Funk & Wagnalls, 1969.

Moore, Jr., Barrington. "Revolution in America?" *New York Review of Books* (January 30, 1969).

Moraes, Dom. "Indian Revolutionaries With A Chinese Accent," *The New York Times Magazine* (November 8, 1970).

Morris, Richard B. *The Emerging Nations and the American Revolution.* New York: Harper & Row, Publishers, 1970.

Mosca, Gaetano. *The Ruling Class.* New York: McGraw-Hill Book Company, 1939.

Mousnier, Roland. *Peasant Uprisings in Seventeenth Century France, Russia, and China.* Trans. by Brian Pearce. New York: Harper & Row, Publishers, 1971.

Mungo, Raymond. *Famous Long Ago: My Life and Hard Times With The Liberation News Service.* Boston: Beacon Press, 1970.

Myerson, Michael. *These Are The Good Old Days: Coming of Age as a Radical in America's Late, Late Years.* New York: Grossman Publishers, 1970.

Nadal, George. "The Logic of the *Anatomy of Revolution,* with Reference to the Netherlands Revolt," *Comparative Studies in Society and History,* II (July 1960), 473–484.

Namier, Lewis B. *1848: The Revolution of the Intellectuals.* Garden City: Doubleday & Company, Inc., 1964.

Nelson, Truman. *The Right of Revolution.* Boston: Beacon Press, 1968.

Neumann, Sigmund. "The International Civil War," *World Politics,* I, 3 (April 1949), 333–350.

―――. *Permanent Revolution.* New York: Frederick A. Praeger, Inc., 1965.

―――. "The Structure and Strategy of Revolution: 1848 and 1948," *The Journal of Politics,* 11 (1949), 532–544.

Neiburg, H. L. *Political Violence: The Behavioral Process.* New York: St. Martin's Press, 1969.

———. "Uses of Violence," *The Journal of Conflict Resolution,* VII, 1 (March 1963), 43–54.

———. "Violence, Law, and the Informal Polity," *The Journal of Conflict Resolution,* XIII, 2 (June 1969), 192–209.

The 1962 Carolina Symposium: Today's Revolutions. Chapel Hill: University of North Carolina, 1962.

Nisbet, Robert A. *Tradition and Revolt; Historical and Sociological Essays.* New York: Random House, Inc., 1970.

Nkrumah, Kwame. *Handbook of Revolutionary Warfare.* New York: International Publishers, 1969.

Nollau, Günther. *International Communism and World Revolution: History and Methods.* London: Hollis & Carter, Ltd, 1961.

Nomad, Max. *Apostles of Revolution.* New York: Collier Books, 1933.

Oglesby, Carl. "The Idea of the New Left," *Evergreen Review* (February 1969).

———. "Revolution: Violence or Nonviolence," *Liberation,* XIII, 3 (July & August 1968), 36–38.

O'Gorman, Ned (ed.). *Prophetic Voices: Ideas and Words on Revolution.* New York: Random House, Inc., 1969.

Oliver, D. *Revolution and World Politics.* Washington: American Educational Publications, 1970.

Oppenheimer, Martin. *The Urban Guerrilla.* Chicago: Quadrangle Books, 1969.

Osanka, Franklin Mark. (ed.). *Modern Guerrilla Warfare: Fighting Communist Guerrilla Movements, 1941–1961.* New York: The Free Press, 1962.

Ottaway, David & Marina. *Algeria: The Politics Of A Socialist Revolution.* Berkeley: University of California Press, 1970.

Palmer, R. R. *The Age of the Democratic Revolution.* 2 vols. Princeton: Princeton University Press, 1959, 1964.

———. *The World of the French Revolution.* New York: Harper & Row, Publishers, 1971.

Patch, Richard W. "Peasantry and National Revolution," in Kalman H. Silvert. (ed.). *Expectant Peoples: Nationalism and Development.* New York: Random House, Inc., 1963.

Paul, Eden & Cedar. *Creative Revolution.* London: G. Allen and Unwin, 1920.

Payne, Stanley G. *The Spanish Revolution.* New York: W. W. Norton & Company, Inc., 1970.

Pech, Stanley Z. *The Czech Revolution of 1848.* Chapel Hill: University of North Carolina Press, 1969.

Petras, James & Maurice Zeitlin. (eds.). *Latin America: Reform or Revolution?* Greenwich: Fawcett, 1968.

Pettee, George S. *The Process of Revolution.* New York: Harper & Row, Publishers, 1938.

Pipes, Richard (ed.). *Revolutionary Russia: A Symposium.* Garden City: Doubleday & Company, Inc., 1969.

Plato. *The Republic.* Trans. B. Jowett. Garden City: Doubleday & Company, Inc., 1960.

Posner, Charles. (ed.). *Reflections on the Revolution in France, 1968.* Baltimore: Penguin Books, Inc., 1970.

Possony, Stefan T. *A Century of Conflict: Communist Techniques of World Revolution.* Chicago: Henry Regnery Company, 1953.

Postgate, Raymond. *How to Make a Revolution.* London: Hogarth Press, 1934.

———. *Revolution From 1789–1906.* London: Grant Richards Ltd, 1920.

Powell, W. *The Anarchist Cookbook.* New York: Lyle Stuart, Inc., 1970.

Priaulx, Allan & Sanford J. Ungar. *Almost Revolution.* New York: Dell Publishing Co., Inc., 1969.

Quandt, W. B. *Revolution and Political Leadership: Algeria 1954–1968.* Cambridge, Mass.: M.I.T. Press, 1969.

Quinana, Segundo V. Linares. "The Etiology of Revolution in Latin America," *The Western Political Quarterly,* IV (1951), 254–267.

Rauschning, Hermann. *The Revolution of Nihilism.* New York: Alliance Book Corp., 1939.

Reich, Charles A. "The Greening of America," *The New Yorker* (September 26, 1970), 42–111.

———. *The Greening of America.* New York: Random House, Inc., 1970.

Report of the National Advisory Commission on Civil Disorders. New York: Bantam Books, 1968.

"Revolution and Social Change; Symposium," *Current,* 118 (May 1970), 3–22.

Revolution and Socialist Construction; Selected Writings of Kim Il Sung. New York: International Publishers, 1971.

Revolutionary Analysis, Strategy and Tactics Today. New York: Pathfinder Press, Inc., n.d.

Riezler, Kurt. "On the Psychology of Modern Revolution," *Social Research,* X, 3 (September 1943), 320–336.

Rights in Conflict: The Violent Confrontation of Demonstrators and Police in the Parks and Streets of Chicago During the Week of the Democratic National Convention of 1968. New York: Bantam Books, 1968.

Robertson, Priscilla. *Revolutions of 1848: A Social History.* New York: Harper & Row, Publishers, 1960.

Robinson, Richard A. H. *The Origins of Franco's Spain: The Right, The Republic and Revolution.* Pittsburgh: The University of Pittsburgh Press, 1971.

Robson, Eric. *The American Revolution In Its Political and Military Aspects, 1763–1783.* New York: W. W. Norton & Company, Inc., 1966.

Rosen, Milton K. *Revolution Today: U.S.A.* Jericho, N. Y.: Exposition Press, Inc., 1970.

Rosenau, James N. (ed.). *International Aspects of Civil Strife.* Princeton: Princeton University Press, 1964.

Rosenstock-Hussy, E. *Out of Revolution.* New York: W. Morrow & Co., 1938.

Ross, James R. *War Within: Violence or Nonviolence in the Black Revolution.* New York: Sheed & Ward, 1970.

Roszak, Theodore. *The Making of a Counter Culture*. Garden City: Double-
day & Company, Inc., 1968.
Rubenstein, Richard E. *Rebels in Eden: Mass Political Violence in the United
States*. Boston: Little, Brown & Co., 1970.
Rubin, Jerry. *Do It! Scenarios of the Revolution*. New York: Simon and
Schuster, 1970.
————. "Yippie Manifesto," *Evergreen Review* (May 1969).
Rudé, George. *The Crowd in the French Revolution*. Oxford: The Clarendon
Press, 1959.
————. *The Crowd in History; A Study in Popular Disturbances in France
and England, 1730–1848*. New York: John Wiley & Sons, Inc., 1964.
Ruiz, Ramon Eduardo. *Cuba: The Making of A Revolution*. Amherst: Uni-
versity of Massachusetts Press, 1968.

Said, Abdul A. & Daniel M. Collier. *Revolutionism*. Boston: Allyn and Bacon,
Inc., 1971.
Sathyamurthy, T. V. "Revolutions and Revolutionaries," *Transition*, 5, no. 21
(1965), 25–32.
Scalapino, Robert A. (ed.). *The Communist Revolution in Asia: Tactics,
Goals, and Achievements*. Englewood Cliffs: Prentice-Hall, Inc., 1965.
Schiffrin, Harold Z. *Sun Yat-Sen and the Origins of the Chinese Revolution*.
Berkeley: University of California Press, 1968.
Schmalhausen, S. D. (ed.). *Recovery Through Revolution*. New York: Covici
Friede, 1933.
Schoenbaum, David. *Hitler's Social Revolution*. Garden City: Doubleday &
Company, Inc., 1966.
Schram, Stuart. (ed. & trans.). *Political Thought of Mao Tse-tung*. New York:
Frederick A. Praeger, Inc., 1963.
Schurmann, Franz. "On Revolutionary Conflict," *Journal of International
Affairs*, XXIII, I (1969), 36–53.
Seale, Bobby. *Seize The Time*. New York: Random House, Inc., 1970.
Seale, Patrick & Maureen McConville. *Red Flag Black Flag; French Revolu-
tion, 1968*. New York: G. P. Putnam's Sons, 1968.
Seton-Watson, Hugh. *The East European Revolution*. New York: Praeger
Publishers, 1965.
————. "Twentieth-Century Revolutions," *The Political Quarterly*, XXIII, 3
(1951), 251–265.
Shaplen, Robert. *The Lost Revolution*. New York: Harper & Row, Publishers,
1965.
Sharabi, Hisham B. *Nationalism and Revolution in the Arab World*. Prince-
ton: D. Van Nostrand Co., Inc., 1966.
Siegel, Jules. "Revolution," *Playboy*, XVII, 3 (March 1970).
Sievers, A. M. *Revolution, Evolution and the Economic Order*. Englewood
Cliffs: Prentice-Hall, Inc., 1962.
Silvert, Kalman H. *Conflict Society: Reaction and Revolution in Latin America*.
New York: Harper & Row, Publishers, 1968.
Singer, Daniel. *Prelude to Revolution: France in May 1968*. New York: Hill
& Wang, Inc., 1971.
Skolnick, Jerome H. *Politics and Protest*. New York: Simon & Schuster, Inc.,
1969.

Smelser, Neil J. *Theory of Collective Behavior.* New York: The Free Press, 1962.

Smith, Robert A. (ed.). *Edmund Burke on Revolution.* New York: Harper & Row, Publishers, 1968.

Snell, John L. (ed.). *The Nazi Revoluton.* Lexington, Mass.: D. C. Heath and Company, 1959.

Soledad Brother; The Prison Letters of George Jackson. New York: Coward-McCann, Inc., 1970.

Sorel, Georges. *Reflections on Violence.* New York: B. W. Huesbsh, 1950.

Sorokin, P. A. *The Sociology of Revolution.* Philadelphia: J. P. Lippincott, 1925.

Southwood, Ken. "Riot and Revolt: Sociological Theories of Political Violence," *Peace Research Reviews,* I, 3 (June 1967).

Spitzer, A. B. *Revolutionary Theories of Louis Auguste Blanqui.* Providence, R. I.: AMS Press, 1970.

Stein, David Lewis. *Living the Revolution: The Yippies in Chicago.* Indianapolis: Bobbs-Merrill Company, Inc., 1970.

Stone, Lawrence. "Theories of Revolution," *World Politics,* XVIII, 2 (January 1966), 159–176.

Straka, Gerald M. (ed.). *The Revolution of 1688.* Lexington, Mass.: D. C. Heath and Company, 1963.

Sydenham, M. J. *The French Revolution.* New York: G. P. Putnam's Sons, 1965.

Sydnor, Charles S. *American Revolutionaries in the Making.* New York: The Free Press, 1965.

Tanter, Raymond & Manus Midlarsky. "A Theory of Revolution," *The Journal of Conflict Resolution,* XI, 3 (September 1967), 264–280.

Taylor, Philip A. M. (ed.). *The Origins of the English Civil War.* Lexington, Mass.: D. C. Heath and Company, 1960.

Templin, Ralph T. *Democracy and Nonviolence.* Boston: Porter Sargent Publisher, 1965.

Thomas, Hugh. "The Origins of the Cuban Revolution," *The World* Today (October 1963).

Thompson, R. *Revolutionary War in World Strategy, 1945–1969.* New York: Taplinger Publishing Co., Inc., 1970.

Timasheff, Nicholas S. *War and Revolution.* New York: Sheed and Ward, 1965.

Tocqueville, Alexis de. *The Old Regime and the French Revolution.* Garden City: Doubleday & Company, Inc., 1955.

Trevelyan, George M. *The English Revolution, 1688–1689.* New York: Oxford University Press, 1965.

Trevelyan, Humphrey. *The Middle East in Revolution.* Boston: Gambit, 1971.

Trotsky, Leon. *The Chinese Revolution: Problems and Perspectives.* New York: Pathfinder Press, Inc., n.d.

––––––. *The History of the Russian Revolution.* 3 vols. New York: Simon and Schuster, Inc., 1932.

––––––. *The Revolution Betrayed.* New York: Pathfinder Press, Inc., 1965.

Tucker, Robert C. *The Marxian Revolutionary Idea.* New York: W. W. Norton & Company, Inc., 1969.

Turner, John B. & Whitney M. Young, Jr. "Who Has The Revolution or Thoughts on the Second Reconstruction," *Daedalus,* 94, 4 (Fall 1965), 1148–1163.

Turner, Ralph H. & Lewis M. Killian (eds.). *Collective Behavior.* Englewood Cliffs: Prentice-Hall, Inc., 1957.

Ulam, Adam. *The Unfinished Revolution: An Essay on the Sources of Influence of Marxism and Communism.* New York: Random House, Inc., 1960.

Untermann, Ernest. *The World's Revolutions.* Chicago: Charles H. Kerr & Company, 1909.

Van Ness, P. *Revolution & Chinese Foreign Policy: Peking's Support For Wars of National Liberation.* Berkeley: University of California Press, 1970.

Venturi, Franco. *Roots of Revolution.* New York: Grosset & Dunlap, 1966.

Voegelin, Eric. "The Formation of the Marxian Revolutionary Idea," *The Review of Politics,* XII (1950), 275–302.

Waelder, Robert. *Progress and Revolution; A Study of the Issues of Our Age.* New York: International Universities Press, 1970.

———. *Obligations; Essays on Disobedience, War, and Citizenship.* Cambridge, Mass.: Harvard University Press, 1970.

Walter, E. V. "Power and Violence," *American Political Science Review,* (June 1964), 350–355.

Walzer, Michael. "Revolutionary Ideology: The Case of the Marian Exiles," *American Political Science Review,* LVII (September 1963), 643–654.

———. *Revolution of the Saints; A Study in the Origins of Radical Politics.* Cambridge, Mass.: Harvard University Press, 1965.

Weaver, Gary R. & James H. (eds.). *University and Revolution.* Englewood Cliffs: Prentice-Hall, Inc., 1969.

Weiker, Walter F. *The Turkish Revolution: 1960–1961; Aspect of Military Politics.* Washington: The Brookings Institution, 1963.

Wildman, Allan K. *The Making of a Workers' Revolution.* Chicago: University of Chicago Press, 1967.

Willer, David & George K. Zollschan. "Prolegomenon to a Theory of Revolutions," in George K. Zollschan & Walter Hirsch (eds.). *Explorations in Social Change.* Boston: Houghton Mifflin Company, 1964.

Williams, Roger L. *The French Revolution, 1870–1871.* New York: W. W. Norton & Company, Inc., 1969.

Wilson, David A. "Nation-Building and Revolutionary War," in Karl Deutsch & William J. Foltz. (eds.). *Nation-Building.* New York: Atherton Press, 1963.

Wittfogel, Karl A. "The Marxist View of Russian Society and Revolution," *World Politics,* XII (1960), 487–508.

Wolf, Eric. *Peasant Wars of the Twentieth Century.* New York: Harper & Row, Publishers, 1970.

Wolff, Robert Paul. *In Defence of Anarchism.* New York: Harper & Row, Publishers, 1970.

Wolfstein, E. Victor. *The Revolutionary Personality: Lenin, Trotsky, Gandhi.* Princeton: Princeton University Press, 1967.

Wolpert, J. F. "Myth of Revolution," *Ethics,* LVIII (1948), 245–255.

Woodcock, George. *Civil Disobedience: Seven Talks For CBC Radio.* Toronto: Canadian Broadcasting Corporation, 1966.

Worsley, Peter M. "The Analysis of Rebellion and Revolution in Modern British Social Anthropology," *Science and Society,* XXV (Winter 1961), 26–37.

Wriston, Harry M. "The Age of Revolution," *Foreign Affairs,* 39 (1961), 533–548.

Yoder, Dale. "Current Definitions of Revolutions," *The American Journal of Sociology,* XXXII, 3 (November 1926), 433–441.

Young, Alfred F. (ed.). *Dissent: Explorations in the History of American Radicalism.* DeKalb, Ill.: Northern Illinois University Press, 1968.

Zeitlin, Maurice. *Revolutionary Politics and the Cuban Working Class.* New York: Harper & Row, Publishers, 1970.

Zinner, Paul E. *Revolution in Hungary.* New York: Columbia University Press, 1962.

Zorza, Richard. *The Right to Say "We".* New York: Frederick A. Praeger, Inc., 1970.